The Rev

*Understanding
the Revelation
with the Old and
the New Testament*

E. W. HEN

TRANSLATIO

elation
OF ST. JOHN

GSTENBERG
OM THE ORIGINAL BY REV. PATRICK FAIRBAIRN

Which things also we speak, not in the words which man's wisdom teaches, but which the Holy Ghost teaches; comparing spiritual things with spiritual.
—1 Corinthians 2:13

CONDENSED & ADAPTED BY MAXWELL HILLIER
© COPYRIGHT MAXWELL HILLIER 2015

Text in
Adobe Caslon Pro
10.5 / 11.5

THE REVELATION OF ST. JOHN,
E. W. HENGSTENBERG
CONDENSED & ADAPTED FOR TODAY'S READER

© Copyright this edition
Maxwell Hillier 2015. All rights reserved.

ISBN-13: 978-0-646-97953-3

Illustrations by Albrecht Durer

This reprint edition is condensed and adapted from:
The Revelation of St John, Expounded for those who search the Scriptures,
(Volumes One and Two)
by E. W. Hengstenberg, Doctor and Professor of Theology in Berlin.
Translated from the original by the Rev. Patrick Fairbairn.
Published 1852. T&T Clark, Edinburgh.

The REVELATION OF ST. JOHN

THE REVELATION OF ST. JOHN

Contents...

1.		AUTHOR'S PREFACE
2.		EDITOR'S FOREWORD
3.		INTRODUCTION
5.		THE DATE
13.		OVERVIEW
17.	1:1-3	**THE TITLE** *What must shortly come to pass*
25.		**FIRST SECTION** *Chapters 1–11* **THREE GROUPS:** *General & Preparatory*
27.	GROUP 1	THE SEVEN EPISTLES *How Shall I Receive And How Shall I Meet Thee?*
29.	1:4-6	1st PART Introduction, salutation
35.	1:7-8	consolatory declarations
37.	1:9–20	2nd PART Historical starting point (verse 9,) charge to write, Christ's appearance
46.	2–3	3rd PART The letters to the seven churches, a commentary on the appearance
59.	GROUP 2	THE SEVEN SEALS, EPISODE CH. 7 *Christ visits the persecuting world with judgments and ruin*
61.	4	The holy assembly sitting in judgment
68.	5	The giving up of the book with seven seals to Christ
76.	6-8:1	The opening of the seals, manifestation of the judgments *contained with...*
81.	7	An intermediate episode to show God's preservation of his people in the midst of judicial visitations, how to attain the heavenly kingdom
91.	GROUP 3	THE SEVEN TRUMPETS, EPISODE 8:2–11:19 *How does the Church stand in reference to the corrupt world?*
93.	8:2–11:19	Group summary
97.	8:2–5	The theme and prelude to the 2nd and 3rd groups
99.	8:6-9:21	Symbols of the plague of war—God chastises the heathen opposition made to his kingdom
108.	10:1–11:13	An episode: the church in reference to the world
118.	11:14–19	The seventh trumpet

121. **SECOND SECTION** *Chapters 12–22*
     FOUR GROUPS: In detail what is to come to pass

123. GROUP 4   THE THREE ENEMIES OF GOD'S KINGDOM
     The dragon, the God opposing worldly power, seven horns denoting seven phases with earthly, physical, demoniacal wisdom, and the persecuted believers

125.	12–14	Introduction
128.	12	First enemy: the dragon: a portrait of Satan
134.	13	Second enemy: the beast from the sea: the God opposing worldly power, with seven horns, denoting its seven phases
142.	13:11-18	Third enemy: the beast from the earth: earthly, physical, demoniacal wisdom
153.	14	Believers assailed by these enemies find consolation in view of God's grace and the judgments ready to befall the enemies

165. GROUP 5   THE SEVEN VIALS
     The seven plagues that accompany the beast, the ungodly power of the world through the course of centuries

167.   15–16   The seven plagues accompanying the beast, the ungodly power of the world through the course of centuries

185. GROUP 6   THE DESTRUCTION OF THE THREE ENEMIES OF GOD'S KINGDOM

187.	17–20	Introduction
189.	17	The announcing of the overthrow of the sixth head, the monarchy of Rome
201.	18	The overthrow of the sixth head, the monarchy of Rome
208.	19:1–4	Praise song at the fall of Rome
211.	19:5–10	Anticipatory celebration of victory over the other enemies
214.	19:11–21	The victory of Christ over the ten kings, instruments of his judgment against Rome, the seventh head of the beast with ten horns
218.	20:1–6	Satan for a time harmless as church reigns a thousand years
224.	20:7–10	Final destruction of Satan
226.	20:11–15	Final judgment on the servants of Satan and the beast, removal of present constitution of world

229. GROUP 7   THE NEW JERUSALEM
     The description of the New Jerusalem

231.	21:1-8	The description of the New Jerusalem
238.	21:1–22:5	The lengthened description of the New Jerusalem

255.   22:6-21   # CONCLUSION
     Come Lord Jesus!

264   Indexes with Appendix: The 70 weeks of Daniel

From the Author's Preface

The Revelation of St. John was for a long time a shut book for me. That it was necessary here to lay a new path; that neither the course pursued in the older ecclesiastical, nor that of the modern Rationalistic exposition was to be followed, I never entertained a doubt. The constantly renewed attempts at fresh investigations resulted only in a better understanding of particular points, but accomplished nothing as to the main theme. I was not the less persuaded, however, that the blame of this obscurity lay not in the book itself, with the divine character of which I was deeply impressed, but in its exposition; and I did not cease to long for the time when an insight might be granted me into its wonderful depths. Several years ago I was visited with what was, in other respects, a heavy season of affliction, which obliged me to discontinue for some months my official duties. I looked about for a rod and staff that might comfort me, and soon lighted on the Revelation. Day and night I pondered on it, and one difficulty vanished after another. At the period of my recovery, there was scarcely a point of any moment respecting which I did not think I had obtained light. I had still, however, after becoming well, to finish my *Commentary on the Psalms*. Then I went to my task with the greater eagerness. The sad times of March 1848, did not interrupt, but rather expedited my labours.

The title shows that this work is intended for all who search the Scriptures. The remarks contain little of a grammatical nature. The text will present no difficulties to cultivated readers, even though not theologians, if they are only animated by an earnest desire to become thoroughly acquainted with the contents of the book.

I am perfectly aware that this work is destined to meet with much disfavour from many who are united with me in faith. The persons whose concurrence I should have most highly prized, are precisely those in whom the exposition of Bengel, to which also I owe more than to any other for the explanation of particular parts, has taken deepest root; insomuch that an attack on it, which has made the Revelation dear and precious to them, will scarcely be regarded by them in any other light than as an attack on the Revelation itself. But I am still not without confidence, that the method of exposition attempted here will by and by make way, especially among those who are disposed to look more profoundly into the OLD TESTAMENT, and in particular into its prophetical writings. For this is absolutely indispensable to a proper understanding of the Revelation. My confidence rests on the conviction, that I have not striven to foist in anything, but to the best of my ability have sought merely to expound and enforce what is written.

In conclusion I commend this work, the deficiencies of which I deeply feel, to Him who has given me strength to execute it thus far, and has rendered to myself a source of edification and comfort.

Professor E. W. Hengstenberg.

Editor's Foreword

Ernst Wilhelm Hengstenberg (1802-1869) was an evangelical Lutheran professor at the University of Berlin, a major figure in nineteenth century Lutheranism, who long stood against the rationalism of his contemporaries. He authored commentaries on the Psalms, Ezekiel, Daniel, John's Gospel and a Christology of the OLD TESTAMENT.

When he wrote his commentary on the Revelation he was troubled by the revolutions of 1848, which threatened the Christian ruling powers. That he could see much in his exposition regarding the significance of these events I leave to the reader to discover. He had already written treatises in 1847-48 entitled *The Beast in the Apocalypse* and *The Thousand Years Reign* in the journal which he had served as editor, Evangelische Kirchen-Zeitung, which form part of this volume. Because the work bore a very close relation to the wants of his time he initially published the first volume, trimmed of investigations on authorship, style and apostolicity, reserving such for the second volume, which he later released. The original lengthy volumes are somewhat impenetrable for a casual approach, particularly for today's reader. So my aim has been to simply present his exposition of the text itself, in an easily accessible format, for today's audience. For these reasons, I also have trimmed the exposition of these investigations, along with much of what concerned his responses to the debates and opinions of his contemporaries and many classical references, thereby reducing two volumes to a concise 266 pages. I have arranged and set the book after the plan of his retrospect, which I have transformed into an overview, along with the chapter on the historical starting point, which has a vital bearing on our understanding of the book. I have also added appropriate sub-headings and some pertinent selections from his other works to complement the exposition, including an appendix on the seventy weeks of Daniel. The translation of the text is the author's. Incidental quotations from Scripture are in *italics* to save the overall clutter of quotation marks. To save page flipping I have placed the Bible text also in the side gutter on pages where it is not in view.

The author is careful to exposit the book in a comparison of its constituent verses and passages under the understanding of holy Scripture being an organic whole. He follows St. Paul's dictum of comparing spiritual with spiritual (1 Cor. 2:13.) As an OLD TESTAMENT scholar, and classical language expert, he is eminently qualified to expound a book that is replete with OLD TESTAMENT references and allusions. It was his hope that his view of the Revelation would make way by and by among those who studied the OLD TESTAMENT. Sadly, however, it appears to have been buried in obscurity since its first publication. My hope is that this publication may serve to answer the hope of our esteemed author. Much of what he has written will sound novel to the modern reader, but the gems in this commentary are worth uncovering. To have not attempted to popularize this forgotten book would be to our loss. I offer this abridgment to all who are interested, in the hope it may revitalize our understanding of the Revelation, that we, as did the author, may find edification and comfort.

–*Maxwell Hillier,*
Editor

REVELATION

Introduction

The starting-point of the book is given in chapter 1:9. St John, who is on the isle of Patmos for the Word of God and the testimony of Jesus Christ, writes to his companions in tribulation. Every thing in the book is adapted to bring *consolation and support to the church in the conflict which she has to wage with heathenism* and its invisible head.

The Apocalypse was intended to disclose the future generally, and not merely under one particular aspect. The older view held it to be a prophetical history of the church in its chief epochs to the end. It did not distinguish *between the general and the special parts of the Apocalypse,* and determined the chief epochs by forcing its own conceptions and historical position on the two groups of the seven seals and the seven trumpets, instead of resigning itself *to obtain from the book itself the rules that should be followed.*

The Revelation is the book by which the Lord verified his promise in John 16:13, to make known the future to his disciples. It is the prophetical book of the NEW TESTAMENT. According to 1:1, it is to show generally what should come to pass. Its object, in 1:7, is the whole coming of the Lord with clouds, *his judicial agency in its continued exercise through the centuries.* It shows the external fortunes and the internal condition of the church.

It shows that from the time of the apostle till the end of the world the conflict with heathenism is of the most decided moment for the church; from it have come its heaviest outward defeats, and its most severe inward temptations; in connection with that also have its most glorious victories been won.

In the Apocalypse heathenism is expressly represented as the proper organ and the chief instrument of Satan. According to 12:3, Satan bears seven heads and ten horns in reflection of his visible image and deputy on earth, the beast, the heathen worldly power. With the overthrow of heathenism also was Satan's power first broken, and during the thousand years at last completely vanquished.

It is important to discern where the Revelation places the nature of heathenism. What is commonly called idolatry did not form the substance of heathenism. In 9:20, idolatry is taken notice of, but it occupies a subordinate position. The really essential element of heathenism is manifest alone from the name of BEAST, which indicates *a want of the living breath of God,* the spiritual nature, and signifies what is low and fleshly (comp. at 13:1.) In close union with this goes its hatred toward God, the open and uncompromising contrariety to Christ and his church (comp. at 20:2), the *impiety,* which breaks forth in the utterance of great things and blasphemies (13:5), and exclaims, *Who is like the beast? and who can make war with him?*—words and utterances, in which the beast, for *himself,* claims the highest dignity and greatness, and not for his idols, which were always the mere fabrication of their worshippers.

The prophetic foresight of the Apocalypse stretches far beyond the period of its composition. It depicts in sharp outlines a series of situations similar to those then existing, and extending even to the final consummation. This also implies, that the author only *primarily*, but not exclusively kept in view the readers and hearers of his own day. With the clear apprehension of the future there is closely bound up a fellow-feeling in respect to it to the church of all times. He, who has had laid open to his view the distresses and sorrows of the future, must also be conscious of an earnest desire to provide for them advice and consolation. Had he looked merely to the first readers, he would never have thought of going so much into detail in announcing the future, or of communicating so much, which could only be fully understood after the fulfilment had taken place. The deep conviction, also, he had respecting the high importance of the book, and which he has expressed in the book itself, shows, that it could not have been intended merely for his own times.

It is *the Revelation of Jesus Christ, which God gave him* (1:1.) The position, which every individual takes up in regard to its subject-matter, determines his salvation or perdition (22:19.) Inspiration in the full sense excludes all limitation in respect to time and place. Chapter 1:3 pronounces him *blessed, who reads and who hears the words of the prophecy, and who keeps those things that are written in it.* According to 13:9-10, 14:12–*here is the patience of the saints, who keep the commandments of God and the faith of Jesus*–the aim of the book is to strengthen believers in patience, and in maintaining faith toward Christ and obedience to God's commandments; *the fearful and the unbelieving* (21:8), who had made shipwreck of patience and faith, being incapable of coming again to the possession of true zeal. At the close of the Gospel of John in 20:31, it says, *But these things are written, that you might believe that Jesus is the Christ, the Son of God, and that believing, you might have life through his name.* As the aim of the Gospel is to lead to faith and patience, so the aim of the Apocalypse is to meet the *dangers* which threaten faith and consequently the life of the soul. It sends the injunction to *overcome* (21:7). The means, it uses to accomplish this aim, the strength and consolation it opens up, are manifold. With the clearness of intuition, with a power, a confidence, and a fullness that overmasters and fills the mind and fancy, it represents how God avenges his people on a persecuting world, conducts them through all persecutions, so that their faith and fidelity does not expire (14:1-5); how he protects them amid the judgments which he causes to alight on the world (7:1-8); how he receives them up to his heavenly glory (7:9-17); how he brings his church to a provisional ascendancy upon earth (the thousand years' reign); how, finally, he erects the new heavens and the new earth, and causes the new Jerusalem to come down out of heaven upon earth. It also describes the dangers and punishments which await apostasy and unbelief.

REVELATION

The date

THE AGE OF LIVING TRADITION

The older theologians proceeded almost uniformly on the supposition, that the Book of Revelation was composed in the closing period of Domitian's reign. There are a series of testimonies for the composition under *Domitian* by various church fathers. Beginning with Irenæus, who says (*B. V. c. 30,*) *For if it were necessary at present to declare plainly his name* (the name of the person indicated by the number 666, 13:18), *it might be done through him, who also saw the Apocalypse. For it was seen not long ago, but almost in our generation, toward the close of Domitian's reign.* According to the beginning of the chapter, *the numbers 666* (*in opposition to the other reading 616*) *bear testimony to having seen John in the face.* He speaks without doubt of a matter generally acknowledged with only a brief indication, silent regarding the persecution and the apostle's exile—confident his readers would supply this themselves.

Clement of Alexandria (*Quis dives § 42,* and in *Eusebius III. 23*) says: *For since he (John) after the death of* THE TYRANT *returned to Ephesus from the isle Patmos, etc.* He implies a tradition: a definite person–*the tyrant,* the Roman emperor of the first century who is named *Domitian.* Origen on Matt. 20:22-23, says: *But the sons of Zebedee have drunk the cup and been baptized with the baptism, since Herod killed James the brother of John with the sword; and* THE KING OF THE ROMANS, *as tradition testifies, condemned the witnessing John on account of the word of truth to the isle Patmos. But John himself instructs us regarding his martyrdom, not saying indeed who had adjudged him to it, yet declaring in the Apocalypse as follows: I, John, your brother and companion in tribulation, etc., and seems to have beheld the Revelation on the island.* The name of *the king* was generally known, from the tradition to which he refers, the analogy in *Eusebius III. 20,* where *the isle* refers to the traditional island Patmos; and also Irenæus, who names Domitian. Origen, without doubts, introduces the testimony of John himself (1:9) only as a confirmation, less complete than the tradition, since the tradition mentions who condemned the apostle. He refers to more sources than the tradition found in the statement of Irenæus, who says nothing of the condemnation of John and his banishment to Patmos.

Eusebius (*B. III. ch. 18* of his *Church History,*) says, *Under him* (Domitian) *tradition relates, that the apostle and evangelist John, who was still alive, on account of his testimony for the divine word, was condemned to reside in the isle Patmos. And* (*B. III. ch. 20*) *then also that the apostle John returned from his banishment on the island, and took up his dwelling again at Ephesus, the tradition of our older men has delivered to us.* And (*B. III. ch. 23*) *John governed there* (in Asia) *the churches, after his return from exile on the island, subsequent to the death of Domitian.* Also in the *Chronicon* under the fourteenth year of Domitian, *The apostle John, the theologian, he banished to the isle Patmos, where he saw the Apocalypse, as Irenæus says.* (On Irenæus and Polycarp see p. 48.)

What Eusebius gives as the testimony of tradition, contains more than stated by Irenæus, and he refers to several depositaries of the tradition. Never once does Eusebius point to any other view regarding *the author* of John's exile, and the time of the composition of the Apocalypse. So there must have been perfect unanimity in the church. Victorinus of Petabio, martyred under Diocletian in 303, declares the composition of the Apocalypse under Domitian, on Patmos as a matter of undoubted certainty. These are all the testimonies on the time of the composition of the Apocalypse belonging to the age of living tradition. They declare with perfect unanimity that John was banished by *Domitian* to Patmos, and there wrote the Apocalypse.

VARIATIONS TO THE TRADITIONAL ACCOUNT

It is only in writers of inferior rank that varying accounts are to be found. Epiphanius is the first, and Theophylact. None of those who deviate from the tradition refer to it, while this is quite common with those who place the exile of John and the writing of the Apocalypse under Domitian, only these indicate the continuance in a definite way. All others speak in a vague manner, and do not venture to go into more exact specification, as expected on supposing one class rested on historical tradition, and the other followed uncertain conjecture. The deviators however are at variance among themselves. The Syriac translation makes the exile of John and the composition of the Apocalypse under Nero, Epiphanius under Claudius, and Pseudodorotheus the banishment under Trajan, who adds, after this, *But others say he was banished to Patmos, not under Trajan, but under Domitian, the son of Vespasian.* Arethas similarly vacillates, while placing the composition of the Apocalypse in 7:1-8 before the Jewish war, yet at 1:6 he makes it to have been written under Domitian. It is tolerably certain that the extraneous grounds which gave rise to these departures from the historical tradition are the ground of conjecture and discovery on the internal field, and a disregard of the weight of most solid testimonies. All the deviators are in agreement of the composition of the Revelation before the era of Jerusalem's overthrow; the chief argument in favour of Claudius from Acts 18:2, and the passage of Suetonius which speaks of the expulsion of the Jews, and this is supposed to have involved the banishment of John to Patmos; with also the passage in Matt. 24:7 on which Rev. 6:5-8 rests. But the more careful examination of the internal grounds, far from invalidating the external testimonies, rather shows the book was composed at no other time than the reign of Domitian.

CONDITION OF THE CHURCHES IN LESSER ASIA

The seven epistles display a time, when the period of the first love is past, we are in later times, in which a gradually advancing corruption had sprung up among those churches. The love which Paul had desired in the Ephesians, has cooled, and is in danger of perishing. Ephesians, written in 61-62, everywhere conveys fresh life, and brotherly *love*. The light in Sardis has almost become extinct. Laodicca had become lukewarm. Such perils endangering even the elect came only at the period to which church tradition assigns the Apocalypse–the reign of Domitian. We have, then, an interval of more than thirty years, during which the apostles had all, except John, gone to their rest. Now a storm of persecution passes over the less firmly established new generation, hence, the Seer writes to his companions in tribulation.

We find, deeply rooted and wide-spread, in the churches the Nicolaitan or Balaamite errors. According to 2:21, the Lord had already given ample time to their operations. In Hebrews we have a temptation and inclination to apostasy to Judaism because of *Jewish* persecution. Here it is a temptation to heathenism by *heathen* persecution. Pergamos is the throne of Satan, the main centre of heathenish persecution. In Thyatira, the promise given shows that the temptation to false doctrine pressed in from heathenism. With the overflowing of the heathen the forecourt of the temple is given up in ch. 11, such as had no deep root, are overcome through heathen persecutions, and drawn to the fellowship of heathen minds. In the time of Domitian a heathen persecution first threatened to destroy the Christians, which did not exist in the reign of Galba, so a victory over heathenism could not have existed before.

In the errors Paul contends with there is no falling away into heathenism and the troubles were chiefly of Jewish origin. The beginning of our heresy meets us in the second epistle of Peter, written shortly before his death; 1:13-14. *The Nicolaitans* here corresponds with *Balaam*, in 2:15-16. The errors belong to the future; yet the first beginnings of the evil are already before the apostle's eyes, indicated in 3:4–a question awakened by the violence of the persecution and the tribulations of the world. In *Jude* these errors are already present. He repeats, and reminds his readers, what Peter had earlier warned. That what was future in Peter had now become present, was the motive to Jude for writing his epistle. (Comp. Jude 17-18, comp. with 2 Pet. 3:3.) In Jude it is said that *certain men had crept in unawares*. We see ourselves here, therefore, brought into a quite isolated region, the path to which only began to be indicated in the latest epistles of the NEW TESTAMENT.

CHAPTER 1:9 CONFIRMS UNDER DOMITIAN

Chapter 1:9 confirms the book was composed under Domitian. It is Christian persecution of a general nature which first happened under Domitian. That under Nero was confined to Rome. Deportations as John had suffered, beside capital punishments, were inflicted under Domitian. Under Nero, there were capital executions at Rome, but not deportations.

The air of martyrdom swims all around us in the Book of Revelation. It could only have been written by one who had experienced martyrdom. That the author was affected by the worldly power of heathendom is evident from the prevailing tone of sadness, and the wrestling character of faith which pervades the whole Book. John was designated a martyr by Polycrates of Ephesus, in *Euseb. v. 24*. The sojourn on the island was fitted for no other purpose than as a place of *banishment*. Chapter 13:10 implies, that when the Book was composed, beside capital executions there were also banishments to different places on account of the faith. See the passages 6:9, 12:11, 20:4 where is denoted faithfulness in confessing Christ in the midst of sufferings.

In Matt. 20:22-23, Mark 10:38 the Lord tells James and John that they should drink of his cup and be baptized with his baptism. From the example of James, and Peter, we expect to find a fulfilment with John, yet tempered by John 21:20-22, according to which a martyrdom involving the loss of life does not come into view. The exile to Patmos is the only event in which the fulfilment can be sought. Origen recognized this in *Matt. Opp. iii.* Jerome refers to John being put into boiling oil—a report which had its rise in the feeling, as if the banishment was not *sufficient* to fulfil the word of Christ.

THE PERSECUTION OF THE CHRISTIANS

The persecution of the Christians, which proceeded from the Roman state and its rulers, forms the historical starting-point of the Revelation. The beast, the world-power, opens *its mouth in blasphemy against God, to blaspheme His name, and His tabernacle, and them that dwell in heaven* (13:6). According to ver. 15 the false prophet has power to compass the death of those who do not worship the image of the beast. Domitian was the first, Caligula perhaps excepted, who among the Romans laid claim to the name of God. Certain approaches to this claim are with the earlier Caesars, particularly Augustus, but there it was the flattery of others which prompted what was done, and the emperor himself rather exercised a restraining influence. But here the emperor took the initiative, and the claim was so extravagantly urged, that scarcely any thing of a similar kind is to be met with among the later emperors, and on this very account Domitian is quite notorious in antiquity. Philostratus says Domitian, *would have himself regarded as the god of all men.* Suetonius says he began his letters, *Our Lord and God commands that it should be done so and so;* and formally decreed that no one should address him otherwise either in writing or by word of mouth. According to Dio Cassias, Nerva caused the gold and silver images of Domitian, which were very numerous, to be melted. Pliny says that Trajan was content with the place next to the gods, but that Domitian raised himself above them, and as if he alone almost had any claim to godhead, chose for his statues the most hallowed sites in the temple, and caused entire hosts of victims to be offered to himself. In the downfall of Domitian Pliny saw an irony in real life on his pretended divinity.

Under Domitian, Christianity had to enter on a struggle of life or death with the imperial power. It is true, we cannot produce distinct historical statements to the effect that Domitian urged his impious claim precisely against the Christians, and considered the honour given to these as a robbery of that due to himself. But this omission is explained from the aversion of heathen authors to Christianity. Still, Dio Cassius says, *Domitian put to death, beside many others, the consul Flavius Clemens, and his wife, Domitilla who was also a relative of the emperor. Both were accused of impiety, for which also many others were condemned, having gone astray after the customs of the Jews. But Domitilla was banished.* That Clemens was a Christian, there can be no doubt. The Christians were classed with the Jews, as very few notable Romans at that time went over to Judaism, but many to Christianity. The sister's daughter of Flavius Clemens is known to have been a distinguished Christian. Suetonius designates Flavius as a man of *despicable inactivity,* a reproach frequently cast upon Christians, because they withdrew from the corrupt civil life of heathendom. This reproach did not apply to the Jews.

That Domitian looked upon Christianity with a jealous eye, may also be inferred from what Eusebius relates as to Domitian causing the relatives of

Christ to be sent for to Rome, because he was afraid of the coming of Christ.

There were *philosophers* who, by their discourses in respect to the emperor's claims, brought others into trouble; and who could these be but the Christians, the only persons who energetically opposed such claims.

A BLOODY PERSECUTION OVER CHRISTENDOM

The Revelation was composed at a time when there was an organized bloody persecution, which extended over all Christendom. Chapter 13:7 is proof, where the beast wars against Christians over the whole earth. In 13:8 all that dwell on the earth worship the beast; in 2:13 the martyr-crown is won far from the centre of the Roman state, and under the magistracy acting as Satan's instrument (13:3); 6:9, where the prophet sees souls slain for the word of God; 17:6, where he sees the woman drunk with the blood of the saints, 16:6, according to which they *have shed the blood of saints and prophets;* 18:20, where God avenges upon the new Babylon saints, apostles and prophets, where in ver. 24 the blood of saints and prophets is found in her. Finally, 20:4, where those who had not worshipped the beast revived again.

The future is in these passages represented as *present*, but only in so far as it was to be a *continuation* of the present. There is no trace of what then existed only within local boundaries, appearing afterwards as a general persecution extending to all Christendom. Comp. besides 7:14. Throughout we see only the aspect Christ presents to the enemies of his kingdom, especially the heathen enemies; the early Jews appear as insignificant opponents, briefly despatched in the epistles. And this coupled with the desire for the coming of Christ, and faith to his imminent approach; show that a general conflict of heathenism and Christianity, of life and death, had already entered. That such a bloody persecution existed under Domitian, is just what might have been expected from the relation in which Christianity stood to Domitian's rigorous claim to divinity. *It was enough,* says Suetonius, *that any word or deed against the majesty of the emperor was objected against any one;* the mere confession of Christianity would appear a capital offence against it. Heathen writers bear testimony to this in cautious and reserved words. Dio Cassius says that Domitian put to death *many others* besides the Flavius Clemens, whose death inferred there were many others; if the emperor treated thus his nearest relatives, how should he have spared others? Nerva punished many delators with death, who, we may be sure, only suffered themselves what they had brought upon others; he set free those condemned for high treason, or were under investigation; and forbade accusations respecting that crime and the Jewish manners to be any longer received. With that prohibition, another (*Nerva c. ii.*) against setting up gold or silver statues, went hand in hand; for the claim of divinity in Domitian, and the persecution of Christians, stood to each other in the relation of cause and effect. Philostratus, complains, that under Domitian a certain class of philosophers had become to others the occasion of death. The notices of Christian authors lead to the same result. In the account of the martyrdom of St Ignatius, it is said, that he with difficulty escaped the earlier storms of the many persecutions that took place under Domitian. Eusebius reports on the authority of Brutius, that *very many Christians suffered martyrdom under Domitian, also saying* that Domitian caused the relatives of Christ to be fetched from Palestine to Rome.

Thus, therefore, we have an excellent historical starting-point in this respect for the composition of the Apocalypse, with the time of Domitian. Under Galba there was no persecution of Christians; that under Nero, was short, and limited to Rome—and it had not been raised against Christians so directly *for the word of God and the testimony of Jesus,* as is here supposed. The Christians, according to Tacitus, were not punished primarily as Christians, but on the ground of beginning the burning of the city, so also Eusebius in his *Church History, ii. 25.* Orosius says, the persecution of Nero spread beyond Rome, but he is a late author, and so less to be regarded, as Tertullian knows only of Rome. In other things he merely copies Suetonius, and introduces but this one circumstance from his own hand. The first epistle of Peter, cannot be used to argue Nero's persecution as widespread. It was written before the persecution of Nero, in which Peter was martyred. The persecutions discoursed of in the first epistle, and the exhortation to stedfastness, are essentially different from those in the Revelation. What in Peter is a subordinate aim, in the Apocalypse is all-predominant: the persecutions referred to in the former are only such as are inseparable from the existence of Christianity itself. Christians are represented as suffering reproach among the heathen, being reviled as evil-doers, 2:12; they have much to suffer, especially in the way of calumny, 2:23, 3:9,16, 4:14. The strongest passage is 5:8-9. But this passage simply indicates, that the heathen mind was then beginning to become fully conscious of the antagonism that existed between it and Christianity, and the threat to its views and feelings; it implies nothing in regard to bloody or judicial persecutions from the heathen state. The Revelation, however, was written in the midst of persecutions, executions, and banishments, as is clear from 13:10, which in comparison with Luke 21:24, Amos 1:6, Ps. 68:19, etc., shows, it is not meant merely imprisonment, but also deportations and exiles, which is also confirmed by 1:9. Nothing of this sort is reported concerning the Neronian persecution. All the sources, Tacitus and Suetonius at their head, make mention only of capital punishments, which were also the only appropriate ones for such a charge. On the other hand, in the persecution under Domitian, banishment, especially to desert islands, is often and expressly referred to. According to Dio Cassius the wife of Flavius Clemens was exiled to Pandatereia. According to him also, Nerva recalled those who had been banished. And according to Eusebius, both in his history and his *Chronicon,* the sister's daughter of Flavius, Domatilla, was for her Christian confession banished to the island Pontia.

DOMITIAN A FIT REPRESENTATIVE

Domitian, above almost every other, was a fit representative of the bloody beast, full of names of blasphemy, and the woman drunk with the blood of saints—comp. 13:17. Pliny describes him as the *most savage monster,* (Panegyr. c. 18) that sometimes gulped the blood of relatives, employed himself in slaughtering the most distinguished citizens, before whose gates fear and terror watched. He was of frightful aspect, pride on his forehead, fury in his eye, constantly seeking darkness and secrecy, never coming out of his solitude, excepting to make solitude. Tacitus (*Agricola, ch. 44,*) mentions Agricola's early death, as a great consolation as *he thus escaped that last period, in which Domitian no longer at intervals and during vacant periods, but constantly, and as with one stroke, made havoc of the state.* Nero, says he (*Philostratus, B. vii. c. 4.*), led the life of a player on the harp and flute, and for such a life little vigour was required. Quite otherwise with Domitian; *he was a man of great bodily strength, and despised the pleasures which music yields, and which tend to soften the mind; he found his enjoyment in the pains and lamentations of others, and thought that the king by night should put an end to all other works, but give a beginning to deeds of murder.*

The view given in 13:10 pervades the Apocalypse. The souls slain for the word cry out for vengeance. And as this cry is heard, we see how God does judge the blood of his servants that had been shed. Even the anti-christian heathen world suspected the greatness of the guilt Domitian had incurred in persecuting the Christians, and the retribution he had in consequence exposed himself to the retributive righteousness of God in Christendom. It could not wholly withstand this, but against its own will and principles was drawn within the sweep of the movement. *The gods,* says Philostratus, 8:25, *drove Domitian from his dominion over men; for he had killed the consul Clemens, to whom he had given his own sister.* Suetonius said, *Especially through this deed, he hastened his own downfall,* and then proceeds to give a long series of pre-intimations that announced beforehand the coming catastrophe.

According to Irenaeus, the persecution was in the closing period of Domitian's reign. Heathen writers (see Juvenal *Sat. iv. v. 153*) agree that the bloody persecution was followed by the death of Domitian. Brutius in Eusebius, and in the *Chronicon Paschale*, states that in the fourteenth year of Domitian, many Christians suffered martyrdom, so the Revelation must have been composed shortly before the death of Domitian. Only this event put a stop to the persecution of the Christians, although Tertullian and Hegesippus represent Domitian as putting a stop to all his persecuting measures, based on the mild treatment which Domitian gave to the relatives of Jesus. It looks from the first very unlike Domitian that he should have come to a better mind; and the closing of the persecution suits much better to Nerva, who is called by Martial soft and good-natured, and who endeavoured to rectify every thing that Domitian had put wrong. According also to Tacitus and Philostratus, it was the death of Domitian which first put an end to his fury. And not till the tyrant had gone did John return from Patmos to Ephesus.

The Apocalypse has no reference to the fall of Jerusalem; its starting-point is the rise of the hostile power of heathenism, its theme the triumph of Christianity over it. Given the prominence Christ's prophecies gave to the fall of Jerusalem and the future development of His kingdom, on which John comments, and that in the time of Galba the fate of Jerusalem was at hand—we should expect the author to comment on it. In the humiliations awaiting the Jewish persecutors in 3:9; not a word respects the fall of Jerusalem. Since the name *Jerusalem* and *Zion* is for the church, if outward Jerusalem and Zion still existed some indication of their fall would be expected. That these names applied to the church, which is represented as the temple (11:1), is easily explained, if the terms now referred to one thing. To the same conclusion points also the analogy of Ezekiel, who received the vision of the new temple and city in the fourteenth year after the destruction of the old ones–see 40:1.

In unison with its place in the Canon, the Revelation must form the key stone to the books of the NEW TESTAMENT, and be separated in particular from the epistles of Paul by a considerable space of time and by the epoch of Jerusalem's fall. This appears from the doctrine that the second coming of Christ and the resurrection were at a great distance from the present time; that in the middle lay a period of a thousand years; before, the overthrow of Rome by the ten kings, the conquest of these kings by Christ, and the destruction of the heathenish world-power; afterward the revival of heathenism, its new conflict with the church, and the glorious victory of the latter. This manner of viewing things is found in 2 Pet. 3:8, where the possibility of the Lord's coming as so long deferred, so regarded in a human aspect as very distant. The earlier writers of the NEW TESTAMENT declare they did not know the time of the Lord's coming. But a decided advance is made in the knowledge, and of such importance, requiring a basis of new circumstances and relations, in particular that the appearance of the Lord to execute judgment on Jerusalem already belonged to the past. So long as this had not taken place, it was difficult to determine what in our Lord's discourses referred to it, and what to the end of the world. The *Verily I say to you, this generation shall not pass away till all is fulfilled,* in Matt. 24:34, must have rendered doubtful the indication of a more distant future by the end of all things, until history had entered as an expositor—until the destruction of Jerusalem as an isolated fact, not connected with a general catastrophe for the world, had shown that there was not an absolute and final, but only a preparatory fulfilment to be looked for. It presented a small scale view of the judgment, which at the actual end of the world was to appear in its proper greatness. Hence, all that our Lord in Matthew prophesies regarding his coming, refers immediately both to the destruction of Jerusalem, and to the end of the world, with all its manifold and recurring signs, preludes, preparations, and warnings; and it is a vain undertaking to try to distinguish mechanically and externally what should be referred to the one event and what to the other. As to the period of the final judgment, no definite marks occur in our Lord's prediction. Till this historical commentary was given, the matter had to hang in suspense, after the example of our Lord, and as appears to have been done by the apostles. It was only when such a commentary had been given that the ground was laid for imparting the new explanations, which are unfolded in the Apocalypse, just as of old when the seventy years of Jeremiah were on the point of expiring, Daniel came forth with his prophecy of the seventy weeks of years.

Some say ch. 11 reflects the fall of Jerusalem or with 20:9, 21:10 that it was still standing, and 17:10-11 determines the period of Galba. But he who assumes for his starting-point the period of Domitian, as having so many solid grounds to support it, may gain an insight into the whole by unbiased and earnest inquiry, and find these passages brought into their true light. A fundamental defect of the theology of the present day, is that criticism comes into play before exegesis has sufficient work, and that the crudest thoughts are proclaimed with naive confidence, and most solid arguments both of an external and internal nature are unscrupulously set aside. This is not the scientific mode of proceeding, however commonly it boasts of being so.

REVELATION

Overview

THE INTRODUCTION

The introduction in 1:1-3 points to the high importance of the book, in which St John acts as the servant and organ of God and Christ. It indicates the subject of the book, which was to show what must shortly come to pass. It is to be the book of the future of the kingdom of God. In pronouncing those blessed who read and hear what is written in it, its practical character is made known, as being throughout intended to promote what concerns the divine life.

THE MAIN BODY OF THE BOOK

The introduction is followed by what constitutes the main body of the book, consisting of seven groups, the seven divided by three and four—three *preparatory* groups, and four which are designed to show *in detail* what is to come to pass. The Apocalypse is not, as many claim, executed on the plan of a progressive and continually expanding whole. The book of Daniel has a plan, and forms a whole; but it is so constructed, that one and the same thing returns again in different ways, and presents itself more and more distinctly to the eye of the reader. It is much the same also with the emblematical portion of Zechariah (1:7, 6:15), which, after Daniel, is most closely related to the Apocalypse, and consists of a series of independent visions, all communicated in one night, and by supplementing one another form together a complete image of the future fortunes of the people of God.

THE FIRST GROUP: THE SEVEN EPISTLES

The first group is that of the *seven epistles*, 1:4—3: 22. It unfolds the practical obligations in view of the near approach of the Lord, which the following groups place distinctly in view; anticipating the question, *"How shall I receive, and how shall I meet thee?"* The seven churches of Asia exemplify what is said for the benefit of the church in all ages.

The group falls into three parts. First, the *introduction*, which after the *salutation* in 1:4-6, delivers *two consolatory declarations*, ver. 7-8. Then, in ver. 9-20, follows *the account of Christ's appearance*, in which John, after indicating the historical starting-point (ver. 9), receives the charge to write to the seven churches. The third part is made up of *the seven epistles* themselves. The substance of the communication contained in them was already prepared by the appearance of the Lord, which bears a double character, one threatening and another consolatory, so the epistles form a commentary on the appearance.

THE GENERAL GROUPS

Next come two groups, the theme of which was unfolded in 8:3-5 thus: *God will hear the fervent prayers of his struggling and suffering church, and cause his judgments to alight on the world.*

All here possesses a general, preparatory character. The *ungodly world*, the earth lifting itself up in rebellion against heaven, appears as the object of the divine judgments. No trace is to be found of Rome or of any other worldly power. The judgments have no individual mark, but are such as continually return in the course of history, as the earth lifts itself up against its Creator.

The *general* groups are necessary because John does not prophesy for the present alone, but for the church in all ages.

From the *special* part we see, that the resistance of the world to the kingdom of God, which formed the immediate occasion of the Revelation being given, was not to be the last. The Roman opposition was to be followed by that of the ten kings. And still further on, after Christ's thousand years' reign, there was to arise the great conflict of Gog and Magog.

Each of these three great divisions of opposing forces falls again into a series of particular acts. The manifestations of God's penal justice, which follow closely on the assault of the adversary, must have much in *common*. This common ground is represented in our two groups—the specific character of which is to be kept apart from all that is individual—*before* the *particular* kinds of opposition, in their separate characteristics, and God's judicial operations in regard to them, come to be spoken of.

It is important to have a right explanation of these two groups, and an edifying application of them, so we can clearly perceive their general and preparatory character.

THE SECOND GROUP: THE SEVEN SEALS

First, we have the group of the *seven seals* in 4:1—8:1.

The arrangement is this: The *holy assembly sitting in judgment* in ch. 4, the *giving up of the book with seven seals to Christ* in ch. 5, the *opening of the seals of the book*, and the *making manifest of the judgments* contained therein in ch. 6 and 8:1. Intermediately, in ch. 7 there is *an episode*, showing how God preserves his people amid his judicial visitations, and helps them attain to his heavenly kingdom.

In what forms the main burden of the group—ch. 6 and 8:1—the church, harassed by the persecutions of the world, has her heavenly king placed before her eyes, as he visits the persecuting world with bloodshed, scarcity, famine, pestilence; and makes all dread the destruction of everything that concerns it, and finally (ch. 8:1) subjects it to ruin.

THE THIRD GROUP: THE SEVEN TRUMPETS

Then follows the group of the *seven trumpets*, 8:2—11:19.

The section 8:3-5 stands by itself as a *prelude*, indicating the point of view out of which this group, as also the preceding one, with which it is united into a pair, ought to be contemplated; and 10:1—11:13, forms an *episode*.

In the main part *the plague of war* is represented under a series of symbols, as that by which God continually, during the course of ages, chastises anew the heathenish opposition that is made to his kingdom. Among the scourges of God this is the most frightful, so a separate group is devoted to it, although war already occurred in the preceding group in order among the other plagues.

OVERVIEW

AN EPISODE: THE CHURCH

In the *episode* we see *the church*. As an enclosure appended to the last verse of ch. 9, it answers the question: *How does the church stand in reference to the corrupt wicked world incorrigible under the heaviest visitations of divine judgment?* It presents an antidote to the doubt respecting the completion of the church, her sinfulness, her proneness to fall in with the world, by assuring the church that a reaction would arise against the tendency to apostatize, and that the judgment upon the church for her backsliding should not annihilate her, but prepare the way for grace to operate.

These consolatory truths could only be represented within the preparatory groups. The temptation they meet is not confined to a single period, but one constantly recurring. In all epochs the corruption of the world has never failed to exercise a disastrous influence on the church. As often as iniquity abounds, and love waxes cold; there is a tendency in those who have remained steadfast, to doubt the completion of the church, their dearest hopes threaten to vanish.

Such, then, is the chief burden of the three groups of the first part.

THE FOURTH GROUP: THE THREE ENEMIES OF GOD'S KINGDOM

The first group of the second part, the fourth group of the book, is that of *the three enemies of God's kingdom*, ch. 12—14. Of these enemies we are presented with first *Satan* in ch. 12, then *the beast from the sea*, the God-opposing worldly power, with seven heads denoting its seven phases, in 12:18, 13:10, and then *the beast from the earth*, earthly, physical, demoniacal wisdom, in 13:11-18.

BELIEVERS CONSOLED

Then in ch. 14, believers, who are assailed by these enemies, leagued together in close fellowship, are consoled by the view of the immoveable condition of those who stand in the grace of God, and the judgments that were ready to befall the enemies.

This ministration of comfort is a general and preliminary representation, and points forwards to another group, in which a more particular delineation was to be given of the victory of Christ. The kernel of this group is manifestly the description of the enemies. The church must learn from it the whole magnitude of her danger, so that she may take to herself her complete armour, may cry from her inmost soul, *Lord have mercy on me,* and after having won the victory, may with heart, mouth, and hands give thanks to her divine helper.

THE FIFTH GROUP: THE SEVEN VIALS

The fifth group, that of the *seven vials* in ch. 15–16, unfolds *the seven plagues,* which during the course of centuries accompany the beast, the ungodly power of the world (the second and third groups had to do only with the corrupt *world*).

THE SIXTH GROUP: THE DESTRUCTION OF THE THREE ENEMIES

The fifth group forms the prelude to the sixth, ch. 17—20, which represents the *destruction of the three enemies of God's kingdom*. This last begins with the beast, the worldly power, and ascends upwards to Satan. Of the seven heads of the beast, five, according to 17:10, had fallen before the prophet's own time–the Egyptian, Assyrian, Chaldean, Medo-Persian and Grecian monarchies. In the prophet's time the church was oppressed through the medium of the *sixth* head, the monarchy of Rome. Ch. 17 announces its overthrow. In ch. 18 we have a *pictorial representation* of it. In 19:1-4 it is celebrated by *a song of praise*. The counterpart is made up of *the anticipatory celebration of the victory* over all the other enemies in ver. 5-10. By these two songs of praise the group is divided into two halves.

THE VICTORY OF CHRIST OVER THE TEN KINGS

In 19:11-21 is related *the victory of Christ over the ten kings*, who were the instruments of his judgment on Rome, the seventh head of the beast with ten horns. With this as the last phase of the heathen world power, the beast himself also, the state of heathendom perishes, and with him, too, his assistant, the beast from the earth.

THE CHURCH REIGNS FOR A THOUSAND YEARS

Ch. 20:1-6 represents, how the first enemy, Satan, is rendered for a time harmless, and how there breaks in upon the church a reign of a thousand years. It has been asked, why this period of a thousand years might not be regarded as one that was frequently to be repeated? The answer is found, as soon as the distinction is perceived between the special part of the Apocalypse and its preparatory groups, which are of a general nature.

From beginning to end this sixth group has a *chronological* development. Although other numbers in the Apocalypse are symbolical, the sixfold repetition of the thousand number alone shows, that it is meant to be taken in good earnest. The number *ten* and what proceeds from it bears the character of a round number in Scripture (as is the thousand), but never the character of a *symbolical* one.

THE FINAL OVERTHROW OF THE WORLD

The *final destruction of Satan* is represented in 20:7-10. After the complete overthrow of the three enemies, there still follows the final judgment on their servants coupled with the removal of the present constitution of the world, as now required by the extirpation of sin, in ch. 20:11-15.

THE SEVENTH GROUP: THE NEW JERUSALEM

The seventh group forms the conclusion of the main portion of the book, and contains *the description of the new Jerusalem*, 21:1—22:5.

THE CONCLUSION

The conclusion of the book, in 22:6—21, which corresponds to the beginning, points to its high importance, and once more brings out its fundamental truth.

THE TITLE

What must shortly come to pass

REVELATION 1:1-3

REVELATION 1:1-3

The title: what must shortly come to pass

THE TITLE

1:1. The revelation of Jesus Christ, which God gave him to shew to his servants, what must shortly come to pass; and he signified it by his angel, whom he sent, to his servant John,

The book is called in verse 1, *the Revelation of Jesus Christ*. The word *revelation*, or disclosing, *apocalypsis*, relates to the word *mystery* or *secret*. Mysteries are the object of revelation, and the territory of the revelation extends as far as the territory of mysteries. The condition of the revelation is the inaccessibility of a matter to the ordinary faculties of the mind. It is also that which has already been made objectively manifest, as the church's own, as communicated to a particular individual. Christian doctrine is superrational (Matt. 11:25, 16:17, John 6:44, Eph. 1:17); flesh and blood cannot produce and exercise it, we have a revelation by which Christian wisdom was the product. The revelations in 2 Cor. 12:1 connect with the visions; Paul received them in ecstasy, was raised to the heavens, and heard unutterable words. In Acts 10, it was in an ecstasy, and by vision, that Peter received the revelation concerning the heathen admission to salvation.

Revelation here and *prophecy*, in ver. 3 correspond with each other. The book is *the revelation of Jesus Christ* and *the prophecy of John*. Its object are the mysteries; its product is the prophecy. The manner of receiving it is revelation, the manner of its delivery, is prophecy. Paul says, *what shall I profit you except I shall speak to you either by revelation or by knowledge, or by prophesying, or by doctrine?* Here is a double pair of corresponding parts; *revelation* and *prophecy*, *knowledge* and *doctrine*. The speaker attains to his knowing by revelation imparted by the Spirit of God. When he gives utterance to this, he is a prophet. Or it may be by learning, meditation, inquiry with the common help of the Holy Spirit; and then his knowing is a *knowledge*, and the utterance a purely intelligent one, working on the understanding. The condition, in which revelation is received differs from that in which the knowledge is matured, so the mode of deliverance in the prophet differs from that of common teaching. That received in ecstasy is delivered in an elevated state of mind; as the delivery stands *immediately* connected with the receiving, and the receiving has not, as was usual with Paul, already wrought into a sort of knowledge.

Revelation is not *eschatological apocalypsis*, or the revealing of the final development of the kingdom of God and the coming of the Lord. By the word itself nothing is indicated here as to the special object of the Revelation of Jesus Christ. But the thing to be supplied, whether counsel, for warning, or consolation, is furnished by the *circumstances* which occasioned the revelation. The starting-point here was the oppression of the church by the world-power, the object of the Revelation of Christ to the apostle can only be what would edify and preserve the church amid persecutions, the adversary's destruction,

1. The revelation of Jesus Christ, which God gave him to shew to his servants, what must shortly come to pass; and he signified it by his angel, whom he sent, to his servant John,

and the church's final triumph.

Revelation, and its prophecy are closely joined with the prerogatives of the apostleship. The prophets are personally identical with the apostles (Eph. 3:5,6.) For it was by the apostles, Peter and Paul, that the truth was conveyed to the minds of Christians by supernatural revelation. History knows nothing of persecutions by the Roman world-power against prophets, *except* against the apostles, Peter, Paul, and John (2 Cor. 12, Eph. 3:3, Gal. 1:12, 2:2.) New truths could only be communicated through the highest gift, *prophecy*, to believers, and be diffused as knowledge and doctrine. Peter, Paul, and John, so pre-eminent above the rest, were also the most highly distinguished by these gifts. The other design of the apostleship was the receiving *the much* that the Lord had still to say to them, after his ascension–John 16:12-13. *The comforter* was to make known the *future* to the apostles. What is written in the Acts of other prophets all bear a *subordinate* character, with no new communication of important truths (11:27, 13:1, 15:32, 21:10.) The author has described himself as an apostle. This prophecy could only have proceeded from one, who among the apostles themselves, held a leading place.

It is the revelation which has Jesus Christ for its author. Of course, this does not exclude a zealous investigation and study of Scripture, a profound reflection on the divine purposes, and an earnest desire for the divine secrets. The Lord Jesus Christ is himself the author, John only holds the pen (ver. 2, comp. 1:10, 4:1, 19:10, 22:16; Gal. 1:12.) None of John's endearing epistolary epithets– *my little children, my brethren, beloved,* are here. He writes here not as of himself, but in the name of Jesus Christ. Much of Revelation is to be found in the old prophecies–referred to in 10:7–but by no means the whole, for God had given the revelation to Jesus Christ. It does not conflict with the formerly given Scriptures; but summarizes all that in ancient prophecy remained to be fulfilled after Christ and the apostles. To disclose the future is not the only design of prophecy. Under the NEW TESTAMENT, Christ has appeared as *the way, the truth, and the life.* The main *source* of higher and clearer views was thus at once laid open to the church, so that knowledge and doctrinal instruction came to prominence. Prophecy was required only for the new things that still remained to be developed.

    1. Which God gave to him.

Revelation is the *act* of communication. Here, it also includes *that which is disclosed*, and to this refers the *which*.

The Son has every thing that the Father has, and yet has nothing but what he has of the Father. John 12:48-49 shows the origin of Christ's word is God, its importance, and the guilt of rejecting it. Also 16:14-15, *All that the Father hath is mine. Therefore, said I, he will take of mine and shew it unto you.* He had said just before, *He will show you things to come.* What Christ had spoken upon earth was ascribed to God, here also in what after his departure was communicated through the Spirit to his apostles.

THE TITLE

1:1. To show to his servants.

The word *showing* is not *making known*, but *causing to see*. The showing refers to things communicated to the internal vision (comp. 4:1, 17:1, 22:1, 6, 8.) To the *showing*, on the part of God, corresponds the *seeing*, on the part of the prophet. The *servants of God* are the prophets, for to them alone belongs the *seeing*.

The prophets, in the OLD TESTAMENT, are named God's servants (comp. 4:1, 17:1, 22:1, 6,8.) For, the sending of the *angel* indicates that the Lord is the *God of the spirits of the prophets*.

1. What must shortly come to pass.

The fulfilment of what is announced in the Revelation is placed in the *immediate* future. According to ver. 3 and 22:10, the time is *near. I come quickly,* says the Lord in 22:7,12, 20, 3:11, 2:5,16. These declarations are opposed to the view of those who would convert the entire book into a history of the time of the end, and confirms the view, which treats it as our companion through the whole course of history.

The beginning in general was ascribed to the immediate future, and such as was to be the beginning of the end. The main burden of the book refers to relations as yet unformed. We are never pointed to the far-distant future; he is secretly working for salvation and destruction, when he seems to be standing aloof; when he executes his judgment we enter into his salvation, and learn what is meant by the *shortly*. Whenever Satan stirs up new wars against Christ and his church, the *shortly* and the *I come quickly*, also spring into new life. In Hag. 2:6, the shaking spoken of took effect in the *immediate* future on the Persian kingdom. The prophet declares the shortness of the time to console us—only that which appears short in the eyes of men was suitable, otherwise it is mockery or deception.

1. And he signified (it) by his angel, whom he sent to his servant John.

He *signified it—not the revelation* but *what must shortly come to pass*. The *he signified,* resumes the *to show* in ver. 1 again. It is said here, as also in 22:6-16, that Christ communicated through his angel to John the knowledge of the future. It is a particular angel who stands beside the angel of the Lord as the mediating agent of his revelations. In Ex. 32:34 we find along with the highest revealer of God—*the angel of the Lord* or *the Logos*, an angel subordinate to him as his attendant. In Daniel the angel of the Lord appears under the symbolical name of *Michael* (see p. 117.) But as he manifests himself in overwhelming majesty, the angel *Gabriel* acts as mediator between him and the prophet, comp. 8:16, 9:21. In Zechariah *the angel who speaks with him* is a standing figure. It is this angelic minister who conducts him from the common state to one of ecstasy, awakens in him the spiritual sense to apprehend what was presented in the vision, and explains it to him, so as to enable him to understand. The angel, in the business of the revelation, is set forth in a quite general way, nothing more is said till we come to the vision of the judgment on the three enemies of God's kingdom, where he is introduced at the very commencement (17:1, comp. 7, 15, 19:9,) and the vision of the New Jerusalem.

1. And he signified (it) by his angel, whom he sent to his servant John.

If the spiritual sense in John was first opened by the angel and kept awake, then he was the mediating agent of the message for him. The mind must be prepared to receive the revelation; the seer must be in the Spirit, 1:10, 4:2. The mediating angel in Daniel and Zechariah, whom John more especially followed, is a pervading one; characteristic to each of them is their announcing, it was thus they were raised into the ecstatic condition. In Dan. 10:16 Gabriel touches Daniel's lips, inspiring him with the higher powers, comp. ver. 10, 8:17. On Zech. 1:9 the *I will make you see what these are* refer to the opening of the spiritual eye and ear of the prophet. Only when this had been done by the *angelus interpres*, could the prophet apprehend the declaration of the angel of the Lord, and the report of the ministering angels. On 4:1, where the angel is spoken of as *awaking* the prophet, like a man out of sleep, between this vision and the preceding the angel had withdrawn for a little from the prophet, and the latter had returned from his ecstasy into the state of common life. The common and the ecstatic condition stand related to each other as sleeping and being awake.

It is not as an *apostle* that John is named here the *servant* of Christ, but as a *prophet*. This is evident from the relation in which *to his servant John* stands here to the preceding expression *to his servants*. Such important revelations were not given beyond the limits of the apostleship. History knows of no other John but the apostle John. In his Gospel John has indicated his name in a gentle way (John, *he to whom the Lord is gracious*) as *the disciple whom Jesus loved*, but here he gives his name expressly. We find the same difference in the OLD TESTAMENT also between the historical and the prophetical writings of the prophets. The history had its security in the joint knowledge of contemporaries; but in prophecy personality is of the greatest moment, and nameless prophecies have no place in OLD TESTAMENT Scripture.

2. Who has testified of the word of God and the testimony of Jesus Christ, what he saw,

John does not speak from himself; he merely testifies of the word of God, as it had been certified to him through *the testimony of Jesus Christ*. In the threatenings, promises, and exhortations of the book we are not to look at the person of John, but remember that it is God who speaks here. The expression is *who has testified*, not: *who testifies*, because the ancients often frame their words to that time when their writings should be read.

The *testimony of Jesus Christ* can only be the testimony which Jesus Christ *delivers*, as the subject-matter of the book comes from the Most High God. Christ *testifies* of what he has heard and seen, and so also do his disciples.

The words: *what he saw*, show that the subject here is of those higher communications which were received in vision by the internal eye. *Seeing* is used thus of the prophetic vision in an entire series of passages of this book, for example, 1:11,12,17,19-20, ver. 1. The feeling of John's own mind, and fancy, is quite excluded. To *see* and to *testify* bear reference one to another. The matters presented to him were partly seen and partly heard. To see is the more excellent. Hence, the prophets were anciently called *seers*, and this book itself has the name of a revelation.

The *who has testified*, regards the apostle's obedience, diligence, and faithfulness in describing *this* revelation, not his gospel.

3. Blessed is he who reads, and those who hear the words of the prophecy, and keep what is written therein; for the time is near.

Blessed, it is said in 22:14, *are they who keep his commandments, Blessed,* in 19:9, *are those who are called to the marriage-supper.* In 20:6, *Blessed and holy is he who has part in the first resurrection.* This refers to the bliss of heaven, and afterwards in the kingdom of glory upon earth. It also comprehends all the good, as the reward of fidelity—the preservation of true believers from the plagues which fall upon the world; 7:1-8, 3:10.

In the conclusion, as in the beginning here, 22:18-19, a twofold threatening is against those who, after Deut. 4:2, 12:32, add to or take away from the book to rid themselves of the obligations of duty. To those who keep what is written, the blessing pronounced on them also has a double reference—preservation amid the plagues and eternal blessedness.

The *he who reads and they who hear,* points to the reading aloud in churches. *Hearing* is the usual way of coming to the knowledge of the book.

The book contains a word of prophecy; not mere citations from the OLD TESTAMENT. The prophecies of the OLD TESTAMENT are pervaded and saturated with references to the books of Moses, by allusion or immediate appropriation, without any formal citations. The *keeping* is the principal thing, to which the blessing belongs, the reading and hearing is the preliminary condition to this. The person who has got to the close of the book has already fulfilled the condition. That every thing is placed in *the keeping* points to the practical character of Scripture prophecy, never to gratify a frivolous curiosity, but to promote the divine life. The true prophet is a counsellor, comp. Numb. 24:14, Isa. 41:28. To the *keeping* belongs repentance, faith, patience, obedience, prayer, watching, steadfastness. The words, *for the time is near,* provide a reason for the call to keep, the time of the fulfilment is near, and consequently the time for rewarding the faithful and punishing the slothful; comp. 1 Pet 4:7, Luke 21:34, Rom. 13:11.

SECTION 1

CHAPTERS 1-11

THREE GROUPS GENERAL AND CONSOLATORY

GROUP 1

THE SEVEN EPISTLES

*How shall I receive
and how shall I meet God?*

REVELATION
1:4–3:22

REVELATION 1:4-6

First part: introduction & salutation

Here we have first the salutation, verses 4-6. The inscription does not belong to the book in general, but exclusively to the seven epistles. Although the conclusion of the whole resembles an epistle; 22:21–*the grace of the Lord Jesus Christ be with all saints*–but the words: *with all the saints*, not *with you all*, as in Paul's epistles, shows here is only an *imitation* of the conclusion of an epistle. Ch. 1:3 pronounces *all without distinction* blessed who hear, read and keep the book; the conclusion is just as general as the beginning; according to 22:7 *all* are called blessed who keep the book. In the middle portion also we everywhere meet with the entire body of the church, with no special respect to the seven churches–in ch. 7 the *one hundred and forty and four thousand* and the *multitudes* represent the church at large, not merely the Asiatic churches; in 11:1 the temple of God symbolizes the militant church, as the New Jerusalem the triumphant state. What is written in the epistles to the churches is only *primarily* addressed to them, because it is not an *accompaniment* to the book, but an *integral part* of the book itself, a book that is destined to the use of all God's servants.

The relation of this first series, the seven letters, to the six following ones is that in the first is unfolded in detail the call, *repent, prepare ye the way of the Lord,* and in the other, *the glory of the Lord shall be revealed, the kingdom of heaven is at hand.* When the Lord is about to bring deliverance to his church, and execute judgment on the world, he also calls his people to prepare themselves by purging out worldly elements in readiness for his work. Throughout this first series, the predominating element is the pressing of practical exhortations in view of the near approach of the Lord; to be effectively done, it must go into the special circumstances of the churches. The *sevenfold* number of the churches indicates the variety of circumstances and the foundation of general applicability.

THE SALUTATION

> 1:4. John to the seven churches in Asia. Grace be to you and peace, from Him who is, and who was, and who comes, and from the seven Spirits which are before the throne.

The author of the epistles indicates his person by the simple name of *John*, a John, preeminent among Johns, that is the apostle. We also think of the apostle John by the seven churches of Asia, that is, *Proconsular* Asia. John writes simply to *the churches of Asia. Seven* churches because it is *his* seven churches. John had a district in Asia, which embraced quite a circle of churches, named by Tertullian *John's nurselings.* The church fathers relate that when the apostles were scattered into different countries, John received for his share Asia, and continued there till he died at Ephesus. After Patmos

CHAPTER 1:4-6   THE REVELATION

4. John to the seven churches in Asia. Grace be to you and peace, from Him who is, and who was, and who comes, and from the seven Spirits which are before the throne.

John went to Ephesus and the neighbouring areas to appoint bishops, start new churches, and appoint some to ministry. The church of Ephesus had been founded by Paul, but John continued to abide there till the times of Trajan. He ruled the churches there. There were other churches in Asia, Colosse, Hierapolis, Tralles, and Magnesia, of whom John may not have been able to have extended his agency.

If Christ had authorized such messages, sharp reproofs and commendations, the churches must recognize the John to be the apostle. For such charges always rest on an official basis. In Clement's account of the youth John gives instructions and reproofs, as a person who has absolute power and authority, and who judges by the most rigid standard, which coincides with the epistles here, in that the *bishop* in the one place, as the *angel* in the other, is made responsible for all that was proceeding in the church. The series of the seven epistles begins precisely with that to the church at Ephesus, where John usually resided.

In all probability the Jewish war which began in 66, interrupting the operations of John in Palestine, took him to Asia Minor. If the Apocalypse had been written under Galba in the year 68 it would supply insufficient time to form the relation we find here, John firmly established and intimately acquainted throughout an extensive district of churches. He must previously have adapted himself to the Grecian culture, he must have visited the particular churches, some distant from one another, he must have resided for a considerable time at each place in order to establish his authority, and must also have frequently returned to confirm it. A series of years must necessarily have elapsed before John could have named the seven churches in Asia *his*, and written to them in the way he does here. John would have not left his fatherland Palestine without some call arising out of *external* circumstances. See Matt. 24:15-20. Had he been *inclined* to do so, he would have done it long before. The character of John is fundamentally faithful; after the death of Paul he would not have transferred his seat to Ephesus on a mere solicitation.

4. Grace be to you and peace,

Peace is always the opposite to strife and war, to hostile pressure, whether the hostility proceed from God or from the creatures. The stress on peace in Scripture arises from this, that believers are threatened by so many hostile powers. A violent outbreak of hostility against the church forms the starting-point here, and all else in the salutation refers to it. Here is not of peace with God, but only of a safe position in regard to the world. The *grace*, which in the Mosaic blessing also precedes peace, is the source of all the benefits belonging to believers, but peace in this strife.

John had entered into the place of Paul, naturally adopting his salutation-formula, which entirely coincides with Romans 1:7. The salutations of James and Jude are different. Peter's comes the nearest to Paul's: 1 Pet. 1:1-2, in unison with other resemblances to Paul, occurring in Peter, as Peter in his first epistle entered into the field of Paul's operations. Still, he lacks *from God, etc.* The conclusion of the Apocalypse has also the greatest similarity to the epistles of Paul. There it is: *The grace of Jesus Christ be with you,* here: *The grace of the Lord Jesus Christ be with all saints.* The deviation was required by the *general* purport of the book. Paul never, like John here, prefixes his mere

FIRST PART: INTRODUCTION AND SALUTATION

name, but always sets forth his dignity. That has already been done in ver. 1, and now a simple salutation, after the manner of Paul, appears here, amplified according to the higher prophetic style, with the necessities of the call for a powerful consolation. From God and Christ comes here a strengthening to an endangered faith, and a bulwark against despair.

4. from Him who is, and who was, and who comes,

These words describe the name of *Jehovah*. This name, properly *Jahveh* (the vowels belong to *Adonai*, which the Jews pronounce instead of it) has the meaning of *the Being*, pure absolute unchangeable existence, that which God is comes into consideration only as conditioning what he is *for* his people. This appears from Ex. 3:13-16. In asking for his name, the people find in that a pledge for his help in distressing circumstances, *not* for satisfying their metaphysical curiosity. *Jehovah* comprises in itself the fulness of all consolation, which is brought up and placed before believers, the prophet's companions in tribulation.

As pure, and absolute, and unchangeable Being, God *is;* he exists in that omnipotence which he serves the good of the church at the present time; he works, in concealment, for her welfare, whatever may seem contrary, the world may triumph over the church lying in apparent helplessness. He *was;* for he has given evidence of his being in the past by deeds of omnipotent love, as in the Egyptian exodus. He *comes;* for he will judge the world and save his church. The stress here is on the last clause, *he who comes*.

In 4:8 the four living creatures cry out, *Holy, holy, holy, is God, the Lord, the Almighty, who was, and who is, and who comes;* as much as to say, who, as by giving matter-of-fact demonstration of his Being in the past and present, he has proved himself to be the *was* and *is*, so will he also come to establish his kingdom over the whole earth.

4. and from the seven Spirits who are before the throne.

The *Spirits* are the Spirits of God. Here the Spirit comes, not according to his transcendence, but his *immanence*–not to his internal relation to the Father and the Son, but to his *mission*.

The designation of the Spirits as *seven* is not derived from Isa. 11:2, where the subject is not, as here, the *active* powers of the Spirit, but his productions or the properties he calls forth, but rather it is taken from Zech. 4:10, where the operations of the Spirit of the Lord appear under the image of *the seven eyes of the Lord, that run to and fro throughout the earth*.

The sevenfoldness merely points to the fullness and variety of the powers, which are enclosed in the unity, with reference to the manifold powers and agencies on the part of Satan and the world, which threaten the church with destruction, as also with respect to the church's manifold straits and necessities, and perhaps to the seven number of the churches which constituted so many fields for the Spirit's efficacious working. Here respect is had only to the manifold *manifestations* of one and the same Spirit. And that this Spirit, manifold in its unity, does not exist together *with* Christ, so that what is here attributed to the Spirit *proceeds from* Christ, is clear from this passage, as the seven Spirits are represented as employed in the service of the church

4. and from the seven Spirits who are before the throne.

of Christ, and from 3:1, where Christ has the seven Spirits of God, and so is almighty to punish or reward, and also from 5:6, where the seven Spirits appear as the seven Spirits of *the Lamb*. The Spirit is not here as knowledge and enlightenment, as both the starting-point and the connection suggest its *physical*, than its *moral* operations.

The seven Spirits form here a mighty bulwark against despair, a compact phalanx, on which all the assaults of the world-power against the church shall break to pieces. The seven Spirits press into the service of the church, delivering and helping, overthrowing and destroying, even to the remotest corner of the earth. No distress is so deep, no feebleness so great, that it may not with them be rectified.

In Zech. 4:6-7 the Spirit of God appears as the power, which carries the building of the temple to its completion in spite of all adverse machinations. It is the same Spirit that moved with creative energy on the waters of the primeval world, Gen. 1:2, Job 34:14, Ps. 104:29-30. It is that power, by which, according to Isa. 4:4, God executes his judgments upon the earth. In the Gospel of John, the Spirit is brought into view chiefly in respect to his moral and religious operations, in accordance with the evangelist's subject. And the same precisely is done here also in 19:10, 22:17, 1:10. The Spirit appears here, not less than the God of nature and Christ, as the well-spring of grace and peace.

The threefold *from*: *from him who is, etc., and from the seven Spirits, and from Jesus Christ*, involves a position of equality, implying an independence of the Spirit, beside the Father and the Son. The derivation of grace and peace from the Spirit not less than the Father and the Son points to the adorable Trinity, and here establishes a close affinity between the Revelation and John's Gospel. As here Christ has the seven Spirits of God (3:1, 5:6,) so in the Gospel the Son has the powers and properties of the Spirit (truth, life), but also the Spirit himself, (16:14-15, 1:33, 3:34.) He is plainly subordinate, as to the Father who sends him, so also to the Son, since the latter also sends him, and since he does not speak of himself, but only what he hears. Further, the Spirit is predominantly viewed in respect to his *operations outwards*—comp. especially John 7:39.

Some identify the seven spirits with *the seven angels* in 8:2, but in the Revelation angels are never called spirits; in 4:5 the seven Spirits are the Spirits of God, in 5:6 the Spirits appear as the seven eyes of the Lamb, and the FUNDAMENTAL PASSAGE in Zechariah is against it.

5. And from Jesus Christ, who is the faithful witness.

A *faithful witness* is a credible and veracious one (comp. Isa. 8:2,) who speaks what he knows and testifies what he has seen, John 3:11. *Christ* is called a witness, because he does not teach at his own hand, but gives testimony to the truth that is in God. The FUNDAMENTAL PASSAGE is Isa. 55:4, *Behold for a witness of the peoples I give him, as a leader and lawgiver of the peoples*, where as here the witnessing is connected with the supremacy. Witnessing embraces all doctrine and revelation, but is here limited in that *grace and peace* are sought from Jesus Christ to the church. The testimony of Christ here has to do with grace and peace. The *leader* and *lawgiver* declare concerning Christ that which inspires the church with courage in the world. Respect is had to the promises like, *Be of good cheer, I have overcome the world, I am with you alway even to the end of the world, The gates of hell shall not prevail against my church.* Such promises are expanded in this book, which discloses the testimony of Jesus Christ; but only under tribulations will they make their due impression on the mind.

> 5. And the first-born of the dead,

The *first-born* in the OLD TESTAMENT is another name for the *first*; as in Isa. 14:30. It is time and precedence in rank, as in Heb. 12:23, and Col. 1:15-18, where the firstborn is explained by expressions, which are put as equivalent: *who is before all, the head, the beginning, who has the pre-eminence,* as also of *the first fruits of them that sleep,* in 1 Cor. 15:20. This passage rests on Col. 1:18, *And he is the head of the body, the church: who is the beginning, the firstborn from the dead; that in all things he might have the preeminence,* from the following reasons: 1. The expression, *the firstborn from the dead,* is preceded by, *the first-born of all creation.* The prefixed explanatory epithet, *the beginning,* intimates, that the mode of expression was somewhat peculiar. 2. There it is *from the dead,* but here simply *of the dead.* The *from–out of,* points to the fact that Christ was the first in moving *out of* the state of the dead. The simple *of the dead* would scarcely have been used but for that other explanatory passage, according to which it is to be understood as meaning, the first among the dead who have attained to life. In 1 Cor. 15:20, we have also *the first fruits of them that sleep.* But the preceding words there, *but now is Christ risen from the dead,* shows how Christ was the first-fruits, or the first among them that sleep. The expression in 3:14, *the beginning of the creation,* points back to the same in Col. 1:15; and indeed so, that *the beginning,* which there comes into the place of the first-born, is derived from ver. 18. Remarkably, it occurs precisely in the epistle to the Laodiceans, who were very closely related to the Colossians.

He was the conqueror of bodily death for Lazarus, so also he is the conqueror of death to his church; which has with him risen out of the grave. Death to the church, since his resurrection, is only a passage to life. This is what from the connection we are here to make account of.

> 5. and the prince of the kings of the earth.

The FUNDAMENTAL PASSAGE is Ps. 89:27, where it is said of the house of David, which had its culminating point in Christ, *And I will make him my first-born, the highest among the kings of the earth.* One is meant, who reigns over the kings of the earth. This he proves by the overthrow of Rome, whose vassal king ventures to his own destruction into a foolish conflict with Him of life and death, and also by the description of the battle of the ten kings and the victory over them in 19:11, in which Christ appears, in verse 16, with the name, *King of kings and Lord of lords.*

Now here is a doxology indicating three other sources of consolation in Christ.

> 5. to him that loved us, and washed us from our sins by his blood,

Firstly, in his love to us it is impossible that he should be unconcerned at our distress, and not bring us help. To fear and tremble in tribulation is to doubt his love, and so rob him of his highest glory, certified by so great and

CHAPTER 1:4-6   THE REVELATION

<small>5. to him that loved us, and washed us from our sins by his blood,</small>

costly a pledge. To believe in his love, is to be sure of his salvation. The love expresses the abiding love, and comprehends the past, the present, and the future. *Second*, those, whom he has made righteous, he will also make glorious. The *washing* marks the taking away of our sins by forgiveness, and the sanctifying power which has its root in this.

6. And made us a kingdom, priests to God and his Father.

6 This points out the *third* source of consolation. It is not the realm, but the dominion. The people of God are, in consequence of their priestly dignity, appointed to govern the world, as in Dan. 7:27.

Even the OLD TESTAMENT knows of an ideal priesthood beside the common one; comp. besides Ex. 19:6, especially Ps. 99:6, Jer. 33:18,22. But the heart of the priesthood is its close connection with God. Whoever has attained to this, he has, with the spiritual priesthood, at the same time acquired the kingly. Essential to this is the exercising of dominion. God cannot suffer them to be overcome by the world. The verses 2:26-27, 3:21, 5:10, 20:6, 22:5 show that we must not think of dominion over others, but only of maintaining the Christian life in a quiet and independent condition, as it is not the supremacy of *the world* which Christ has acquired for his people. Here the emphasis rests on the kingdom, and the priesthood comes under consideration only as the necessary basis. The kingdom which Christ has acquired for his people was fitted to console dismayed Christians. It was even then manifesting itself. Every heathen won over to the kingdom of God, every martyr who maintained with success the conflict with the world, was a proof of it. But, however important might be the conquests which were then in process of being made on the territory of heathenism, such were only a small pledge of the glorious realization, which should not reach its climax till the whole heathen world lay at their feet. A view of this royal priesthood and priestly kingdom, and undaunted courage before the persecuting heathen world, ought now to fill them.

6. To him be honour and power for ever and ever. Amen.

The words are a *declaration*, the *Amen* an asseveration of the truthfulness of what is said. It is an unquestionable fact, on which anxious minds might strengthen themselves. The *honour* in connection with the *power* is not the ascription of praise, but the glory. As an antidote against timidity and despair under suffering, Peter also points, in 5:11, to the honour and the person of Christ. A leaning on Peter in the close of the salutation, whose doxology is imitated also in Jude 25, with an enlargement as here in 5:13, corresponds to the leaning on Paul at its beginning. The epistle of Peter was also addressed to the churches in Asia. There is a chain-like connection of the later writings of the NEW TESTAMENT with the earlier, which is no more than the example of the OLD TESTAMENT might have led us to expect.

After the salutation, and before he comes to the main subject, John still gives two weighty and appropriate utterances. With two torches he sends a gleam of light beforehand into the dark abyss of terror and dismay.

REVELATION 1:7-8

Consolatory declarations–introductory statements

FIRST INTRODUCTORY STATEMENT

1:7. Behold he comes with clouds, and all eyes shall see him, and they that pierced him, and all the tribes of the earth shall wail over him. Yea, Amen,

St. John here looks back especially to Matt. 24:30 which again rests upon Dan. 7:13, and Zech. 12:10, from which is taken *they shall wail*, and *they shall see*. John had Matt. 24:30 more in view, as there the two passages of Zechariah and Daniel are united together. Instead of *in the clouds of heaven*, we have a more exact reference to Daniel: *with* the clouds; and the clause from Zechariah, *and they who pierced him*, is omitted by Matthew. While in the declaration of our Lord both the FUNDAMENTAL PASSAGES are woven together, here the territory of both is still preserved distinct.

The *Behold he comes with the clouds*, points to Daniel, the rest to Zechariah, the *clouds* with which the Lord comes are the shadow of the judgment, and announce his anger, threatening thunder and lightning, see Isaiah 19:1, Ps. 97:2, Ps. 18:10, Nahum 1:3. That the Lord comes with clouds, renews itself with every oppression of the church by the world. The FUNDAMENTAL PASSAGES where the Lord comes upon the clouds to the judgment of Jerusalem, show it is not merely his coming at the last day, and that the words do not point to a visible appearing. He comes *from henceforth;* so that his whole concealed agency towards the destruction of Jerusalem is comprehended under his *coming*. But if there this refers to the judgment on Jerusalem, and here primarily to that on Rome, then the judicial activity of the Lord in its whole compass, according to its different objects and manifestations, is indicated. It is terrible to the world, and joyful to the church. We have the connection between the redemption and the judgment in Luke 21:27-28. The PASSAGE of Zechariah treats of the penitential mourning of Jerusalem over the Messiah, who had been slain by its guilt. The passage here, and Matt. 24:30 are a sacred parody on that of Zechariah, showing that, beside the salutary repentance of which he speaks, there is another Judas-like repentance of despair; besides the free looking to him who was pierced, there is another not free, which it is impossible for unbelief to escape. The *who have pierced him,* John 19:37, to the piercing with the spear, considered here, is to be viewed not simply as the work of the soldier, but the common deed of those who share the similar state of feeling, and their deeds against Christ in his members. They *shall wail over him,* on account of what they have perpetrated against him, and what they have now to expect from him.

The expression of affirmation in two words, *Yea, Amen,* serves, according to 2 Cor. 1: 20, to give it additional strength. The double *Amen* in the Hebrew and in John 1:51, is analogous. Such a liveliness of asseveration was here perfectly in its place. For the visible presented a strong objection against what was affirmed. There follows now in ver. 8 the second introductory statement of what the prophet had to say for the consolation of the church in its faint and distressed condition.

SECOND INTRODUCTORY STATEMENT

8. I am the Alpha and the Omega, says the Lord God, who is, and who was, and comes, the Almighty.

The *Alpha* as the first and the *Omega* as the last letter in the Greek alphabet, denotes the beginning and the end. Corresponding to this is *the first and the last* in 1:18, 2:8. In 21:6 the two expressions, *Alpha and Omega, beginning and end,* occur together; and in the full-toned conclusion at 22:13, we have the whole three, *Alpha and Omega, first and last, beginning and end.* The fact that *the beginning and the end* never occur elsewhere but in connection with Alpha and Omega, while the latter, and the other expression also, *the first and the last*, are found alone, shows that *the beginning and the end* is only to be regarded as an accompaniment of *Alpha and Omega*. And these words are appropriated to this purpose, because they begin with the first and the last letters of the Hebrew alphabet, and so fitly indicate in what character the Alpha and Omega here come into consideration—only in respect to their place in the alphabet. The speaker is not Christ, but neither is it God the Father in contrast to Christ, but God in the undivided oneness of his being, without respect to the difference of persons.

The great question which then agitated the minds of believers, was about whether the world would maintain the ascendancy, which it then claimed and seemed to possess; or whether it should belong to the God of the Christians. This is answered by the *I am the Alpha and the Omega*. The emphasis is to be laid upon the *Omega*. It is as much as: *I am as the Alpha, therefore also the Omega*. The beginning is the surety for the end. The unconditional supremacy of God over the world, which is placed before our eyes by the Beginning, since God made heaven and earth, since he spake and it was done, commanded and it stood fast, is also brought again into notice by the end. If any one finds the end a cause of vexation, let him only lose himself in the beginning; let him dive into the word, *Before the mountains were brought forth, etc.*, and his anxiety will disappear. Let the world enlarge itself in the middle as it may, the church knows from the beginning, that the victory at the end must be God's.

The epithet, *Lord God*, corresponds to the OLD TESTAMENT combination, *Jehovah Elohim*, i.e. Jehovah the only God, the sole possessor of Godhead, Jehovah besides whom there is no God and no Saviour. The words that follow in the latter part of the verse unfold what is contained in the *Lord God;* and with a twofold respect corresponding to each: *Who is, and who was, and who comes,* the substance of the Lord; and *the Almighty,* the substance of God. The OLD TESTAMENT *Zabaoth*, which corresponds to it, serves along with *Elohim* to prevent all narrow views respecting Jehovah, all that would shut him up into a limited sphere. It was such a God, that belonged to the beginning, and such also must necessarily belong to the end; and the church can smile at those who would put themselves in opposition to him.

REVELATION 1:9-20

Second part: historical starting point, the charge to write, Christ's appearance

SUMMARY

The introductory section is followed by a narrative, verses 9-20, telling how John had received from Christ the commission to write to the seven churches, and containing an extended representation of the appearance of Christ, which was admirably fitted to prepare the minds of men for the contents of the epistles—to dispose sinners to repentance, and to kindle hope in the bosoms of the desponding. It proclaims with emphasis at once, *Fear,* and *Fear not.*

HISTORICAL STARTING POINT

1:9. I John, your brother and companion in tribulation and in the kingdom and patience of Jesus Christ, was in the isle that is called Patmos, for the word of God and the testimony of Jesus Christ. 10. I was (there I was) in the Spirit on the Lord's day, and heard behind me a great voice as of a trumpet.

The *I John* is in imitation of Daniel's style, who alone among the prophets says, *I Daniel.* John thus attaches himself to Daniel, in a similar position, indirectly designating himself an apostle. For prophets on equal footing with the writers of the OLD TESTAMENT could only be found among the apostles. Scripture is no fortuitous assemblage, but an organic whole, John connects what he wrote at once with his NEW TESTAMENT predecessors, and with the last prophets of the OLD TESTAMENT, Ezekiel, Daniel, Zechariah, whom he followed as the author of the first and only prophetical book of the NEW TESTAMENT.

As *father* in his epistles he addresses them as his *children,* but here *brother* points to the common participation in suffering. The *tribulation* could only consist in persecution, for John, the *companion in tribulation,* is on the island of Patmos *for the word of God and for the testimony of Jesus.* Besides, the *Jesus Christ* belongs to all the three, the *tribulation, the kingdom,* and the *patience.* Here, as in the FUNDAMENTAL PASSAGE of Col. 1:24–John writes to the same circle of readers, and the whole verse is full of references to Paul's epistles–in both alike, the tribulation denotes what Christ suffered partly in person and partly in his members, and what he still has to suffer. Here it is the personal tribulation or steadfastness of John and of those to whom he wrote. A *companion* (only found also in Paul) is one who partakes along with others. But one cannot partake of the tribulation which Christ himself has suffered. The sufferings of Christ also in 1 Pet. 4:13, are not merely the sufferings which Christ personally endured. The *tribulation* of Christ, *the kingdom of Jesus Christ* can only be that which belongs to him, partly in

9. I John, your brother and companion in tribulation and in the kingdom and patience of Jesus Christ, was in the isle that is called Patmos, for the word of God and the testimony of Jesus Christ.	person, partly in his members. In like manner, the *patience* of Christ is that, which he has personally manifested, and manifested in his members. It is a spiritual force and energy, whereby one is fortified to endure something, and bears up under it, a steadfast endurance of things contrary to the faith and truth of the gospel—comp. 2 Tim. 2:12, where the patience stands in opposition to the denying, and Luke 8:15, where those who bear fruit in patience are contrasted with those, who believe for a time, but in temptation fall away. The same three things are united together in Acts 14:22, where the brethren are exhorted to continue in the faith, and that through much *tribulation* they must enter into the *kingdom* of God; comp. also Rom. 8:17.
10. I was (there I was) in the Spirit on the Lord's day, and heard behind me a great voice as of a trumpet.	10 To be *in the Spirit* means being in the element and state of the Spirit. In a sense all Christians are so, but here it is in the highest sense, in which the natural life is entirely overcome. Parallel is Paul's being in a trance, Acts 22:17, comp. 10:10, 11:5. Opposed is Peter's being again *in* or *with himself* in Acts 12:11, after *the angel departed from him*.

The *I was in the Spirit on the Lord's day*, primarily refers only to the first series, which is a whole by itself. At the beginning of the second series we have the corresponding: *I was in the Spirit*, 4:2. However the contents of the whole book were communicated on the same day. For the day of the Lord is closely connected with the contents of the following visions. Zechariah also receives the entire series of his visions, which are formally independent of each other, in a single night. The book shows everywhere the marks of great art and careful preparation. But in the state of ecstasy holy men were raised far above themselves in an extraordinary condition. Much appears to us art, which was quite natural and easy to them, such as their arrangements according to symbolical numbers.

The key to the right understanding of *the day of the Lord* is supplied by ver. 5, where Christ is called *the first-begotten from the dead*, and by ver. 18, where the resurrection is the pledge that he will quicken his people out of death. These passages prove, 1. That *the day of the Lord* is the day of the resurrection, as the day on which Christ was manifested above all others as *the Lord*, comp. Rom. 1:4. 2. That it was so named, not because of what the church should do on that day, but because of what the Lord did on it, as a figure and pledge of what he is still going to do on it. For this reason it is to be sanctified by the church, and John has so responded to this call, to render himself capable and worthy of receiving the Revelation.

On the very first weekly return of the resurrection-day the apostles gathered together, to remember the event of eight days before, if haply the Lord might again appear; and the day was distinguished anew by a manifestation of the risen Lord, John 20:24-29. Paul, in 1 Cor. 16:2, singles out the first day of the week for contributions. On that day the Christians met to celebrate the Supper, Acts 20:7. Seven days before had Paul arrived there: he would a second time observe the sacred day in the midst of them. The weekly observance was accompanied with the yearly festival. The most credible testimonies show the Passover feast peculiar to Lesser Asia was introduced there on the authority of John. The knowledge possessed by the ancient church of the internal connection between the resurrection of Christ and his second coming, led to a particularly energetic celebration of that yearly festival. Easter day was a very suitable one for receiving the Revelation, the fundamental idea being that Christ will come to deliver his church from death. Since the

SECOND PART: STARTING POINT, CHARGE AND APPEARANCE

weekly commemoration of the resurrection had then begun, everyone must naturally think of that, when he hears of *the day of the Lord*, and the yearly festival could not have been designated in this simple manner, but must have had some mark of distinction, as it is called by the Fathers *the holy, the great, the splendid day of the Lord*.

John hears behind him *a voice*. This took place because he must *first* hear. Had he immediately seen, he would not have been able to hear, but as in Isa. 6:5, he would have fallen prostrate on the ground; comp. ver. 17. But here the reference to the church must presently come forth.

The great voice is as of a trumpet. The OLD TESTAMENT use of the trumpet was the sign for calling the people together, intimating the Lord had something to say to them; comp. Num. 10:2, Ex. 19:16-19, Joel 2:1, where in expectancy of the day of the Lord, Israel is called by the sound of the trumpet before an angry God, and Joel 2:15, Matt. 24:31, 1 Thess. 4:16, where the trumpet calls the members of the church before the Lord at his second coming. So here also the trumpet summons the church to his throne, to receive the word of warning and consolation.

THE CHARGE TO WRITE

> 11. What thou seest, write in a book, and send it unto the seven churches which are in Asia; unto Ephesus, and unto Smyrna, and unto Pergamos, and unto Thyatira, and unto Sardis, and unto Philadelphia, and unto Laodicea. 12. And I turned round to see the voice which spake with me. And, when I turned, I saw seven golden lamps.

The *I am the Alpha and the Omega, the first and the last*, derived from ver. 8 and 18, are wanting in the best manuscripts. It is only at ver. 12 that John turns round to look after the voice which spake with him, so he would not yet know who the speaker was. John must *write what he sees*, not what he may yet see. The seeing has already begun; the hearing also is comprehended in the seeing in the larger sense. By the *book* here is what is written to the end of chapter three. The name of the book, βιβλιον, *little* book, shows it is not the whole book. For, in 5:1, we find the book with the seven seals. The *seven*, as is clear from ch. 2 and 3, fall into three and four. *Ephesus, Smyrna, and Pergamos* stand together, contending for the primacy in Asia. Ephesus stands at the head as John's seat, as centre of the circle. From Ephesus it proceeds northward to Smyrna and Pergamos. Then from Pergamos as the most northerly point it goes south-east by *Thyatira, Sardis, Philadelphia*, to *Laodicea*, which lies almost in the same parallel of south latitude with Ephesus, but farther east. The apostle takes the same course in his actual visits (comp. 2 John 12, 3 John 10.) While writing to the seven churches, John had the example of the seven Catholic and the fourteen Pauline epistles (including Hebrews, which, if not directly, had Paul as its source.) That John was instructed to send to the churches, shows that he wrote out what he saw on the spot.

12 He *turns his head* to learn about the voice, from whom it proceeded. He sees first the churches and then Christ, in his relation to the churches. The seven churches are indicated by the *seven lamps*. In the sanctuary there was a candlestick with seven lamps, Ex. 25:37, in Zech. 4:2 it is an image of the church. The oil throughout the Bible is the symbol of the Spirit of God.

>12. And I turned round to see the voice which spake with me. And, when I turned, I saw seven golden lamps.

The candlestick, as the bearer of the Spirit, is the church. The light, the operations of the Spirit, streaming from church into darkness. The symbol declares what the church is, and what it ought to be. After saying in Matt. 5:14, *Ye are the light of the world,* Christ adds in ver. 16, *Therefore let your light shine before men. Seven* is in Scripture the number of the oath, the covenant. The *gold* denotes the glory of the church. The blossoms of flowers, the church's joyful blossoming and prosperity. Here are seven *individual* lamps. The candlestick with the seven lamps is a symbol of the whole church, but here it is only seven particular churches, in which the church was reflected but not the church at large. The seven churches constitute one whole, but only a separate section of the church standing under John. The seven epistles form part of a book, which is destined for the whole church. Like other apostolic epistles, our epistles likewise refer to special relations. It is the part of the church by means of its theological expositions to extract from the particular, the general, and again make application of this to the particular.

The seven churches are no more representatives of all other churches, than were the churches to which the other apostles wrote. Of the two hostile forces the Christian church has to contend, Judaism, a false slavery, and Heathenism, a false freedom of spirit, only the latter is brought into notice, as it had then power and influence in the churches to which the apostle wrote. This belies those who see in the seven epistles a prophecy of the seven ages of the church, for, among these ages there are some, in which the Judaistic element has wrought the greatest devastations in the church. Those who perceive in the epistles a pre-intimation of the church's states in the last times, cannot easily dispose of this argument. For Judaism has a very tenacious existence, and will assuredly never altogether abandon the field to heathenism.

CHRIST'S APPEARANCE

>13. And in the midst of the seven lamps one who was like a Son of man, who was clothed with a long robe, and girt about the breast with a golden girdle. 14. But his head and his hair were white as white wool, as the snow, and his eyes as a flame of fire. 15. And his feet like clear brass, as if they glowed in an oven, and his voice as the sound of great waters. 16. And had seven stars in his right hand; and out of his mouth went a sharp two-edged sword, and his face shone as the sun in its strength. 17. And when I saw him, I fell at his feet as one dead, and he laid his right hand on me, and said: Fear not. 18. I am the first and the last; and the living, and I was dead, and behold I am alive for evermore, and I have the keys of hell and of death. 19. Write therefore what thou hast seen, and what is, and what shall be done afterwards. 20. The mystery of the seven stars, which thou sawest in my right hand, and the seven golden lamps. The seven stars are angels of the seven churches, and the seven lamps are seven churches.

Here we see, not the actual form of Christ, but aspects of Christ's nature, his glorious majesty and his punitive righteousness, adapted to the seven churches, and to all in similar states and circumstances, to bring them to repentance, and console and encourage them. What he afterwards says to them in word, he prefigures to them through his appearance. Christ appears *in the midst of the seven lamps* as the guardian and the judge of the church.

The expression, *like a Son of man,* refers to Dan. 7:13, where he was given the dominion over the world. As he was only *like* a Son of man, there was another part of his Being, which far surpassed the human, as the whole succeeding description explains.

The *long robe* was not the sign merely of priestly, but also of kingly dignity. Here Christ is shown as king and judge. A king is more exalted than a priest. Both the *long robe* and the *golden girdle* have respect to Daniel 10:5, speaking of *Michael* or of the Logos. A golden buckle on one's girdle, and being clothed in purple, is the mark of royal state. Christ appears here not in a state of full activity, in 2:1 he *walks* amid the seven lamps. The seven angels also in 15:6, in active service, are girt about the breast.

14 The mentioning separately of the *head and hair*, while in Daniel it is simply the hair of the head, is to be explained from the contrast in respect to the feet in ver. 15. In ver. 13 we have the clothing, in ver. 14 and 15 the uncovered parts. The FUNDAMENTAL PASSAGE for the first half, is Dan. 7:9. The blinding *whiteness* of the *hair* (*as snow*, as a glittering splendour,) denotes his holiness, majesty, glory, as is clear from the *eyes like a flame of fire*.

The second half rests on Dan. 10:6, speaking of *Michael, the Logos*. The eyes like a *flame of fire* denote the energetic character of his punitive righteousness, as fire is the image of anger. The eyes as *torches of fire* appear in the midst of warlike accompaniments, between the countenance like lightning, and the arms and feet like burning brass, ready to destroy everything that comes in their way. We have the same in Daniel 7:9 which forms the basis of the first half. After the words already quoted, it follows there, *His throne was pure flame of fire, and its wheels burned with fire*. The Lord appears there to execute judgment on the world. His holiness and glory, shadowed forth under the colour of his clothing and his hair, shows that no one can escape. His punitive righteousness imaged by the flame of fire shows his will to punish adversaries. There comes the admonition, *Be afraid*, and also, *Be not afraid*. In 19:12 the words, *and his eyes are as a flame of fire*, are followed by, *and in righteousness he judges and makes war;* while in ver. 15 he is represented as *having a sharp sword going out of his mouth*. In 2:18, eyes as of a flame of fire, and feet like burning brass, are united together, and both appear as the ground at once of threatening and of promise to those in Thyatira.

15-16 This respects his great power, bringing all under him, as with the thrust of a burning hot bar of metal. *Clear brass*, in the sense of heated brass, *chalkolibanos*, is an enigmatical term, formed by John himself in a peculiar manner.[1] The words, *as if they glowed in an oven*, are explanatory. The *voice*, is that with which he chides his enemies whether within or without the church, and which for them utters the thundering and destructive cry: Thus far, but no farther. *The voice as the voice of many waters*, is from Dan. 10:6, coupled with Eze. 43:2. Comp. also Ps. 93:3-4. The *stars* denote rulers. In ver. 20 they signify the overseers of the seven churches with a *power over the community*. That Christ has the stars in his *right* hand, marks his unconditional power over them. No one can deliver them out of his hand, when he will punish; but

---

1. The *chalkolibanos* corresponds to the *burnished brass* of Eze. 1:7, and Dan. 10:6, *clear light brass*–not in the sense of shining or glittering brass, but of brass in a glow-heat, as the explanatory clause *as if they glowed in an oven*, and also *his feet are as pillars of fire*, in 10:1; as is clear also from the preceding clause in Dan. 10:6, *and his face was as the appearance of lightning, and his eyes as flames of fire*. They sparkled like *burnished brass*, not glittering but emitting sparks. Having thus ascertained the sense, we understand the derivation, which is that from χαλκο, chalko, brass, and לבנה, λιβανο, libanos, whiteness, here used of the whitish glitter of much heated brass. The words nowhere occur except here and in 2:18, showing that John had formed it, and that it was of an enigmatical description.

16. And had seven stars in his right hand; and out of his mouth went a sharp two-edged sword, and his face shone as the sun in its strength.	no one can pluck them out of his hand, if they remain faithful. The descriptions of Christ bear a two-fold respect, the words, *who holds the seven stars in his right hand*, underlies the threatening in ver. 5 not less than for the promise in ver. 7. The *sword* here is the destroying power of the word, which proceeds from the Almighty. It denotes the resistless energy of Christ's power in punishing his enemies, internal and external, as made clear from ch. 12 compared with ver. 16; the two-edged sword is directed against the false seed in the church, and in 19:21, it brings destruction to the anti-christian heathen power. In this he appears as one possessing divine power. For it belongs to God to slay with the word of his mouth. The *face* of Christ is as *the sun shining in his strength*, when nothing veils his splendour in the clear sky. The visage has respect to the stars, which pervades the whole description of Christ's appearance. As the splendour of the sun is to that of the stars, so the glory of Christ transcends that of his servants.
17. And when I saw him, I fell at his feet as one dead, and he laid his right hand on me, and said: Fear not.	17 John recognizes that the glory of the Lord and the energy of his righteousness have the church as well as the world for their operations, and, penetrated by the feeling of his personal sinfulness, sinks overwhelmed to the ground. Under the OLD TESTAMENT, such immediate intercourse with heavenly beings, even with angels, filled with terror the minds even of his holiest servants. The fervid appearance of the Lord's glory which Isaiah saw in ch. 6– comp. *smoke* in ver. 4, primarily had respect to the ungodly he was sent to as a messenger of wrath. Yet he cried out, *Woe is me, for I am undone, mine eyes have seen the King, the Lord of Hosts.* As also with Ezekiel, and Daniel also, when Gabriel comes to him. But Dan. 10:7 comes nearest to the passage before us; Daniel falls on the ground when he sees Michael, the angel of the Lord, in his burning glory, and in verse 10, *and lo! a hand touched me and set me on my knees, and on my hands.* The outward touch is to be regarded as the symbol of the angel's agency in raising the prophet.
18. I am the first and the last; and the living, and I was dead, and behold I am alive for evermore, and I have the keys of hell and of death.	18 After the fear had been removed from the Seer, he is directed to the consolatory and elevated import, which the appearance of the Lord has for him and the church. Three glorious predicates meet us here, which are to inspire a joyful hope, *the first and the last, the living, the possessor of the keys of death and of hell. I am the first and the last* expresses what is included in full Godhead, His being the *first* refers to the creation of the world, I also am *the last:* all that has been made shall at the end lie at my feet, and no one that abides in me needs to vex himself about it. *The living* is also a peculiarly divine predicate, especially *he who lives for evermore*, which is used of the Most High God. Purposely and intentionally, everything is in the Revelation attributed to Christ which belongs to the Supreme God, to show he is equal to God in power and glory. The living is at the same time the life-giving. His life is the pledge to his church that she cannot remain in death. That Christ had been dead is a security for the living and the life-giving. His life is gloriously manifested by the victory over death in the resurrection. And through this he first properly became the source of life for the church. Christ has *the keys of death and of hell.* He opens and no one shuts, he shuts and no one opens. With the keys he shuts death and hell for his people, that they may not go there; but he opens them for Satan and his servants, and thrusts them down there. Hades respects *dead sinners*. So natural death is here regarded as the punishment of sin and associated with the second death. From this Christ keeps his own by keeping them steadfast amid the trials and persecutions which Satan and the

SECOND PART: STARTING POINT, CHARGE AND APPEARANCE

world bring upon them so they are not tempted above measure.

19 John must first write *what he saw,* which we find written in 1:11-18. He had seen the Lord in his fiery indignation, helping his own people, threatening destruction to the world and the unfaithful among his professing people, the seven stars in his hand, and the seven golden candlesticks, in the midst of which he walked.

<small>19. Write therefore what thou hast seen, and what is, and what shall be done afterwards.</small>

He must further write what *is*; the internal state of the seven angels and the seven churches, as is done in the seven epistles. This also is an important object of prophecy, with which the holy men of the OLD TESTAMENT occupied themselves as much as with the unveiling of the future. The *reality* of things is not less concealed from the natural eye than the future. Through prophecy the unbeliever is judged, the secrets of his heart made manifest.

John, finally, must write what *shall be done afterwards.* This is the second part of the contents of the seven epistles. Along with discoveries of the real state of the churches, these contain announcements of the coming of the Lord, threatenings against the insincere, promises to those who should overcome, all in close connection with the condition of the particular angels and their several churches.

Here is not the introduction to the *whole* book. The command here is a resumption of the command in ver. 11, as the *therefore* plainly shows. What was already seen were the seven lamps with the Lord in their midst, and the seven stars. The word must point to the present state of the lamps and stars in their relation to the Lord and their future fate. *Then*, it is only in this view that ver. 20 fits properly in to the preceding context. The idea that *what shall be hereafter,* as referring to 4:1 onwards to the end of the book is inadmissible if the preceding context is limiting the import of *what shall be afterwards.* Further in 4:1 to the end, we have an entirely new beginning, new in respect to both the state of inspiration and the scene.

20 John must write *the mystery of the seven stars,* and what in respect to them is now and shall come to pass afterwards. Ch. 2:1 is but a specialising of the command, which is given here generally. The words *the mystery . . . golden lamps,* determine more exactly the sphere of the *what thou sawest, what is and shall be done afterwards,* cutting off every kind of false meaning. By *mystery, secret* is always meant in the NEW TESTAMENT, things and doctrines inaccessible to the natural man, only apprehended with God through his internal and external Revelation. Even as an objective revelation a mystery remains laying beyond those who have not received the Holy Spirit; as, in spite of the revelations given by John, the fleshly and impenitent in the seven churches are in darkness regarding the stars and lamps, with earthly and superficial views. The mystery is not *formal* in nature, solved by a mere explanation. Such would be an enigma, but no secret. The formal explanation of the stars and the lamps, is a hasty sketch, preparing the way for the extended illustration of the secret in chapters two and three; discovering there the concealed depths of the heart, and the disclosure of the future.

<small>20. The mystery of the seven stars, which thou sawest in my right hand, and the seven golden lamps. The seven stars are angels of the seven churches, and the seven lamps are seven churches.</small>

The αγγελο of itself can signify both angels or messengers; but in the Revelation it always has the sense of *angel*. In the OLD TESTAMENT stars and angels often form together the heavenly hosts of God. The *angels of the churches* could only be those God had *sent* to the churches, to whom their charge is intrusted. But *messengers* of the churches could only be deputies whom the churches themselves had sent. The *stars* indicates an authoritative power, unsuitable for

20. The mystery of the seven stars, which thou sawest in my right hand, and the seven golden lamps. The seven stars are angels of the seven churches, and the seven lamps are seven churches.

a deputy. The angels in the seven epistles are the *soul* of the churches, of which *the deputies of the churches* are not, and the churches themselves are represented under a separate symbol, that of the *lamps*. We must think of the messengers of God to the churches as translated: *the angels of the churches*. In Eccl. 5:6, the priesthood is denoted *the angel*, in order to mark his high dignity and the impropriety of any levity in his presence. He stands as God's representative.

The *angel* implies that the sending is of God. In Mal. 3:1, *messenger*, in reference to Ex. 23:20, is *angel*, yet only an *earthly* messenger can be meant, the prophet, the divine messengers preparing the way for the Saviour. But the name of the *heavenly* messenger designates the earthly, that the grace of God, the origin of salvation, and the dread responsibility of rejecting what was to be provided might be apparent. If we must translate, *my angel*, then we must understand of *the angel of the Lord* what is said in Mal. 2:7-8, *For the priest's lips must keep knowledge, and they should seek the law at his mouth; for he is the angel* (the *messenger*) *of the Lord of Hosts*. For, the two passages stand closely related to each other. If in these three passages the messenger must give way to the angel, so in Isa. 42:19, we should also translate, *Who is blind but my servant, and deaf as the angel, whom I send*, in Isa. 44:26, *Who fulfils the word of his servant, and executes the counsel of his angel;* in Hag. 1:13, *And he spake to Haggai, the angel of the Lord, in a message of the Lord to the people*—rather so as the word, being used of divine messengers, elsewhere always denotes only angels. We must, however decide entirely for the *first* view, for the transference of the mere name of *the angel* to the overseers of the several churches. Angels as purely ideal forms occur in this book, in 16:5, *the angel of the waters* is mentioned in a figurative sense; as also in 16:8, *the angel who has power over fire;* in 21:12, the Lord's protecting guardianship over the new Jerusalem as embodied in the *twelve angels* at its gates. Also John 5:4, in which the symbolical appears in the midst of the factual narrative. But if the Seer introduced here such purely ideal angelic forms, it could only have been as embodiments and personifications of the power of God as exercised in behalf of the churches. Angels, however, as they are here considered *beings of a higher sphere*, to whom epistles are addressed, who are partly rich and partly poor, partly steadfast, partly lukewarm, partly admonished to be faithful, and to repent, who have a local habitation (2:13,) who, as the admonition to be faithful unto death presupposes, could die—are a nonentity with no analogy in Scripture. Against the supposition that angels are personifications of *the churches*, the symbol of the stars does not apply to the churches, but only to the *presidents*; as also the praise for the angel of the church of Ephesus for his contendings against false teachers—which only suits those who had the charge and oversight.

The angels of the churches, formally but one, denoted in reality a number of persons, not only the bishop, but the elders and deacons. In the OLD TESTAMENT passages the ideal person of an angel denotes *the whole body* of priests and prophets. John, in the narrative formerly given, makes the bishop responsible for individual souls. Paul regarded the elders of Ephesus as those on whom the spiritual state of the church entirely depended. In 1 Pet. 5:1-5, Peter writes to the elders as *ensamples of the flock*. We must include the presbytery of 1 Tim. 4:14, as Polycarp begins his epistle to the Philippians: *Polycarp and the elders that are with him, to the church of God which dwells at Philippi*, but, on the ground of what is indicated in 2:19, we must also add the *deaconship*, as Ignatius, in his epistle to the Philadelphians, says, *especially if you are at one with the bishop, and the presbyters and deacons that are with him.* If the angels are considered thus, the passage 2:5 can easily be understood. If all that hold office in an organized church have become degenerate, the church itself must have sunk into a low condition, and every thing be ripe for judgment.

As for the age of episcopacy, nothing certain can be obtained from what is said here of the angels. Whether we have to think of the state, which presents itself to us in Acts 20, as still continuing,—a college of presbyters on a footing of equality, or whether a bishop with more or less of superior power already standing at the head, we have no sufficient data for determining.

REVELATION 2–3

The third part: the letters to the seven churches, a commentary on the appearance

INTRODUCTION TO THE SEVEN EPISTLES

One of the functions of prophecy is to make manifest the secrets of the heart. Along with the promise goes the admonition; Isaiah's commission to comfort comes in the second part of his prophecies, but with the announcement of salvation the call to repent and the admonition to be faithful is constantly combined. And so also in the New Testament. John from chapter 4 onward reveals the salvation Christ has for his suffering church to vindicate them and raise them to glory. Before this he must prepare the saints for the purpose of Christ, for the great events of the future. He must remove the idea that the *name* of Christians forms the wall between them and the world, and call forth the spiritual state of things which alone can render the coming of the Lord salutary, to awaken the slothful and unfaithful to repent, and admonish the faithful and diligent to persevere to the end.

Each epistle shares, 1. a command to write to an angel of the church; 2. A glorious title of Jesus Christ; 3. An address to the angel of the church; wherein is (1) a testimony of its mixed, good, or bad condition; (2) an admonition to repentance or to steadfastness; (3) an announcement of what is to take place, for the most part of the coming of the Lord; (4) a promise to those that overcome, along with the words *he that has an ear, let him hear what the Spirit saith to the churches.*

The address is in plain language, speaking primarily to the contemporaneous church in Asia and their angel, while Christ's promise is in a flowery style, in the third person of those who then, and in future times, should overcome.

Two of the churches are in a mixed state, two very corrupt, two very healthful in condition, all hold a pattern for profitable and salutary instruction. Whether one be dead as Sardis or well as Philadelphia or the Apostle John himself, this book is serviceable to him.

There are twelve promises; in the third, fourth and sixth is a double promise and in the fifth a threefold one, all distinguished by: *I will give, I will not blot out, I will confess, I will write.* For those that overcome, the enjoyment of the highest good, or freedom from the greatest troubles, is proffered. The one is included in the other, when some one part of blessedness and glory is expressed, the whole is to be understood. That part is particularly expressed which refers to the virtues and deeds in the preceding address. Some things are mentioned only here, as *the manna, the confession of the name, the inscribed name of the New Jerusalem, the sitting upon the throne.* Some things find a resemblance to what is after found in the representations of Christ–*the secret name,* 19:12, *the heritage of the nations,* 19:15, *the morning star,* 22:16. Others occur afterwards, *the tree of life,* 20:12, 21:27, *remaining in the temple,* 7:15, *the name of God and the Lamb on the righteous,* 14:1, 22:4.

He who holds the seven stars in his right hand
EPHESUS

> 2:1. To the angel of the church in Ephesus write: These things saith he who holds the seven stars in his right hand, who walks amid the seven golden lamps. 2. I know thy works, and thy labour, and thy patience, and how thou canst not bear them that are evil, and hast tried those who say they are apostles and are not, and hast found them liars. 3. And hast patience, and hast borne for my name sake, and hast not fainted. 4. But I have against thee that thou hast left thy first love. 5. Remember therefore from whence thou hast fallen, and repent and do the first works. But if not, I come to thee (shortly) and remove thy lamp out of its place, if thou repent not. 6. But this thou hast, that thou hatest the works of the Nicolaitans, which I also hate. 7. He that has an ear let him hear what the Spirit says to the churches: He that overcomes, to him will I give to eat of the tree of life, which is in the paradise of my God.

The servants of Christ (the *angel,*) at Ephesus in which Paul had laboured longer than any place else, to which he after committed to Timothy (1Tim. 1:3,) had not fully responded to his exhortation (Acts 20:31); they had responded with great zeal against the *grievous wolves,* but had forgotten their *first love.* It is not accidental that in this first epistle predicates are attributed to Christ showing his unrestricted power over the seven churches. The first, from 1:16, the *holding the stars,* stronger than the *having* there, shows no one can pluck them from his hand, whether he is minded to protect or destroy them, and the second predicate comes from 1:12, where he *is* in the midst of the lamps, while here he *walks* in the midst of them, showing his continued activity, that he is everywhere at hand whether the occasion may require him to chastise or to help her. A glance at him who walks in the midst of the lamps is the best antidote against a false security as well as despair.

2-3 Seven times in the epistles we hear the *I know,* referring respectively to their works, tribulations, dwelling-place, and love. Here the *works, labour and patience* that he knows refer to the angel's zeal against false teachers. This letter details the angel's conflict with false teachers, his shortcomings, and appropriately as the first letter, in reference to the tree of Genesis, the promise of the tree of life to the overcomer. The evildoers' evil consists in that they *say they are apostles and are not but are liars*. The angel's virtue is shown in his just hatred against the evil of the false teachers, and the *works* of these heretics. Verse 6 connects closely to verse 2. The angel has resisted the temptation to bring heathenism and Christianity together, his opponents have responded in hatred, which he bears in *patience,* and he maintains a *hatred* for the works of these heretics, without a hatred for their persons.

4-5 The angel has denied love and faith as his energies have been focussed into a narrow field, in a defence of orthodoxy and is in danger of having the root and ground of his Christianity vanishing away. The seriousness of this is the threatening that the lamp would be removed, and taken elsewhere, with the church vanishing from its place.

CHAPTERS 2–3   THE REVELATION

<small>6. But this thou hast, that thou hatest the works of the Nicolaitans, which I also hate.</small>

6 The old Jewish errors that Paul had to deal with are gone, and the church is free from Judaism. There is still a synagogue of Satan, but the temptation and danger now comes from heathenism, and gnostic heresies. Gnosticism began in Paul's time with Hymænius and Philetus' denial of the bodily resurrection, in their maintaining a purely spiritual view, with no concern for the physical material. The separation of the spiritual from the body gave the heathen gnostics a basis for a spirituality unaffected by the actions of bodily lusts, giving a license to licentiousness and idolatry, where morals and law were unnecessary. The false teachers here are called *Nicolaitans*, which is a Greek version of *Balaamites*. The name *Nicolaus* means *Conqueror of the people*, while that of *Balaam*, *Destroyer of the people*. Balaam caused the Moabite women to seduce the people to licentiousness and idol worship. This is connected with the later reference to Jezebel. The Nicolaitans attempt to smuggle heathenism and gnosticism into the church, their works, like the Moabite Balaamites, which the angel hated, issued in fleshly freedom, unrestricted liberty to all authority and law. Their doctrines, allied to their works and deeds are idol offerings, fornication, and a heathenish mode of life.

<small>7. He that has an ear let him hear what the Spirit says to the churches: He that overcomes, to him will I give to eat of the tree of life, which is in the paradise of my God.</small>

7 The *Spirit says to the churches*–plural, these principles are for all churches, the Spirit is a new principle, who would teach them all things, the *ear* meaning the spiritual sense of the mind, and a deeper spiritual understanding.

The promise, *He that overcomes* is repeated through all the epistles and in 21:7, and here for victory against all opponents, in particular over the Nicolaitans. The *eating of the tree of life* is pledged as a gift, in contrast to a sensual heathen enjoyment, as a promise of eating spiritual food in Paradise.

He that was dead and is alive again
SMYRNA

> 8. And to the angel of the church at Smyrna write: These things saith the first and the last, he that was dead and is alive again. 9. I know thy tribulation and thy poverty (but thou art rich), and the blasphemy of those, who say they are Jews and are not, but are of the school of Satan. 10. Fear not what thou wilt suffer. Behold the devil will cast some of you into prison, that ye may he tried, and ye shall have tribulation ten days. Be thou faithful unto death, and I will give thee a crown of life. 11. He that has an ear, let him hear what the Spirit says to the churches: He that overcomes, shall not be hurt by the second death.

Here, in contrast to Ephesus, there is no call to repent, just the encouragement to *fear not* and *be faithful*. It appears that the *angel of Smyrna* was the disciple of John who was appointed bishop by the apostles, Polycarp, who a young Irenæus saw, and who lived to a great age, finally suffering a glorious martyrdom.

8 The predicates are from 1:18, the Lord appears to John as *the first and last, he that was dead and is alive again*, which sets the tenor of this letter as consolatory to those who will suffer persecution and undergo martyrdom. The faithful will conquer with Christ at the last, and must not suffer themselves to be cast down, if they are presently depressed.

9 The *poverty* sits between the *tribulation* and the *blasphemy*, and this is *known* by the Lord, who knows those who are his, only the Christians bear the marks of fellowship in his kingdom. The Jews delude themselves that they

are the Lord's own, yet in reality the epithet, *the school of Satan*, fits them as being adversaries of the church, *Satan* being the persecutor and murderer of the righteous, Satanism meaning antagonism.

10 The *devil*, Satan's title as calumniator (Job 2:6, Zech. 3:1,) will cast some of them into *prison*, the Jews in calumnies against them (Justin, Tryphon,) will act as false accusers before the heathen magistrates, in blasphemy and hatred of Christ and the church. So tribulation from the heathen rises against the angel, and poverty from litigations renders them helpless and oppressed (Jas. 2:5-7.) But *thou art rich* in heavenly fruit, *polycarpus* being here an allusion to the blessed Polycarp.

The persecution is announced beforehand, with the consolation, *Fear not what thou wilt suffer*, as the Lord shows the rod before the smiting. The persecution will be *ten days*, a long short period, after which the sufferers will attain blessedness. The being *tried* is an evil and dangerous thing as from the Devil, but from God it is good and salutary, proving experienced warriors of God. If the choice is between death and damnation, then *be faithful to the death*. The *crown* is not a crown of victory, as heathen allusions are not to be resorted to in the Apocalypse, but the badge of royal dignity, of rich and glorious life and eternal blessedness. Paul, Peter and James mention this crown, James agrees with John with the crown *of life*. And this *overcoming* immunizes them from the *second death*, the lake of fire or hell, or what the Lord calls *Gehenna*. The fits and starts of persecution alternate with revival—at the martyrdom of Polycarp the persecution stopped.

He which hath the sharp sword with two edges
PERGAMOS

> 12. And to the angel of the church in Pergamos write; These things saith he which hath the sharp sword with two edges; 13. I know thy works, and where thou dwellest, even where Satan's seat is: and thou holdest fast my name, and hast not denied my faith, even in those days wherein Antipas was my faithful martyr, who was slain among you, where Satan dwelleth. 14. But I have a few things against thee, because thou hast there them that hold the doctrine of Balaam, who taught Balak to cast a stumbling-block before the children of Israel, to eat things sacrificed unto idols, and to commit fornication. 15. So hast thou also them that hold the doctrine of the Nicolaitans, which thing I hate. 16. Repent; or else I will come unto thee quickly, and will fight against them with the sword of my mouth. 17. He that hath an ear, let him hear what the Spirit saith unto the churches; To him that overcometh will I give to eat of the hidden manna, and will give him a white stone, and in the stone a new name written, which no man knoweth saving he that receiveth it.

Here there is more praise than blame, as they are faithful amid difficulty, yet warned about the mischief of the Balaamites. The *sharp sword* appears from 1:16, and is for the impenitent. The angel is to be afraid of the sword on account of his people, or be assured of its victory over his enemies.

Pergamos was the principal seat of persecution against Christians in Asia, perhaps due to the strength of individual heathen heretics.

13 The *faith* of Christ means the faith in Christ, not fidelity, but holding fast. The angel has not denied this faith. The preceding valorous conduct of Antipas is placed to the angel's account. Antipas means *against all*, similar

to Antikosmos: a man of contention against the world. Perhaps it is Timothy named Antipas here. Timothy's name means to fear God, which is also to be against the world, he was martyred in 97 AD, while strenuously opposing heathenish disorder.

> 14. But I have a few things against thee, because thou hast there them that hold the doctrine of Balaam, who taught Balak to cast a stumblingblock before the children of Israel, to eat things sacrificed unto idols, and to commit fornication.

14 Although free from heresies, the Lord needed the angel to be more energetic in resisting the Balaamites. Verse 14 talks of the Balaamites and verse 15 the Nicolaitans, and they are talking about one heresy, not two, as the sense of verse 15 is, *so and in like manner as Balaam taught so there are also those who hold Balaam's doctrine* (of the Nicolaitans).

Balaam was a seer in the time of Moses, and Balak was king of the Moabites, who had a contention against the children of Israel and wished a curse to be placed upon them. Balaam taught for Balak, in the interest of Balak, to please him. The Lord had commanded Israel to destroy the Midianites, but they spared the Midianite women who had caused Israel to be unfaithful to the Lord (Num. 25:1-3, Num. 31:16,) in committing whoredom, idol worship to Baal-Peor and eating their sacrifices.

The gnostics had a false spiritualism, holding everything corporeal to be indifferent. Paul had taught if viewing idolatry as a nothing then eating idol meat sold in the shambles was a matter of Christian liberty. The heretics however, were seducers, idolaters and whoremongers, participating in heathen festivals and idol offerings (*Iraenius*.) Fornication was a mark of these heathen festivals, eating the sacrifices, as a means of advance into their secret doctrine (*Eusebius*).

> 15. So hast thou also them that hold the doctrine of the Nicolaitans, which thing I hate.

15 These heretical Nicolaitans practise the same doctrine as Balaam, as they sought to win the favour of ethnicizing heathens, breaking down the limits between the church and the world.

> 16. Repent; or else I will come unto thee quickly, and will fight against them with the sword of my mouth.

16 If the angel fails to repent in this little thing, and show greater zeal in recovering the seduced backsliders, he too may be punished. The Lord's *I will come* here is not an obvious coming, but power exercised secretly. The Lord *will fight with them*, that is the Nicolaitans who hold the doctrine of Balaam. The *sword of my mouth* refers to the story of Balaam who with his seducing company was slain with the sword (Num. 31:8, Josh. 13:22,) and foundational to this was the avenging sword of God and his Logos (Num. 22:23,) as the mad Balaam was restrained by the dumb ass speaking.

> 17. He that hath an ear, let him hear what the Spirit saith unto the churches; To him that overcometh will I give to eat of the hidden manna, and will give him a white stone, and in the stone a new name written, which no man knoweth saving he that receiveth it.

17 In allusion to idol offerings, *to him that overcomes* is promised the gift of eating *the hidden manna*. With heavenly bread they must lose their relish for idol offerings. Whoever denies self and fleshly delights will experience much in heavenly things, of which others must be deprived. Manna has respect to the life to come, and is promised to *he who overcomes*, and, in verse 26, *keeps my works to the end*. However there is a completing there of whatever has begun here. Unlike natural manna it is hidden, a hidden treasure, the life hid with Christ in God, a foretaste in this life promised by Christ. This contrasts with the Nicolaitans' wish to introduce heathen mysteries and sensual lusts into Christianity.

The *white stone* is writing material where a new name is written. Not the white of innocence but the shining white (comp. 4:4.) The stone connects with the promise of a *new name*. *New* is an apocalyptic word— a new name, song, heavens, earth, Jerusalem—all new. The burden of the old gives it a sweet sound. It is derived from Isa. 62:2, 65:15, *thou art called by a new name*. No particular name is meant, only that it is more glorious than the old one.

This parallels 3:12, the overcomer with a new name in a new state of things—*we shall be like him.*

No one knows but he who receives it, it is a secret unspeakably more precious than the Nicolaitan secrets. Christ only knows his name (19:12.) They persecute because the world knows us not as they know him not.

He who has eyes as a flame of fire, and his feet like to clear brass
THYATIRA

> 18. And to the angel of the church at Thyatira write: These things saith the Son of God, who has eyes as a flame of fire, and his feet like to clear brass. 19. I know thy love and thy faith; and thy service and thy patience; and thy last works more than the first. 20. But I have against thee, that thou sufferest (that woman) thy wife Jezebel, who says she is a prophetess, and she teaches and seduces my servants to commit fornication and to eat things offered to idols. 21. And I have given her time to repent, and she will not repent of her fornication. 22. Behold I throw her into a bed, and those who commit fornication with her into great tribulation, if they do not repent of their works, 23. And her children will I put to death; and all churches shall know, that I am he who searcheth the reins and hearts; and I will give to every one among you according to your works, 24. But to you I say, the others that are at Thyatira, who have not such doctrine, and who have not known the depths of Satan, as they speak; I will not throw upon you another burden, 25. But what you have received hold fast till I come. 26. And he that overcomes and keeps my works to the end to him will I give power over the heathen. 27. And he shall rule them with a rod of iron; as the vessels of a potter shall they be broken to shivers: even as I received of my Father. 28. And I will give him the morning star. 29. He that hath an ear, let him hear what the Spirit saith unto the churches.

Lydia, a seller of purple, was from Thyatira (Acts 16:14,) a colony of the Macedonians. Jezebel could be regarded as her Satanic counterpart. The Roman road from Pergamos southeast to Sardis led by Thyatira. The title *Son of God* is presented to the angel of Thyatira, which with verse 27 refers to the second psalm. *His eyes are as a flame of fire,* and *his feet like to fine brass,* as appears from 1:14, the flame is not for light, but to consume, the feet a threat to those secure persons who tread the Son of God underfoot–he will tread *them* underfoot.

19 Here, unlike Ephesus, *love* is first, reflecting the female beginnings of this church. *Faith* is paired with love, as faith is the root of love. Three pairs here-love and faith; service and patience; last and first works. The deaconship service is connected to an active patience and perseverance. The last works are of love. Reference is made here to 2 Pet. 2:20 (which rests on Matt. 12:45,) the *more than* (πλειονα) is very similar in sound to the *worse* in *the latter end is worse* (χειρονα) *with them than the first.* Peter's discourse has respect to the Nicolaitans, so it follows, *that does not hold of thee, which is true of the Nicolaitans.*

20 Hearty, loving people may still allow evil to have its progress, as they have suffered the woman *Jezebel.* She was the daughter of the King of Zidon, the wife of King Ahab of Israel, who had murdered the prophets, introduced idol worship to Israel, and with Balaam she personifies heathenish seduction, false doctrine and heresy. She is *that woman,* the *wife* of the angel,

the weaker half (1 Pet 3:7,) or that part of the governing body of the church infected with the heresy. She says she is a prophetess, her father was high priest of Astarte, her whoredoms and witchcraft were many (2 Kings 9:22) and her followers introduced Baal worship with great enthusiasm. The gnostics falsely pretended to inspiration. Here she seduces the laity, *my* servants, to false doctrine. The seducing to idolatry marked Balaam—to adultery, Jezebel. The spiritual adultery often goes with the bodily, especially in a demoniacal excitement. 2 Kings 9:30 with Jer. 4:30 shows this connection with Jezebel. Eze. 23:37 says *with their idols they have committed adultery*.

21-22 The adulteress was hardened and impenitent. From the bed of infamy she is thrown into a sick bed of pain. The adulterers, *those who commit fornication with her,* and the children, are the followers and children—*her children* are the recipients of false doctrine, as this probably refers to Isa. 57:3, *sons of the sorceress, seed of the adulterer and the whore*. John calls believers his children, Peter calls Mark his son, in figurative expressions.

23 Literally *I will kill with death* shows the earnestness of the threatening, this is derived from Lev. 20:10, *he that commits adultery shall die the death*. The *all churches shall know* is in an emphatic irony on their gnosis (ver. 24.) They should help all churches to the right and profitable gnosis, which object is that Christ *searches the reins and hearts*. This derives from Ps. 7:9, *prover of the hearts and reins art thou, righteous God*. This *proving* and *searching* points, not to God's omniscience, but his righteousness, in that he is not indifferent toward good and evil. The gnostics pride themselves at penetrating hidden things while expressing contempt at common Christians, now they must face Christ penetrating their inmost being. *I will give to every one of you according to your works* (Ps. 62:12, Matt. 16:27, Rom. 2:6, 2 Pet. 3:17,) is most appropriate in the presence of the lawless who think they can do as they please.

24 *The others* are those who have kept free from Jezebel, *who have not known the depths of Satan*. The *having known* the heretics took in an exalted, laudable sense, but John uses it in a low, scandalous one, as the depths are those of Satan. The Lord holds the overseers responsible for the evil. The gnostic's principle was, in going into the depths of Satan, to become familiar with everything shameful, as Eusebius, commenting on the Simonians said, *their deeper secrets were full of folly and madness, unspeakable on account of their horrid filthiness and obscenity*.

The threatening was for the apostate party, not the true. The *other burden* contrasts to what they now had and should hold fast. The Pharisees bound burdens on men's necks (Matt. 23:4,) and the Judaizers laid a yoke upon the disciples' necks (Acts 15:10.) The lawless party abused Paul's doctrine of liberty, accusing the church of Pharisaism or Judaism, applying to moral law what bore respect to the ceremonial, always speaking of burdens which one seeks to lay upon you. This does not admit of flying off with the lawless on the pretext of Christian liberty. The apostolic council would lay no other burden (Acts 15:28-29) except to forbid eating of idol offerings and fornication—what the lawless party regarded as a burden.

25 To the *and* at the beginning of verse 26 correspond *and keeps my works to the end*, resuming the *hold fast till I come* of verse 25. The *keeping* contrasts with self-willed thoughtless forgetting. Christ's *works* have preceded us by his example, opposite to these works are those of 22:15. For each individual the end is the period of his death, when it can only then be said, *I* *have overcome.* The *till I come* is either the Lord's advent and the judgment, or events in history, as at the destruction of Jerusalem or the fall of Rome.

26 By an abuse of 1 Cor 8:9, 6:12 the gnostics confessed dominion over the world, seducing Christians to the corruptions of heathenism (2 Pet. 2:19.) They sought to overcome lust by gratifying lust (acc. to Clemens of Alexandria). Porphyry said *he who is an ocean of power receives everything into himself and is not defiled.* But in fact it is he who resists such false and destructive sentiments, abiding steadfast to the law, that shall come to an ascendancy over the heathen world. Where the Church conquered and *kept*, it overcame heathenism, where it did not, it soon disappeared.

26. And he that overcomes and keeps my works to the end to him will I give power over the heathen.

27 On *tending the heathen with a rod of iron* see 12:5 and 19:15. The promises are very strong here, as the Nicolaitan seduction was exceedingly formidable at Thyatira, as seen by the length and earnestness given regarding the heretics, and Jezebel's being named the wife of the angel.

27. And he shall rule them with a rod of iron; as the vessels of a potter shall they be broken to shivers: even as I received of my Father.

28-29 *The morning star* is the image of a glorious dominion, *star* is constantly used in this sense in this book. It is here connected with the rod, or sceptre (Num. 24:17,) *a star comes out of Jacob, and a sceptre rises out of Israel and shatters.* It denotes dominion over the heathen. In the ORIGINAL PASSAGE (Isa. 14:12,) the bearer of the world power, the king of Babylon is named *the bright morning star.* When the church remains steadfast, the world must change places with it. The previous verse, 27, deals with dominion over the heathen. Christ is called the *morning star* in connection with his royal supremacy in 22:16. Allusion is made to the pretensions of the Nicolaitans who promised a new light, the dawn, the morning star of knowledge, and called themselves shining stars. However in reference to Isa 14:12, 15, Jude 13, and 2 Pet. 2:17 describe the false teachers as *wandering stars for whom is reserved the blackness of darkness forever.*

28. And I will give him the morning star. 29. He that hath an ear, let him hear what the Spirit saith unto the churches.

He who has the seven spirits of God and the seven stars
SARDIS

3:1. And to the angel of the church at Sardis write: These things saith he who has the seven Spirits of God, and the seven stars: I know thy works, that thou hast a name that thou livest, and art dead. 2. Be wakeful, and strengthen the rest that is ready to die; for I have not found thy works complete before my God. 3. Remember, therefore, how thou hast received and heard, and keep it and repent. If thou wilt not therefore watch, I will come as a thief and thou wilt not know at what hour I shall come on thee. 4. But thou hast a few names in Sardis, who have not defiled their garments; and they shall walk with me in white garments, for they are worthy. 5. He that overcomes, the same shall be invested with white garments; and I will not blot out his name out of the book of life; and I will confess his name before my Father and before his angels. 6. He that has an ear to hear, let him hear what the Spirit says to the churches.

Here the angel has a name that he lives, and is dead. The Lord addresses the few living Christians who still remain there. Though sorely tried they are exhorted to be faithful, in view of the glory awaiting them. The *seven Spirits of God* are the powers of the Spirit working in creation (see on 1:4.) Because Christ has the seven Spirits he also has the *seven stars*, that is the rulers of the church, who are subject to either his displeasure or his love. This unconditional and unlimited power to punish or reward forms the foundation

CHAPTERS 2–3   THE REVELATION

to verse 3. The name of *life* is inseparable from the pastoral office, *thou hast a name that thou livest*, yet without faith and love, which are the manifestations of spiritual life—death has the ascendancy of the angel, he is near death (Matt. 8:22.) Paul refers to this death in Rom. 6:13, Eph. 2:1,5, 1 Tim. 5:6, Heb. 6:1, 9:14.

2. Be wakeful, and strengthen the rest that is ready to die; for I have not found thy works complete before my God.

2 *Be wakeful*, Eph. 5:14, has both elements of death and awaking—*awake thou that sleepest and arise from the dead*. It is to awake and to remain awake, to *watch*, as in 1 Thess. 5:10, Matt. 24:42, 25:13. John here as Peter in 1 Pet. 5:8, would have the words of Jesus in mind, *Watch and pray that ye enter not into temptation. Strengthen the rest that is ready to die*, that is the laity, who were in danger, alludes to Eze. 34:4, *the weak have ye not strengthened*, regarding the careless keeping of the Lord's flock. The *works* are by which at the last everything is to be determined, he that does the Father's will and keeps Christ's commandments shall enter and find God's love (Matt 7:21, John 14:21.) The angel appeared pure before men and his own sleeping conscience, but was not justified *before my God*.

3. Remember, therefore, how thou hast received and heard, and keep it and repent. If thou wilt not therefore watch, I will come as a thief and thou wilt not know at what hour I shall come on thee.

3 He is called to *Remember, therefore*, since the case is so bad with him, as opposed as he is to the pure doctrine delivered to him which requires living faith and cordial love. *How thou hast received*—not the manner but what the nature or tendency of what has been received or heard, to *keep* what has been given, 1 Tim. 6:20, 2 Tim. 1:14, Rev. 2:26, and especially Col. 2:6, *as ye have therefore received Christ Jesus the Lord so walk ye in him*. The second *therefore* of verse 3 joins to the *repent: if thou, therefore*. If you will not do so *I will come as a thief*, here and in 16:15, from Matt. 24:42-43, *in such an hour as ye think not the Son of Man cometh*. Elsewhere it is *the day of the Lord* that is coming, 2 Pet. 3:10, 1 Thess. 5:2, 4.

4. But thou hast a few names in Sardis, who have not defiled their garments; and they shall walk with me in white garments, for they are worthy.

4 It was not to the credit of the angel that there were *a few names in Sardis, who have not defiled their garments*. The *names* have respect to *thou hast a name* in verse 1. To be named a *Christian* is to keep oneself unspotted from the world. There were only a few among them of which the bearers did honour to their name, as name founded in reality. Many were defiled, as Sardes had become a Sordes, in contrast with 14:4, *they were not defiled with women*, women used figuratively for sin. Garments are a symbol of the state of a person, in 7:14, we have the pure state of the baptized where they have *washed their robes and made them white, for they are worthy*, white garments being given as a reward as also in 6:11, 7:9. By contrast those who shed the blood of saints are worthy of blood to drink in 16:6, and their persecutions are a token of God's righteous judgment that the saints may be counted worthy of the kingdom of God (1 Thess. 5:24.) Remarkably, in Sardis and Laodicea, the two most debased churches, there are no Nicolaitan speculations. This is explained in that what was sinful in gnosticism proceeded from the general corruption pervading heathen life. In speculative errors, there is always a spiritual element, however unspiritual, in which the conflict with it quickens, while common worldliness and indifferentism exert a deadening influence. For followers of false doctrine the spiritual excitement can be a transition to spiritual life.

5. He that overcomes, the same shall be invested with white garments; and I will not blot out his name out of the book of life; and I will confess his name before my Father and before his angels.

5 In verse 5 we have a three-fold promise all which runs into 2 Thess. 1:5, *he will be deemed worthy of the kingdom of God, for which he has suffered*, or of Acts 13:48, *he shall be of those who are ordained to eternal life*. The second promise, *I will not blot out his name out of the book of life*, rests upon Ps. 69:28,

54

which rests in turn on Ex. 32:32, *blot me out of thy book,* which is as much as to be devoted to an untimely and sudden death. For this the believers are spared.

The third promise, *I will confess his name before my Father and his angels* rests on Matt. 10:32-33, Luke 12:8-9, where *father* is in Matthew and *angels* is in Luke, while here, both are present. This whole epistle is in the words of Christ which he spoke while yet on the earth.

He that hath the key
PHILADELPHIA

> 7. And to the angel of the church in Philadelphia write: These things saith the Holy, the True, he that has the key of David, who opens and no one shuts, who shuts and no one opens. 8. I know thy works. Behold I have given before thee an open door, and no one can shut it; for thou hast a little strength, and hast kept my word, and hast not denied my name. 9. Behold, I give out of Satan's school of those that say, they are Jews and are not, but lie. Behold I will make them, that they shall come and supplicate before thy feet, and know that I have loved thee. 10. Because thou hast kept the word of my patience, I will also keep thee from the hour of temptation, which shall come upon all the world to tempt those that dwell upon the earth. 11. Behold I come quickly—Hold what thou hast, that no one take thy crown. 12. He that overcomes, him will I make a pillar in the temple of my God, and he shall not go out any more. And I will write upon him the name of my God, and the name of the New Jerusalem, the city of my God, that comes down from heaven from my God, and my name the new.

Justin, in his discourse with the Jew, Tryphon, §17, thus reproaches the Jews, *Other nations have not so much guilt in their unrighteous dealings toward us and Christ as you, who are also the authors of the bad prejudice which they raise against the Holy One and us, who are sprung from him.* From this bitter feeling of hostility from the Jews, the feeble community here had much to suffer. But the Lord consoles them, no one can rob them of possession of the Kingdom, ver. 8, but many that give themselves out proudly to be the only true people of God will humbly sue for reception into the calumniated church of Christ as the only church, ver. 9. Steadfastness in persecutions preserves them in the soon impending judgment, ver. 10-11; at the end will be eternal blessedness, ver. 12, so in view of the promise, do not faint, but fight with vigour, ver. 13. The name of *the Holy* belongs only to God who is exalted above all the calumnies and blasphemies of the Jews. Another exclusively divine predicate is *the True.* 1 John 5:20, along with John 14:6, show that he is the truth, this demonstrates Christ's oneness with the Father.

The Jews boasted of possessing the keys of the kingdom in an external succession, but the keys are perpetuated in David for his house, in Christ. The king's castle was in Zion, David dwelt in the upper house in the fort, next to the tower and he called it the city of David (2 Sam 5:9.) Jeremiah had been shut up in the prison of the king of Judah's house (Jer. 32:2.) The prophet Micah (4:8) considers David's tower as the symbol of the dominion of David's race. In Ps. 101:2, 7, David talks of *my house* where deceitful workers will not enter in, and the faithful will dwell with him. The house of David had a key, which Christ owns, Isa. 22:22. Eliakim represents those to whom Christ gives the keys, not Christ—Matt. 16:19. The house of David is the symbol of the kingdom of David, and the kingdom of Christ is the continuation and *completion of this,* as Luke 1:32. As the root and offspring of David, Christ has *the key of David*, which is the key of the kingdom of heaven. The key of death and hell in 1:18 is connected here, as he who is in David's house is secure against death and hell, and in Matt. 16:19 we have the keys in the retaining and forgiveness of sins, given to the disciples in John 20:23. It is the *Eliakim* who determines who is admitted in.

8 There are three points of commendation now from verse 8–the *works*, the *keeping of Christ's word with a little strength*, and *the not denying of his name*. The three *beholds* in verses 8-9 indicate a progression to the future. Not *I give* but *I have given*. They have a little strength in weakened beginnings, yet what is given has already been given, so it cannot mean a door of mission strength. The *open door* then refers to the *opening and shutting* in verse 7, personal membership in the house of David, or the kingdom of God. This is in face of those Jews who would deny them the kingdom.

9 *I give a gift*–that is, some of the Jews of Satan's school who recognize their vain pretensions. This serves as a limitation on Paul's conversion of all Israel, there will be a sediment of the synagogue of Satan to the end. This rests upon the promise of Isa. 60:14 where the Jews now renounce any homage to themselves and their synagogue, and willingly do homage before the church, recognising the promise respects the church and the Lord is in her midst. I give *now* in the present, and in the future *I will make*, and so it will happen.

10 The *word of my patience* is not all Christian doctrine, but Christ's declaration of patience and stedfastness declared in Luke 21:19, 8:15, and especially the kernel-declaration, *he that continues to the end shall be saved* (Matt. 10:22, 24:13,) as preservation against the judgments upon the world. He will also *keep thee* in protecting his own on earth and in the enjoyment of future glory. *Temptation* regards both believers and worldly people. The plagues on Egypt are described as temptations (Deut. 4:34, 7:19, 29:3) in which the Egyptians proved impenitent. The proving renders manifest the believers' faith and love, the worldly people their impenitence and hardness of heart, with the abyss of perdition opened to their view. Here it is not a promise only to Philadelphia, but is of force for the church universal, as chapter 7 and verse 9 makes clear. Christ gives the choice, we either suffer from the world or suffer with it. The Roman Empire had transgressed, where the Christian church had its seat, and was to be visited with the temptation.

11 Christ *comes quickly* where there is sin and hostility toward him. The *crown* is that of life, and the chosen already possess it in faith, and God keeps it for them to be bestowed at his coming, but Jews and heathen may rob us of it if we are not on our guard.

12 *The temple of my God is* the triumphant church which abiding in two states, the regeneration on the glorified earth (Matt. 19:28,) and the final state of blessedness in heaven, yet internally united. *A pillar* does not specify distinguished Christians but Christians generally, because to be a conqueror and a Christian is the same thing. The clause, *and he shall no more go out*, explains it as an unchangeable stability—however *the servant does not remain in the house* (the church) *forever* (John 8:35.) *My God* is repeated *four* times here in a respect of the four letters of Jehovah. *I will write upon him*–that is, the conqueror, not the pillar. *The name of my God* is the name of Christ and of the Father (14:1.) In *the New Jerusalem*, as its citizens. And *my name the new*, which is 19:16, *King of kings and Lord of lords*. Now received into fel-

The faithful witness and the firstborn from the dead
LAODICEA

14. And to the angel of the church at Laodicea write: These things says Amen, the true and faithful witness, the beginning of the creation of God. 15. I know thy works, that thou art neither cold nor hot. I would that thou wert cold or hot 16. But because thou art lukewarm, and neither cold nor hot, I will spue thee out of my mouth. 17. Because thou sayest, I am rich and have enriched myself and need nothing; and knowest not, that thou art wretched and miserable, poor, blind, and naked. 18. I counsel thee, to buy of me gold, that has been purified in the fire, that thou mayest be rich; and white clothing, that thou mayest put on, and that the shame of thy nakedness may not appear; and eye-salve, to anoint thine eyes, that thou mayest see. 19. Whomsoever I love, them I rebuke and chasten: be zealous, therefore, and repent. 20. Behold I stand at the door and knock. If any one hear my voice and open the door, I will go into him, and sup with him and he with me. 21. He that overcomes, to him will I give to sit with me on my throne; as I have overcome and have sitten down with my Father on his throne. 22. He that has an ear let him hear what the Spirit saith to the churches.

The angel of the church at Laodicea, for which Paul had fought a good fight (Col. 2:1, 4:15,) had imagined themselves to be the foremost, but in reality they were the farthest from salvation–they had become lukewarm, blind and naked. They need a hearing ear for the great secrets, to suffer themselves to be drawn to repentance. The Hebrew *Amen* is everywhere used adverbially. In Isa. 65:16 the God of the verily is he whose words and deeds have always the verily impressed on them. The verily is he who in all he says in disclosing the concealed depths of the heart in threatening and promising can always add with the fullest right the verily. This verily frequently occurs in the Lord's discourses, particularly in John, this points to the fullness of truth that dwells in him as the true. The *true witness* in 1:5 is there to console despairing saints faced with a powerful world, with faith in his promises. Here we think mainly of the certainty of his threatening and rebuking testimony, and also to the promises in verses 20 and 21. The *beginning* is the living beginning where it had its root and source of being, as also God and Christ are named the end. Named the beginning in relation to the creatures, Christ is omniscient in the knowledge of his works (Heb. 4:13,) almighty in his power to reward or punish them. Against the Arian view, which held Christ to be a creature, is Col. 1:15-18, compare on ch. 1:5, where he is the author of creation as he is here, compare on 5:13.

This predicate of Christ—the *arche* of the *ktisis* of God may allude to *Archippus*, who, in Col. 4:17 compared with Philemon 2, is the overseer in Laodicea, the first bishop of the Laodiceans, ordained, it is said, by the apostles. Paul's admonition sounds suspicious.

15-16 Coldness is the love produced by self, while heat, that which is kindled by the Holy Spirit; compare the fire of Luke 12:49 and Acts 2:2-4, and the love in Rom. 5:5. In the Song it is called the vehement flame of the Lord, *with coals of fire*. It is the condition of those who stand in relation to himself, being cold, one is conscious of being cold with a hearty desire to be hot. It goes with *blessed are they who are poor in spirit*—blessed are they who in their own feeling are cold in spirit. To become warm, one must first have been cold. As the being blind in John 9:41. Being cold is preferable to being lukewarm. Lukewarm is sickness, not to be tolerated as a transition state—*I would that thou wert cold.* Lukewarm water promotes to spewing. The accusation of lukewarmness has its ground in verse 17, but verse 18 is not a conclusion to this verse. The judgment against them is in connection with their high minded conceit, self satisfaction, lack of sensible conviction of sin or earnest desires after pardon and sanctification.

17 They imagine *riches*, but spiritual riches are meant, 1 Cor. 1:5, 4:8, 2 Cor. 8:9. *I have enriched myself*, the ORIGINAL PASSAGE is Hosea 12:8, *Ephraim says I have become rich and have found substance*. Either they had low ideas of the calling of Christians, or could point to showy virtues. How one can have and do everything points to the example of the Pharisees whose *I thank thee, etc.* the Laodiceans responded, and received also along with them the condemnation of heaven, *ye are they who justify yourselves before men; but God knows your heart*, see also 1 Cor. 13:1. The three actual wants correspond to the three imaginary distinctions. But beforehand the whole condition of the Laodiceans is condensed into the *par excellence, wretched and miserable*. The reproach of *blind and naked*—compare Matt. 15:14, 23:26, shows they pride themselves on their knowledge, pretend to a higher knowledge, as Colossians shows, but they could not see they were beggars.

18 The *buy* of verse 18 is from Isa. 55:1. The merchandise is the giving up the imagination of their own excellence which had not known the coldness and therefore the warmth, and having the conviction that in one's own strength nothing is done. The *gold* signifies tried faith. This is connected with 1 Pet. 1:7, compared with James 1:3 where faith is tried and purified. *That thou mayest be rich*—their faith could not go through a trial, it was a faith of the fancy, not a heart faith. *White clothing* is the Christian virtues, only found in fellowship with Christ, compare 3:4. *Eyesalve* is the illuminating grace of the Holy Spirit. The third thing, the seeing, is true spiritual knowledge, this is contrasted with superficial show knowledge.

19 *I rebuke and chasten*, represents the penetrating force of the preceding address after it had wrought its necessary effect. *Whomsoever I love*, the Laodiceans had still not reached the last step—its candlestick still remained. Allusion is made to Prov. 3:11-12, also quoted in Heb. 12:5-6. *Be zealous and repent*. Repentance is not a mere insight into one's poverty and nakedness, but a change of mind, from lukewarm through to cold to hot zeal of love. It needed an entire change of mind.

20 *Behold I stand at the door and knock*. The first part of the verse is from Song 5:2. The spiritual state of the person is the same in both passages. *If anyone hears my voice*. The bride is between sleeping and waking, corresponding to the lukewarm state. She can't overcome her slumbering inactivity, and delays to let the bridegroom in. We see the grief of a soul that has driven the Lord from it. The second part of the verse, *I will go into him*, points to the Song. 4:16 and 5:1 is the foundation of *I will sup with him and he with me*. Song 2:3 is the foundation for *and he with me*.

21-22 The overcomers will be received into his dominion, those that afflicted them will lay prostrate under their feet. Comp. on 1:9, 2:26-28; and in regard to the *as I have overcome* see 5:5, 7:17, 22:1, Phil 2:9, Heb 12:2.

GROUP 2

THE SEVEN SEALS, WITH EPISODE

Christ visits the persecuting world with judgments and ruin

REVELATION 4:1–8:1

REVELATION 4

The holy assembly sitting in judgment

GROUP SUMMARY

In chapter 4 the seer is snatched up to heaven, and sees there a holy assembly, in which all points to the judgment, which, for the benefit of his sorely oppressed church, the Lord is going to execute upon the ungodly world. What the whole scene suggests is then brought clearly out in ch. 5, where a book with seven seals is delivered to Christ for the purpose of being opened, containing the judgments to be inflicted on the world. This opening follows, and the judgments, one after another become manifest in ch. 6 and in 8:1, while ch. 7 forms an intermediate episode, which represents the preservation of the faithful in the midst of the judgments which alight on the world.

UP TO HEAVEN THROUGH THE OPEN DOOR

> 4:1. After this I saw, and behold a door was opened in heaven; and the first voice, which I had heard speaking with me as a trumpet, saying, come up hither, and I will show thee what must be done after these things.

After this, after John had written the seven epistles. In going up to heaven through the open door, John, ver. 2, is in the Spirit. The ORIGINAL PASSAGE is Eze. 1:1, *the heaven was opened, and I saw visions of God*. What is said there in ver. 3, *The word of the Lord came to Ezekiel ... and the hand of the Lord was there upon him*, is parallel. Since the Messiah's time, heaven has been opened (Matt. 3:16, John 1:51;) so his servants can ascend there to learn the secrets of God. For us to handle divine things is entirely in the power of the Lord Jesus Christ. To seek to ascend by one's own might is the part of Lucifer. The voice as a *trumpet* in 1:10 and here, belonged to Christ, who unfolds everything to the prophets.

A COUNCIL AND JUDGMENT REGARDING THE UNGODLY WORLD

> 2. And immediately I was in the Spirit, and behold a throne lay in heaven, and upon the throne one sat. 3. And he that sat was to look upon like a jasper and sardius stone; and a rainbow was round about the throne in sight like to an emerald. 4. And round about the throne four and twenty thrones; and sitting on the thrones four and twenty elders, clothed with white garments, and on their heads golden crowns. 5. And from the throne proceed lightnings, and voices, and thunders; and seven torches of fire burn before the throne, which are the seven Spirits of God,

Here the second vision begins, and it completes itself at 8:1, where in 8:2 another vision will start. John sees God the Father sitting on the throne.

CHAPTER 4   **THE REVELATION**

3. And he that sat was to look upon like a jasper and sardius stone; and a rainbow was round about the throne in sight like to an emerald.
4. And round about the throne four and twenty thrones; and sitting on the thrones four and twenty elders, clothed with white garments, and on their heads golden crowns.

3 The two stones represent two different properties of God, terrible and frightful—the jasper his glory and holiness, the dark clay red sardius, not the blood colour, but the fire of God's anger. Around the throne was an emerald rainbow, the green predominant as showing the divine condescension and forbearance.

4 The twenty four elders are ideal representatives of the church, the one Israel of God, perpetuated in the New Testament, under the twelve patriarchs and the twelve apostles (Matthew 19:28, comp. Luke 22:30, Rev. 20:4.) They also appear as co-regents with God in 11:16, representing the whole church of believers, the sitting on the throne in 3:21 is of this. It is the privilege of the Christian, that nothing comes to pass which he does not will, every thing that he does will—that he triumphs in God over all hostile powers, and with him rides upon the high places of the earth, and sees the whole world lying under his feet. The crowns are kingly (6:2, 9:7, 14:14; comp. Matt. 27:29, John 19:12,) the glittering white garments (comp. Matt. 17:2, Mark 9:3, Luke 9:29, Matt. 28:3, Luke 24:4, Acts 1:10, comp. 10:30, 1:14, 19:8, 15:6, comp. 19:14) being the glory of God imparted to the righteous (1:14, 3:18, 6:2, 7:14, 19:8, 11, 20:11.) The elders are there in the governing, not priestly capacity, their assembly shows the episode pertains to the church.

5. And from the throne proceed lightnings, and voices, and thunders; and seven torches of fire burn before the throne, which are the seven Spirits of God,

5 The lightnings and thunders from the throne are pre-intimations of judgment, the seven torches of fire (comp. 1:14, 2:18, 19:12, 10:1, 20:10, 21:8, 14:10) show the operations of the Spirit of Christ in chastisement and destruction, as the Old Testament describes them as consuming and burning (Zech. 12:6; Judges 15:4-5; Dan. 10:6, comp. 8:10.)

THE CRYSTAL SEA AND THE CHERUBIM

> 6. And before the throne was a sea of glass, like crystal. And in the midst of the throne and round about the throne four beasts, full of eyes before and behind, 7. And the first beast was like a lion, and the second beast was like a calf, and the third beast had a face as a man and the fourth beast was like a flying eagle. 8. And each of the four beasts has six wings, and round about and within they are full of eyes, and have no rest day and night and they say: Holy, holy, holy is the Lord God, the Almighty, who was, and who is, and who comes. 9. And when the beasts give glory and honour and thanks to him who sits on the throne, who lives for ever and ever, 10. the four and twenty elders fall down before him who sits on the throne, and worship him who lives for ever and ever, and cast their crowns before the throne, and say, 11. Lord, thou art worthy to receive the glory and the honour and the might; for thou hast made all things, and through thy will they were and are created.

The seven lamps of fire and the sea are mentioned together; both *before the throne*—afterwards, at 15:2, there is again a sea of glass; and instead of the seven torches of fire, the sea itself is *mingled* with fire. The sea is a product of the torches of fire. God by his Spirit brings about the execution of what is right. In ch. 15 the song was sung by those who stood on it; sign and word go together. Accordingly, it denotes the great and wonderful works of God, his righteous and holy ways, his just deeds become manifest. The sea of glass is an anti-type to the Red Sea, as an image of the great judgment of God. THE ORIGINAL PASSAGE here is Ps. 36:6, *Thy judgments are a great flood.* The judgments are judicial acts through which God destroys the wicked and aids his people. Against the flood of human wickedness stands the great flood, the broad ocean of the divine judgment (Gen. 7:11, the only other passage where the *great flood*, occurs,) the deluge, in which the judgment of God appears as in reality a great flood. Twice had the sea served as an embodiment of God's judgments, which are here described as *immeasurable* under its image—at the deluge, and when the Egyptians were drowned in the Red Sea, referred to in ch. 15. The words, *before the throne*, rest on Ps. 89:14, 97:2, *righteousness and judgment are the foundation of thy throne*, that is, God's dominion maintains itself on the territory of what is just and righteous. These two passages rest on Ex. 24:10, *And they beheld the God of Israel, and under his feet there was like the work of white* (clear glittering, comp. on ver. 4) *sapphire, and like the heaven itself in purity*. They explain the symbol there. Upon these again rests Eze. 1:22, *And there was on the heads of the beasts something like a cloud, like the look of crystal, terrible* (a great blinding splendour), *expanded over their heads above*. Above this cloud stands the throne of God, according to ver. 26. Here in Ezekiel the crystal signifies the terribleness (comp. Hab. 3:2, *Lord, I heard thy doing, I was afraid,*) the awe inspiring greatness and glory of the divine executions of judgment. Also according to 22:1, *And he showed me a stream of water of life, clear as crystal*, it is not the transparency, but the *shining clearness* of crystal that is considered (comp. 21:11.) Different from the *crystal*, the *glass* designates the rectitude and purity of the divine judgments—comp. 21:18, 21, *as pure* or *transparent glass*. In Ex. 24:10 too there is found a double point, the *clear splendour* and its *purity*. To the purity of glass, as indicative of righteousness and truth, corresponds, in 15:3, the *righteous and true are thy ways*. And to the clear and blinding glitter of crystal, indicating the frightfulness and glory of the acts of judgment, corresponds the *great and wonderful are thy works. Lord God Almighty. Who would not fear thee, Lord, and glorify thy name!* The measureless character of the divine judgments, a view, if dreadful to the world, consoles the church, which in the depths of this sea should lose all its cares, and sorrow, and pain, to disregard the sea of the nations, and have it open for this glorious mirror, this holy sea before the throne of God. In Scripture the *sea* signifies agitation and trouble; but here the idea is changed, by the transparence and the likeness of crystal.

The Cherubim are seen in the OLD TESTAMENT in the symbolical forms of the law and in Ezekiel. The signification comes from the name here given to the Cherubim, called *Zoa, living beings*, as those in Ezekiel. Consequently they are *the representation of living beings, of all that is living on the earth*. God appears enthroned above the Cherubim, in order to show his absolute supremacy over all that is earthly, as the *God of Hosts, Sabaoth*; pointing to the dominion of God over the heavenly powers, as the other to his dominion over the earthly. The God, with the Cherubim under the throne, who is preparing to judge the world, is the God of the whole earth, whom all that lives and moves on it obeys, and who can turn all it contains into weapons of vengeance against the apostate. The Cherubim are *not* superior angels. They are connected with the elders, distinguished, not only from the angels, but also from all angels, as is done in 7:11, *all the angels stood round about the throne, and about the elders **and** the four beasts*. In ch. 5 the whole assembly before the throne, is divided into two choruses, beasts and elders formed one, ver. 8, and the angels the other, ver. 11. (* *See footnote at end of chapter.*)

The Cherubim never do the service of the messengers, the ministering spirits. Their business is only that of *being*, first, *under* the throne of God (not

CHAPTER 4   THE REVELATION

6. And before the throne was a sea of glass, like crystal. And in the midst of the throne and round about the throne four beasts, full of eyes before and behind,

supporting it), then of *symbolizing* the truth that God is the God of the whole earth and of the spirits of all flesh, and that of praising and glorifying God. They have a part in prefiguring the judgments, which are to fall upon the earth, as at the opening of the seals in 6:1, they call out to the Seer, *Come and see*, and in 15:7, they stretch out the seven vials to the seven angels. They come as representatives of the earth, which is to be affected by the divine judgments. The Cherubim were *four*, because four is the signature of the earth. Scripture describes nature by the four quarters of the world, Ps. 89:13, the four corners of the earth, 7:1, 21:13. In Ps. 148, of those who praise the Lord on the land, there are four times four, and four in particular of living creatures. We find the same four of living creatures in Gen. 7:21, 23. In Ezekiel 1:6 the four beasts have each four faces and four wings.

In the first description of the Cherubim, Ezekiel says in 1:18, that the felloes of the wheels connected with the cherub were full of eyes, while in the second description, 10:12, he says in unison with John, *And their whole flesh, and their backs, and their hands and their wings, were full of eyes round about.* In Rev. 5:6, we see the Lamb has seven eyes, *which are the seven Spirits of God that are sent forth upon the whole earth*—comp. Zech. 4:10, where the operations of the Lord's Spirit are set forth as the seven *eyes of the Lord, which run to and fro in the whole earth*. The eye is the organ, the *corporeal image* of the Spirit. Being full of eyes indicates that the whole living creation is *inspirited*. In Scripture, all life, intellectual, spiritual, *and* physical also, is of God, the source of life, the God of the spirits of all flesh (Num. 16:22, 27:16; Heb. 12:9; comp. Gen. 1:2, 2:7; Eccl. 12:7, Ps. 104:29.) The eyes of the Cherubim, symbolising the powers of God working in creation, encourage the pious, and bring terror to the wicked, so we see why in ver. 8 there is a repeated allusion to the eyes in connection with the song of praise by the Cherubim: this song forms a commentary on their being full of eyes, round about and within. The eyes cannot denote wisdom and knowledge.

7. And the first beast was like a lion, and the second beast was like a calf, and the third beast had a face as a man and the fourth beast was like a flying eagle.

7 The *lion* and the *eagle* begin and close the series. The order here is different from Ezekiel. As the most warlike among the four beasts, they are the strongest matter-of-fact prophecies of the impending destruction over the world (comp. in regard to the lion Isa. 21:8-9, in regard to the eagle here 8:13.) In the second place, it is not the ox that is mentioned, but the *calf*, as was the case also in Eze. 1:7. So here the ox represents cattle generally, as also the designation of *flying* for the eagle represents all winged creatures–not the *act* of flying, but the *power* of flight. The other beasts were not throughout, but only in the face, unlike man. Each of the beasts had his peculiar visage, and the third that of a man's countenance; but *the human form belonged to them all*. This is implied in its being said of the third, not that it was *like* a man, but that it *had the face as of a* man. The likeness of a lion, an eagle, and a calf, in the others, is confined by this to the face. Eze. 1:5 said, *and this is their appearance, they have the form of a man*—a man's erect gait and hands. In Rev. 5:8, 19:4, the beasts fall down with the elders, incongruous if two were quadrupeds. From the position given to man in the creation, the human type must predominate in the personification of all living, and the rest be content with a representation in the countenance alone. The Cherubim of Ezekiel have each the four faces of these beasts, but these beasts, are intimately connected together, forming one beast-existence, which Ezekiel calls *the living* (1:20-22,) and it is no matter whether all the properties belong to each of the

THE HOLY ASSEMBLY SITTING IN JUDGMENT

four, or singly in each.

8 The Cherubim here have *four* wings like the Seraphim in Isaiah 6, Ezekiel has *six*. They serve to glorify God, to terrorize his enemies and console his friends. The three pairs of wings and their use display the excellencies in a holy creature, their humility and obedience. They honour, fear and respect the divine holiness, since, covering their faces, they do not look boldly, but show humility, veiling themselves before God's splendour, and also readiness, in obeying the divine commands. They do not say, *holy art thou*, but *holy is He*. They cover their feet, from God's sight, though sin free yet in a creaturely abasement. They fly and move about in full activity, praising the Lord and executing his will. All this serves to glorify God. Their wings are in line with their eyes, and their thrice exclamation of *holy*. The clause *they are full of eyes round about (in front) and within (in the back parts)* stand in close connection with what follows; and because they are wholly penetrated by the powers of God, therefore, etc. The words, *they have no rest day and night, saying*, alludes to Ps. 19:2-3. As the heavens unceasingly declare the glory of the God of hosts, so also do the Cherubim or the earthly creatures. The *holy, holy, holy*, taken from Isa. 6, and is in Ps. 99, a threefold woe to the world which has this God for its enemy (comp. 8:13,) and a threefold *lift up your heads* to the church, which stands under his protection. *Holy, holy, holy*, according to his glory as manifesting itself in *our* state of being, evident from: *they are round about and within full of eyes*; and also ver. 9, where the beasts give honour and glory to God, and also *thanks*, which they could only do if they celebrated God's holiness on the ground of their own existence.

Holiness is not merely the highest purity in God, but it rather denotes the infinite exaltation of God above all that is created and finite. This is clear from the reference the Cherubim make to their own existence, and also from the epithet, *the Almighty*, which has respect to holiness as its ground: *holy*, because all-ruling and *almighty*. When God is called *Holy*, his separate, peculiar excellence is indicated—composed of his divine properties, their splendour throwing everything else into the shade, since God stands apart from all: he is, and he works by himself, from himself, in himself, through himself, for himself. (See 1 Tim. 6:15-16.) Therefore he is the first and the last, the one and eternal, living and blessed, infinite and unchangeable, almighty, all-seeing, wise and true, righteous and faithful, gracious and compassionate. So *holy* and *holiness* are much the same as *God* and *Godhead*; and as one says of a king: *his Majesty*, so the Scripture says of God: *his Holiness* (Heb. 12:10.) The Holy Spirit is *God's* Spirit. *The holy* is often used as a name, when God is spoken of (Isa. 40:25; 1 Sam. 2:2; Ex. 15:11.) As God swears by his name and soul, so he also swears by his holiness, that is, by himself. He is sanctified when he is known and worshipped as the true God. This holiness is often named *the glory*; often are his holiness and glory celebrated together (Lev. 10:3; Isa. 6:3.) The *Almighty* is the description of him to whom *Holy*, was applied, and the *reason* why it was applied. The beasts say: *God the Almighty*, for which the elders say: *our God*, ver. 11. *The Almighty!* often so named in the Revelation, because he there shows himself in his power over all. The expression: *who comes*, refers, according to the PARALLEL PASSAGES (see in 1:4) to the future developments and triumphs of the kingdom of God, who, as he has shown in the past and present what he was and is by displays of his glory and almightiness, so he will also come to introduce the kingdom over the whole earth—comp. 11:17.

8. And each of the four beasts has six wings, and round about and within they are full of eyes, and have no rest day and night and they say: Holy, holy, holy is the Lord God, the Almighty, who was, and who is, and who comes.

On the ground of the declaration, *Holy, holy, holy is the Lord God the Almighty*, prophecy may be said to be based. He that has preserved his holiness will also come, without any one being able to prevent his arrival. So all in the verse, the wings of the Cherubim, their eyes, their ceaseless *holy, holy, holy*, serves to revive the spirits of the church before a persecuting, apparently omnipotent world, and lay a foundation for the following vision of the seven seals.

9 In the OLD TESTAMENT style, glory, strength, greatness, etc., are given to the Lord, in the sense of being *ascribed* to him (comp. Deut. 32:3, Ps. 29:1, Ps. 96:7.) According to this usage, *glory and honour*, referring to what is peculiarly God's, might be joined with the *thanks*, which proceed from the Cherubim; the former are given in the acknowledgment of God, the latter in the offering of praise. In the elders' song of praise, likewise, *power* might be put in the room of *thanks*. The Cherubim, in whose formation divine power has unfolded itself, give thanks for this unfolding, the elders satisfy themselves with a simple ascription of praise on account of it.

10 It is not said, the elders *laid aside* their crowns, but that they *cast them down;* as a burden to wear in the presence of God, feeling their littleness and unworthiness. All who truly reign in the church wish no glory or honour to themselves. The four beasts do not precisely say, *thou art holy*, etc., but they reverentially turn away a little, and say: *Holy, holy, holy is* the Lord, but when the four and twenty elders fall down, they exclaim: *Worthy art thou*.

11 The adoration of the Cherubim turns on God's almighty power in *creation;* and so does that also of the elders, indicated by the article, *the* glory, etc., showing that the elders respond to the doxology of the Cherubim. There is also a background reference to the glorious completion of his kingdom, which God must as certainly bring about as he made the world. The adoration is given to him as sitting on the throne, and addressing himself to the execution of the world's judgment. Similarly has the creation already been mentioned in the NEW TESTAMENT, being *the foundation and basis of all other displays of goodness, which are in a manner the continuation of it*. So in Ps. 104 the celebration of God's praise from the works of creation awakens confidence in the church in regard to the final victory of the righteous over the wicked, of the church over the world, which had the ascendancy at the time the Psalm was composed. In Jer. 10:11 it is said, *The gods that have not made the heavens and the earth, these shall perish from the earth and from under heaven* (Comp. also Isa. 43:1; Acts 4:24.) In the Revelation the creation appears as a pledge for the completion of the kingdom of God in 10:6 and 14:7. The Creator must necessarily be the Redeemer of his people, and the judge of the apostate. If any one holds fast by the article of the creation, he will not doubt the completion of God's kingdom. The *Thou hast made*, marks the creative energy of God. As this was accomplished by a mere word, it was quite appropriate to bring out the result by the express words, *They were and are created*. In Gen. 1:7 also it is said, *And God made the firmament, and divided between the waters under the firmament and above the firmament, and it was done so*. See besides Ps. 119:90, Ps. 33:9. The general predominance of the number *three* in ver. 8-11 is noticeable: *Holy, holy, holy; the Lord, God, Almighty; who was, who is, and who comes; glory, honour, thanks; they fall down, they worship, they cast; thou hast created, they were, and are created*.

Such is the prophet's description of the divine holiness and glory, and the manner in which these are celebrated by those who are so near him, and yet look upon us as their companions. He is a holy God with whom we have to do. If the beings who dwell so near about his throne act so reverentially toward him, how much more humbly does it behove us to conduct ourselves! Were our hearts but penetrated with a just dread of him, we should also come to possess an assurance of his favour, confidence in him, desire after him, delight in him, and a more zealous endeavour to do what is pleasing in his sight.

---

* The CHERUBIM occur in the OLD TESTAMENT 85 times. The Scripture nowhere gives us a direct explanation of the cherubim. In Gen. ch. 3 they meet us with the first man. They are an image in which the piety of the primeval world represents the nature of surrounding things. The only correct definition of the nature of the cherubim must equally suit all the passages of scripture in which it occurs. The divine prophets saw not the very essence of the invisible things, but only certain likenesses and patterns–see Eze. 1:5. The beings of whom the cherub is composed belong to the creatures of the visible world that form the upmost and highest of its three kingdoms–the kingdom of organic, warmblooded physical life. The cherubim is not a figure of God himself, its essential character is to be a creature in its highest stage–an ideal creature. The cherub is creation individualised, only God is above it, it is the being in which the glory of God manifests itself. It does not include the Hosts, the heavenly creatures. They are characterised by two things: a *multitude*, Eze 1:24, and as *the living*, Gen. 2:7, 9:16, Eze. 1:20-21, 10:15, 20. The number four represent the classes of the animal world, the signature of the earth–see Gen. 7:21, Ps. 148, Eze. 1:7, Rev. 4:7.

The human type must preponderate as the crown of creation–Gen 1; in the tabernacle, all is human except the wings; in Ezekiel the human face faces the east, the front and chief quarter. Lions, kine and cherub prefigured on the laver bases in 1 Kings 7:29. The cherub of Solomon have only the birds-wings, with man in the whole figure. Lions and oxen are not expressly represented except on the bases. The signature of the Almighty Lord of nature is impressed on the ark, the walls, and the furniture. The animal life culminates in man, lion, ox and eagle, also the plant life in palm and flowers–1Kings 6: 29 and Eze. 41:18. The palm is according to the Arabs the blessed tree. It cannot bear to remain on the earth but hastens to heaven like man. The herb culminates in the flower, the king of the trees is the palm.

In Eze. 1:22, 26, the vault or firmament is upon the heads of the living creatures, above the terrible crystal is the place of the throne of God. The vault is a type of the heavens–see Gen. 1:1, Isa. 40:22, Dan.12:3. Therefore the cherub under the vault can only represent the terrestrial creation. Isa. 42:5 portrays the heavens as stretched out and the terrestrial creation spread forth under it.

In Ps. 80:1 *He who sits on the cherub*, is also *the God of Hosts;* they are coordinate expressions, always occuring together and in connection with God–the Lord of heavenly powers appears beside the Lord of the earthly, see 1 Sam. 4:4, 2 Sam. 6:2. *He who sits* is also joined to *the elohim*. The God of Israel is designated as the absolute deity, possessor of the fulness of the Godhead. 1 Sam. 4:4, Ps. 80:1. He is *the God*, the maker of heaven and earth–see 2 Kings 19:15. The sitting of God over the cherub shows that the world power can have no advantage over God's people. He not only sits, but he rides, that is, he takes action. He flies on the wind, Ps. 18:10, which represents the power of nature. The Lord of all that lives is at the same time He who gives way, course, path to clouds, air and winds–Eze.10:13, Isa. 5:28. Fire comes from within the wheels Eze. 10:6, Ps. 148:8, *fire, and hail, snow, and vapour, stormy wind fulfilling his word*. The powers of nature serve God along with the cherub in the story of Job. The creature and the powers of nature work equally for the end appointed by God, for salvation or destruction, both equally dependent on the Spirit of God moving them.

In Eze. 1:16, 10:12 and Rev. 4:6 the cherub is all covered with eyes, representing the powers of nature under the guidance of divine providence. The wind appears to go where it will, but in truth it has no independent will, the powers of nature in their action on the world, and their relation to man, are not subject to blind chance, but are guided by deliberate counsel–that reason is in them, because above them. The cherub is the being that represents the multiplicity of the works of God. Everywhere is law, order, design guided by intelligence. The whole living creation is penetrated by the Spirit, where the Spirit is is also reason, end, design. The seven eyes of the Lord are the powers of God, the radiations of his providence. They penetrate the whole earth to counteract the dangers from every quarter to the Kingdom of God.

In Revelation the elders are the representatives of the church. If they are purely ideal beings, an ideal element will also be present in the cherubs that are joined with them; and those will be astray who simply see in them real beings. The four beasts have a claim to the first place, because they represent the genus, while the elders form a species of that genus. They are not angels. See Rev. 5:11, Rev. 7:11, where angels and beasts are different entities.

–Condensed from the author's treatise on the cherubim, in his Commentary on Ezekiel.

REVELATION 5

The giving up of the book with seven seals to Christ

In this chapter we have first the presentation of a book, sealed with seven seals, which is delivered to the Lamb, that is, Jesus Christ, to be opened, ver. 1-7; then, the celebration of Jesus Christ as the Lamb who was slain and must open the book with the seven seals, consisting of doxologies and songs of the heavenly hosts, ver. 8-14. The doxologies belong partly to the beasts and the elders, ver. 8-10, partly to the angels, ver. 11-12, and partly to all creatures, ver. 13. The sequel to this solemn glorification is the response of the beasts, and the worship of the elders, ver. 14. It would be more correct to say that ver. 9-12 contain the celebration of the Lamb's praise by the four beasts, the elders and the angels, and that in ver 13-14 the Father and the Son are glorified by all creatures, through the concurring voices of their representatives, the elders and the beasts.

THE PRESENTATION OF THE BOOK TO THE LAMB

5:1. And I saw on the right hand of him who sat upon the throne, a book written within and without, sealed with seven seals, 2. And I saw a strong angel proclaim with a loud voice: Who is worthy to take the book and to break its seals? 3. And no one in heaven, nor on the earth, nor under the earth, could take the book and look therein. 4. And I wept much, that no one was found worthy to take the book, nor to look therein. 5. And one of the elders spake to me: Weep not; behold the lion, who is of the tribe of Judah, the root of David, has overcome to take the book, and to break its seven seals. 6. And I saw (and lo!) in the midst of the throne and of the four beasts, and in the midst of the elders, a Lamb standing, as if it had been slain; and it had seven horns, and seven eyes, which are the seven Spirits of God, sent into all lands. 7. And he came and took the book out of the right hand of him that sat on the throne.

The prototype of this book is in Ezek. 2:9-10, which in turn rests on Jer. 15:16. The *book* contained the word Ezekiel had to announce, and was the archetype of the book of his prophecies. The book here likewise is the archetype of the section of the seven seals in the Revelation. Ch. 10:2 also rests more closely on Ezekiel, as the subject is an *open* book which also respects the fate of a degenerate church, has to do with the world in the church, while the book here contains the judgment upon the *world* by itself; and that book was eaten by the prophet. It is not the archetype of the whole of the Revelation from chap. 6, but only the seven seals, 6–8:1, which come entirely to an end at 8:1. The Revelation is composed of a series of independent portions, and an entirely new series begins at 8:2. If this book were the archetype of the whole Apocalypse, we should have nothing new to begin that second book at ch. 10.

Its being *written within and without*, properly within and *behind*, bookrolls were usually only written within, when the inner side did not suffice, then the exterior was brought into use, all intimating its varied contents does not mean it is not limited to 6:1—8:1, as it is only a sketch of the contents of the book, with much between the lines. The judgments, in rough outlines, consist each of a vast assemblage of many single calamities, which were fully noted in the original.

The book was as still in motion *to the right hand* of him who sat upon the throne, it was not usually there. The *out of the right hand* in ver. 7 corresponds to the *in the right hand* here. Being in the *right hand* of him who sat on the throne shows that it is judicial in nature, as 4:4 makes clear it affects the enemies of the church. Vitringa concludes from this image that nothing takes place in the world and the church, which has not been determined in God's counsel and judgment.

The being *sealed with seven seals*, signifies that the divine decrees, before they are executed are shut and concealed from angels and men. In Isa. 29:11; Dan. 8:26, 12:4, 9, a shut and sealed prophecy is all one with the dark and incomprehensible. The darkness of the future was complete, sealed all over. Whenever a seal was removed, a portion of the contents became known. The seven seals are the *theological* cause of the inaccessible character of the book. By opening, not reading, each seal, a successive portion of God's decrees or judgments upon the world were made manifest. The book was a roll on which outside seven seals were impressed. What was seen at the opening of each seal indicate the contents of it. That it was God's judgments on the enemies of his church, is clear from ch. 4. The *public* presentation of the book had no bearing on its decrees being executed. In the Old Testament shut or sealed books, or prophecies, refer only to the difficulty of understanding them. In ver. 3 and 4 the *opening of the book* is only the condition of the seeing. The whole book is the Revelation of Jesus Christ, which God gave him to *show* to his servants, what must shortly come to pass. So in it is not the executing, but only the making known of God's decrees.

2 A strong angel was chosen because of the loud voice, to be heard in the heavens, the earth, and under the earth; hence powerfully in all regions of being. Those, who heard it, would be forced to think of their weakness.

3 The inhabitants of the three kingdoms of creation are, in like manner, united together in Phil. 2:10, both showing the subordination of all to Christ; the Seer might have this passage in view. The book contains the decrees of God, as can belong to no created being, but only to Christ, who was in the beginning with the Father. Religious knowledge can only be attained through fellowship with Christ, the one mediator. See John 1:18, John 3:11-13, Matt. 11:27.

4 The tears of John were not from unsatisfied curiosity, but from the same cause as those of Mary, in John 20:11,13; and with the grief of the disciples on the way to Emmaus (Luke 24:21.) The terrible Roman power had thrown itself upon the church to crush it; comp. 13:7. John, who here represents the church, is in solitary banishment. It appeared the kingdom of Christ was coming to an end. It went with John, as it had done with the disciples in Luke 24. He had heard the words, but his faith in them has failed. The Lord had taken from him all he formerly had, to show him he had nothing but what was his through undeserved grace, that he might more gloriously experience the divine consolation. Bengel says, without tears, the Revelation

CHAPTER 5   THE REVELATION

was not written, neither can it without tears be understood. Whoever goes to it merely as an interesting production of the apostolic age, will everywhere stumble in darkness. If we take this view of the weeping we get rid of the notion that detailed disclosures of the future are given in the seven seals; and regard them as for inspiring the soul with confidence respecting God's judgments on the world, and the victory of faith.

<small>5. And one of the elders spake to me: Weep not; behold the lion, who is of the tribe of Judah, the root of David, has overcome to take the book, and to break its seven seals.</small>

5 The *elder* represents the whole church of the completely righteous. From the testimony yielded by this to Christ, out of rich experience, consolation first comes to the fainting Seer, and a fainting church on earth, and then also from the action of Christ himself.

The *overcoming* is not so much getting, or attaining but the idea of a victory, as Christ is designated *the lion of the tribe of Judah*, a warlike image; in the FUNDAMENTAL PASSAGES, Gen. 49:9, where Jacob declares Judah as a warrior and a conqueror under the image of a lion. He also shows the Messiah would come from Judah. David also was a hero and a conqueror. In ver. 9 the *being slain, etc.,* corresponds to the *conquering* here. And John 16:33 gives farther confirmation. But the connection is not directly his victory over sin, the devil, and the world, as the conquering is immediately joined to the opening: *he has overcome to open*, or *in opening*. He had victory over sin and Satan, through death and blood, for by this alone was Christ worthy to open the book. The opening of the book is, therefore, a reward for having finished redemption.

The second designation of Christ, as *the root of David*, accords with the preceding one. In Christ the race of David, as the hero and conqueror, lived anew, see Ps. 18:29, 37. The *root* here, and in 22:16, marks the product of the root, through which the root makes itself seen: its shoot, as seed, is very often used for the product of the seed. The Messiah is named, in Isa. 11:10, *the root of Jesse*, as the one in whom the family of David, that had sunk into the lowest condition, again flourished, as is displayed by 11:1, and 53:2, where the likeness of the shoot of a plant, refers to the Messiah as sprung from a family which had once resembled a proud and stately tree, but now had become one of the lowest.

<small>6. And I saw (and lo!) in the midst of the throne and of the four beasts, and in the midst of the elders, a Lamb standing, as if it had been slain; and it had seven horns, and seven eyes, which are the seven Spirits of God, sent into all lands.</small>

6 What the elder had announced is now exhibited. The elder showed John a lion, and yet John sees a little lamb. What there derogates from his majesty is ascribed to him under the image of *the lion*. Only here Jesus is named in prophecy a lion, precisely before he is called *a lamb*. So when we think of him as a lamb, we should also regard him as the lion. He is a little lamb, with respect to the elders, the aged patriarchs, as Jesus died at a tender thirty three— see 12:5. The image of a lamb is found only with John's gospel, John 1:29, 36, John 21:15. In 19:36 the OLD TESTAMENT Paschal lamb (Ex. 12:46) is transferred to Christ. Christ appears here as a slain lamb, who had conquered to open the book through his sufferings as the God-man by which he made reconciliation. The lamb represents Christ's innocence and righteousness (1 Pet. 1:19,) quiet patience and meekness in suffering. Comp. the FUNDAMENTAL PASSAGE Isa. 53:7, Acts 8:32. The prophet sees the dead lamb now living, standing with the marks of slaughter, comp. 1:7. Because the lamb had been slain, it was worthy to open the book (Phil. 2:8-9.) After his resurrection Jesus still had the crucifixion wounds. It is a mark of renown for a warrior to have wounds and scars, for his followers to follow in his steps.

The *seven spirits of God* are the eyes of the lamb. As the lion precedes the lamb, so here again allusion is made to the entire fullness of divine power and strength of Christ for the destruction of his enemies and deliverance of his people. The *horns* symbolize victorious power, comp. Ps. 148:14. The *seven horns* shows that this strength was combined in him with the greatest fullness. The *seven eyes* are not wisdom or omniscience, because in 4:6 they symbolize rather the powers of God put forth in creation. That the lamb has the seven Spirits of God (comp. 1:4, 3:1)–the Spirit of the Father is also the Spirit of the Son; all divine powers stand in him; with all divine omnipotence, showing the divine glory of our Redeemer. The naming of *the seven Spirits of God* does not refer to the nature of the Spirit, as there is but one Spirit (Eph. 4:4) so the seven points to gifts and operations. Here all power in heaven and on earth is given to Christ. As he also said: *all that the Father hath is mine;* so the seven Spirits of God, namely, of our Heavenly Father, are also the eyes of the Lamb. The seven Spirits are sent over all the earth. This rests on Zech. 4:10, where the spirit of God is there, not in the oneness of his being, but the multifariousness of his operations. This guards against despair. Should the whole earth rise against the church, Christ, her head, has the seven Spirits of God, that are sent over the whole earth, and whose secret, yet irresistible influence, nothing on the earth can resist, however it may exalt itself.

7. And he came and took the book out of the right hand of him that sat on the throne.

7 The future could never be concealed from him, who has the seven Spirits of God. The Word, who in the beginning was with God, has part in everything that is God's. The lamb takes the book, opens it and imparts its contents to John, and to the church. But all these hang on Christ's atonement, as the foundation of every gift for the church. The Spirit, who imparts to the church insight into the future, was first poured down after Christ's ascension. In John 7:39, it is said that believers will receive the Spirit, who would be given after Jesus was glorified. In John 16:7,13, he goes away that the Spirit will come, who will lead into all truth, and he will show things to come. Only if any one is truly in Christ, he has a clear look into the future. And so John, who represented the fainting church of his time, being for the *moment* not in Christ, was oppressed by the heavy burden of sufferings and persecutions, that he wept as if no one were able to open the book.

THE CELEBRATION OF THE LAMB

> 8. And when he took the book, the four beasts and the four and twenty elders fell down before the Lamb; having every one harps and golden vials full of incense, which are the prayers of saints.

The order was first the taking of the book, then the solemn ascription of praise, and finally the opening of the seals.

The words: *and having every one, etc.* refer to the elders only, not to the Cherubim; the harps, are found in the hands of the church (comp. 14:2, 3, 15:2;) the *golden vials full of incense,* which are the prayers of saints, are in the hands of the *heavenly* representatives of the church. The Cherubim's song of praise is only to God as the almighty Creator, 4:8. The words in ver. 9, *Thou hast redeemed us, etc,* are not suitable for the beasts. The cherubim never in the proper sense *bear* the throne, not even in Ezekiel: how could they in that case fly with it? That the throne moves above them so as to admit of its being said in a certain way to be borne by them, only images the truth that the Lord is the absolute ruler of the earthly creation.

CHAPTER 5   THE REVELATION

<small>8. And when he took the book, the four beasts and the four and twenty elders fell down before the Lamb; having every one harps and golden vials full of incense, which are the prayers of saints.</small>

The elders came forth as the speakers of the chorus, which was formed of them and the four beasts. Both are connected together by an internal bond. The elders represent the church, redeemed from the earth, *out of every kindred, and tongue, and people, and nation.* They are the bloom of the earthly creatures represented by the Cherubim, specially of the human race.

The elders have each harps and golden vials full of frankincense, the prayers of saints. The vials with the harps float softly on the hands. The harps accompany the new songs, the prayers proceed on this. Even now the church has in the one hand a harp, and in the other a vial. Without vials no harps. Without prayer no occasion for thanks. The harps are first, as the subject is mainly adoration and praise, because the new song, mentioned in ver. 9, must be accompanied with the harp. Smoking sweet smelling *frankincense* symbolizes believing prayer (comp. Ps. 141:2, Eze. 8:11, Rev. 8:3; Luke 1:10.) The words: which are *the prayers of saints* refer only to the vials, not the incense. But the vials are brought into notice in connection with their use. *Prayer* is here supplicatory prayer. The saints pray according to the historical starting-point of the book and the PARALLEL-PASSAGE, 8:3-4, for the support of the church in the midst of persecution, its completion, and the execution of judgment upon the enemies; comp. 6:10. By the *saints* are primarily the saints on earth, comp. 13:7,10, but also the saints in glory—comp. 11:18, 18:20, who entreat God to accomplish the redemption and perfection of his church below. Now, prayer rises as a precious incense. The elders as representatives of the church are not mediators, they only present their prayers before Christ. The Lamb, is himself worshipped by the elders as the only Mediator between God and man. They fall down with the Cherubim before the Lamb, extol him by their songs on their harps, direct to him their prayers for redemption: all a proof of the true and essential Godhead of him, *to whom has been given a name above every name, that at the name of Jesus every knee might bow, of those who are in heaven and on earth and under the earth.*

THE LAMB'S PRAISE BY
THE BEASTS, ELDERS AND ANGELS

<small>9. And they sing a new song, saying: Thou art worthy to take the book, and to open its seals; for thou wast slain, and hast redeemed us to God by thy blood out of every kindred, and tongue, and people, and nation. 10. And hast made us kings and priests to our God, and they shall reign on the earth. 11. And I saw, and heard a voice of many angels round about the throne, and about the beasts and the elders, and their number was ten thousand of ten thousands and thousands of thousands, 12. And they speak with a loud voice: The Lamb that was slain is worthy to receive the power, and riches, and wisdom, and strength, and honour, and glory, and blessing.</small>

The elders sing a *new song* (Isa. 42:9-10, 43:18-19; Ps. 33:3, 40:3, 96:1, 98:1, Rev. 14:3.) New work, new song. The subject of the new song is the opening of the book, the new act of grace, given the church to revive hope and confidence, when her way was hedged in, because no one could open the book and break its seals. The *they* in the next verse shows that the elders appear as representatives of the church; and also 1:6. The reading *them,* for *us,* corresponds to the us, and the *we shall reign,* in the following verse. The *kindreds, tongues, and peoples,* point to the tables in Gen. 10. This marks the ecumenical character of the work and church of Christ. In the same direction points also the number *four* in Gen. 10—comp. ver. 5, 20, 31-32, being the signature of the *earth*. The *kindreds* are not the tribes of Israel, evidence Gen. 10:5,18,12:3 in the Septuagint. The tone of the Revelation is one so thoroughly ecumenical, a respect to the Jews would be unsuitable.

10 They do not say: *Thou hast made us thereto, and we shall reign*, although they themselves must be understood in what is said. Thou hast made them, namely the redeemed, a kingdom and priests by virtue of this very redemption. The reading: *kings*, not a *kingdom*, is best: they confess that they hold their crowns only in fief; they wonder that Christ has conferred such honour on such persons, with the same humility that David praises the grace of God, in Ps. 8, in granting royal dignity to his poor creature, man. But if the elders, as representatives of the church, in 4:4, bear crowns on their heads, Christians might here also be called kings. We may compare also the diversity in the two readings at 1:6. We must rather explain: *kings even now*, but kings still more gloriously in the future, when the meek shall inherit the earth. The kingdom of the saints has its stages, as that of the Lord, comp. 11:17.

The *and they shall reign* follows the designation *priests*, showing that the priestly and the royal dignity are conjoined together; he who is priest is also king spiritually. In John's time, the words *they shall reign*, must have appeared incredible; but the saints anticipated with their hope that great revolution of things which came under Constantine. The FUNDAMENTAL PASSAGE is in Dan. 7:27, where the power over the kingdoms is given to the saints. We can either explain: they shall reign *over* the earth, by comparing 2:26, Matt. 2:22; or *on* the earth. Even if we follow the latter, according to ver. 13, we need not exclude 20:6, where the saints reign in heaven with Christ a thousand years. Its being on the earth does not necessarily require the seat of the kingdom to be on the earth; this only is implied, that the earth is the sphere of their government, their domain. But 22:5 points to the final consummation.

11 The holy beasts are like a part of the throne itself, although they are living. The elders, however, are nearer the throne than the angels, *because the matter in hand concerns the church on earth*. The angels, because they are spirits, so far agree more with the nature of God than ours. But because the Son of God has become man, men also have an honour which the angels have not. That the angels encompass, not only God but also the elders is because they are God's servants for the good of the kingdom of his anointed upon earth (comp. Ps. 34:7; John 1:51; Heb. 1:14.) The ORIGINAL PASSAGE is Dan. 7:10, where the thousands stand after the ten thousands, showing that in enormous multitudes distinctions vanish. After the myriads stand also the thousands in Ps. 68:17-18, where in like manner reference is made to the angelic hosts as agents in the administration of God's kingdom on earth.

12 We must supply: *and so to open the book*. For, it is in regard to the opening of the book, that the praise of Christ is here celebrated.

In ver. 9 it is said: *Thou art worthy*, and now: *The Lamb is worthy*. And so again in ver. 13. The songs more immediately belong to the Lamb. Here, the mode of representation is more an objective one, there the direct address carries more of feeling. The encomiums mentioned are seven, corresponding to the same number of God in 7:12, and the ten number of encomiums in regard to God in 1 Chron. 29:11-12. These seven encomiums are as one word,

CHAPTER 5 THE REVELATION

<small>12. And they speak with a loud voice: The Lamb that was slain is worthy to receive the power, and riches, and wisdom, and strength, and honour, and glory, and blessing.</small>

standing together under a single article.

The Lamb is worthy to *take* or *receive* the power, etc., they ascribe to him, in the acknowledgment and celebration of it—comp. on 4:9. Mention is made also in Eph. 3:8 of *the unsearchable riches of Christ*. On account of these riches he possesses glorious gifts, which are discoursed of in ver. 9-10, and can impart them to our poverty (comp. John 1:16-17.) The *blessing* denotes objectively manifold blessings, as in Rom. 15:29, where the blessing of the gospel is spoken of. But that it is used here as an encomium, appears from the corresponding *thanks* in 4:9, and the connection in which it stands with the thanksgiving in 7:12. The word is intentionally placed here at the end, and in ver. 13 at the commencement of the whole enumeration. It points to this, in what sense the power, etc., are taken, in the acknowledgment.

THE FATHER AND THE SON ARE GLORIFIED BY ALL CREATURES

13. And every creature, that is in heaven, and on the earth, and under the earth, and in the sea, and what is in them, heard I all saying: To him that sits upon the throne, and to the Lamb, be blessing, and honour, and glory, and power for ever and ever, 14. And the four beasts said, Amen. And the four and twenty elders fell down and worshipped.

In ch. 4 there were two songs in honour of Jehovah, in ch. 5 two also in honour of the Lamb; and this concluding song of all creatures has respect to both together, therefore combines both adorations into one, and accordingly rounds off the whole scene. The praise itself is of four parts, so that it possesses a doxological roundness of parts, and just the four, indeed, of the universe that here speaks. The ORIGINAL PASSAGE is Ps. 148, where everything in heaven and earth that reflects God's glory, is summoned to praise him. It begins in heaven with the angels, and through the stars passes to the clouds. The lifeless there praise God by their simple being, as also in Ps. 103:21, 19:1. So the praise of the Lamb can be ascribed to all the different parts and orders of creation, as he participated in the creation of the world (John 1:3,10, comp. John 17:5, 1 John 1:1, Heb. 1:2-3, Col. 1:15-17.) In this book itself Christ appears as *the first and the last*, 1:17, *the beginning of the creation of God*, 3:14.

Here there is no more mention of the opening of the book, but the whole scene runs out into the general praise of God and the Lamb. The addition: *and is in them*, points to this, that we are not to think merely of the earth in its mountains and valleys, but also in its smaller things, which have their abode in it. The *all*, not everything, is used on account of the personification. The *blessing*, which ends ver. 12, forms the beginning here.

14 This *Amen* was said by them to all that was contained in the adoration of the whole creation. They took it up, affirmed it to be good, expressed their satisfaction with it, and so it went back again from the outermost circle to the throne. Within the circle the four holy beasts and the elders had begun the celebration of praise, from them it went forth, came to the circle which was formed by the multitude of angels, and then to all creation. And now when the whole has ceased, the four holy beasts say, Amen; that is, Let it be so, it should and it shall be so to all eternity. The saying of Amen and worshipping is the inferior position. It was customary in the temple and syna-

gogue for the whole assembly to say *Amen* to the prayers and doxologies read by the priests, or the minister of the synagogue. This custom passed over to the church, and remained there for a long time; comp. 1 Cor. 14:16, and the second Apology of Justin Martyr, where it is said, *And the president, according to his ability, pours out prayers and thanksgivings, and the people respond, saying Amen.* This humble position the four beasts and the elders could not occupy generally and from the first, but only after the chief business, in which they played the first part, had been already finished. When those had come forth, who stood in the most general relation to God and the Lamb, and performed also their part, then the four beasts and the elders took up the subordinate position of respondents. The concluding theme of praise returns back to the fundamental fact, the creation, upon which every other rests, and with the celebration of which a beginning was made in ch. 4. Here too those, who in the adoration of ver. 8-12 had to remain silent, could take a part. The response of the four beasts to their song of praise is first mentioned, because they are the representatives of an important part of creation, the living creatures upon earth. In ver. 8 they had stood along with the elders, because the living earthly creation represented by them is the natural basis of the church; here they respond to the acclaim of the whole creation.

The addition: *him who lives for ever and ever,* is feebly supported by the codices, and has been derived from 4:9-10, without attending to the essential difference between this passage and that. There the praise is ascribed to the Father alone, here it is ascribed to him that sits on the throne and *the Lamb;* so that such an addition would be unsuitable.

After the first five chapters of the book, Bengel felt that not much had come by way of the historizing approach of interpreting the Revelation, which he and others adopted, in disclosing much of human history, although it was the substance and design of the book to show what was to come to pass, but now with the following chapters such things have come. He regarded, however, that the vast majority of Christians, not being learned, could not enjoy his exposition. But such a book as this is not to be intended for the narrow circle of the learned, which should have led him to subject that mode of interpretation to a severe ordeal, for what renders a book unintelligible to the unlettered Christian, also renders it unsatisfying to the learned. Even the resources of a Bengel have not succeeded in preventing many parts of his exposition from being no farther edifying, than as an antiquated compend of universal history.

REVELATION 6:1–8:1
The opening of the seals, manifestation of the judgments, with an intermediate episode–
REVELATION 7

THE FIRST SEAL–CHRIST ON THE WHITE HORSE

6:1 And I saw that the Lamb opened one of the seven seals. And I heard one of the four beasts say as with a voice of thunder: Come and see. 2. And I saw, and behold a white horse, and he that sat on him had a bow, and a crown was given him, and he drew out conquering, and that he might conquer.

The four first seals resemble and connect to each other. The beasts say *Come*, and a horse was given a colour and given to its rider. In the three last seals the beasts and horses are not mentioned. The beasts are announced because they represent all living beings on the earth, amid which the judgments were to be inflicted.

2 The first seal comes with a voice of thunder announcing the God-man conqueror, carrying everything before him. The first appearance, as it introduces a higher dignity, says, *Come and see* to John while the next seals have only, *Come.* This rests on Ps. 66:5, *come and see the deeds of God,* and in John 1:39 the *come and see* being the second word heard from Jesus by John and Andrew. The rider on the *white horse* is Christ, the crown is the badge of royal dignity, and points to Christ who in ch. 19, *has a name written . . . King of kings and Lord of lords.* The *end* of Christ's war and victory there corresponds with the *beginning* here. Christ appears at the head, the following figures are means for accomplishing his victory. The *white* is the colour of Christ's lucid splendour. The other colours foreshadow what the other riders do. The *crown* is *given* to the kingly rider, for his warlike victorious march.

The court of judgment has opened this group, the book being God's judgment over the world for the deliverance of his people. It is from this that the white rider brings terror to a world hostile to Christ, and in his train follows the three scourges of the wrath of God, as presented to David, in 2 Sam. 24:13, *war, famine, and pestilence.* Seeing its king thus, the church is consoled in its tribulation.

THE SECOND SEAL–BLOODY DISCORD

3. And when he opened the second seal, I heard the second beast say: Come, 4. And there went forth another horse, which was red, and it was given to him that sat thereon to take peace from the earth, and that they should kill one another; and there was given him a great sword.

The *red horse* is bloody discord, the colour that of the blood. It is a harbinger of Christ's victory and breaks the confidence of the world.

THE THIRD SEAL–MOURNING AND SCARCITY

> 5. And when he opened the third seal, I heard the third beast say: Come. And I saw, and behold a black horse; and he that sat thereon had a pair of balances in his hand. 6. And I heard a voice in the midst of the four beasts say: A measure of wheat for a denarius, and three measures of barley for a denarius; and do not hurt the oil and the wine.

The *black* indicates mourning. A *voice* comes from the midst of the beasts as it is concerned with them as they represent all the Living.

6 A *measure* is the soldier's daily allowance, a *denarius* a day's wages, *barley* is for the poor, being three times cheaper; corn, *oil* and *wine* are the three essentials of life. It is a time better for oil and wine than for barley and wheat, which indicates a moderate scarcity, not yet hunger–when it is weighed, it is a sign there is not too much. All seasons, crops and events are subject to Christ, the course and issue of things, the operations of war and peace and the course of nature are to do with the Divine judgments.

THE FOURTH SEAL–DEATH

> 7. And when the fourth seal was opened, I heard the voice of the fourth beast say, Come, 8. And I saw, and behold a pale horse, and he that sat on him, his name is death, and hell followed after him. And power was given him to kill the fourth part on the earth, with the sword, and hunger, and with death, and by the beasts of the earth.

The *pale horse*, a pale green, is death, *hell* follows as death's hearse. Here are four instruments of death, the *death* being the pestilence and other desolations. It is limited to a *fourth part*, fearful judgments are still to come. These are to chastise and break the world's pride, restrain its persecuting zeal and convert what is to be converted, to lay at the feet of Christ the Conqueror.

THE FIFTH SEAL–CATASTROPHES TO THE FINAL JUDGMENT

> 9. And when the fifth seal was opened, I saw under the altar the souls of those who were slain for the word of God and for the testimony which they had. 10. And they cried with a loud voice and said: How long, Lord, thou holy and true, dost thou not judge and avenge our blood on those who dwell on the earth! 11. And there was given to every one of them a white garment, and it was said to them that they should rest yet for a time, until their fellow servants and their brethren, who should also be killed as they were, should fulfil.

As the seals are laid open they disclose Christ as a conqueror. These four seals are preliminary judgments, not signs of the second coming in general. Here now a general judgment begins to shake the ungodly world power, preparing the way for the sixth and seventh seals. The prayer of this seal has a definitive relation to the sixth, as the final overthrow was not yet. What here *begins* is accomplished afterwards under the seventh seal, after the premonitory signs have under the sixth assumed an extensively threatening character. The substance of the fifth seal is such catastrophes as bring to view the final

9. ... I saw under the altar the souls of those who were slain for the word of God and for the testimony which they had.

judgment, connected with the glorification of the church. The souls are not souls in the intermediate state, but murdered souls, in their blood, as much as the *blood* stands in verse 10. The *altar* here is in the heavenly sanctuary, the altar of burnt offering (14:18, 16:7,) not incense (8:3-4, 9:13.)

10. And they cried with a loud voice and said: How long, Lord, thou holy and true, dost thou not judge and avenge our blood on those who dwell on the earth!

10 Here the seer has primarily in view the Roman world, which killed his fellow martyrs. The *how long* called for great shakings of the Roman empire, see Ps. 35:17, Ps. 94:3. But with the immediate fulfilment, the prophecy comes to life again, when a new anti-christian power, indicated in 20:7, follows the Roman, so providing consolation for the church that shall then groan under persecutions. Here the subject is not the souls, but the slain. The FUNDAMENTAL PASSAGE is Ps. 79:10, which points back to Deut. 32:43. God, as Christ said, does avenge his people, see Matt. 7:1-2, 23:35-36, and Luke 18:7-8, which shows revenge is agreeable to God's nature, and the wish for it acceptable, if from a God glorifying motive.

11. And there was given to every one of them a white garment, and it was said to them that they should rest yet for a time, until their fellow servants and their brethren, who should also be killed as they were, should fulfil.

11 The suppliant martyrs receive *a white garment* in answer to their prayer, as this could not at present receive a complete fulfilment, see on 6:2, 4:4 on the white as the colour of lucid splendour. The white garment is the clothing of the blessed generally, they go from this life immediately into the life of glory. They must be satisfied with the heavenly glory till when the kingdom of glory would be set up on the earth. The *resting* (comp. Mark 6:31, 14:41, Luke 12:19, Matt. 11:29,) is not simple resting and ceasing, but a resting and refreshing of themselves from the sufferings and troubles of this life, comp. 14:13. As there the resting corresponds to the blessed, so does it here to the white garments. The blessedness and glory before the resurrection consist especially in the resting–as also in ch. 7, in the representation of the state of the blessed before the resurrection the negative element is the predominating one: *they shall hunger no more, nor thirst any more, neither shall the sun light on them, nor any heat, and God will wipe away all tears from their eyes.* Resting from the troubles and annoyances of the earthly pilgrimage–this is a blessed earnest that God will certainly give to his people a rest in most intimate fellowship with Christ; for otherwise dying could be no gain to them, Phil. 1:21. In the expression *till they should complete or fulfil* we must supply their course or their work, see Paul, Acts 20:22-24, 2 Tim. 4:6-8, Rom. 15:19, Luke 9:31, Acts 13:35, 12:25, 14:26. Because these are *their fellow servants,* God must not have a partial respect to them, they must be satisfied with the white clothing, and the rest after their labour, until opportunity has also been given those to deserve the crown of righteousness, who should fight the good fight and love not their lives unto death, during the further persecutions that should be carried on by the beast under the Roman dominion, under the ten kings, and lastly under the assaults of Gog and Magog. One must be very much captivated by Jewish representations, if by the fellow servants one understands the future martyrs from the heathen, and by the brethren those that should come from the house of Israel. The Apocalypse knows nothing of such a distinction.

The groups of the seven seals and the seven trumpets bear a general and comprehensive character, nothing refers specially or exclusively to the Roman empire. The special references to this belong to the later groups. The judgment, which through its frightfulness seemed to bring the end into view, was a presage, that the final judgment would come when the world, through its continued persecution of the church, had filled up the measure of their sins.

THE SIXTH SEAL—SUMMARY

The sixth seal follows now in verses 12-17. First, in ver. 12-14, the plague is described which alights upon the ungodly world, as completed in the number *seven*, divided by the four and three; the earthquake, the sun becoming black, the bloody moon, the falling stars of heaven—the disappearing heavens, the mountains and islands moved out of their places. Then in vers. 15-17 the indescribable anguish by which they were seized, which these facts produced upon those who were affected by them.

The subject here is not the final judgment. The things which in verses 12-14 appear to carry one over the boundaries of the present world, are figurative in representation, which is evident from verses 15-17 where we are still in the existing state of things. Only by the figurative style does it become clear why the heavens, mountains, and islands are brought together. We are still at the sixth seal, the seventh follows where the final judgment must first enter. For, according to the starting-point of this group, and the whole contents of the book, the seals cannot reach farther than the judgment. The kings of the earth, etc. are in great trouble and despair; but the deadly blow has not struck at the close. Here there is no resurrection of the dead and the tribunal of Christ. That this judgment is a preparatory one, appears from the ORIGINAL PASSAGES of the OLD TESTAMENT, and likewise Christ's word in Matt. 24:29, the text on which the Seer comments. Men still live after the catastrophe; and the manifestation of Christ, corresponding here to the seventh seal, only appears afterwards. Those who, not perceiving that the Revelation falls into a series of independent groups, think that the seventh seal comprehends the whole of the rest of the book. So lengthened a course of things could not have followed the sixth seal if this were taken in its natural import. If we do not stand here exactly at the final end, we yet stand at the *beginning* of the end. The *great day of his wrath* is immediately before the door; and ch. 7 can only come as an episode between 6:17 and 8:1, where the dawn of that day is announced. The two verses are very closely connected together, and in ch. 7 we have only a repetition of what belongs to an earlier period. Historically this section is realized in the impending terrible convulsion of the Roman world-power, whose persecution occasioned this book, and whose approaching overthrow was comforting to the church. This also appears in 16:18, under the symbol of a mighty earthquake. Here in its general features, is more fully detailed in the following groups. But the prophecy does not come to an end with this first realization. It continually revives anew, whenever a new persecuting world-power steps into the place of the Roman, as another of this kind, *Gog and Magog*, are named in this very book. The ORIGINAL PASSAGE also, Matt. 24:29, has had more than one fulfilment—the first a provisional one, which John already saw in the overthrow of Jerusalem, a more general one in the breaking up of the Roman state; the most extensive one is still future, and may already be descried in its beginnings.

THE SIXTH SEAL–THE PLAGUE ON THE UNGODLY WORLD

12. And I saw when he opened the sixth seal, and there was a great earthquake, and the sun was black as sackcloth of hair, and the whole moon was like blood. 13. And the stars of heaven fall to the earth, as the fig tree casts its unripe fruit, when shaken by a strong wind. 14. And the heaven departed as a scroll when it is rolled together, and every mountain and island were moved out of their places.

The *earthquake* is a symbol of the destroying omnipotence of God, every earthquake and storm are as prophecies in act concerning God's judgments. The shining of the heavenly lights are a symbol of the grace of God, their extinguishment a prelude to the divine judgments. The *stars of heaven* are a symbol of the greatness and splendour of worldly rulers, the heaven is the princes' heaven, the order of kings and nobles, the stars are individual princes and nobles. The *strong wind* is the storm of God's judgments. The *mountains and islands* are the kingdoms of the earth. The main point here is the state of mind indicated, the consciousness of guilt with thoughts of an avenging God.

THE INDESCRIBABLE ANGUISH BY WHICH THEY WERE SEIZED

15. And the kings of the earth, and the great men, and the captains, and the rich and the strong, and every bondman and every freeman hid themselves in the caves and in the rocks of the mountains. 16. And say to the mountains and to the rocks. Fall on us, and hide us from the face of him, who sits on the throne, and from the wrath of the Lamb. 17. For the great day of his wrath is come, and who is able to stand?

Here we have seven classes divided by the three and the four, three of the governing party, then the possessors of dignity in civil and military life. The *kings* are kings who breathe hostility to God and Christ, the *great men* are all that is brilliant, great and mighty, those who speak in matters of state policy, who often rule over kings, the *strong* are those who are often self-willed and insolent, full of self-confidence, who ask nothing of the Almighty. Here the proud enemies of God, even those normally undismayed in fields of slaughter can be seized with fear and trembling, and creep into vaults and such like places. The patience and meekness of Christ encouraged them to be against him, instead of being drawn to repentance, but now the *Lamb* is the Lion. That the day is said to have *come*, meaning it is already as good as present, yet still no infliction of judgment, not come yet, as we are at the sixth seal, not yet the seventh. Here OLD TESTAMENT prophecies are carried over into the NEW TESTAMENT, here showing we cannot confine the NEW TESTAMENT prophecies to their more immediate object.

REVELATION 7

An intermediate episode: a people preserved amidst judgments, how to attain the Kingdom

CHAPTER SUMMARY

We have *an episode* before us in this chapter. The judgments that threaten the world, were developed in a lengthened series under the first six seals. It might seem to the faithful also living in the world, as if they could hardly escape. These painful cares are here met by *a double consolation: first*, that God protects them while war and terrors of every kind overspread the world, 7:1-8; and *then*, a view is opened into that celestial glory, which awaits the chosen after the short tribulation of the present time, vers. 9-17.

First, in regard to the portion, vers. 1-8, verse 1 shows us precisely where the place of this scene is. The winds have still not moved, the judgments on the world are yet to take effect. But these begin with the very first seal, and not merely with the sixth. So it is here what is to take place before the accomplishment of that which is announced in the opening of the sixth seal.

Those who think that the faithful are here secure against the tribulation, spoken of in what follows, or who refer the security only to the judgment of the sixth seal, have—apart from the consideration that we cannot go out of the group of the seven seals, which stops at 8:1—this against them, that judgments have not already preceded; there is so far only guilt in the world, not punishment.

The *four* number of the angels and the winds points to a variety and fullness in the divine judgments, such as are found to exist only when we take into account the sixth seal.

The regressive character of this portion, has proved a stumbling-block to many expositors. The earth here appears still unhurt. The world's destruction and the church's preservation are co-ordinate to each other; in the general dissolution taking place in the world's destruction is also represented the foresight to be exercised in the church's preservation.

To a church fainting under the persecutions of the world the Seer had announced the judgments, through which God would avenge his servants on the world, and break its rebelliousness and pride. But out of this consolation a new fear arises. The church is still in the world, and must, it seems, be involved in those judgments. The fifth seal would awaken this fear. If the proud tree must fall, under whose shelter men dwell, there appears no hope of safety for the elect.

To meet this new temptation a new consolation is brought in. God will protect his own children even during these frightful plagues, as he delivered Lot, as he slew Egypt and spared Goshen; as he promised Zerubbabel amid the shakings of the world to make him as a seal-ring; as in Zech. 9:8, after a representation of the judgments looming on the countries around Judah, and

Persia. Christ had guaranteed safety to his disciples under the persecutions they were to experience, and in the midst of the judgments by which the world was to be visited, Matt. 24:22.

GOD PROTECTS THE FAITHFUL WHILE WAR TERRORIZES THE WORLD

> 7:1. And after these things I saw four angels standing on the four corners of the earth, holding the four winds of the earth, that the wind should not blow on the earth, nor on the sea nor on any tree, 2. And I saw another angel ascend from the rising of the sun, who had the seal of the living God, and cried with a loud voice to the four angels, to whom it was given to hurt the earth and the sea, saying, 3. Hurt not the earth, nor the sea, nor the trees, till we have sealed the servants of our God in their foreheads, 4. And I heard the number of those who were sealed, an hundred and forty and four thousand, that were sealed out of all the tribes of the children of Israel, 5. Of the tribe of Judah were sealed twelve thousand; of the tribe of Reuben were sealed twelve thousand; of the tribe of Gad were sealed twelve thousand. 6. Of the tribe of Asher were sealed twelve thousand; of the tribe of Naphthali were sealed twelve thousand; of the tribe of Manasseh were sealed twelve thousand, 7. Of the tribe of Simeon were sealed twelve thousand; of the tribe of Levi were sealed twelve thousand; of the tribe of Issachar were sealed twelve thousand, 8. Of the tribe of Zebulon were sealed twelve thousand; of the tribe of Joseph were sealed twelve thousand; of the tribe of Benjamin were sealed twelve thousand.

1 The *angels* let the wind go, it is given them to hurt the earth and the sea. The preservation of the righteous and the destruction of the wicked both belong to the good angels. The divine judgments bring storms of suffering and temptation, for destroying, scattering is the consequence. They break in from all sides. The *sea* is the sea of nations. The *trees* are kings, magnates, the common symbol of the great, the angels hold the winds, the hurting of the trees brings injury to those under their branches, however, Christians are preserved from such destruction.

2 The *angel* is Christ sent by the Father as Comforter of his afflicted church, like the Old Testament logos he constantly appears as the Angel of the Lord, the heavenly mediator. As the rising of the sun marks the heavenly regions, so Christ, who possesses the glory of God, is the spiritual sun, the true light which enlightens every man. In Malachi 4:2 the sun is righteousness itself, or salvation as a matter-of-fact justification and manifestation of righteousness. But He through whom the righteousness was to be imparted to God's people, with whose appearance righteousness was to be manifested like the sun, is according to 3:1, the Angel of the Lord, the heavenly mediator of the covenant. He has *the seal of the living God*, like Ezekiel's man with an inkhorn, symbolising protection to the godly in the midst of the judgments on the wicked. Some things are sealed to make inaccessible, here it is to confirm individuals as the servants of God, to make them secure from calamities that alight on the children of this world. The seal is the seal of the living God, as life giving. The *loud voice* proclaims the determined and absolute will, as Jesus cried with a loud voice, *Lazarus come forth*. The four angels took part in the sealing, in that they held the winds till it was completed. As a symbolical act it was completed before the commencement of the plagues, by which the

ungodly world was judged. The simple idea is, that amid all the judgments which befell the world for its sins, God protects his own people. The sealing refers to the entire duration of the Christian church, even to its final completion, to the entire duration of the world, even to its final destruction. Therefore, it has not yet lost its significance. For now it is full of consolation, as the sixth seal is beginning to be realized anew in a manner never seen before.

4 The *I heard* here coincides with *the great multitude which no one could number* of ver. 9. The number is not statistical but purely theological. A *great multitude which no one could number* is appropriately indicated by this number. *Twelve* is the signature of the church—the woman with the crown of twelve stars, twelve gates, foundations, two sources of the church in patriarchs and apostles, making twenty four elders. The number is multiplied, and then by *thousands*, in which we can see the faith of patriarchs and apostles multiplied in their successors. The solidity of a number so perfectly square shows the immutability of the truth of God and of his apostles. The same *an hundred and forty and four thousand*, preserved amid the plagues coming upon the earth, meet us again in 14:1, 3, in their state of heavenly glory; in the same state, in ver. 9, only that the number is not expressly repeated.

The *sealed* are *out of all the tribes of the children of Israel*. That the Christian church is what is meant by Israel and his tribes, as the legitimate continuation of ancient Israel, appears from the omission of Dan, and the equality of the numbers in the small and the great tribes, and in ch. 11 from the effacing there of all tribe-distinctions. Here the children are not in a Jewish sense but an Israelitish-Christian sense. Even in the Old Testament, though descended from Jacob, they are cut off from their people. The prophets announced the inclusion of believing heathen with the exclusion of the false seed. To understand by these simply the Jewish Christians, is the greatest arbitrariness. Here it is the inclusion or the exclusion of the adopted children, who *through faith* have become incorporated. The enumeration of the particular tribes has only an *ideal* import, to embody the thought that the preservation extends alike to all parts of the church. The Saviour himself took the lead in designating his church by the name of Israel, Matt. 19:28, and chose his apostles with a respect to the number of the tribes of Israel. The name arose out of a consideration of the continuity of the church.

5-8 The tribes are united in pairs together. The birth determines the order in the eight last, four closely related brotherly pairs after their mothers. The two leaders, Judah and Reuben, are placed beside each other, then with Simeon and Levi. Precisely as the tribes here, the apostles are arranged in pairs, Matt. 10:2-4, for similar reasons; at the head stand two pairs of brothers, with an express reference to this relationship.

The Danites after possessing the land, introduced into their territory a false worship (Judges 18,) which continued through centuries. Ezekiel, ch. 48, in determining the positions of the tribes, assigned the most remote place on the north to Dan, the farthest from the sanctuary. John excludes Dan *altogether*. In similar fashion the name *Joseph* was substituted for *Ephraim*, and the name of *Judas Iscariot* was dropped out because of his apostasy. Instead of Ephraim stands Joseph, after Manasseh, the other son of Joseph, had been named. In Judges 17 the Ephraimite Micah had set up the false worship, which passed over to the Danites. They opposed the sanctuary in Zion, and the dominion of David's house and line; bringing a deadly division on Israel. So *Joseph* is put a security, that Ephraim should not, like Dan, suffer extinction.

Judah, the fourth of the sons of Leah, stands here at the head, over Reuben, the firstborn, because, *our Lord sprang from Judah;* and Christ is *the lion of the tribe of Judah.* This tribe was distinguished, by the promises from Jacob, Gen. 49:10, and from Nathan, who announced to David the perpetual dominion of his line, and consequently that of Judah, 1 Chron. 17:11-14.

Levi, so distinguished in the blessings of Moses, after Judah, is mixed up with the others without any superiority. The shadow work has passed away, the Levitical ceremonies abolished, all now are priests, showing the precedence of Judah rested on nothing but its relation to Christ. Now *there is neither Jew, nor Greek, nor Gentile.*

The foundation of the arrangement of the tribes stands in the order of the birth of the sons of Jacob. But there is a series of departures from this, which as a whole are ruled by one principle—namely this, that in the kingdom of Christ difference of birth, external privilege avails nothing; the same principle, on which the doctrine of Paul in Eph. 3:6 rests, *That the Gentiles should be fellow-heirs and of the same body, and partakers of his promise in Christ by his Gospel.*

ORDER OF BIRTH:
Of Leah: Reuben,
Simeon, Levi, Judah.
Of Bilhah: Dan, Napthali.
Of Zilpah: Gad, Asher.
Of Leah again: Issachar, Zebulon.
Of Rachel: Joseph, Benjamin.

ORDER OF THE APOCALYPSE:
Of Leah: Judah, Reuben.
Of Zilpah: Gad, Asher.
Of Bilhah and Rachel: Naphthali, Manasseh.
Of Leah again from her earlier sons: Simeon, Levi.
Of Leah the two last-born: Issachar, Zebulon.
Of Rachel: Joseph, Benjamin.

There is found a complete intermingling of the sons of the different women, and in particular of the sons of the maids with those of the proper wives. By this the sons of Rachel, the humanly beloved, are placed on an equality with the sons of Leah, who was hated.

In the PARALLEL PASSAGES in Ezekiel, in the two enumerations also of the sons of Jacob given by him in ch. 48, the whole arrangement is theologically constructed, and pervaded by the same principle. There is an intentional intermingling of the sons of the maid-servants and the wives, and of the latter again among each other, in 48:31-34. All birth-prerogatives are broken through. In 48:1-7 and 23-29 the tribes are divided into two groups, the one of seven, and the other of five, a division of the twelve, which we often meet with in the arrangements of the Psalms. In the middle of the two groups is the sanctuary. The first group is closed by Judah, the second commenced by Benjamin, so that the nearest to the sanctuary are the two tribes, which remained true after the apostasy of Israel—Benjamin certainly but in part.

AN EPISODE: A PEOPLE PRESERVED IN THE MIDST OF JUDGMENTS

INTRODUCTION TO VERSES 9-17

In the midst of the plagues, which are destined to befall the world, the elect were assured of safety in the preceding context. But this can still only preserve them from the worst. That the execution of judgment on the world must bring heavy troubles on the Lord's people, in the first instance in the catastrophe of Judea, which John saw lying behind him, was plainly implied by our Lord in Matt. 24:19-22. And how can it be otherwise, since the guilt of the world is not foreign to them, since they struggle with the sin which reigns in the world, and they also need the sufferings, which fall with a destructive severity on the world, in order to be tried and purified, and withdrawn from an undue love to the world. So then a new consolation is still required for believers, and this is furnished in the section before us. The good reaches its end. Those who were before assured of preservation amid the judgments that are decreed against the world, are here presented before us in that heavenly glory which awaited them. If they have in many respects to suffer here with the world, what boots it? since the white garments, and the palms, and the waters of life, are sure to them.

THE CELESTIAL GLORY
AWAITING THE CHOSEN AFTER TRIBULATION

> 9. After these things I saw, and behold, a great multitude, which no one could number, of every nation, and tribes, and peoples and tongues, standing before the throne and before the Lamb, clothed with white robes and palms in their hands. 10. And they cried with a loud voice and said: The salvation to our God, who sits upon the throne, and to the Lamb! 11. And all the angels stood round about the throne, and about the elders, and the four beasts, and fell down before the throne on their face, and worshipped God. 12. Saying. Amen, the blessing, and the glory, and the wisdom, and the thanksgiving, and the honour, and the power, and the strength, be to our God for ever and ever. Amen! 13. And one of the elders answered and said to me: Who are these clothed with white robes? And whence came they? 14. And I said to him: My Lord, thou knowest it. And he said to me: these are they, who come out of the great tribulation, and have washed their robes and made their robes bright in the blood of the Lamb, 15. Therefore are they before the throne of God, and serve him day and night in his temple, and he who sits upon the throne shall tabernacle before them. 16. They shall not hunger any more nor thirst any more; neither shall the sun light on them, nor any heat, 17. For the Lamb in the midst of the throne shall feed them, and shall lead them into life-fountains of waters, and God shall wipe away all tears from their eyes.

The *multitude that no one could number* is a characteristic description of Israel or the church. It is not simply heathen Christians as opposed to Jewish ones in vers. 1-8.

Some say the *palms* are palms of *victory* like conquerors in the Olympic games. But here celebrates not victory for the redeemed but the surpassing grace of God's salvation. The palms are those of *the feast of tabernacles*. The children of Israel at this festival were to bring green branches of palms, and take other trees, in order to rejoice before the Lord seven days in a feast of joy for the concluded harvest. The fresh green twigs of trees are always an expression of joy, as in where the people expressed through palms their salvation joy,

CHAPTER 7 THE REVELATION

9. After these things I saw, and behold, a great multitude, which no one could number, of every nation, and tribes, and peoples and tongues, standing before the throne and before the Lamb, clothed with white robes and palms in their hands.
10. And they cried with a loud voice and said: The salvation to our God, who sits upon the throne, and to the Lamb!
11. And all the angels stood round about the throne, and about the elders, and the four beasts, and fell down before the throne on their face, and worshipped God.

when the Saviour rode into the earthly Jerusalem, so now do the elect, in the heavenly Zion with Christ—comp. 14:1.

The custom of bearing the palms *in the hand* is from 2 Macc. 10:7, where after the temple had been consecrated, the bearing of the palm branches was an expression of joy for deliverance. The feast was, according to Lev. 23:43, in thanksgiving for the Lord's preservation of Israel in the wilderness, purifying them for the possession of Canaan. The anti-type then is kept by those who, after having escaped the troubles and dangers of their pilgrimage through the wilderness of life, have reached the heavenly Canaan, the place of their rest, with no hunger nor thirst any more.

10 Here we have the words of the thanksgiving of the redeemed. The word signifies deliverance and freedom from all mischief and adversity: but along with this there is also an overflowing of joy and glory. *The salvation* forms the contrast to *the great tribulation*, out of which they have been taken. Allusion is made to the name of Jesus, as when the multitudes exclaim at the entry of Jesus into Jerusalem, *Hosanna to the Son of David;* let his name, Jesus, be verified, let there be salvation to him, and through him, to us. Why they call Christ *the Lamb* is evident from ver. 14, in that His holy atoning blood is the source of their salvation.

11 The glory of God has most singularly manifested itself in the leading of his church through the wilderness of the world to the heavenly Canaan and Zion, so that the angels could not remain unconcerned in the matter. Their voice was heard at the birth of Christ, so now they could not be silent, when the holy work, which had its unpromising commencement in the birth of Christ, has reached its close. If they rejoice over the glory of God, in the conversion of a single sinner, so much also in the final safety and well-being of his whole church.

The worship is addressed to God in Christ (the Lamb, ver. 17, is in *the midst* of the throne.) Christ is not expressly named, as the same doxology had already been uttered of him in 5:12. In connection the two last words there are intentionally made the first here. The same words are repeated here, with *thanksgiving* here instead of *riches* there, as a mark of independence.

12. Saying. Amen, the blessing, and the glory, and the wisdom, and the thanksgiving, and the honour, and the power, and the strength, be to our God for ever and ever. Amen!

12 The first *Amen* expressed an accord to the praise of the redeemed, and so marks the sphere in which the glory of the Lord has unfolded itself. In the encomiums the seven are better divided into the three and four. For, by the first division, the *thanksgiving* appears at the head of the second group, and serves, like the *blessing* in the first, as an explanation of the following epithets—shows, that God must receive the honour etc. in the commendation given of them. On the other hand, in 5:12, the seven is divided by the four and the three: *power and riches, wisdom and strength, honour and glory, blessing.* The reverse order was naturally to have been expected, as the beginning here connects itself with the end there. *Power and riches* then stand together, as *riches and strength* in 6:15, *wisdom and strength*, as *counsel and strength* in Isa. 11:2. The twin pair, *honour and glory*, remain together. Finally, in that case *blessing* stands alone, and the internal is also externally represented.

13. And one of the elders answered and said to me: Who are these clothed with white robes? And whence came they?

13 John had not asked but his whole conduct betrayed that he burned with desire to get an exact account of the attractive appearance of the persons in white clothing. The answer to the silent question is thrown into the form of a verbal question, with the view of calling forth John's request for information, and the confession of his inability. Christ used this way with his disciples

and others to get at their heart, and loose their tongue. The *who* and *whence art thou*, was in ancient times the regular question to friends on their arrival. The questions are afterwards answered in the reverse order, first the *whence*, then the *who*.

14. In the speech of John there is a discreet request for information. John, in a state of holy wonder, addresses the elder as *his lord*, in the presence of the glory of the Lord, which shines upon the blessed, so that the expression of veneration at last returns to the Lord himself. So Lot addressed the angels by the name *Adonai*, which properly belongs only to God; and in Isa. 45:14, the Gentiles who desire salvation fall down before the church because God is only in her. In the NEW TESTAMENT this address always occurs as an expression of veneration and dependence. The Greeks address Philip thus (*Lord, we would see Jesus*), because they transferred the glory of the master to the disciple. The most advanced, who still dwell here in flesh and faith, can only look up to the perfectly righteous.

14. And I said to him: My Lord, thou knowest it. And he said to me: these are they, who come out of the great tribulation, and have washed their robes and made their robes bright in the blood of the Lamb,

By *the great tribulation, the plagues of the world* are to be understood, which bring with them troubles also for the elect. In the ORIGINAL PASSAGE, Matt. 24:21, *For there shall then be great tribulation, etc.* the subject there, too, is the judgments to be brought on the world, which necessarily involve the elect in sufferings along with others. The subject in 3:10, *the hour of temptation*, cannot be persecution, for the temptation appears as a future one, while the persecution raged at that very time. If persecution, there would be mention of fidelity and steadfastness, but only the general marks of believers are given.

The *washing* denotes the obtaining of pardon of sin through the blood of Christ; the *making bright* sanctification which springs out of reconciliation. In the symbolical rites of the law, and in its explanation in Eze. 36:25, the washing and sprinkling with water is an image of the forgiveness of sins. *Filthy garments* (the clothing a symbol of the *state* of a person) were, in the OLD TESTAMENT, borne by sinners, clean ones by the justified.

Here instead of the water *the blood of Christ* is put, to indicate that it is here forgiveness as rooted in the atonement. We have a commentary in 1 John 1:7, 5:6, *This is he who came by water and blood, Jesus Christ, not by water only* (forgiveness without satisfaction), *but by water and blood;* John 19:34, the water and blood from Christ's side.

To the making of the garments *bright* corresponds in the passage of Ezekiel referred to, ver. 26, the *giving of a new heart and a new spirit* (after the purging away of their sins); and in John, the *walking in the light*, 1 John 1:7, *not sinning*, 2:1, 3:6, 9, *keeping one's self*, 5:18, *doing the will of God*, 2:17, *doing what is well-pleasing before him*, 3:22, *keeping his commandments*, 5:3.

The courageous *witness-bearing* springs from the sense of forgiveness as obtained through the blood of the Lamb, as a particular manifestation of the sanctified life denoted by the bright garments. Here the white is the colour of the righteous, which streams forth in the splendour of their virtues.

15. *Therefore*, because they have been prepared for it by the blood of the Lamb. The delineation of the blessedness is completed in a threefold three: they are *before the throne, they serve, they are tented*—they *hunger not*, they *thirst not*, they *suffer no heat*—the Lamb *feeds* them, *leads* them, *wipes* them. The foundation for this lies in the *three* number of the Mosaic blessing on the chosen people, which, with those here, has reached its complete fulfil-

15. Therefore are they before the throne of God, and serve him day and night in his temple, and he who sits upon the throne shall tabernacle before them.

CHAPTER 7   THE REVELATION

15. ...and he who sits upon the throne shall tabernacle before them.

ment. Here it is not the happy condition of the perfectly righteous *on this earth* represented. This section can unfold nothing that lies absolutely beyond the seventh seal.

He will tabernacle upon them is as much as: *he will perform to them the part of a tent.* The tent, therefore, is the Lord himself. The tabernacle consists, in the grace of the Lord abiding with his people and protecting them—in the Shekinah. God was called by Moses the dwelling-place of his people amid the troubles of life. Here also there is an allusion to the feast of tabernacles: in that blessed time there shall be an infinitely glorious tabernacle.

16. They shall not hunger any more nor thirst any more; neither shall the sun light on them, nor any heat, 17. For the Lamb in the midst of the throne shall feed them, and shall lead them into life-fountains of waters, and God shall wipe away all tears from their eyes.

16-17 The FUNDAMENTAL PASSAGE for ver. 16, and the two first members of ver. 17, is Isa. 49:10. There are only two important deviations from the ORIGINAL PASSAGES.

1. Instead of *He that has mercy on them,* we have here, *the Lamb in the midst of the throne.* What is said of Jehovah in the prophet is appropriated to Christ. The *in the midst of the throne,* has respect to Christ as sitting on the right hand of God, as equal in might and glory with the Father; as also his having the seven Spirits of God, receiving divine worship, having applied to him directly what in the OLD TESTAMENT is written of God. It accords also with what in the Gospel of John is written of the Word of God (comp. here 19:13,) who in the beginning was with God and was God, of the oneness of Christ with the Father, of his being in the Father, and of the Father being in him, in 14:10-11. The full Godhead of Christ is suitable here, because only from this point of view could Christ have been substituted for God in the ORIGINAL PASSAGES, and because Christ could no otherwise bestow the highest good on his people than as the possessor of essential Godhead.

2. Instead of simple *watersprings* as in the ORIGINAL PASSAGES, we have here *life-fountains of waters. Spiritual* fountains of water are meant. *Life* with John is life in full vigour undisturbed by anything painful or unpleasant, but blessed life, as God the source of life gives it, raised above all creaturely weakness. *Life* is consequently another term for salvation. That by the introduction of this single word, Isa. 12:3 is combined with the ORIGINAL PASSAGE into one whole, most suitable, as the figure of that passage was at the feast of tabernacles embodied in the symbolical action of pouring out water. An allusion to this here was natural, as the palms and the tabernacles had already preceded (ver. 15.) The salvation or life, which through that rite is the privilege and hope of the people of God, is in the fullest measure secured to them here by him, who as the Lamb is at the same time the true shepherd. They now receive in truth what was only imaged by the literal waters of the wilderness. For, these were a type of the well-springs of salvation, which the Lord opens in all ages for his people in the wilderness of trouble, and most gloriously when the period of their pilgrimage is over.

It is precisely in the gospel of John that the passages occur, in which the blessings of salvation, which the Lord gives even in this life to his people, are denoted by *not hungering, not thirsting, the true bread* and *the living water*—comp. 4:14-15, 6:35, 7:38. In them also respect is had to what the Lord formerly did for his people in the wilderness. This starting-point is distinctly marked in 6:30-31. In regard to the substance, *hunger* and *thirst* indicate the unsatisfied need for salvation, the *sun* the glow of tribulations—comp. 16:8-9.

The conclusion of ver. 17: *and God shall wipe away,* etc., is taken from Isa. 25:8. These words return again, not without reason, in 21:4, with a slight intentional variation. For instead of, *out of* the eyes, it is there *from* the eyes. Such small differences almost constantly occur in the borrowings and repetitions of Scripture. They serve to prevent the appearance of a lifeless adoption. In 21:4 the subject of discourse is the *regeneration*, the kingdom of glory upon earth, to which the words in the ORIGINAL PASSAGES refer, and in which they are to find their only complete and ultimate fulfilment.

THE ENEMIES OF CHRIST ASTONISHED

> 8:1. And when he opened the seventh seal there was silence in heaven for an half hour.

These words are to be connected with the close of ch. 6. As all the seals contain scenes of judgment, so the silence here denotes the dumb astonishment of the raging enemies of Christ and his church. Now, we have actually three prophetic passages, in which *silence* is found in a similar connection as here.

First, the proper FUNDAMENTAL PASSAGE, on which the two others are dependent, Hab. 2:20, *And the Lord is in his holy temple, be silent before him all the earth.* Then Zeph. 1:7, after the representation of a frightful judgment of the Lord upon the earth: *Be silent before the Lord, for near is the day of the Lord.* Finally, Zech. 2:13, *Be silent, all flesh before the Lord, for he is raised up out of his holy habitation.* The announcement of a glorious manifestation of God precedes, by which he was to humble the heathen world, especially proud Babylon, and raise his people out of the dust of abasement. So the meaning is, all flesh, which has raged loud against the Lord and his church, shall be brought to *silence*, like that of Pharaoh when he sank with his host into the Red Sea.

In regard to his coming for judgment, there is a corresponding declaration in Matt. 24:30, *then shall the tribes of the earth howl,* that *howling* of the ungodly world corresponds to the *silence* here. Both imply absolute annihilation; and both alike come into play at intervals through history, but at the end alone reach their perfection. As often as a power manifests itself in opposition to God and Christ and the church, a whole series of preparatory divine judgments begins to be developed (the six first seals,) and then at last descends the fatal blow. The whole process terminates in the dead silence and dreadful howling of the creature that had presumed to revolt against its Creator and Redeemer.

The *heaven* here comes into notice only as the visible theatre. In reality the silence belongs to the earth. The *half hour* is not the time of the actual accomplishment, but the time of the *symbolical* representation. Hence the half hour, as this seal is the one that brings the final decision, is a *long* time. The first seals followed quickly on one another, probably each occupying a single moment. The period occupied in receiving the whole Revelation was probably the space of a day (comp. on 1:10,) as Zechariah received in one night the whole series of visions, which together present a complete image of the future fate of the people of God, 1:7—6:15. The entire cycle, too, of the prophecies in Ezekiel contained in 33—39 belong to a single day, which is described in 33:21-22. From this meaning, it follows that here there can follow no continuation, but only a new beginning. The oppression of the church by

1. And when he opened the seventh seal there was silence in heaven for an half hour.

the world-power is the starting-point and the pole of the whole Revelation. But that power we see here lying shattered on the ground. New scenes may possibly be disclosed, in which other aspects of the great conflict between God and the world shall be made known. Such must be expected; for here everything is of a general character, and we should lay down the book with an unsatisfactory feeling, if we were at the close. In particular, the final catastrophe is very imperfectly described by the thought, which is here rendered prominent—the profound silence of the lately so noisy world. All bears the impress of a prelude of a general plan, which is afterwards to be followed up by the further development—one that shall go more thoroughly into the history of that world power, whose persecutions formed the immediate occasion of the Revelation. But the action cannot possibly be continued farther on the same scene.

GROUP 3

THE SEVEN TRUMPETS WITH EPISODE

How does the church stand in reference to the corrupt world?

REVELATION 8:2–11:19

REVELATION 8:2–11:19

How does the church stand in reference to the corrupt world?

GROUP SUMMARY

The distribution of this group is as follows. Verse 2, *and I saw the seven angels, who stand before God, and to them were given seven trumpets,* supplies the place of a superscription. It presents immediately before our eyes those from whom all action proceeds in the great drama that follows. Next comes, in the vision of the incense-offering angel, a kind of prelude, ver. 3-5. Then begins the work of the seven angels. The plagues of the four first, vers. 6-12, alight upon the *earth,* the *sea,* the *rivers,* the *heavens,* and thus compose together one whole, embracing the entire territory of creation. The three last trumpets are likewise bound up together. After the four first have been brought to a close, they are announced in 8:13 by an eagle, which proclaims a threefold woe on the inhabitants of the earth. The fifth trumpet and the first woe is contained in 9:1-12; the sixth trumpet and the second woe in vers. 13-21, on which follows an episode in 10:1—11:13, so that the concluding formula is only given in 11:14. Then comes at the close of the whole the seventh trumpet and the third woe, in 11:15-19.

The three last trumpets, by being designated as the three last woes, are represented relatively to the four first, as greatly the more important and frightful; and in accordance with this is their more lengthened description. The fifth trumpet, or the first woe, takes up almost twice as much space as is devoted to the whole of the first four together. Only in the third woe, the seventh trumpet, do we find a shorter description than expected; the reason of which shall afterwards be considered.

Again, on the first six trumpets in relation to the seventh—leaving out of view the point of some of them belonging to the woes—there is impressed the character of the half and incomplete. In the first four trumpets the third part of the sphere on which the injury alights is uniformly mentioned. The locusts under the *fifth* trumpet torment, according to 9:5,10, *five* months, the five being the signature of the half and incomplete, in contrast to the last trumpet and the last woe, when the mystery of God is finished, which he has revealed to his servants, the prophets, 10:7. In the sixth trumpet the third part of men is again killed. The Revelation was occasioned by a severe oppression of the Christian church through the heathen world-power; so we expect such a revelation as will bring destruction to this hostile power, but salvation to the church. Then, the introductory vision of the angel with frankincense, in 8:3-5, shows that God will hear the fervent prayers of his afflicted church, and send his judgments against the world. The six first trumpets are preparatory to the seventh, they all lead to the fact, that the kingdom of the world has become the Lord's and his anointed, 11:15. The plagues were designed to punish and extirpate the enemies of God's people, so that the kingdom might be prepared for Christ and his saints. This group stands by itself separate and complete; as evident from a comparison of the prophecy, 8:5, with the fulfilment, 11:19. At the close of the vision we stand at the last end. At the beginning we stand at the first commencement, in 8:1 we see the world-power shattered on the ground. Here, we have another series of catastrophes, which bear the signature of the *half* and *incomplete*, and only at the seventh trumpet are we at the same point when the seventh seal was disclosed. In the sixth seal even, where all was in dreadful convulsion and approaching its end, such catastrophes could not follow, as are indicated here in the first four trumpets. The world-catastrophes represented here could only run *parallel* to those described in the earlier group. But though independent, it bears a near connection between this group and the preceding one. The beginning: *And I saw the seven angels,* connects with the introductory vision of the angel with incense as a sort of bridge with what goes before; the seven angels with the trumpets are formally linked together with the seven angels, and materially associated with them. The theatre here is presupposed as a thing known from the preceding context, 4:1: John still finds himself in heaven. But this group likewise points forward to what is to follow; as appears in a double respect.

First, the final catastrophe is delineated here with greater brevity than the other preliminary ones, being confined to 11:19. This was because the more extended representation of the final catastrophe was reserved for later, as also the brevity is an enigmatical one, pointing to a later commentary. Further, the Revelation was seen in the midst of the *Roman* persecution. As with the earlier prophets, say Isaiah 13, we expect on the general representation of judgments on the world, a special disclosure of the ungodly world-power in particular. But this is as little found here as in the group of the seven seals. All the judgments befall the inhabitants of the earth, under whom the Romans are certainly comprehended, but never solely intended. But this group, like the preceding one, for the most part retains a kind of general character, suitable in an introduction to the closing prophetical book of Scripture, though it could not continue to stand at that.

None of the great prophets of the OLD TESTAMENT remained thus at mere general enunciations. With all of them, indeed, the special rests on the general as its foundation; only it does not stand there. There is, besides, in Revelation a twofold special reference to the contents of the later groups. The voices of the seven thunders in 10:4, which John for a time was not to write, but to seal up, point to a later group, in which it is going to be reported concerning the time of the mystery of God, as he has announced it to his servants the prophets. And the beast which ascends from the abyss, which suddenly meets us in 11:7, is a riddle that finds no solution within this group. These indications pointing forwards to the following groups correspond to the not less intended allusion to the group of the seven seals in 9:4.

As for the relation of this group to the preceding one, the commonest and most frightful scourge through which the vengeance of heaven discharges itself on the apostate earth is *war*. The other plagues, hunger and pestilence, appear only in its train. In the preceding group also war has broken out, but only on a like footing with the other plagues. This second introductory group, however, is entirely devoted to it. To the last trumpet, that of the final victory, all here is only an expansion of the words of our Lord in Matt. 24:7, *Nation shall rise up against nation, and kingdom against kingdom.*

The loud stirring noise of the trumpet is the essential characteristic. It is described as *a cry*, for example in Lev. 25:9, fittingly accompanied with a *loud* cry; comp. Josh. 6:5, Zeph. 1:16, Isa. 58:1, Hos. 8:1. Finally, it appears from the use of trumpets in the sacred music, Ps. 47:5, at the paschal feast in Ps. 81:3, at the consecration of the walls of the city in Ps. 150; bringing in the ark, 1 Chron. 15:24 (comp. 2 Sam. 6:15,) consecrating the temple, 2 Chron. 5:12-13, the solemn restoration of worship, 2 Chron. 29:26-27; finally, in Ezra 3:10, Neh. 12:35. They are always mentioned in connection with other very noisy instruments. In 2 Chron. 30:21 *they praised the Lord with instruments of strength,* bearing a strong loud stirring sound; with trumpets, having respect to 29:26-27. This accords with Num. 10:10. Hence, festivals and trumpets were inseparably connected together. As the festival day was related to other days, so the sound of the trumpet to other sounds.

The sound of the trumpet has no definite peculiarity, or connection with the Sabbath-idea. In the Sabbatical year there was no sounding of trumpets, nor at the Sabbath of weeks. It points to the more excited religious feeling, peculiar to festive occasions generally, particularly of those feasts which marked the commencement of a new period of time. According to Num. 10:9-10 the blowing with trumpets is a *call of the congregation,* and not a remembrance or an announcement on the part of God. Else, the blowing with trumpets would be by the priests, not the people. The trumpets sounding throughout the land in the year of jubilee on the day of atonement merely intimated, through the strong, far-resounding sound of the trumpet, that an important time for the land had come in. The fiftieth year was thereby consecrated, Lev. 25:10, set apart from the number of the rest. The more definite purpose is intimated in the proclamation of liberty throughout the whole land for all its inhabitants, mentioned in that passage. Only in this connection did the loud sound become at the same time a joyful one.

Of the use of the trumpets for what the Lord has to say to the church, it is treated in Num. 10:2-8; where we have the assembling of the congregation and decamping. Of their use in what the church had to say to God, in times of distress or on festival days, is treated in ver. 9-10. In the former case, the sound of the trumpet might announce a joyful subject, a great salvation; like the falling of the walls of Jericho; or to give notice of great tribulation, as in Joel 2:1, where the day of judgment is announced by trumpets. But it can only be in respect to important transactions, such as were of general significance that they are used; whether great catastrophes or important tidings, from the Lord, as the common note of a summoning before the Lord. The trumpets had the loudest, strongest, most powerful tone, and so were used, where the Lord had to say something important to his church, or where the church came before him in a particularly lively and excited state of feeling. The trumpets stand related to the other instruments, as the Lord's servants to the ordinary members of the church, as the feast-day to the other days. In the section before us the more immediate import of the trumpet-sound is determined by the starting-point of the book, which was the oppression of the church by the heathen world-power. Accordingly by the trumpets only great catastrophes can be denoted, through which destruction should be brought to the world, and salvation be first prepared for the church, and then actually brought in. The trumpets here are *exciting* for all—*joyfully* exciting for the church, *frightfully* exciting for the world. Such generally is the signification of the trumpets here. Three special references may still be supposed.

By combining the *seven* number with the trumpets we are reminded of the conquest of Jericho in Josh. 6, where the Israelites march solemnly round the city with the ark and seven priests blowing trumpets, each day once, but on the seventh day, seven times, then the walls fell. What was done at the fortress of Jericho, guarding the entrance into Canaanite territory, symbolized what should be done with the Canaanitish power. Faith saw in the last trumpet-blast at the walls of Jericho, along with these, the whole state of the Canaanites, apparently so strong and invincible, falling to the ground. Jericho then stands as a type of the world-power generally, the overthrow of which ensues on the blowing of the seventh trumpet, in which all the preceding ones culminate.

After seven times seven years it was ordained in the Mosaic law, that the year of jubilee should be proclaimed by trumpets—the year, when the Lord announced himself as *proprietor*—the year, when every one returned to his possession (Lev. 25:13)—the year of freedom and of restoration for all the distressed, who looked for it with anxious longing. This year appears even in the OLD TESTAMENT, in Isa. 61:1-2, as a type of the redemption from the slavery of the world, *the year of the Lord's grace and the day of the vengeance of our God, to comfort all that mourn.* Such consolation breaks in here at the sounding of the seventh trumpet.

Finally, the trumpet stands in a close relation to the excited character of war, and is peculiarly the warlike instrument—comp. Zeph. 1:16; Jer. 4:19, 42:14; Ezek. 7:14. Hence also, among the catastrophes to be inflicted by the Lord, which were denoted in general by the blowing of the trumpets, it was especially suited for announcing the tribulations of war that were impending from the Lord.

REVELATION 8:2-5

The theme & prelude to the second and third groups

A SUPERSCRIPTION

8:2. And I saw the seven angels, who stand before God, and to them were given seven trumpets,

This verse supplies, as it were, the place of a superscription. It presents immediately before our eyes those from whom all action proceeds in the great drama that follows. The vision of the incense offering angel, section 8:3-5, stands by itself as a kind of *prelude*, indicating the point of view out of which this group, as also the preceding one, with which it is united into a pair, ought to be contemplated; and 10:1—11:13, forms an *episode*. In the main part the plague of war is represented under a series of symbols, as that by which God continually during the course of ages chastises anew the heathenish opposition that is made to his kingdom. Among the scourges of God this is the most frightful, so a separate group is devoted to it, although war already occurred in the preceding group in order among the other plagues.

The seven constantly *stand* before God as the elect angels, unlike all others who appear at seasonable times to execute his commands (Job 1:6.) Similar is the seven princes among the servants of the king of Persia, *who saw the king's face and sat the first in the kingdom,* Esther 1:14: comp. Ezra 7:14. It is the same with *beholding the face of the Father in heaven,* Matt. 18:10, and the entering in before the glory of the holy one, which in Tobit 12:15, is affirmed *poetically* of the seven most distinguished angels. What is said in 1 Cor. 15:41 of the varying glories of the heavenly bodies is involved in the distinction of angelic orders. God's creations are no democratic chaos, they everywhere form organisms, in which a gradual rise takes place from the lower to the higher. The position Satan entered into supposes that before his fall he was furnished with powers or prerogatives that ennobled him far above the other angels, with an exalted dignity. The seraphim of Isa. 6 point to a distinction of rank, as they stand before the throne of God, their name, the nobles or *principes*, indicates an exalted place, as do the angel-princes in Dan. 10:13. Gabriel is distinguished as such in Luke 1:19. In the *thrones, dominions, principalities, powers,* in Col 1:16, 2:10, comp. Rom. 8:38, Eph. 1:21, 3:10, 6:12, we see different ranks in the angelic world, although Paul opposes prying into specific distinctions. In 1 Pet. 3:22, beside the general name of angels, *principalities and powers* are mentioned, and in Jude ver. 8 (comp. 2 Pet. 2:10) *dominions and majesties* are spoken of among the angels. The seven number of the trumpets determined the *seven* number of the angels, as no other scripture passage teaches this.

A PRELUDE OF THE INCENSE OFFERING ANGEL

3. And another angel came and stood beside the altar, and had a golden censer; and much incense was given him, that he might give it to the prayers of all saints on the golden altar before the throne. 4. And the smoke of the incense went up to the prayers of the saints from the hand of the angel before God, 5. And the angel took the censer and filled it with fire from the altar, and poured it out upon the earth. And there were voices, and thunderings, and lightnings, and earthquakes.

In the times of the first persecutions the Christians prayed in earnest; as in Jas. 5:16-17. The angel's agency here is a symbolic figure, not substantial, and belongs to the character of the vision, which must give a *visible* shape. In 7:2, 10:1 and 13:1, the angel is Christ, but here he cannot be understood as Christ, as there is no distinguishing predicate, or anything in what he does that sets him above the rank of ordinary angels. If prayer embodied itself in frankincense, there must be a heavenly representative of believers above to present the frankincense. *The altar* here cannot be the altar of burnt offering, only the altar of incense can be meant. Even in Lev. 16:12, the incense-pan was filled with coals from off the incense-altar. A *golden censer* was a sign and instrument of what the angel had to do. Much incense was given to the angel. By the *prayers* are to be understood such as those in Joel 2:17, Ps. 9:19, Ps. 79:11-12, sparing his people from the heathen reproach. According to 5:8 frankincense is a symbolic embodiment of prayer. By *all saints*, it is those in earth and in heaven, as the prayer concerns them both. The angel causes the incense of the prayers of the saints to ascend, but also the fire of God's wrath to come down.

The golden altar is *standing* before the throne. The *veil* is also existing here, as appears from 11:19, 15:5. The whole of the heavenly sanctuary fashioned itself to John after the personal eye-sight of the temple at Jerusalem, as an undivided whole. It is said expressly the altar was before the throne. Therefore, beside the sanctuary, in which was the altar of incense, there must also have been the Most Holy Place.

4-5 The *angel* is as a days-man, Job 33:23. In ver. 3 and 4 he represented the church, and brought its petitions before God. Here he brings God's answer to the requests of the church—so he throws God's fire down upon the earth. According to John 1:51 (comp. Gen. 28:12,) the angels first ascend up from Christ in his humiliation, and his militant church, bringing their petitions before the throne; then descend down and bring the answer and help and the vengeance on the enemies.

The internal connection between the fiery prayer, and the fiery indignation consuming the adversaries, is shadowed forth by the circumstance, that of the same fire of the altar, with which the frankincense was kindled, there was taken and thrown upon the earth. *Fire* is here, as usually in the Apocalypse the symbol of the holy wrath and judgment of God.

The *fire*, the *voices*, etc. have here only a typical, a prophetical character. The fulfilment of the prophecy begins with the first trumpet and closes with the last; comp. 11:19. In 4:5 the voices, lightnings, and thunders are likewise, not the judgment itself, but its symbolical announcement, of which the seven seals are the realization.

REVELATION 8:6–9:21

Symbols of the plague of war, God chastises the heathen opposition made to His Kingdom

THE FIRST FOUR PLAGUES ON THE EARTH, SEA, RIVERS AND HEAVENS

8:6. And the seven angels with the seven trumpets prepared themselves to sound. 7. And the first (angel) sounded. And there was a hail and fire mingled with blood, and they were cast upon the earth. And the third part of the earth was burnt, and the third part of the trees was burnt, and all green grass was burnt. 8. And the second angel sounded. And like a great mountain burning with fire was thrown into the sea. And the third part of the sea became blood. 9. And the third part of the living creatures in the sea died, and the third part of the ships was burnt. 10. And the third angel sounded. And there fell a great star from heaven, which burned like a torch, and fell upon the third part of the rivers, and upon the fountains of waters. 11. And the name of the star is called Wormwood. And the third part of the waters became wormwood. And many men died of the waters, because they had become bitter. 12. And the fourth angel sounded, and the third part of the sun was smitten, and the third part of the moon, and the third part of the stars, so that their third part was darkened, and the day did not appear for the third part of it, and the night in like manner.

The angels, with the seven vials went their ways, 16:1-2, but those with the trumpets stay in preparation, and even when they sound, still stand before God. The prayers of the saints are a necessary pre-existing condition of their preparing themselves. The angels do not inflict the punishment, they merely announce it. Only at the sixth plague is there an active angelic agency, where the four angels loosed, yet the angel with the trumpet does not inflict punishment, but the *four angels* do.

7 John beholds concentrated in a great and fiery hail-storm the desolations of the war, which through the centuries bursts anew against the world at enmity with God. The prototype was the seventh plague upon the enemy of God's people, Pharaoh, in Ex. 9:23-25.

The *fire* is the fire of wrath and war, kindled by the anger of God. The *mingled with blood* shows it as war as desolating and consuming.

This prophecy respects the whole earth, it is not limited to any single war, but it is a species before us personified as an individual; but only a *third part of the earth* is destroyed by it, because it is still not the final judgment. The threefold division of the destroyed corresponds to the threefold division of the instruments of destruction. The following context describes more exactly what on the earth was affected by the burning.

The *trees* denote the high and mighty. The *grass* indicates *the people* (Isa. 40:7.) Trees and grass, in 9:4, designate the high and low, princes and subjects. The *green* refers to the cheerful bloom and prosperity, which continued till the plague (comp. Job 5:25; Ps. 72:16.)

CHAPTERS 8–9   THE REVELATION

8. And the second angel sounded. And like a great mountain burning with fire was thrown into the sea. And the third part of the sea became blood.
9. And the third part of the living creatures in the sea died, and the third part of the ships was burnt.

8–9 The person who *throws* is God. The *like* indicates it is not a natural mountain. *Mountains* are a common symbol of kingdoms (Ps. 76:4, 68:16, 65:6, Zech. 4:7—*mountain being Persia*, 17:9.) The *great mountain burns with fire*, the fire of wrath, the lust of war and conquest. The mountain is cast into *the sea*, symbol of the world and the nations (comp. on 6:14, 13:1, 17:15.) Mountain and sea are connected together (Ps. 46:2-3, comp. Ps. 65:6-7, Matt. 21:21.[2]) Symbolically it means that the apostate kingdom greedy of plunder shall be itself plundered. The invasion of the Roman empire in 250 AD is only one fulfilment in an entire species of divine judgments before us; the fulfilment of this prophecy is still in progress.

The *sea becomes blood* refers to the first Egyptian plague, as a symbolical pre-intimation of the killing of the first-born, as the blood and the dying of the fish being in both places connected together.

Men appear in the scriptures under the image of *living creatures in the sea* (Ps. 104:25, Isaiah 27:1, Hab. 2:14, Ezek. 29:3-4, 47:8-9, Matt. 4:18-19, Luke 5:1-11, John 21:1-14, Matt. 13:47.) In Ezekiel, the waters of life come into the sea. The healing life-giving stream contrasts to the burning death-bringing mountain here, the saving net of Christ contrasts with the destructive net of the Chaldeans, the healing tree Moses put into the water, to the great star which makes the waters bitter. Those who refuse restoring grace are doomed to judgment and destruction. The same person directs the quickening stream into the sea, and throws into it the burning mountain.

10. And the third angel sounded. And there fell a great star from heaven, which burned like a torch, and fell upon the third part of the rivers, and upon the fountains of waters.
11. And the name of the star is called Wormwood. And the third part of the waters became wormwood. And many men died of the waters, because they had become bitter.
12. And the fourth angel sounded, and the third part of the sun was smitten, and the third part of the moon, and the third part of the stars, so that their third part was darkened, and the day did not appear for the third part of it, and the night in like manner.

In Ps. 104:26 we find immediately after the words quoted above, *There go the ships*. In symbolic language possessions in common are indicated by *ships*, as in these many persons are together, having one aim, risk, profit and loss. In the symbolical action in Mark 4:36, Matt. 8:23, Luke 8:22, the ship is the church. Here we are rather to think of cities and villages than states; since for *states* the symbolical term in the Apocalypse is *islands*.

10 The symbol of *the star* has the meaning of *ruler* (comp. on 6:13, 1:16, 2:1, 28, 3:1, 9:1, 12:1,4.) It *falls from heaven*, whence comes every good gift, and every destructive result; for the earth is dependent on heaven for salvation and perdition. The falling in 9:1, is unexpected. The *fire* with which the great star burns is the fire of wrath, war, and plunder. As the *sea* is masses of people, the water of *rivers* is affluence, prosperity, and success; God causes the waters of the world's commerce and prosperity to dry up, but those of his church to flow. The *fountains* beside denote the sources of the prosperity.

11 The star, burning like a *torch* and named *Wormwood*, contrasts the wood with which Moses, as a type of the Saviour, made the bitter water sweet, as in ver. 8-9, the *great mountain burning with fire* contrasts with Ezekiel's life-stream.

12 The glittering splendour of the heavenly lights represents a prosperous happy state, a symbol of God's grace and salvation, and their *darkening*, of distressing times, that is, the tribulations of war, as is also the whole group. The being *smitten* of God is the cause, the *darkening* is the effect. A *third part* denotes long periods of time, in which distressing times alternate with better ones. In the seventh trumpet the sun, moon, and stars are *wholly* smitten. Here *a third part* interferes with the shining. Two bright sections are followed by a dark one.

---

2. One might suppose the destruction of Jerusalem and dispersion of the Jews in 70AD an example of a mountain thrown into the sea—*Editor*.

SYMBOLS OF THE PLAGUE OF WAR

THE THREE-FOLD WOE ANNOUNCED BY AN EAGLE

> 13. And I saw, and heard an eagle flying through the midst of heaven, and saying with a loud voice: Woe, woe to those who dwell upon the earth before the other voices of the trumpets of the three angels, which are yet to sound!

The trumpets of the four first angels were not previously announced with their contents, but the three last are. Under the four first, tribulations had already happened; yet were not called woes. But now great lamentations come in succession, and it is declared, that although the first four trumpets have reached to the four ends of the earth, still three woes under the trumpets of the three last must be endured (or *pass by*—they are salutary to the church), before the final seventh trumpet.

The *eagle*, in the OLD TESTAMENT, is a symbol and messenger of the divine judgment, especially against hostile oppression (Deut. 28:49, Hos. 8:1, Hab. 1:8, Jer. 48:40, Ezek. 17:3, Matt. 24:28.) *The Lord will bring against thee*, it is said in the ORIGINAL PASSAGE, Deut. 28:49, *a people from afar, from the end of the earth, as the eagle flies*. The *flying* is used of the eagle in 4:7, and of the angel in 14:6. The eagle here forms a contrast to the *dove* in John 1:32. John sees the *eagle flying in the midst of heaven*, to be heard by the whole earth, as also in 19:17, where an *angel* stands in the sun.

CHAPTER 9:1-12 STRUCTURE

We have in 9:1-12 the fifth trumpet, the first woe. A new image of war, the awful scourge with which God chastises the apostate world: *A star fallen from heaven with locusts*. First there is the appearance of the locusts; then the injury they occasion, ver. 3-6. After this we have a description of them, ver. 7-10, which again at the close connects itself with the injury they occasion. And the close of the whole leads back to the first beginning, the *leader* of the locusts, ver. 11. There is only added farther in ver. 12 a short sentence placing a boundary-line between this trumpet and the next. The absence of all individual traits shows we have not a particular historical event, but a general vivid image of the tribulations of war.

THE FIFTH TRUMPET AND THE FIRST WOE

> 9:1. And the fifth angel sounded. And I saw a star fallen from heaven upon the earth, and to him was given the key of the pit of the abyss. 2. And he opened the well-pit of the abyss. And there arose a smoke out of the pit, as the smoke of a great oven; and the sun and the air were darkened by reason of the smoke of the pit. 3. And out of the smoke came locusts upon the earth. And to them was given power, as the scorpions of the earth have power. 4. And it was said to them, that they should not hurt the grass on the earth, nor any green thing, nor any tree, save only the men who had not the seal of God on their foreheads. 5. And it was given to them, that they should not kill them, but that they should be tormented five months; and their torment was as the torment of a scorpion, when it strikes a man. 6. And in those days shall men seek death and not find it; they shall desire to die, and death will flee from them. 7. And the locusts are like horses, which are prepared for war, and upon their heads are crowns, like gold, and their faces like the face of men. 8. And they had hair as the hair of women, and their teeth were

as those of lions. 9. And they had coats of mail like iron coats of mail, and the rustling of their wings as the rustling of chariots of many horses, running to battle. 10. And they have tails like scorpions, and there are stings in their tails; and their power is to hurt men for five months. 11. They have over them as king the angel of the abyss; whose name in Hebrew is Abaddon, and in Greek he has the name Apollyon, 12. One woe is past; behold! there come two woes more after it.

9:1. And the fifth angel sounded. And I saw a star fallen from heaven upon the earth, and to him was given the key of the pit of the abyss.

The *star* denotes a *ruler*, no single historical person; but an *ideal* person, who appears in history in a whole series of real individuals, Napoleon, for example.

In 8:10 the Seer beholds the star as he falls, here *after* he has fallen. All comes down from heaven *upon earth*. It is different from that of Satan's falling from heaven. That the key was *given* to the star shows the star was intermingled with the human form. The *abyss*, properly *bottomless deep*, is the receptacle of demons and the proper abode of Satan, the source and centre of demoniacal influence upon the earth. The *well-pit* of the abyss is the communication connecting the lower world with the earth, and opens out toward the earth. The wicked are sunk down, like Korah, through the medium of the well-pit opened by *the star from heaven*, (ver. 11 also *the angel of the abyss*) where the evil spirit ascends from hell to the earth. If the earth shuts itself out from heaven by proclaiming its ungodliness, in righteous judgment hell shall be opened by heaven, and, in the place of human wickedness and for its punishment, there shall come that of demons. This is brought in by particular Satanic individuals, angels or messengers from hell, set by God in the fitting positions where they have the opportunity of spreading through a wide circle the hellish spirit. As heaven, so also hell is opened by particular personages, who are, as it were, an incarnation of the hellish spirit. *Here*, however, it is a different incarnation of the hellish principle that comes primarily into consideration.

2. And he opened the well-pit of the abyss. And there arose a smoke out of the pit, as the smoke of a great oven; and the sun and the air were darkened by reason of the smoke of the pit.

2 The *smoke* denotes the hellish spirit which penetrates to the earth, especially the Cainite spirit of brotherly hatred. Smoke is the product of fire. The fire denotes rage and hatred, the thirst of destruction. The *smoke* very thick, like that *of an oven*, is from Gen. 19:28, Ex. 19:18. A different smoke from frankincense—the prayers of saints, which rises from earth to heaven; where this smoke falls, or where it ascends *against* any one, there constantly bursts forth that hellish smoke. The *darkening of the sun and the firmament* here also denotes the sad and distressing times, which come upon the earth in consequence of the power given to the hellish Cainite spirit.

3. And out of the smoke came locusts upon the earth. And to them was given power, as the scorpions of the earth have power. 4. And it was said to them, that they should not hurt the grass on the earth, nor any green thing, nor any tree, save only the men who had not the seal of God on their foreheads.

3-4 The *locusts* do not come from hell, but they proceed out of the hellish smoke, from which their body, previously in existence, is *quickened* and made thirsty for destruction. Invading hosts are compared to locusts, which *overspread the land*, as a *multitude*, from which *locusts* in Hebrew derive their name (Judges 6:5, comp. 7:12, Jer. 46:23, Jer. 51:27, comp. Ps. 105:34-35.) They have a special starting-point in the locust-devastation in Egypt. The Egyptian plagues are prophecies in action, the analogous future is represented under the image of the past, in which it had its pledge.

Amos in 7:1-3 beheld the approaching divine judgment, consisting of a hostile invasion, under the image of a swarm of locusts. Under the related image of swarms of flies and bees, are hordes of enemies (comp. Isa. 7:18; Deut. 1:44; Ps. 118:12.) Here it is a *warlike* connection. The four preceding trumpets announce hostile devastations, as do also those that follow. A ruler and conqueror is indicated by the star fallen from heaven, who opens hell and sends forth the smoke, out of which the locusts proceed, identical with the angel of the abyss in ver. 11, who is called the *king* of the locusts. The succeeding trumpets agree with this, so the subject must be the same; that of hostile devastations.

To the *horses prepared for war* here in ver. 7 correspond in ver. 16 the *myriads of horsemen;* to the *lions' teeth* in ver. 8, the *heads of lions* in ver. 17; *coats of mail* are mentioned alike in ver. 9 and ver. 17; and the *tails like scorpions* in ver. 10 have their correspondence in the *tails like those of serpents* in ver. 19.

The image of the locusts is not sufficiently comprehensive, so the idea of malice required the addition to the symbol, of *scorpions*. When it is said that *power was given to them, as the scorpions of the earth have power,* it shows that in nature everything destructive has its mission from God—comp. Gen. 3:17, where the earth is cursed for man's sin, and Isa. 11, according to which in the *regeneration* of the earth, everything violent and destructive shall vanish from it. The scorpions of the earth form the contrast to these scorpion-like locusts sent forth from hell.

Natural locusts are destructive to plants and trees. In 8:7, we saw the green grass and the trees designating persons of distinction. The *trees* correspond to the kings, nobles, etc. Trees and *grass* denote the high and the low, princes and subjects. Men generally are also denoted by the *grass* and the *trees*, yet not believers, as is clear from the limitation that follows. The human family is divided into the sealed, and those *who have not the seal of God on their foreheads*. All excepting the sealed are under divine judgment, and the sealed out of the tribes of Israel comprehends all believers. The *grass*, etc. here is not literal things in nature preyed upon by locusts.

5-6 The *not killing* is not as if none were to be killed; but those who are not killed alone draw attention, because their number is much the greater and their lot the harder, ver. 6.

In the four first trumpets, and the sixth, the third part of men are mentioned as the object of the plagues, but here not so. Hence the *fifth* here marks this trumpet as incomplete in its character compared with the seventh. For this the fifth number is well adapted as the signature of the half, the incomplete, as the broken ten. *Five months* are named, because only five compared to the year's twelve produces the idea of a proportionately long continuance and frightfulness. It denotes a very long period, and still not the longest.

They resembled scorpions in their malice to torment men; comp. Eze. 2:6, and, therefore, by a righteous judgment of heaven, their torment becomes like the torment inflicted by a scorpion. In verse 6 the earnestness in their desire for death appears from its repetition a second time. Ch. 6:16, in the vision of the seals is parallel, and the ORIGINAL PASSAGE is Jer. 8:3.

7-9 The first clause is literally: and the likenesses of *the locusts are like*. The prefixing *the likeness* shows the Seer leaves other things concerning them in order to describe their likeness. Four verses are devoted to this. First we have their likeness in regard to their appearance as a whole, then only particular features.

The *horses* are occupied by their riders, so that they correspond to the horsemen in ver. 16. Only when the riders sit upon them, are they prepared for war. Behind the veil of the locust symbol the real nature of the thing meant appears, in an infusion of symbol and the reality into each other. They appear

5. And it was given to them, that they should not kill them, but that they should be tormented five months; and their torment was as the torment of a scorpion, when it strikes a man. 6. And in those days shall men seek death and not find it; they shall desire to die, and death will flee from them.
7. And the locusts are like horses, which are prepared for war, and upon their heads are crowns, like gold, and their faces like the face of men. 8. And they had hair as the hair of women, and their teeth were as those of lions.

9. And they had coats of mail like iron coats of mail, and the rustling of their wings as the rustling of chariots of many horses, running to battle.

like locusts, and yet also like a frightful mass of horses and horsemen.

The *crown* is the mark of royal dignity, dominion, being *upon their head* mark them out as a sovereign people in their relation to strangers (comp. 2:10, 3:11, 4:4, 6:2, 12:1, 14:14.) To the crowns correspond the designation of their leader as *the star that has fallen from heaven to the earth.* In *his* dominion is their dominion, as in the kingly dignity of Christ is that also of believers. For he is the head, they are the members. They have the feeling of kings over the inhabitants of the plundered countries. *Their faces resemble those of men*, since the fierce countenance of a man looks through the visage of the locust. In reality they were human countenances. Unruly *hair* designates one as giving free scope to lusts and passions, with no hindrance to natural desires, a symbol of savage wildness. The *teeth* resembling *those of lions*, is from Joel 1:6, which comparison suits spiritual locusts, raging enemies, but not natural ones. The *iron coats of mail* indicate the difficulty of attack at these horsemen. The *horses* here also, as in ver. 7, are occupied by their riders, partly sitting on their saddles, partly on light chariots. The *chariots* are an appurtenance of the cavalry. It is not *of many horse-chariots,* but only: *of the chariots of many horses*. The numerousness of the chariots is concluded from the numerousness of the horses.

10. And they have tails like scorpions, and there are stings in their tails; and their power is to hurt men for five months.
11. They have over them as king the angel of the abyss; whose name in Hebrew is Abaddon, and in Greek he has the name Apollyon,

10 This verse reverts to ver. 3-6, from the description of the locusts to what they were to accomplish. Bengel remarks, *The tails of the locusts are not only like the tails of scorpions, but like the scorpions themselves, as the tails of the horses in ver. 19 with their heads are not only like the tails of serpents, but like the serpents themselves.*

11 In Prov. 30:27 locusts have no king, but these have one. The *star* in ver. 1 corresponds to the *king*. We can the less doubt respecting the identity of the king and the star, as the retrogressive movement begins even in ver. 10. As there in connection with the tails of the locusts the subject of ver. 3-6 is resumed, so this verse looks back to ver. 1-2. For the identity of the king and the angel we cannot think of Satan himself, for Satan has his angels, but he is not himself called an angel. There is no other infernal king, who could be designated as *the angel of the abyss*. The article denotes either this angel of the abyss, an ideal person, who becomes manifest in a multitude of real personages, as already known from what had gone before, or as the angel *par excellence*—comp. on 3:17.

It is not the messengers, but the *angel of the abyss*, that is here spoken of, as the angels of the devil, who reside in the darkness of hell. The name of the higher messengers of hell is transferred to the lower, in order to create a salutary dread of them, as we speak of a corporeal Satan (12:7, Matt. 16:23, Matt. 25:41, 2 Cor. 12:7, 2 Pet. 2:4, Jude 6.) The king has on one side, according to ver. 1, a divine mission. But the hellish one, alone rendered prominent here, was also indicated in ver. 1-2. For, if he opens the well-pit of hell, and lets out the smoke, he certainly does, apart from the divine mission, a devilish work, what betokens a Satanic disposition, and a hellish employ.

Abaddon means *destruction*, and occurs in the OLD TESTAMENT in connection with death and the grave. Here it appears as a name of him, who has become a kind of personal, embodied destruction, synonymous with *Apollyon*, the *destroyer*. The names of Abaddon and Apollyon, the destroyer, stand related to the name *Jesus*. The name *Antichrist* stands directly opposed to the name of Christ; and not less directly opposed to the name of Jesus or *Saviour*

SYMBOLS OF THE PLAGUE OF WAR

is that of Abaddon the *destroyer*. On those, who despise Jesus, the Saviour, inevitably comes the destroyer.

12 In 9:13-21, we have the sixth trumpet, the second woe. Four angels, bound in the Euphrates, are set loose, to execute God's vengeance. They overspread the earth with horsemen. The third part of men are destroyed. But the world continues impenitent. Since they will not turn back to him who smites them, they must expect this word to be verified, *For all this his anger is not turned away, but his hand is stretched out still.* The world's sinfulness calls aloud for the seventh trumpet, the last woe.

12. One woe is past; behold! there come two woes more after it.

THE SIXTH TRUMPET AND THE SECOND WOE

> 13. And the sixth angel sounded. And I heard a voice from the four horns of the golden altar, before God, 14. which spake to the sixth angel that had the trumpet, Loose the four angels, bound by the great river Euphrates, 15. And the four angels were loosed, who were prepared for the hour, and day, and month, and year, that they might kill the third part of men. 16. And the number of the army of the horsemen was twice ten thousand times ten thousand, I heard the number of them. 17. And thus I saw the horses in the vision, and them that sat on them, having coats of mail of fire and hyacinth and brimstone; and the heads of the horses were as the heads of lions, and out of their mouths went forth fire, and smoke, and sulphur. 18. By these three plagues was the third part of men killed, by the fire, and by the smoke, and by the brimstone, which issued out of their mouth. 19. For the power of the horses is in their mouths and in their tails, for their tails are like serpents, and they have heads, and with these they do hurt. 20. And the rest of the men, who were not killed by these plagues, repented not of the works of their hands that they should worship demons, and idols of gold, and silver, and brass, and wood, and stone, which can neither see, nor hear, nor walk. 21. And they repented not of their murders, nor of their sorceries, nor of their fornication, nor of their thefts.

The *voice* is that of the altar *itself*, like the eagle in 8:13 not an actual existence, coming out of its four horns. It is the place of *the prayers of saints*.

14 The *four* number has respect to the four angels in ver. 14, and the four number of sins in ver. 21–all bear the impress of comprehensiveness and intensity. The four number of the sins constitutes the foundation, the four number of the horns and the angels stand related to these as the effect to its cause. *Angels*, without any predicate, are always *good* angels, as here, employed in punishing the wicked, the being *bound*, points to the long-suffering of God, which restrained the punishment, and gave space for repentance. The *four* number of the angels bears respect to the four ends of the earth, the universal character of the divine judgment. The *Euphrates* is the river, from beyond which through history the scourge of God came forth upon Asia.

15 The *preparation* proceeds only from God. They were already in preparation for a definite period, and when it arrived, after the wickedness of the world had become full, the *loosing* took place, and they were to begin their work. An ascent is made from the lower to the higher, in the *for the hour, and day, and month*. When I know that something has happened about nine o'clock, I know less than if the year had been mentioned to me. God determines exactly the periods.

16-17 The whole of the plundering hordes is here, as in the preceding trumpet, represented under this image, foot soldiers included.

17. And thus I saw the horses in the vision, and them that sat on them, having coats of mail of fire and hyacinth and brimstone; and the heads of the horses were as the heads of lions, and out of their mouths went forth fire, and smoke, and sulphur.

The *four hundred millions* exclude all idea of a particular war, we have here to do only with a personified species. In Ps. 68:17, *the chariots of God* are thousands multiplied by thousands. There it is the *invisible* war-chariots of Jehovah, drawn by hosts of angels. These earthly hosts are as dependent on every nod of God, as those heavenly ones. They, too, are led by angels. In both places alike the hosts of God are employed in his service against the world. He *heard their number*, because it was so great a one, that no one could number it—comp. 7:9. The description begins with the horsemen and then passes over to their horses. *And them that sat on them,* for: namely, *them that sat on them.*

The wild exasperation, the thirst for murder, rapine and desolation, are pictured in the colours of the *coats of mail* on the horsemen, and especially in the *fire*, and *smoke*, and *sulphur* which came out of the mouth of their horses.

The signification of the colours of the coats of mail is determined by what proceeds out of the mouth of the horses: to the *coats of mail of fire* corresponds the fire, which must therefore be imaged by them; to the *hyacinth*-coloured (deep blue hyacinth), the smoke; to the *brimstone-like*, the sulphur. The *lion-heads*, fearful and appalling. The *fire* is the fire of wrath, the *smoke* the inseparable accompaniment of fire—in Ps. 18:8, as here, the fire-wrath goes out of the mouth—the (burning) *brimstone* points to the unpleasant character of this fire: the fire of hell. If fire and smoke alone had been mentioned, an honourable wrath might have been indicated, so the *sulphur* here is quite necessary to a complete characteristic.

18. By these three plagues was the third part of men killed, by the fire, and by the smoke, and by the brimstone, which issued out of their mouth.

18 The *these* refers to the things that had first been named–their wild spirit of ferocity and murder, for, the not being killed, is there to be limited to the majority, who here also remain in life; and in ver. 6 there, it is represented, not as the better, but as the worse lot. The perishing are those who have not the seal of God spoken of in ver. 4.

19. For the power of the horses is in their mouths and in their tails, for their tails are like serpents, and they have heads, and with these they do hurt.

19 The clause, stating *the power* to be *in their mouth*, connects what is still to be said of their *tails*. The injurious and destructive tendency farther embodies itself in the symbol of the *serpent tails*; like *the old serpent*, on account of their cunning, malicious wickedness, as opposed in some sense to the *lions* in ver. 17; agreeing also in this, the serpents are *behind*, where one suspects no danger. It is not said of the tails of the serpents, that they had heads, but of the tails of the *horses*. These resemble serpents, which have grown to the tails, and have the head free for biting.

20. And the rest of the men, who were not killed by these plagues, repented not of the works of their hands that they should worship demons, and idols of gold, and silver, and brass, and wood, and stone, which can neither see, nor hear, nor walk.

20-21 We may compare Pharaoh, whose servants said to him in vain, *Dost thou not see, that Egypt is destroyed;* and Isa. 9:13, *And the people return not to him that smites them, and the Lord of Hosts they seek not.* A similar spirit of impenitence under divine judgments is given in 16:9, 11, 21. The opposite applies, however, in the degenerate church, 11:13. Along side the world, which here is the subject of discourse, the church exists, and is also, indeed, much tainted by the worldly spirit, but by the judgments of the Lord it is awakened to repentance; see ch. 11.

We have here a tenfold description of idols, divided by the seven and the three, and the first again by two and five. That by *the works of their hands*, it is not actions that are denoted, but works generally, as is clear from Deut. 4:28, *And ye shall there serve idols,* **the works of men's hands,** *wood and stone, which see not, and hear not, and eat not, and smell not;* Ps. 115:4-7, *Their gods are silver and gold,* **the work of men's hands,** 135:17.

The hard expression: *Repent of the works,* is softened by what follows immediately after. According to this it is as much as, *repent of their worshipping the works of their hands, demons and idols.* By the *demons* we can only understand evil spirits, according to the usage of the NEW TESTAMENT.

The *worship* of idolatry, on the one aspect, is a rude image-worship. The several heathen gods have no existence beside the material one in their statues, the works of men's hands. But in the other, the idolatrous service has a demoniacal background, where the allurement to give honour to those *Elilim*, those nonentities, proceeds from the powers of darkness, and since they constitute the spiritual background in the matter, the worship may be regarded as in a measure performed to them.

The demoniacal nature of the Revolution and the rage for freedom has opened many eyes in our days, that were hitherto shut, to perceive the existence of a kingdom of darkness.[3] It is quite similar in respect to the worship of idolatry. Airy phantoms, nonentities, were what came into immediate contact with men's consciences, but behind these a real power lay concealed, and one of terrible energy. The demoniacal background continues through all ages, even to the end of the world.

The works of the hands are set first, for, the subject is not about a direct and conscious worshipping of demons. On the transgressions of the first table there follow now those of the second. The former were completed in the number ten, and these latter are comprised in four. The four, on account of the four quarters of heaven, is next to the ten, the signature of the comprehensive, the complete. The two first sins are against the fifth commandment, according to Luther's reckoning (*thou shalt not kill,*) the sixth by the original text, or the first of the second table; the two last are against the sixth and seventh (*thou shalt not commit adultery, thou shalt not steal,*) or the seventh and eighth respectively.

Sorcery appears here among the transgressions of the second table, in connection with open *murders*, and is therefore viewed not in its religious aspect, but as one of the means by which a neighbour might be secretly injured, and injured in respect to his life. *Fornication* is the spirit of licentiousness, whence proceeds the transgression of the precept: *Thou shalt not commit adultery.*

21. And they repented not of their murders, nor of their sorceries, nor of their fornication, nor of their thefts.

---

3. The Revolution of March, 1848 in Europe, presented to the author the duty of expounding this book's rich treasury of counsel and comfort—*Editor.*

REVELATION 10:1–11:13

An episode: the church and the world

CHAPTER SUMMARY

The seven angels with the seven trumpets form a prophetic picture in itself complete, bringing matters fully to an end, as was the case also with the preceding group of the six seals; and after it an entirely new beginning follows, the vision of *the three enemies of the kingdom of God*.

In this section, 10:1—11:13 forms a sort of episode; and 11:14 connects itself with 9:21. The prophet sees a strong angel descending from heaven, ver. 1. First by a *symbolical action*—having his right foot planted on the sea, the left on the earth—and then by an *express word*, coupled with an oath, this angel announces, that under the trumpet of the seventh angel the full and perfect realization of all the promises made to the church concerning her final victory over the world, and the kingdom of glory, should be accomplished, ver. 2-7. Then he gives to the prophet a little book of painful contents, which should enable him and the church to bear that first business with a courageous spirit. He swallows the little book, is thereby enabled to utter the prophecy, which follows in 11:1-13, and by which the contents of the little book are made known.

The church has become subject to the power of the world, externally and partly internally, connected with it for the persecution of the true confessors of the faith. The elect abide steadfast under trial. Those who stand loosely to the church fall under it. Through the course of the external and internal pressure of the world on the church, witnessing proceeds by the grace of God. And the reformation of the church, prepared by this, has been brought about by God's visitations of judgment, by which the seed scattered by the faithful germinates, grows and brings forth fruit.

The *interlude* here between the sixth and seventh trumpets has its correspondence in the vision of the seven seals, which is united with this into a pair, and in common with it, is of a preparatory and introductory character, in the *episode* between the sixth and seventh seals. There, too, the focus is turned from the world, with the fates of which, according to the historical starting point of the book, its chief scenes have alone to do, to the church; as is the case also here.

A STRONG ANGEL DESCENDS FROM HEAVEN

> 10:1 And I saw another mighty angel come down from heaven, clothed with a cloud: and a rainbow was upon his head, and his face was as it were the sun, and his feet as pillars of fire:

The other angel can only be Christ (**see footnote at end of chapter.*) In verse two he comes down to plant his foot upon the sea and earth to show his approaching possession of both.

The *cloud* is a foreshadowing of judgment to primarily the world, to which the threatening immediately belongs. The cloud calls both joy and fear, the wound it makes is healed by the *rainbow,* which is the symbol of divine grace returning after wrath. The *face like the sun* marks the angel as the possessor of the glory of the Lord (comp. on 1:16, Heb. 1:3; 2 Cor. 4:6,) symbolic of the preservation of the divine glory in judging the world and the church (Ex. 23:21-22,) yet with grace (Hosea 11:9.) The *feet* are *pillar* like and *fiery,* like clear brass (1:15, 2:18, 3:12,) which displays the *massive* character in the immoveable steadfastness of the heavenly conqueror against all resistance of his enemies, while the fire its *consuming*. The pillar of fire and cloud in Ex. 13:21 symbolizes the Lord's judgments on his enemies (Ex. 13:21.)

THE PROMISES OF VICTORY OVER THE WORLD TO BE ACCOMPLISHED

2. And he had in his hand a little book open: and he set his right foot upon the sea, and his left foot on the earth, 3. And cried with a loud voice, as when a lion roareth: and when he had cried, seven thunders uttered their voices. 4. And when the seven thunders had uttered their voices, I was about to write: and I heard a voice from heaven saying unto me, Seal up those things which the seven thunders uttered, and write them not. 5. And the angel which I saw stand upon the sea and upon the earth lifted up his hand to heaven, 6. And sware by him that liveth for ever and ever, who created heaven, and the things that therein are, and the earth, and the things that therein are, and the sea, and the things which are therein, that there should be time no longer: 7. But in the days of the voice of the seventh angel, when he shall begin to sound, the mystery of God should be finished, as he hath declared to his servants the prophets.

The book in chapter 5:1 contained the judgments on the world, the *little book* here concerns the destinies of the church; there the victory of the church over the world, here the injuries sustained by the church from the world. Verses 2-7 meet the doubt and disquietude which the little book raised. Should a church tainted by the world be worthy of attaining victory over the world? The consideration of the church's sinfulness is the rock on which the hope of a completed salvation threatens to be shipwrecked.

The planting of the *foot* on anything is a symbol of taking possession and maintaining with invincible power (Dan. 12:5-7, Ps. 8:6, Ps. 110:1, Josh. 10:24.) In Daniel, Michael appears as standing on the Tigris, signifying his power over heathendom. The *sea* is used here as the sea of the nations. The *feet* are placed on the sea and *the earth*; presupposing a revolt against God must have existed, for in the next group the beast arises out of, not a literal sea, but the sea of nations.

3-4 The *roar of the lion* expresses God's wrath against his enemies. This is carried forward by the *seven thunders,* which respect the frightful judgment of God, whether merely threatened or executed, toward the sea and the earth. In John 12:29 the thunder shows that the name of Jesus shall be glorified by judgment on the world. He had cried out *with a loud voice* on the cross, *It is finished,* so here the voice announces the victory of the church and the subjection of the world, as founded in the work of the cross. The meaning of the thunders is temporarily shut up, until the foundation for understand-

5. And the angel which I saw stand upon the sea and upon the earth lifted up his hand to heaven,
6. And sware by him that liveth for ever and ever, who created heaven, and the things that therein are, and the earth, and the things that therein are, and the sea, and the things which are therein, that there should be time no longer: 7. But in the days of the voice of the seventh angel, when he shall begin to sound, the mystery of God should be finished, as he hath declared to his servants the prophets.

5 The *whom I saw stand* details the placing of the foot on the sea and the earth, as in Dan. 12:5-7, where the angel raises both hands to heaven, here only the right hand, as he holds the book, which points back to Deut. 32:40-41 where the Lord pledges vengeance for his people (comp. with Ps. 102:24.) The object of the oath is that *no time more shall be,* time being here *delay,* between the seventh trumpet and completion of the kingdom, as ver 7 shows (Isa. 13:22, Hab. 2:3.) In the earlier trumpets were a delay in the completion of the kingdom, the fainting church is tempted by doubts regarding the nature and extent of the delay, so this meets that doubt.

6 *He who lives forever,* as his protection is eternal, all opposition must give way and vanish.

7 *Mystery* denotes the absolute inaccessibility to ordinary sense and discernment, which is fast bound within the circle of the present. The *mystery of God* here is of a joyful nature, it is literally *as he has evangelized the prophets* and respects the dominion of Christ over the sea and earth, and the inheritance of the servants of God. Concealed here, it is apparent when it actually appears in 11:15,18 (Matt 22:29.) Unaware of God's power to radically change the present state, the church feels its sins, as if the world were to always triumph in its ascendancy, so the joyful completion is marked as a mystery.

LITTLE BOOK OF PAINFUL CONTENTS

8. And the voice which I heard from heaven spake unto me again, and said, Go and take the little book which is open in the hand of the angel which standeth upon the sea and upon the earth. 9. And I went unto the angel, and said unto him, Give me the little book. And he said unto me, Take it, and eat it up; and it shall make thy belly bitter, but it shall be in thy mouth sweet as honey. 10. And I took the little book out of the angel's hand, and ate it up; and it was in my mouth sweet as honey: and as soon as I had eaten it, my belly was bitter. 11. And he said unto me, Thou must prophesy again before many peoples, and nations, and tongues, and kings.

Notwithstanding the little book, the church's victory over the sea and the earth remains certain. Ezekiel 2:10 shows the contents of the book as having a mournful character, to do with the sins of a degenerate church and the judgment due it. It is painful for the seer, as in ver. 9-10, 11:1-13, where the church falls away. As the rainbow consoles despite the cloud, the angel's standing on the sea and earth consoles in relation to the little book.

9-10 The seer swallows it that it might go into his body, as in Ezekiel 3:3, where the divine truth is taken into his inmost being, the consequence being that he becomes God's spokesman. The *sweetness* is ascribed to the *mouth,* the *bitterness* the *belly.* The passage in Ezekiel rests on Jer. 15:16, where the words were joy and rejoicing, to be God's spokesman was unspeakably sweet and delectable, the mouth is the organ of God's orator (Isa. 6:5,7, 59:21.) In Ps. 19:11 commands are sweeter than honey. The bitterness, literally *bitter in the body,* denotes the sharp pain produced by the word committed to him, which Eze. 3:14 describes as embittered, in a vexatious sadness and holy indignation (Jer.15:17, Eze. 2:10. Eze. 3:14.) We too must eat and swallow it, not only that which is agreeable to us, *thy law is in my heart*, literally my entrails (3:3, Ps. 40:9.) The pain was named before the joy as it would overcome the joy, then the joy was mentioned before the pain. Without eating the little book one cannot prophesy, but having eaten it one must do so, so Paul also must testify–Acts 23:11.

11 The prophet prophesies *again*, as in the seven seals, and six first trumpets. There, as the peoples were visited by judgments, here as they overflowed the church to seduce her into apostasy and drew down judgment. In this respect this is prophesied upon the peoples and nations. The prophet in 11:1-13 announces in the fulfilment of this command to prophesy, the outer court is given to the Gentiles, who tread the holy city; the beast wars with the two witnesses, the peoples and nations see their corpses three days and a half, and rejoice over them. The *four* number here points to its ecumenicity, it forbids us to confine this to one event in history. The *many kings* (17:12, 19:19, 16:14) takes it out of the seer's time, where *one* king was ruling–the Roman emperor. These heathen kings return in the ten kings who serve the beast who war against Christ.

VERSES 11:1-13

Chapter 11:1-13 falls into two divisions. The first, ver. 1 and 2, gives the promise, that the faith of the elect shall not expire; the second, ver. 3-13, certifies the uninterrupted continuance of the office of witnessing. Christ's words in Matt. 13:20-21, present the naked thoughts of this passage. The outer court had its correspondence in him who *hears the word, and anon with joy receives it; yet has he not root in himself, but endures for a while, for when tribulation or persecution arises because of the word, by and bye he is offended.*

THE PROMISE OF ENDURING FAITH FOR THE ELECT

> 11:1. And there was given to me a reed like a stick, saying, Rise, and measure the temple of God, and the altar, and them that worship therein, 2. But the court, which is without the temple, throw out and measure it not, for it is given to the heathen, and the holy city shall they tread down forty and two months.

The *temple* proper denotes those who are filled with the spirit of the church, the outer *court* those who are superficially affected (John 2:19; Mark 14:58; Eph. 2:21-22; 1 Tim. 3:15; 2 Cor. 6:16; 2 Thess. 2:4; Heb. 3:6.) The *measuring* is determined by the opposite *throwing out*, being measured as far as the preservation is to go. Ezekiel measured the restored temple (Eze. 40.) Beside the sanctuary as the believer's ideal abode is *the altar*, that is of burnt offering. It is transferred from the outer court in an ideal figure. Under the abiding constraint of love believers offer themselves in a free-will sacrifice (6:9-11.)

2 Those externally related tread *the outer court* (Isa. 1:12). The *treading down* of the city causes the court to be *given up to the heathen*, and thrown away. As in Daniel the *forty and two months* signifies the dominion of the world over the church, the seven symbolizing the church, the broken seven, the three and a half (12:6, 14, 13:5.) John saw this happening, and in vision, the

last in 20:7-9, which we have now before us. So the prophecy verifies itself anew, those affected by the evil, find here consolation and warning. As an example of our prophecy a great degeneracy in the Christian church preceded the Diocletian persecution, many were shaken by it, many more apostatized; yet true believers and martyrs remained steadfast.

UNINTERRUPTED CONTINUANCE OF WITNESSING

> 3. And I will give to my two witnesses, and they shall prophesy a thousand two hundred and sixty days, clothed in sackcloth. 4. These are the two olive-trees and the two lamps, which stand before the Lord of the earth. 5. And if any one will hurt them, fire goes out of their mouth and devours their enemies; and if any one will hurt them, he must in this manner be killed. 6. These have power to shut up heaven, that it rain not in the days of their prophecy, and have power over water, to turn it into blood, and to smite the earth with all plagues, as often as they will. 7. And when they shall have finished their testimony, the beast that ascends out of the abyss shall make war with them, and shall overcome them, and shall kill them. 8. And their corpse shall lie upon the street of the great city, which is called spiritually Sodom and Egypt, where also their Lord was crucified. 9. And they of the peoples, and kindreds, and tongues, and nations, shall see their dead corpse three days and an half, and shall not suffer their corpses to be laid in the grave, 10. And they that dwell on the earth shall rejoice over them, and make merry, and send gifts one to another, because these two prophets tormented them that dwell on the earth. 11. And after the three days and an half the Spirit of life entered into them from God, and they stood upon their feet, and a great fear fell upon those who saw them. 12. And they heard a great voice from heaven saying unto them, Come up hither. And they ascended to heaven in a cloud, and their enemies saw it. 13. And at the same hour there was a great earthquake, and the tenth part of the city fell; and in the earthquake seven thousand names of men were killed; and the rest were affrighted, and gave glory to the God of heaven.

In the second part of the section, ver. 3-13, the church is assured by the speaker, being Christ, the strong angel, with the *I will give*, that her witnessing gift continues in times of darkness and worldly intermixture. The *two witnesses* are ideal persons who appear in a multitude of real ones. The *two* number comes from Moses and Elijah (ver. 5-6, Ex. 7:15-25, ch. 8–11, 1 Kings 19:17, 17:1,) who appeared on the mount with Christ before John and the others, representing the witnessing of the Old Testament, the apostles that of the New (Matt. 17:1-3.) The two never stand isolated, as the disciples were sent by two together; there were Moses and Aaron, Joshua and Caleb, Zerubbabel and Joshua, Haggai and Zechariah, in order they might mutually strengthen one another. The *sackcloth* was a mourning garment of hair, with John the Baptist and Elijah, in mourning over the desolation of the church and the holy city (Matt. 3:4.)

4 The two witnesses bear the name of *lamps* and *olive trees* as the concentration of the light of the church, and as an instrument of divine grace to her.

5-6 Here the wrath and power of the witnesses shows itself, what Moses and Elijah had done separately is done here by the two at once, reaching to all visible nature, *heaven*, the *waters* and the *earth*. Where the oil is there is fire, one and the same spirit manifests for both salvation and vengeance. The Lord has put his word in their mouth, which resembles a hammer, that breaks the rock in pieces. At the word of Elijah fire came down and consumed his adversaries; and the mockery of the people who heard Jeremiah

(5:14) changed into bitter lamentations, when his words assumed Chaldean flesh and blood, who besieged and destroyed the city. Whatever strikes in hostility against God and his witnesses shall be consumed in vengeance, *he must in this manner be killed.*

7 The *beast that ascends out of the abyss* is mentioned here by anticipation. He is extensively described in the fourth group: the three enemies of God's kingdom, ch. 12—14; and in the sixth, the judgment on the three enemies, ch. 17—20. That it is in notice here shows the Revelation is not a regularly progressive history. The *beast* denotes the ungodly heathen state. By it here is meant the reviving of the ungodly heathen power at the close of the thousand years' reign, or, the whole of the ungodly power is here denoted by the most prominent part, which the Seer had already before him in his day. The brutal character of the ungodly power discovers itself more and more in the present age. What is said here of the witnesses of Christ, was exemplified in Christ himself, only when he had finished his testimony did the darkness receive power, when it was good for the church that he should go away.

8-10 The *great city* is not literal Jerusalem, but Jerusalem as degenerate on account of the ascendancy of the world. The New Jerusalem is the purified and glorified church. The *spiritual* Jerusalem is compared to *Egypt* on account of the religious corruption in early Israelitish history; by *Sodom*, on the other hand, the morals are constantly referred to (Eze. 23:3, 8, 27. ORIGINAL PASSAGES–Sodom: Deut. 32:32; Isa. 1:10; Eze. 16:46, 48; Jer. 23:14.) When the church is overrun by the world, then seeming faith, half faith, and false faith, play the part of giving up the true witnesses of the Lord to unbelief for crucifixion. The *three days and an half* are in imitation of the history of the Lord, whom his servants must follow, and also point, like the three and an half years, to the seven as the signature of the kingdom of God on which account the half day is added.

These prophets *tormented* those on the earth, although a little flock, their words had an ally in the hearts and consciences of their hearers, who gnash their teeth in hatred. The declaration: *These two prophets tormented*, is a touchstone, to know whether one fulfils his office in the right spirit and with proper zeal. So long as all speak well of us, or let us go unmolested, we are still not in the right state, and can look for no fruits from our operations. He who torments not also blesses not, the ground must be first pierced by the plough before the seed can be sown in it.

11-13 The triumph of the witnesses here described after their apparent defeat, is taken from the history of Christ, whose ascension to heaven is attested here, prefiguring the destiny of his people, and possesses for them the character of a matter-of-fact prophecy (comp. ver. 8, Luke 24:51, Acts 1:9, Mark 16:19.) On *a great fear fell on those who saw*, see Matt. 27:54; and on *at the same hour there was a great earthquake*, see Matt. 27:51, 54, 28:2. A reviving always succeeds the death. Repentance is produced by the divine judgments on the church, not by crying peace, peace with such as prophesy out of their own hearts, but, with Habakkuk, to pray to the God of the degenerate church to revive righteousness and holiness in it, and pray, *in wrath remember mercy*. The witnesses stand before the Lord of the *earth*, and he to whom the glory is given is called *the God of heaven*, with whom, as the Alpha and Omega, rests all hope of a blessed result.

THE TEMPLE AND THE HOLY CITY
—JUDAISTIC VIEWS

According to some the temple and the holy city must not be the symbol of the church; but the vision must refer to the external temple, and the literal Jerusalem, and the fates of the restored temple and the Jerusalem of the last times. Yet at the time of the vision there is no trace of Jerusalem and the temple being in ruins, nor any future rebuilding here or elsewhere in the book.

This literal method of exposition is not agreeable to scripture. It is a kind of revival of the Jewish-Christian tendency in the ancient church—the idea that the converted Jews in it are to form a sort of spiritual nobility in the church, and that for them a separate, distinguished and most illustrious part of it. It is a worm in the fruit of the Jewish mission, as it nourishes a natural pride, misleading them to form a peculiar brotherhood among themselves, and prevents them from properly incorporating themselves with the general society of the Christian church.

We should cease to change Jewish Christians into Christian Jews. The heathen who were converted to Christ were grafted into the Jewish olive tree, and have taken on them, as it were, the person and form of the Jews; so shall the Jews, who in the latter days shall be converted to Christ, be grafted into the church of the heathen, or rather become incorporated with the mystical and spiritual Jews, and without any difference possess along with them the same condition in the kingdom of Christ. All are one in Christ. There is no distinction between Jewish and Gentile Christians in this book, under the new economy all distinction of races in matters of religion is taken away.

Romans speaks of the blessing which the conversion of the Jews shall bring to the church of the future, but nothing whatever of a new church from the Jews, of the restoration of Jerusalem or the rebuilding of the temple, nor generally of a return to the old beggarly elements, which have been completely swept away by Christ and his blood, placing all nations on a footing. We Christians in the first instance apply to the New Testament. In the Old Testament what appears to favour the modern Judaistic view rests on the want of a proper understanding. If any one concludes that whenever Israel is spoken of, the Jews are meant, he may prove much, but little good will be done by such a light and superficial mode of expounding the scriptures. What the Spirit has spoken must be spiritually understood. Even the promises given the patriarchs do not respect the children of Israel as opposed to believers from among the heathen—an olive tree, a people of God stands from first to last—an Israel in which the false seed is excluded, and into which believers from among the heathen were adopted.

Another view maintains the temple was still standing because the Revelation was composed before the destruction of Jerusalem, and that the patriotism of John cannot embrace the idea of a complete destruction of the city and temple, though he sees an approaching judgment, so he lightens the matter—of the temple only the outer court is given up, and of the city only the tenth part. But John would stand quite alone from any blind partiality for his people. The prophets before the Chaldean desolation predicted this desolation, and after the Babylonian captivity they predicted a second total desolation when the sin had reached its maturity. Christ rests on these prophecies as he predicts the days of vengeance in Luke 21:22, Matt. 24:15, alluding to Dan. 9:24-27, where Daniel pointed to a second desolation when the city and temple still lay in ashes. The last of the prophets, Malachi, was entirely of a threatening character–he prophesies the Lord would come and smite the land with a curse after Elijah would come. *That* Elijah, John the Baptist, threatens a baptism with fire, then Christ himself declares its destruction in Luke 19:43-44, and in Matt. 24:2, that of the temple.

John was raised far above the territory of mere Jewish sympathies. These are to be found out of Judaism only among half Christians, with those who, in the meagre acquaintance with the glory of Christ, have never attained to the full knowledge of the difference between Judaism and Christianity. The position the apostle takes toward the unbelieving Jews in the letter to Smyrna is as strong and offensive as could well be. They are plainly characterized as unworthy of the name of *Jews*, and belonging to the *community of Satan*. That it is not single individuals of improper character discoursed of, but the whole fraternity as such, is evident from the expression *Satan's synagogue*, a parody of *Jehovah's congregation* with which they flattered their vanity (Num. 16:3.) See also John 8:44. To John and other believing Jews, the temple was but only a den of robbers, as Christ had said in Matt. 21:13. It is denied the name of temple, he recognizes none to be Jews but the Christians, and can own no other temple but the Christian church. In John's time the nobler elements of Jewry had long been absorbed by the Christian church; the synagogue of Satan retained only the dross (Eze. 24:1-14 KJV.) The fall of a tenth part of the city could not have produced the effect of leading such to glorify the God of heaven, tribulation is fruitless for such, it can only produce rage in such characters, the dark zealot-spirit. The Revelation knows of no prerogatives belonging peculiarly to the Jews in the kingdom of God; Gentile Christians have perfectly equal rights imputed to them with the Jewish brethren, John makes no account of any distinction between Jewish and Gentile believers, he knows of only one holy Catholic church. To say this section contains Jewish patriotic fantasies cannot possibly be right. Ch. 5:8-10 shows us that there is neither Jew nor Greek, the kingdom of God draws its members out of all the peoples of the earth to the possession of the same rights, it has its foundation in the worth that is here ascribed to Christ's blood. All Judaism has its roots in defective views of redemption. He who sees Christ the lamb of God who takes away the sin of the world is thereby raised above the contracted and partial Jewish spirit.

In ch. 7:1-8 we see the tribes of Israel sealed. This may, to a superficial view, prove the precedence of the Jews. However Abraham, Isaac and Jacob are the fathers of all believers–from the very beginning of the arrangements respecting salvation to the end of the world, there is but one people of God, the sons of Abraham and of Israel, from the number of whom they are excluded, who give way to a spirit of unbelief and backsliding, even though they have been born among them, while on the other hand those who have faith, wherever they may have been born, attain to equal rights with the native members. In Matt. 19:28 Christ uses the twelve tribes of Israel not in the ordinary Jewish sense, but rather to denote the whole church of God, the calling of the apostles being to all nations, Matt. 28:19. The mode of epistolary address followed by James, and Peter, addressing their letters to the twelve tribes scattered abroad, and the elect strangers scattered abroad, would not exclude the Gentile Christians (as appears from the Acts and Paul's epistles) nor include the unchristian Jews–they addressed both the genuine original sons, and the sons by adoption. This manner of contemplation was followed by John in 21:24; all are received without distinction of nation. The honour of the Jews being the kernel and trunk of the people of God, even under the New Testament, is accorded to them in all scripture, and the communication of the gospel to the heathen was made by believing Jews. If we tear asunder the two testaments we leave the old to be regarded as primarily destined for the Jews, and retain only the new for the Christian church in a very imperfect manner. The prophet in no doubt speaks of the 144,000 in the spiritual or Christian sense; to represent the whole company of Christians, taken out of all nations.

For John, the things of Judaism serve only as the forms of and symbols under which he represents the Christian, all these analogies cannot mean that what he means by the temple cannot be the temple at Jerusalem, he must intend by what corresponds to it on the Christian territory, the Christian church. That by *Israel* is not denoted corporeal descendants of Jacob, but the entire body of true Christians. *Jew* in this book denotes one who is so in secret, circumcised in heart, a true confessor of the faith. The priests are not the Levitical, but all Christ's faithful people, who have been made priests to God (1:6, 5:10, 20:6.) The temple serves as a designation of the church of Christ. It is not merely *a* temple, but *the* temple or tabernacle of God discoursed of. All saints in earth and heaven have access to it (3:12, Heb. 12:22, 13:6, Phil. 3:20.) The temple with the ark of the covenant (7:15, 11:19, 15:5) as the heavenly symbol of the church, implies the prophet sees the church under the same symbol.

As with the temple so with Jerusalem–it never denotes the city in the vulgar sense, but always the church. By *the beloved city*, which in 20:9, is to be encompassed and besieged by a revived heathenism at the close of the thousand years, is meant the church. The church of the future world is called the *new Jerusalem* in 3:12, 21:2,10–the new Jerusalem in contrast, not to the old material one, but to the spiritual beloved city in its imperfect condition here, from which this section tells us of its need for renewal.

The heavenly Zion, with its 144,000 perfected saints in 14:1-5, presupposes the existence of an *earthly* Zion, in which believers are prepared through tribulation. If the triumphant church takes the name *Zion*, so must also the militant. The spiritual use of the language is also employed elsewhere in the NEW TESTAMENT, the temple is designated the *Christian church* in Gal. 4:26 and Heb. 12:22.

The seven epistles reflect the internal state of the church, and in delineating the preserving and protecting agency of God over it, the command to measure the temple here is allied with the injunction to *be faithful unto death* in 2:10, and the *keeping of the word of patience* and being kept from *the hour of temptation* in 3:10. Similarly the *throwing out of the temple court* and *not measuring* it, allies nearly to the *removing of the candlestick*, and the *I will spew thee out of my mouth*. The subject of a great sifting of the church, yet never wholly to perish is frequently unfolded in the epistles. To refer this to Judaism, instead of the church, is discordant.

The placement of this passage between the sixth and seventh trumpets, makes sense if rightly interpreted as the Christian church, given the trumpets have to do with the world power, which has encroached upon the church. A literal temple and city would be out of place to the context.

The appearance of the angel of the Lord in this episode (10:1-11:13) serves a double purpose– the completion of the judgment upon the world, and the glorifying of the church-how dreadfully the temple and Jerusalem would be imperilled by the world, yet they should still be preserved. These two parts would lose all internal connection whenever by the temple we understand the Jewish one.

The two witnesses are equally hated by the world power of the beast, and brought to death—the judgment comes on the degenerate holy city because of the despite done to their testimony. Between the world power and the Jews there existed no internal connection, but the church had been leavened to a large extent by the spirit of the world. According to ver. 7 the beast who persecutes the witnesses has to do, not with the literal Jerusalem, but with *the saints* (13:7-8.) In 13:2 the dragon wars against the redeemed (12:10.) The literal Jerusalem was no longer the theatre for the two witnesses. It had ceased to be the centre of the church at Christ's death, *Behold your house is left unto you desolate,* Matt. 23:38. The seven epistles proclaim the complete separation of the church from Jerusalem and its temple. The designation of the two witnesses as the two olive trees and the two lamps determine the region of their agency to be that of the Spirit and grace of God. The ecclesiastical tradition for the composition of the book under Domitian is affirmed (see p. 6.) The punishment of the Jews had already passed, Judaism had already been overthrown, the focus here is the overthrow of heathenism, we have here holy ground with no room for patriotic imaginations. The comforting assurance is given us of the preservation of the church amid all temptations–our own preservation, if we do not loiter about the court, but press into the kingdom, into the temple itself.

---

* We must first of all consider the OLD TESTAMENT doctrine of the Angel of God, or of Jehovah, who is represented as far above the sphere of the inferior angels, of whom are predicated all the attributes of the true God, who speaks in His name, claims for himself the honours due to the Eternal, and is addressed and treated as God. In Ex. 23:21, he is designated as *the Angel in whom is God's name*, i.e., his nature as historically unfolded and attested; in Isa. 43:9 he is spoken of as *the Angel of His Presence* (or face), i.e., the Angel in whom God appears, in opposition to the inferior created angels; in Josh. 5:14 as Captain of the Lord's Host, on account of his Godlike majesty and glory (in ver.15, he attributes to himself Divine honours, and in 6:2 is called Jehovah,) the powers of heaven, material and spiritual, the stars and angels, are subject to him. He appears surrounded by the latter, who are attentive to his words in the first vision of Zechariah, as the Protector of the covenant people (comp. ver 11,) the mediator between them and God. The Angel of the Lord occurs first in Gen. 16. Wherever an appearance of Jehovah is spoken of, we are to consider this as accomplished through the medium of his angel, see Gen. 16:7, *and Jehovah appeared unto him,* adding: *in His angel,* see 18:1. In Gen. 28:11-22, Jehovah appears to Jacob. In 31:13, the Angel of God calls Himself *the God of Bethel*, in reference to the occurence related in ch. 28. In Hos. 12:3, he who wrestled with Jacob is called *Elohim*, as in Genesis, but in ver. 4, he is *the Angel*–the ground for mentioning the Angel must lie in the presupposition, that all revelations of God occur through the medium of his angel. The *angel of the Lord* occurs in Zechariah and Malachi, in connection with the doctrine concerning Christ. Zech. 11 announces a personal appearance of the Angel of the Lord in the midst of His people, and the taking of the office of shepherd under him. Mal. 3:1 foretells that the *Angel of the covenant* will come to his temple. That John's doctrine of the *Logos* is related to the OLD TESTAMENT doctrine of the Angel of the Lord, can be the less doubted, since he refers to this frequently. Christ appears with unusual frequency as *sent* by God, by which expression is everywhere intimated the personal identity of Christ with the OLD TESTAMENT Angel or Messenger of the Lord. In John 1:11, he rests on the doctrine of the Angel of the Lord, when he designates the covenant people as the property of Christ, and in John 12:41, he says, without further explanation, that Isaiah saw the glory of Christ, while in the OLD TESTAMENT it is the glory of Jehovah which is spoken of.

–*Condensed from the author's Commentary on the Gospel of John, regarding the Logos, ch. 1.*

REVELATION 11:14-19

The seventh trumpet, the third woe

CHAPTER SUMMARY

11:14. The second woe is past; behold, the third woe comes quickly.

We have now in 11:15-19 the seventh trumpet, the third woe. The trumpet of the seventh angel sounds, and the blessed in heaven triumph, that now the universal dominion of their God and his Christ appears immediately in prospect, ver. 15. The heavenly representatives of the church, the four and twenty elders, give thanks to the Lord, that he now comes in his kingdom to execute judgment on the ungodly world, as also on the dead (raised to life again), and to reward the righteous, ver. 16-18. The catastrophe follows; the confidence of the blessed and of the elders is not put to shame; the strong angel who, in 10:6-7, had declared, that at the sounding of the seventh trumpet the completion of the mystery of God should take place without delay, keeps his word, ver. 19. The conclusion of the vision of the seven trumpets points back to its beginning. In 8:3-4, the prayers of the saints call for the judgment of God on the world; here the saints give thanks that the wrath of the Lord has come. In 8:5 voices, and lightnings, and thunders, and earthquakes, come forth as a symbolical announcement that the world's judgment is approaching; in ver. 19 this symbolical announcement goes into complete fulfilment: amid lightnings, and voices, and thunders, and earthquakes, and great hail, the ungodly world is brought to ruin.

THE SEVENTH TRUMPET,
THE BLESSED TRIUMPH AS CHRIST APPROACHES

11:15. And the seventh trumpet sounded. And there were great voices in heaven, saying, The kingdom of the world has become our Lord's and his anointed's, and he will reign for ever and ever.

The *great voices in heaven* proceed from the great multitude which no man could number, who are called to reign with their Lord and his anointed, as in 5:10 (15:2-4, 14:3.) The *kingdom* is here in the active sense of dominion. He has come to the government, and shall continue to exercise it forever upon the earth. The world's time of supremacy and oppression has come to a final end. The kingdom has *become*, since the trumpet has sounded, the consequence is anticipated, though not attained till verse 19, it is guaranteed by the divine promise, the oath of the angel. This fact here celebrated is founded in the redemption of Christ (comp. 12:10) but now it comes fully into reality.

It is *the Lord's and his anointed's*—the Son's, as in Acts 4:26, and Ps. 2:2. The conflict depicted there has come to an end. *Anointed* is equivalent to *king*, the anointing denotes the gifts of the Holy Spirit upon his servants, as Saul, and David (1 Sam. 10:1, 16:13, 1 Kings 19:16, Ex. 28:41.) Prophets and priests were anointed, but most of all kings, when used absolutely it only denotes *the* king. His future dominion was long foretold (Ps. 22:28, 24:1, Obadiah 21, comp. Zech. 14:9, Dan. 2:44, Dan. 7:13-14, Ps. 2, comp. ver. 18.) This is also connected with the dominion of the saints, as indicated by the *our* Lord. If states are emancipated from the dominion of Christ and grace, there will only be the dominion of judgment.

THE ELDERS GIVE THANKS FOR THE COMING JUDGMENT AND REWARD

16. And the four and twenty elders, who sit on their thrones before God, fell upon their faces and worshipped God, 17. Saying, We give thee thanks, Lord God, the Almighty, who art and wast; because thou hast taken thy great power and dost reign, 18. And the nations were angry, and thy wrath is come, and the time of the dead to be judged, and to give reward to thy servants, the prophets, and the saints, and to those that fear thy name, small and great, and to destroy those who destroy the earth.

In 4:4 the elders assembled before God to adore and praise him, as he prepares himself to judge the world. Here they celebrate the judgment as executed, the final victory over the world, representing those who shall reign upon the earth (5:10.)

17 God is addressed in the unity of his being, the *Almighty* unfolds what is contained in *God*, the *who is and was* explains *Lord*, equal to Jehovah; the same designations are in 1:8, plus the *who comes*. The elders give thanks, because they partake of the power and dominion which God enters on. The *power* is the means by which the kingdom has been won over the ungodly powers. The *taking* forms the contrast to the *leaving alone*. He always possessed the power, but hitherto had not exercised it. To *reign* is to enter on the government. See Ps. 93:1, where the Lord comes in his kingdom against the world's revolt. The *Lord reigns* alludes to the form used at the proclamation of earthly kings, which shows it is not the existing government of the Lord here, but a new revelation of his supremacy (Ps. 96:10, 97:1, 99:1.) The allusion to the Psalms implies, that what the church now has immediately in prospect is the same that had long ago been prophesied; the hopes and expectations of the fathers were now to be gloriously realized. The three first petitions in the Lord's Prayer, as prophecies, receive their complete fulfilment.

18 The overthrow of particular phases of the ungodly power point forward to the final one, when this power itself lies stricken under the judgments of God. The wrath of the heathen, *the nations were angry*, is the time of provocation for the wrath of God. It pervades all history, and then at the end of history it finds its full recompense. It is rooted in the wrath of Satan, they have shed the blood of saints and prophets (12:17, 16:6, 18:24.) The chief phases of the wrath of the heathen are the wrath of Rome, of the ten kings and of Gog and Magog, 20:7-9. That here is the final judgment on the dead previously raised to life again is clear from 20:12-13, in the second death, where, only the bad dead are *judged* according to what is written in the books as records of guilt, according to their works (16:6, 18:24.) The book of life is opened to show they are not written in it. This judgment of condemnation is the product of the wrath of God, as in John 5:24, 29. In John 3:17 to be judged forms the contrast to be saved (1 Pet. 4:6, 1 Cor. 11:31-32.) By *those who corrupt*

18. And the nations were angry, and thy wrath is come, and the time of the dead to be judged, and to give reward to thy servants, the prophets, and the saints, and to those that fear thy name, small and great, and to destroy those who destroy the earth.

the earth, it includes those sinners who are living. The execution of judgment brings redemption along with it. The *reward* of the faithful is that the earth is cleared of its persecutors and oppressors, now the meek possess it (Matt. 5:5, 10:41-42.) Of those who receive reward are two classes–*servants of the Lord* and *those who fear his name,* each with two subdivisions–the first, *prophets and saints;* the second, in reverse order, *the small and the great.* Believers are called God's *servants*, by the *prophets* here are teachers, as witness bearing is called prophesying in 11:3. The *saints* is the common designation of all Christians, those whom God has taken out of the territory of the profane world into the elevated condition of his own people (13:7,10, 14:12, 17:6, 20:9.) *Those that fear the Lord* are the entire multitude of believers. They *fear thy name,* as the name is the product of his doings. The *small,* as prophets beside saints (Matt. 10:42, 18:6,10,14; comp. Luke 9:46.) The extended description meets the misgivings of those who feel too little, weak and wretched, to appropriate any share in the reward. In Ps. 115:10-13, set over against the house of Aaron are *all the rest that fear the Lord* (Ps. 112:1, 22:23.) The reward of the saints is that their persecutors are brought to destruction. Here alludes to Gen. 6:11-13, where the earth is corrupted and full of violence, and so, the Lord declares, *I corrupt (destroy) them with the earth.* They corrupt the earth not mainly by idolatry, but by violence and persecuting the church. As the reward is to the great and the *small,* so the judgment also falls upon all the *destroyers* without distinction, the deceivers and deceived, the ringleaders in mischief, and their instruments.

THE CATASTROPHE FOLLOWS, THE STRONG ANGEL KEEPS HIS WORD

> 19. And the temple of God was opened in heaven, and the ark of his testimony was seen in his temple; and there were lightnings, and voices, and thunderings, and a great hail.

Here the *naos* is the whole *heavenly* temple as consisting of the sanctuary and the most holy place. It is *opened* fully when the veil is removed which separated the sanctuary from the holiest. The ark is called *the ark of testimony,* with the law, and the ark of the covenant, which had the symbol of atonement, the *capporeth,* on which the covenant was founded. It covered the ark with its testimony and spiritually covered the people's sins (Ex. 25:16, 22, 26:33.) When the ark is made visible, the meaning can only be that the covenant receives its most signal accomplishment. The open exhibition of the ark shows the terrors next described as about to burst upon the earth had their foundation in the love of God. God now, remembering his holy covenant, shall give to his people, that being redeemed from their enemies, may fearlessly serve God (Deut. 10:8, 31:9, 25-26; Josh. 3:6, 4:9.) The five number of the *lightning, etc.* is signifying the half, the incomplete, pointing to the supplement it will receive in the later groups. The *earthquake* marks the shattering of the ungodly world power. Ch. 16:18-20 forms a commentary on it. The *hail* is an image of divine judgment having entered upon his enemies (Isa. 30:30, 32:19; Ps. 18:12,13, Ex. 9:24, comp. Ps. 78:47-48, Jos. 10:11.)

SECTION 2

CHAPTERS 12-22

FOUR GROUPS IN DETAIL WHAT IS TO COME TO PASS

GROUP 4

THE THREE ENEMIES OF GOD'S KINGDOM

The dragon, the God-opposing worldly power, seven horns denoting seven phases, with earthly, physical, demoniacal wisdom, and the persecuted believers

REVELATION 12–14

REVELATION 12–14

The three enemies of God's Kingdom

INTRODUCTION

The Revelation of St John gives no regularly progressive disclosure of the future, advancing in unbroken series from beginning to end; but it falls into a number of *groups*, which supplement each other, every successive vision giving some other aspect of the future, but which are still formally complete in themselves, each proceeding from a beginning to an end.

At ch. 12 we have the commencement of a new group, for at the close of ch. 11 we are brought to the last end; so that the Seer, if he will not conclude his book, must commence anew. For it is a description of the last end, regarding the development of the kingdom of God, for 11:15 anticipates what was immediately to follow, *The kingdom of the world has become (the kingdom) of our Lord and his Christ, and he shall reign for ever and ever.* The four and twenty elders, the ideal representatives of the church in heaven, say in prospect of what is presently to be done, *We give thee thanks, Lord God the Almighty, who art and wast, that thou hast taken thy great power and reignest.* The *and art to come,* which before the last end has so deep a meaning, and spoken with strong emphasis, appears now as antiquated, so there is only a past and present in the kingdom of God. The elders say further, in ver. 18, *Thy wrath is come, and the time to judge the dead, and to reward thy servants, the prophets and the saints, and those that fear thy name, the small and the great, and to destroy those who destroy the earth.* Such, surely, have the time of the last judgment, and the consummation of grace immediately in prospect.

What we now, according to 11:15-18, expect—the appearance of the Lord, the final victory of God's kingdom, the resurrection of the dead, the last judgment, the glorification of the church—all this is represented in ver. 19 as *having entered*, but only by way of *gentle* indication, which few have understood. For, the Seer would reserve the more particular delineation of these last things for a *later* part of his book, and precisely by the enigmatical brevity with which he here treats them, would set expectation on the stretch regarding that more particular delineation in reserve. *And the temple of God* (it is said) *was opened in heaven, and the ark of his Testament was seen in his temple; and there were lightnings, and voices, and thunderings, and an earthquake, and a great hail.* The temple in heaven is a symbol of the church, the ark of the covenant a symbol of the gracious relationship in which the Lord stands to his church; that it has become visible, imports that this relation is now in a glorious manner maintained, and becomes manifest to view. All that the Lord does toward the realization of this, and in suspending judgment over the church's enemies, is here concealed under the lightnings, and voices, and thunderings, and earthquake, and great hail—exactly as in 8:1 by *the silence,* where the closing scene appears under the same kind of veil. So the end of the vision reverts to the beginning, as a certain proof that we have here a termination before us. What is said in 8:5, *And the angel took the censer and filled it with fire from off the altar, and threw it upon the earth; and there were voices, and thunderings, and lightnings, and an earthquake,* is a prophecy, which we here see brought to fulfilment.

But if we must be still within the compass of the seventh seal at the end of ch 11, it is very strange that no reference whatever is made to what goes before 8:1; the seven trumpets have entirely the appearance of an independent position, and never make any allusion to the seals. The silence in 8:1 belongs to the seventh seal. The seven trumpets are not to be drawn into the circle of the seven seals. The description belonging to the other seals in proportion to this, would then embrace the contents of four entire chapters; while, the events of most of the other seals are declared in simple delineations. If the trumpets were subordinated to the seals, and contained the issues of the seventh seal, there would have been no need for a new preface or an introductory vision, as the vision of the sacrificing angel, 8:3-6, is a sort of prelude, heralding the new scenes, that were soon to present themselves to John. If we have a new beginning at 8:2, the Revelation cannot be a regularly progressive and continuous whole, a view that has been most pernicious to the right exposition of the book. At chap. 12 we are entirely cut off from the earlier series of representations, so we would have to construct groundless hypotheses, to build a bridge out of our own materials. Attempting to bring the whole of what follows even to the end of the book within the compass of the last trumpet and of the last woe, is unavailing because after ch. 11 no word is said about a trumpet or a woe; the first six trumpets and the two first woes have so limited a range; and the immediately following portion, ch. 12–14, has not at all the character of a trumpet and a woe. As certainly as at the end of ch. 11 we stand at the final close of things, so certainly do we find ourselves at the beginning of ch. 12 thrown back to the commencement of the NEW TESTAMENT economy; so that it is vain to speak of a continuous representation.

The sufferings of the Lord's people first pass before the soul of the prophet, which were endured before the birth of Messiah; then follows the birth itself, then the ascension, and the description, how through the accomplished atonement of Christ the power of Satan has been broken. And though we should consider all this as an introduction, which is its real character, as shall presently be made to appear, yet it does not conduct us over the very first beginnings of the Christian church. The starting-point in that case is the present of the Seer, the time of the Roman persecution, and the tendency of the section appears to be, to direct those, who had to suffer under the persecution, to the grace of God, which was to preserve the church through all the coming troubles, ver. 6, 14, and at last bring the persecution to an end by the overthrow of the persecuting power.

Having thus determined the relation of this section to the preceding context, we shall farther endeavour to fix its relation to what follows. A new scene opens to us with the beginning of ch. 15. The section of ch. 12–14, or the fourth group, is occupied by the three enemies of God's kingdom; the capital enemy Satan, who, as such, to indicate his great power, appears in heaven, 12:1-17—the beast, who arises out of the sea, the symbol of multitudes of people, the ungodly world power, 13:1-10—and the second beast out of the earth, the earthly, sensual, demoniacal wisdom, 13:11-18. The fourteenth chapter consoles the faithful, who are to be tried and oppressed by these enemies, by pointing to the blessedness in heaven, which awaits them, ver. 1–5, and to the judgment, which is to be executed on the enemies at the close of all. But the representation given of this judgment is of a very general kind; the detailed account of the divine judgment on the three enemies is reserved for a separate group, the sixth, ch. 17–20, which in a reverse order ascends from the beasts to Satan, and for which the fifth group, the vision of the vials in ch. 15–16, forms a sort of prelude.

According to the historical starting-point of the Revelation, as it is unfolded in 1:9, which declares the book to have been written by John during the Roman persecution; and according to its designs as announced in ver. 1, to show to the servants of Christ, what must shortly come to pass; farther, according to ver. 19, *Write what thou hast seen, and what is, and what shall be done hereafter,* and according to 4:1, *Come up here, I will shew thee, what shall be done after these things,* which show that the point as such cannot be the proper object of the things here unfolded, we must regard what is said in 12:1-5, 7-12, only as introductory. What Christ has accomplished in the past comes here into consideration only in so far as it formed the basis of confidence and blessing to his oppressed people in their present troubles–comp. ver. 11, where this aim comes plainly out; where it is announced that the glorious victory of Christ, described in the preceding context, is only to be taken into account so far as it is the foundation of victory to Christ's people in the hard conflict which they have to maintain with the dragon. Verse 6 and vers. 13-15 have respect to the present and the immediate future; vers. 16-17, to the more remote future. In this whole representation there are such unmistakeable allusions to the history of the child Jesus and his mother, and the tyranny of Herod, in Matthew 2, that this chapter receives from it a new confirmation.

REVELATION 12

First enemy: the dragon, a portrait of Satan

THE CAPITAL ENEMY SATAN INDICATES HIS POWER, APPEARS IN HEAVEN

12:1. And there appeared a great sign in heaven: a woman clothed with the sun, and the moon under her feet and on her head a crown of twelve stars, 2. And she was with child and cried, and was in travailing pangs, and in great pain to be delivered. 3. And there appeared another wonder in heaven and behold! a great red dragon, that had seven heads and ten horns and upon its head seven crowns,

John always saw things in signs and enigma; the church under the image of *a woman*, Satan under that of *a dragon*. So *sign* is used also in 15:1. Those who keep standing at the outward appearance, not penetrating into the idea concealed behind it, are apt to accuse others of a false spiritualism. The word *sign* is used otherwise in Matt. 24:30, where the *sign of the Son of Man* is his appearance, comforting in his nature, yet unspeakably frightful, as a prophecy in action of judgment and salvation—comp. the connected declaration, *And then shall all the tribes of the earth mourn.* The sign (*a great sign,* in 15:1: *a sign great and wonderful,*) appears in heaven. The object of the religion is in heaven, and the subject of this vision, the church of the NEW TESTAMENT, has its place with Christ in heaven. Her pregnancy and the birth is heavenly; in heaven she is assaulted and defended, vers. 4-7. The heaven is here the theatre, where every thing passed before the eye of the prophet. To be in the Spirit and to be in heaven is the same; comp. Ezek. 1:1, *The heavens were opened, and I saw visions of God;* here 4:1-2, where, as the realization of the call, *Come up hither (into heaven,) I will shew thee what shall be after these things,* it is stated, *And immediately I was in the Spirit;* then, ch. 8:1.

The *woman*, or Zion, is the one indivisible community of the Old and New Covenant, the Israel perpetuated in the Christian church, out of which the false seed has been cast by its unbelief in the now manifested Angel of the Covenant, while the believing heathen have been received into it—comp. ch. 7:4. That the church here was seen in the type of the virgin Mary, is rendered probable by ver. 4. The *sun* is that of the visible heavens, and signifies the glory of the Lord, and as such is it here in view. In Isa. 60:1, this already appears under the image of a great light, *Arise, shine, for thy light is come, and the glory of the Lord is risen upon thee.* Of Christ it is said, in Matt. 17:2, *And he was changed before them, and his countenance shone like the sun, and his raiment was white like the light.* In this book, 1:16, *his countenance was as the sun shineth in his strength.* And of the New Jerusalem, the church in its state of exaltation, it is said, in 21:23, *And the city needs not the sun nor the moon to give light to it, for the glory of the Lord illuminates it, and the Lamb is the light of it.* To be shone upon by the glory of the Lord, belongs to the nature of the church; but in the present, as with Christ in his state of humiliation, it is a veiled one.

The *crown of twelve stars* denotes the twelve Israelitish patriarchs– not the apostles, for the woman has this crown *before* the birth of her Son. They are ideal representations of the tribes, which continue in the church of the New Covenant; comp. Eze. 47:22-23, where the stranger is to be equal with the Israelite. Their names are on the gates of Jerusalem in 21:12. Elsewhere the *twenty four elders* correspond to the stars, the number indicates the adding of the apostles.

2 The prophets showed the troubles preceding the appearance of Christ under the image of severe pains falling upon Zion, the church of God (Mic. 4:9-10, Jer. 4:31, 30:6, 49:24, Isa. 26:17, Hos. 13:13.) Sorrows call out anxious longing and prayers for the kingdom of God. The suffering must culminate before the first and the second coming of the Lord–as with the great tribulation (Matt. 24:21.) In our day the beginning of troubles has already entered, the divine wrath is lowering. Jer. 31:15 shows Zion under the tyranny of the Romans and Herod. Zion's cry is described in the song of Zacharias (Luke 1:68) where the need for redemption hails the redeemer.

3 The two first groups, the seals and the trumpets have a general and introductory character. In the first eight chapters is no description of Satan. Now he is introduced as the chief enemy of the kingdom of God and Christ. The *dragon* is the sovereign of the marine animals (Ps. 74:13-14.) In the spiritual sea of the world he is the conquering and reigning power, having earthly princes as his instruments (Isa 27:1, Jer. 51:34, Eze. 29:3-4.) He is *red*, as the murderer of men from the beginning, author of all plundering ambition and bloodshed, and fury against the church (John 8:44, comp. 1 John 3:12.) The *seven heads* and the *ten horns* of the dragon denote the seven phases of the hostile world-power—the seventh head divided into ten horns. Satan bears this image as a reflection of his visible representative upon earth. The OLD TESTAMENT commits the earthly world-power, the dragon, to Satan, as its moving principle.

CHRIST'S CHILDHOOD

> 4. And his tail draws the third part of the stars, and throws them upon the ground. And the dragon stood before the woman that was ready to be delivered in order to devour the child as soon as she had brought forth,

Stars are rulers; their being *cast down* is their being conquered and overthrown (ORIGINAL PASSAGE–Dan. 8:10.) His *throwing* the stars on *the earth* shows the dragon's destroying agency in former times as the animating principle of the conquering world kingdoms. The *third part* denotes a great multitude. The dragon seeks to *devour the child*, as with Moses, and the innocents of Bethlehem, in order to destroy the one hated child. The wicked one is always at hand to strangle the nascent life (Ex. 1:16, 2:2. Matt. 2:1-12.)

CHRIST'S ASCENSION

> 5. And she brought forth a son, a male, who was to tend all the nations with a rod of iron. And her child was snatched up to God and his throne. 6. And the woman fled away into the wilderness, where she has a place prepared of God, that they

CHAPTER 12 THE REVELATION

might there nourish her for a thousand, two hundred and sixty days.

5. And she brought forth a son, a male, who was to tend all the nations with a rod of iron. And her child was snatched up to God and his throne.

The allusion here is to *Zion* in Isa. 66:7, the *man-child* is not a single person, but denotes manly vigorous fresh growth in God's people. By that manly son Christ that other ideal manly son could be produced.

Ruling the nations with a rod, accomplished at 19:15, is a threat to the heathen. This alludes to Ps. 2:9, where he will *bruise* the heathen, the LXX has *tending*. The office of the anointed is to tend, Ps. 78:71-72, unless refractoriness to Christ demands a bruising.

In ver. 4 the dragon stood ready to devour before the birth, which continues after he continued his persecution for a season to before the child was caught up, from the temptation to the cross. The *snatched up* denotes the ascension of Christ (comp. 11:12,) from oppression and judgment was he taken away, to the heavenly throne of God, symbol of his dominion over heaven and earth (FUNDAMENTAL PASSAGE-Isa. 53:8, parallel 5:6–*a lamb standing*: Luke 24:21.) His reign is presently a concealed one. What seemed to cast off hope here is the means to its accomplishment.

6. And the woman fled away into the wilderness, where she has a place prepared of God, that they might there nourish her for a thousand, two hundred and sixty days.

6 No particular *wilderness* is meant, only a contrast to cultivated land. It means the preservation of the church under the cross, in spite of persecutions and privations. It is a spiritual sojourn and leading through the wilderness (Hos. 2:14; Ezek. 20:34-38; Jer. 31:1-2. Deut. 8:2-5.) Its characteristic feature is the temptation, where the thoughts of many hearts are revealed. The *nourishment* is spiritual, the flesh fares ill. The ideal mother of Jesus, the church in its flight, was typified by the *flight* of Mary there. The *thousand, two hundred and sixty days* are the three and a half years, which in Daniel and here signify the apparent victory of the world over the church. it has no historic meaning, but as related to the number seven, it is mercifully a broken short period appointed for afflictions.

CHRIST'S ATONEMENT

7. And there was a war in heaven: Michael and his angels fought with the dragon, and the dragon fought and his angels, 8. And he overcame not, and his place was no more found in heaven, 9. And he was thrown, the great dragon, the old serpent, who is called the devil, and Satan, who deceives the whole world; he was thrown on the earth, and his angels were thrown with him.

Michael is no other than Christ, the Word, who in the beginning was with God, and from the first has mediated in all transactions respecting the church on earth. His name means *who is like God,* in him is God's glory represented (Ex. 15:11, Ps 89:6.) The derisive imitation of his name in 13:4, *Who is like the beast?* implies this name denotes an incomparable greatness and power. The being like God is affirmed of God in John 5:18 and Phil. 2:6. In Daniel he is the angel of the Lord or Logos, whose description in Dan. 10:5-6 is transferred to Christ in Rev. 1:13-15, and 10:1. Daniel falls down before him, as does John, in terror. The conquering of Satan here by Michael is attributed in the gospels to Christ. A created angel would be taking the glory from Christ, if Michael was not Christ. In Jude he says to the devil, *The Lord rebuke thee,* as the captain of the Lord's hosts–he is called *Michael* here, not Christ, because the victory over Satan belongs to Christ after his divine nature not his human–comp. 1 John 3:8. His name bridges the Old and New Testaments as the great Prince who fights for the church in Dan 12:1–the prelude and prophecy of this one here. There was a war, where Michael makes the onset, the dragon then fights back. Michael and Satan are the proper factors of history, all others are subordinate agents and instruments.

The controversy between Satan and the Angel of the Lord, that is Michael, in Zech. 3:1 shows us the nature of the battle-the sinfulness of the people. Satan demands they be given up to him farther, but the ground of this is taken away by imparting the forgiveness of sins, declaring a richer participation and deeper confounding of Satan would take place under the Messiah. There the angel is on the defensive, here he is on the offensive. As soon as Christ became Christ Satan fights against him and the beginning work of redemption. He tempts Christ in the wilderness, then withdraws, appearing in fearful violence when Jesus suffered. Satan has nothing in Christ (John 14:30-31), as Christ is without sin, and Satan's territory only extends as far as sin does. He had acquired over sinful men a right in consequence of the fall, but with the conflict with Christ had lost it, and received judgment as a murderer and robber (John 12:31-32, John 16:11.) The obedience of Christ to the cross ends in the final overthrow, after the ascension of Christ and his return from the Father.

8-9 Because Satan did not overcome he was *no more found in heaven*. His power is broken by the blood of Christ, because forgiveness of sin is obtained. All that is powerful is transferred to heaven. This refers to Isa. 14:12, the King of Babylon the visible image of the dragon here. As in Dan. 8:10, where mighty kings appear as stars, so their fall from power is denoted by the casting on the earth. Eph. 6:12 talks of wicked spirits, with much power and dreadful cunning. The *he was thrown* precedes the *he was thrown upon the earth*, in a complete unrecoverable overthrow, the being *on the earth* did not mean more power, merely his rage was increased (comp. ver. 12-13, 12:12-13, 1 Pet. 5:8, John 12:31, 1 John 3:8, Luke 10:18, Luke 11:21-22.)

The enemy appears here under four names. The *great dragon* is at the head before the *old serpent*, because he comes as the prince of this world, the animating principle of the ungodly world power, shown in the OLD TESTAMENT as the dragon. The persecution by the world power forms the starting point. He is called the *old serpent* because of what he did so craftily at the beginning, murder (Gen. 3:1-5, John 8:44, also he sins, 1 John 3:8, he deceives, 2 Cor. 11:3.) The *who is called* transitions us from the matter-of-fact to the proper names, being the *devil*, the calumniator and accuser of the faithful, and *Satan*, the adversary, who leads astray the whole world and stirs them up against the kingdom of God (20:3, 8, 10.) As for the *angels with him*, their prior state and operations is not made known.

CHAPTER 12 THE REVELATION

THE CHURCH TRIUMPHANT, PERFECT IN HEAVEN, REJOICES IN SALVATION

> 10. And I heard a great voice in heaven which said: Now is come the salvation, and the power, and the kingdom of our God, and the power of his Christ; because the accuser of our brethren is cast out, who accuses them day and night before God, 11. And they have overcome him by the blood of the Lamb and by the word of their testimony, and have not loved their lives to the death, 12. Therefore, rejoice ye heavens, and those who dwell therein! Woe to the earth and the sea, for the devil is come down to you, and has a great wrath, because he knows that he has a short time.

10 The *great voice* is their brethren, 19:10. The saints in heaven are those who rejoice thus over them, (comp. on 11:15.) The *now is come*, that is, in this is contained the germ and the pledge of all that follows. The *salvation*, by which the saints were delivered, the *power*, by which the enemy was overthrown, the *kingdom*, which displays God's majesty.

11 They have *overcome him* as they are now able to do so (parallel is 1 John 2:13-14.) The victory is certain because of *the blood of the Lamb*, and *the word of their testimony*—comp. Matt. 10:32-33, *Whosoever confesses me before men*, etc. The *witness-bearing*, derives from the consciousness of pardon obtained through the blood (comp. 1:5, 5:9, 1 John 1:7,9, 2:2.) They *dwell therein* spiritually with God in his sanctuary, appearing here and in 13:6 as tabernacling or dwelling in a tent (2 Pet. 1:13-14.)

12 *Therefore* the church triumphant in heaven *rejoices*, because of the salvation, which is obtained by the church militant on earth, as they express their joy in vers. 10-11. The context was that which the church had obtained through the overthrow of Satan—the church on earth also have their citizenship in heaven (Phil. 3:20, Eph. 2:6, Heb. 12:22-23.) Those who dwell in heaven and on earth, are those affected by the blasphemies of the beast, and calumniated by him as evildoers (1 Pet. 2:12, 3:16, 4:14.) Those in heaven enjoy peace, the earthly are still exposed to the assaults of Satan, sorrow and tribulation, yet kept in trial and prepared for glory (1 Pet. 1:7.) The *sea* here is figurative, denoting the sea of the peoples, the restless world (7:3, 8:8, 12:12, 13:1, 16:3, 21:1.)

A PAINFUL SOJOURN WITH A BOUND SET TO IT

> 13. And when the dragon saw that he was thrown upon the earth he persecuted the woman who had brought forth the male (child.) 14. And to the woman were given the two wings of the great eagle, that she might fly into the wilderness to her place where she is nourished a time, and times, and half a time from the face of the serpent.

He *persecuted the woman* because she had given birth to the son, his conqueror, now beyond his reach. Hatred of Christ is in Satan and his instruments the foundation of their hatred of Christians.

14 Verse 14 corresponds to the sixth, where what was said there is here resumed again after her situation was described, with the addition of the *eagle's wings* and the replacement of the *time, two times and half a time*. The wings occur in Ex. 19:4 and Deut. 32:11 as the means whereby they are brought into the wilderness to God. In Eze. 17:3 the kings of Babylon and Egypt appear as a great eagle. The Lord is the true great eagle. The *wilderness* here is a place of security. The *where she is nourished* implies a state of privation, where God must provide in a supernatural way.

By the *times* it is *two* times, as a definite number is demanded, of which the two is logical, the *times* stand between the *one time* and *the half time*. While the sojourn quickens and purifies, and is accompanied with something painful, it is consoling to know it has a bound set to it, the three and a half in relation to the seven suggests a small period of time (Dan. 7:25,) which corresponds to ver. 12, *he knows he has a short time*. In Daniel 7:24-27 this particular time is the period when the little horn was to temporarily obtain the victory over the saints, yet finally ending well for them. Through this prophecy, which refers to the last great conflict and victory of the kingdom of God, the three and a-half signifies the temporary subjection of the Lord's people running out into victory. The little horn will effect a total revolution in changing times and laws–comp. Dan. 2:21, where the *he changes times* is used of God. The saints will be given *into his hand for a time, and two times, and an half time*. But then shall be a reversal, where the saints will have dominion forever.

She has her nourishment so long in *the face of the serpent*, he cannot come at her with persecution.

THE HOSTILE OVERFLOWING OF THE CHURCH

15. And the serpent cast out of his mouth water as a flood after the woman that he might drown her, 16. But the earth helped the woman and opened its mouth, and swallowed up the flood, which the dragon cast out of his mouth. 17. And the dragon was wroth with the woman and went to make war with the rest of her seed, who keep the commandments of God and have the testimony of Jesus (Christ.)

The *water* in 17:15 is an image of the peoples. Under the figure of an overflowing the idea of an overwhelming is represented, as in regard to the Chaldean invasion, *Behold waters come out of the mouth, and become an overflowing flood* (Ps. 124:4-5, Jer. 47:2, Ps. 18:16; Isa. 8:8; Jer. 46:7-8.) Verse 16 shows this is the hostile overflowing of the church, the commencement of which gave rise to this book—the Roman persecution (to which refers 1 Pet. 5:8.) The *serpent* is named here, in regard to its cunning, the poor world has been deceived by it, unaware it is driven on by Satan, and conceives it acts independently in the persecution of the church, advancing its own interest, while it is only working for its own destruction (Gen. 3:1.)

16 The matter reversed as *the earth helped the woman*. Another earthly power rose up against those who persecuted the church, bringing their persecutions to an end, as the Medes and Persians brought an end to Babylon. In chapter 17 Rome was to be destroyed by the ten kings, which were themselves *of the earth*, and gave their power to the beast (17:17.)

17 The *rest of her seed* are those who survived the hostile overflowing or were not affected by it. The ten kings give their might to the beast and later battle against Christ. Believers serve God in a new and willing spirit, and this is called *keeping the commandments of God*. God is indulgent in regard to the conduct of his children on earth, which is often so faulty in an obedience to his commands.

REVELATION 13:1-10

The second enemy: the beast from the sea, the God-opposing worldly power with seven horns—its seven phases

CHAPTER SUMMARY

St. John, in the second and third groups, gave a general representation of the divine judgments to come on the ungodly world. He would now go more particularly into the victory of Christ and the overthrow of the world.

The preceding chapter had spoken of the persecution of the church by the dragon. Here, we learn, how he carries on the work, not by assuming a personal bodily form, but by preparing for himself a powerful instrument on earth—by rendering the heathen and especially the Roman power, serviceable to his designs, and in it taking, as it were, flesh and blood.

The three enemies of God's kingdom, to which the whole group refers, are not co-ordinate with each other; but the second is the vassal and instrument of the first (13:2,) and the third is the abettor of the second (13:12.) The immediate enemy of the saints is the second, but this has an invisible head, making the conflict with him so severe and dangerous—and a *visible* auxiliary. The church should faint before these enemies, but the Lord said: *Be of good cheer, I have overcome the world, and the prince of it*. This word forms the theme, which is enlarged upon in the following visions.

The arrangement of the section before us is the following. We are first presented in 13:1-2, with a full delineation of the enemy, in which his past, present, and future history, are brought together, as with the first enemy. Respect is also had to the past, to set the present in its true light—comp. on 12:2. The prophet sees a beast with seven heads and ten horns rise out of the sea, to which the dragon gives his strength, and his throne, and great power. This represents the God-opposing power of this world in its seven phases—the seven being again subdivided. This is clear from the diadems, insignia of dominion on the horns; and the names of blasphemy on its heads. The several heads denote the phases of this power, made evident in the FUNDAMENTAL PROPHECY of Daniel (ch. 7,) where the plurality of world-powers is exhibited by a succession of different beasts. Here only one beast appears, combining the properties of all the beasts in Daniel. The seven heads denote the particular manifestations of the worldly power in its hostility to God, from Pharaoh down to Rome, the ungodly power in the time of the prophet, and even to the new heathen power, which, according to his later announcements, is yet to tread in its footsteps.

The second part of the section, ver. 3-8, concerns the state and action of the enemy in John's time. One of the heads of the beast, is, as it were wounded to death. The ungodly Roman power having, along with the power of the world in general, had received a deadly stroke through Christ–*I have overcome the world.* But the deadly wound was again healed: the heathen state comes anew, at least apparently and for the time, to the possession of power, as John had found, banished by the Roman antichrist to Patmos. The whole earth follows, as if nothing had happened, in wondering admiration the beast, that appeared to possess unbroken power, and is allowed to blaspheme and persecute, ver. 5; the former is represented at greater length in ver. 6, and the latter in ver. 7. So the earth falls into two parties—the majority of the worshippers of the beast, and the small flock of the Lamb, ver. 8.

An admonitory conclusion, in ver. 9-10, points the eye of the church, under these threatening and perilous circumstances, to the divine recompense, and charges her to wait for it in faith and patience.

A FULL DELINEATION OF THE ENEMY

> 13:1. And I was placed upon the sand of the sea, and saw a beast rise up out of the sea, having ten horns and seven heads, and upon his horns ten crowns, and upon his heads the name of blasphemy. 2. And the beast which I saw, was like a panther, and his feet as the feet of a bear, and his mouth as the mouth of a lion. And the dragon gave him his power, and his throne, and great authority.

This is not a continuation of ch. 12, but a new scene, showing by what medium Satan accomplishes what had been described in ch. 12. The *I* that *was placed,* is John, not the dragon. This is confirmed by the FUNDAMENTAL PASSAGES, Dan. 8:2 and 10:4. John was *set* there in the spirit beside the sea, as in 17:3 and 4:1. The sea now exhibited a remarkable spectacle. The *sand* is not the seashore, but a great multitude on whose condition and destiny the beast, that was going to arise out of the sea, should exert an influence (20:8, Rom. 9:27, Heb. 11:12, Gen. 22:17, Isa. 48:19, Job. 6:3.) The *sea* designates the sea of peoples, the restless world, the agitated state of human affairs (comp. 6:14, 7:1,3, 8:8, 10:2, 16:3, 20:13, 21:1, FUNDAMENTAL PASSAGE-Daniel 7:2.) *And behold the four winds of heaven strove on the great sea,* shows it as multitudinous and restless. The mountains, or conquered kingdoms are in the heart of the sea (Mk. 11:23.) The masses of people are kept in constant motion by their pride and ambition; comp. Isa. 57:20, *the wicked are like a troubled sea, that cannot rest* (Ps. 93:3-4, Ps. 46:3-4, Isa. 57:20.)

Beast is not simply the attribute of wildness, as the false prophet appears gentle, but rather consists in the want of the divine image, the properly and distinctively human, the want of the living breath of God–Gen. 1:26-27, the ascendancy of the flesh, carnality and corruption, it behaves in a bestial manner. In Daniel, worldly, godless, irreligious kingdoms are represented under the image of a beast. In 7:17 four kings arise *out of the earth*–the earthly origin agrees with the bestial. In 7:4 the first beast was taken from off the earth. A mind directed toward the earth is characteristic of a beast. Nebuchadnezzar was reduced to a beast in intellect and appearance, see 4:13-14, 34, where it characterizes man to lift adoring eyes to heaven in praise, but in contrast a beast is senseless and indifferent or hateful toward the divine.

This beast is a compound of the several in Daniel, as showing that power in its entireness. The seven heads are seven ungodly kingdoms which follow one another in succession (17:9-10.) The beast that bears these heads indicates the ungodly power in general. It *carries* the great whore Babylon (17:3, 7;)

CHAPTER 13:1-10   THE REVELATION

1. And I was placed upon the sand of the sea, and saw a beast rise up out of the sea, having ten horns and seven heads, and upon his horns ten crowns, and upon his heads the name of blasphemy.

Rome is only the possessor for the time of the ungodly power of the world, and not the beast itself, but a particular head of it, which five others precede, and one follows. In 11:7 it arises out of the abyss to make war, overcome and kill. It could not arise out of the abyss without, at the same time, arise out of the sea, nor vice versa.

The *abyss* is hell, the seat of Satan, the original source of all evil on earth, all that erects itself in opposition to God and his kingdom. From there the beast proceeds, though more immediately out of the sea. The dragon that gives him his power, his throne, his great authority, is the moving agent in his ascending from the sea. The beast, which immediately arises out of the sea, more remotely out of hell, comes down also from heaven, as the *angel of the abyss* (9:11,) and at the same time, as the *star from heaven* (9:1.) Nothing comes from the abyss and the sea without at the same time comes from heaven, comp. *It was given to him* in ver. 5, 7.

Because John sees the beast come up, he consequently sees the horns first, before the head, so the best reading, as in the second clause also, is *the beast has ten horns and seven heads*. 17:9 gives the meaning of the heads, the mountains symbolize kingdoms, seven kings or kingdoms, or seven phases of the ungodly power of the world.

Daniel in chapter 7 shows the phases of the world-power, from his own times, by the *number* of beasts in the vision, while John, however, saw the whole ungodly power under the image of one beast, while he represents its *phases* under the image of the heads of this beast. Yet there is some plurality of heads in Daniel, in chapter 7:6, where the four phases of the third monarchy are symbolized by the four heads of the third beast. In ver. 3 he sees four great beasts arise simultaneously out of the sea. The succession is indicated by local position, rather than sequence of time. The beast Daniel sees immediately before him is the Chaldean of his day. He sees it all from its commencement so that he could view the parts in relation to the whole. There the beast rising out of the sea has the seven heads one after another in a historical manifestation of the beast, but in the symbolical representation here set before us the heads exist together, otherwise John could not see the horns which belong to the last head on his first rising up. The beast has but one active head at any particular time, the others have only a historical or a prophetical import. According to 13:3 one of the beast's heads is wounded and healed, but in ver. 12 and 14 the wound and healing belong to the beast itself, so the beast has no existence separate from its heads.

Four of the seven heads are clear from Daniel: the *Chaldean, Medo-Persian, Grecian* and *Roman* kingdoms. Another head, the seventh with ten horns, or kingdoms, was to arise, according to Daniel, out of the fourth monarchy. These five then were to extend till the end of the ungodly heathen power of the world. At the time of the *sixth* head this prophecy was given, which according to 17:10 is the Roman. The first two heads must then be before the Chaldean, being *Egypt* and *Assyria*, which frequently in the OLD TESTAMENT oppressed the kingdom of God. Zechariah, who lived under the Persians, saw four horns (1:18-21) denoting four oppressors, Egypt, Assyria, Babylon and Persia (comp. Isa. 52:4-5, coupled together in Isa. 10:24-26, 11:11-16, 19:23, 27:13, Hos. 9:3, 11:11, Jer. 2:18,36, Zech. 10:10-11, Isa. 27:13.)

Horns denote power (5:6,) so the ten horns are ten powers, Daniel 7:7-8, 17:12, which shows they are ten kings or kingdoms. They are on the seventh head, showing it will be a divided ungodly world power. The ten horns in Dan. 7:7-24 correspond entirely with John, denoting kingdoms which spring out from the Roman empire. The only difference is *the little horn*. If the ten horns are kingdoms, not persons, then this horn is also a power not an individual. The beast comes to an end with the overthrow of the ten kings by Christ, but the little horn re-appears after under another form at the close, as *Gog and Magog*. Daniel makes no mention of Christ's victory over the ten horns, and their conversion to Christianity, nor the thousand years reign. A thousand years would intervene between the last enemy but one, so it was appropriate to let the ten horned beast perish, and give the last ungodly power a separate name and independent position.

Here on his horns were ten *diadems*–the insignia of royal dignity, and on his heads *names of blasphemy*. What was on the horns was described first as these first became visible as the beast rose. The horns only belong to the seventh head. 12:3 shows that the heads bore diadems as well as the horns. They belong to Satan as a reflection of his agent the beast. Against this Christ bears many diadems in 19:12. The *names of blasphemy* refer to the assumed supremacy over the world, and consequently involve the diadems, and vice versa. For the horns do not hold dominion under God, they belong to the beast whose nature is godlessness, rebellion, presumption and blasphemy–in 17:3 the whole beast with its heads and horns is full of the names of blasphemy. The diadems define the sphere of the blasphemy in that it consists in the assumption of independent sovereignty. The *name of blasphemy* is the name which belongs to Christ alone: *King of kings and Lord of lords*, this is usurped by the beast (19:12,16,) who vaunts himself as the independent lord of the world. Every name is a name of blasphemy by which the creature makes an inroad into the territory of God. It reaches its fulfilment when the person comes into a conscious relation to God, opposes his *I am the Lord* with an impious, *I am the Lord.* Such was Pharaoh, who had long called himself *Lord*, but it became blasphemy when he said, *Who is the Lord that I should hearken to his voice?* (Ex. 5:2.) Again with Rome, the blasphemy never reached its consummation till his assumption of the title was directed against Christ. The blasphemy presupposes God has a name and has manifested himself.

2 The *beast* here is compounded of the different beasts in Daniel 7, which has respect to Jer. 5:6, but the wolf is a *bear*. Here is the ungodly power of the world as a *whole*, while Daniel presents its *different phases*. As in Jeremiah, the beasts are used to present a composite animal. Only the three first beasts of Daniel have a definite form, and are also in the beast here, as the last beast is non-descript. Nothing depends on the order of the beasts, as here they are reversed from Daniel, they equally belong to Egypt, Babylon, Rome. It merely portrays the nature of the ungodly world power. Unlike Daniel, John does not begin with Babylon, but with Egypt, to use all three beasts to represent a blood-thirsty disposition.

2. And the beast which I saw, was like a panther, and his feet as the feet of a bear, and his mouth as the mouth of a lion. And the dragon gave him his power, and his throne, and great authority.

The *panther* (leopard) shows terrible and savage energy (Hab. 1:8; Hos. 13:7; Isa. 11:6, Jer. 13:23.) In its main bulk, bar the head and feet, the beast resembles a panther. In Hebrew it is *dark-spotted* in body–an emblem of spiritual staining (Jer. 13:23.) The bear *devours much flesh* (Dan. 7:5.) It has the feet of the *bear, and stood upon one side;* to assault with his fore-paws; while the *lion* uses his mouth. To the beast formed after this manner *the dragon* gives his power, throne, and authority.

2.... And the dragon gave him his power, and his throne, and great authority.

The *dragon* is Satan *as the prince of this world*. His throne is his dominion upon earth exercised by means of the throne of the beast (16:10.) The *power* is the natural power, of retainers and earthly resources; the *throne* is worldly supremacy; and the *authority* is its assumed right to command whatever it might please. In John's gospel Satan is the *prince of this world*, here he is the *dragon*. What Satan here gives to the beast, he there promises to Christ (Matt. 4:8-9.) In Luke 4:6, Satan declares that the power and glory *is delivered to him*, which belies an independent principle of evil; his power and authority is derived—it comes from hell, yet descends from heaven, is subject to divine direction, and not merely divine permission. He is but a servant of God. Even its abuse also is of God, when turned to lawless conquest or to the cruel persecution of the church in a chastisement for her sins, to perfect her through the cross in sufferings, in preparation for her destiny.

THE STATE AND ACTION OF THE ENEMY IN JOHN'S TIME

3. And (I saw) one of his heads as killed to death, and the stroke of his death was healed. And the whole earth wondered after the beast, 4. And worshipped the dragon, because he gave the power to the beast, and worshipped the beast: Who is like the beast! and who can make war with him! 5. And a mouth was given him, which spoke great things and blasphemies, and power was given him to do forty and two months. 6. And he opened his mouth in blasphemy against God, to blaspheme his name, and his tabernacle, and those that dwell in heaven. 7. And it was given him to make war and to overcome them. And power was given him over every tribe and people, and tongue and nation. 8. And all that dwell upon the earth shall worship him, whose name is not written in the book of life of the Lamb that was slain, from the foundation of the world.

St. John saw *the head* as *wounded to death*, with the scar of a mortal wound, going round the throat, indicating the head had been cut off. The *as* here corresponds to 5:6, *a lamb as it had been slain*. It signifies *killed*, always a violent death (comp. 1 John 3:12; Rev 5:9, 6:4,9, 18:24, 13:8.) Later it would rise out of the abyss where it by death had been sent (17:11.) As the lamb had been slain so had this beast.

The head that John saw is that which the beast bore in the time of Christ and John, the sixth, or the Roman empire, as the deadly stroke was inflicted on the beast through the atonement of Christ. Whatever brings destruction to the dragon, or Satan, in his relation to the world, and his dominion, must also inflict on the beast a deadly wound. The epochs of the beast correspond with those of the dragon. In ch. 12 Satan as possessor of the world's power, received a severe blow though Christ and his atonement. In ver. 9 the great dragon stands first before the old serpent, because Satan here is the prince of this world, the animating principle of the world power, represented under the symbol of the dragon. What the prince of this world experienced fell upon his instrument. Whatever destroys the dragon's power must also be fatal to the beast. The wound comes from Christ, after the beast was healed he magnifies himself in violence and blasphemy in revenge upon Christ and his church. In former times the overthrow of one head was succeeded by the rise of another, here the victory of Christ was the one event by which the whole beast was smitten in one head; the beast then must have existed at the time of Christ's death, this serves to refute those who understand by the beast a power of a later period–the Papacy.

The healing of the beast must have been hard on John, whom Christ had assured he had conquered the world and cast out its prince, Antipas had been killed, John was in banishment. The *wondering* of the earth comes in spite of the death and also the healing; yet a sad presentiment that it was over with the ungodly power of this world accompanied the preaching of the gospel throughout the heathen world. From this we can explain the rage of persecution.

4 They *worshipped the dragon because he gave;* a distinction being observed between the giver of the power and the bearer of it. The worship of the dragon was under the form of an idolatrous service which, according to 9:20, has a demoniacal, Satanic background.

The property of being *incomparable* belongs only to God and to Christ, who is connected by oneness of nature, and appears under the name of Michael, *who is like God* (Ex. 15:11, Ps. 89:6; Isa. 40:18, Rev. 12:7.) They make the beast, to which the dragon gives his power, or the beast in his connection with the dragon, a *Michael*, and scornfully challenge the *true* Michael and his servants to measure themselves with him. God had raised Christ from the dead, reviving and energizing his prostrate church. A similar resurrection seemed now to be wrought by the dragon in favour of the beast, so his adherents shout: *Who is like the beast, and who can make war with him?*

5 The *it was given* is consolatory, in that it is God who moves our enemies; it appears in three pairs; two of the first beast, ver. 5 and 7, and one to the second, ver. 14-15. God does not give the inclination to blaspheme, but only the liberty and conditions to indulge in this inclination. In Dan. 7:8, 20 a mouth is attributed to the little horn speaking *great things;* here *blasphemies* are also added, like, *Who is like the beast?* The *forty and two months* signifies the world's temporary dominion over the church (see 11:2, comp. 12:6,14.)

6 *Blasphemy against God* is committed in three ways: when anything is attributed to him, which is contrary to his holiness; when anything is disowned that rightfully belongs to him; and when anything is ascribed to the creatures, which belongs to him alone.

The *name* of God is the product of his acts, revelation and historically manifested glory (Ps. 20:1, Deut. 28:58, Ps. 22:31, 23:3, 74:10, 83:16.) When we hear his name, we remember all that he has done. God is *named* the *God of Jacob;* he has made himself known in this character, and through deeds has gotten a name that is glorious and terrible. His election is not hidden, but revealed, confirmed by deeds. The most fearful blasphemy of his name is when his revelation in Christ is consigned to lies and sin, and when the Scriptures, the record of God's acts and words of which his name is composed, are attacked.

Here the temple is the *tabernacle*, the church (11:1) under persecution in the wilderness (comp. 12:6,14.) Without the name there is no tabernacle, and where the name is, there is the tabernacle. The church assembles about a manifested God who has gotten a name (Isa. 63:14,) which reached its perfection in Christ; and in this she finds union. Jerusalem, the holy city, the mother of all believers (Gal. 4:26,) is in heaven (12:12, Phil. 3:20, Heb. 12:22, Rev. 21:2,10, 3:12.) *Those who dwell in heaven,* are the *saints* in ver. 7, 10. Here we have blasphemies, in ver. 7 active persecutions. Believers on earth are prin-

6. And he opened his mouth in blasphemy against God, to blaspheme his name, and his tabernacle, and those that dwell in heaven.	cipally meant, as they bear the blasphemies of the beast and his adherents; and are calumniated as evil-doers (1 Pet. 2:12, 3:16.) Blasphemy against God is of three kinds: the blaspheming of his *name*, which is converted into an empty one by transmuting history into poetry and lies; the blaspheming of his *tabernacle*, which is bereft of a present God (comp. Ex. 25:8; Matt 28:20,) and changed into a building of man, unworthy now of bearing the name *tabernacle of meeting*; finally, the blaspheming of those *who dwell in heaven*, denying they possess his Spirit, and changing them from saints into evil-doers, thus blaspheming God, who dwells in them through his Spirit. These three kinds of blasphemy always go hand in hand. They have now again become rampant, since the beast of Daniel in the little horn has once more come upon the stage, and Gog and Magog have taken the place of the beast in the Apocalypse.
7. And it was given him to make war and to overcome them. And power was given him over every tribe and people, and tongue and nation.	7 This verse alludes to 11:7, there it is a riddle, but here it is explained. There the object was *the testimony*, here it is the believers. The FUNDAMENTAL PASSAGE is Dan. 7:21, *I beheld, and the same horn made war with the saints and overcame them*. The reference to this is consolatory; for in ver. 22, Christ comes and *the saints possess the kingdom*. What is said in Daniel primarily of the little horn is here applied to the beast, though that little horn corresponds with the Gog and Magog of 20:8. So what is said here of the beast, his conflict with the church and his victory over it, holds good respecting Gog and Magog. This accounts for the brevity in describing Gog and Magog. What is indicated there, is to be extended and filled up from the delineation of the beast, whose activity, interrupted for a thousand years, is again resumed by Gog and Magog.[4] Then the description of the beast acquires an entirely new meaning. It no longer relates to things past, but respects our conflicts and inspires us to stand fast in them. The *power* consists in this, that all nations must either worship the beast or suffer persecution and death. We have the *four* number of the tribes, people, etc. (5:9, 7:9, 10:11, 11:9; 14:6, 17:15.)
8. And all that dwell upon the earth shall worship him, whose name is not written in the book of life of the Lamb that was slain, from the foundation of the world.	8 They shall worship *him* (not it,) that is, the king (17:10,) the Roman emperor. The *shall worship* shows the matter was in the act of becoming. The worship is not purely external, but an inward veneration, holding the power of the beast to be divine, by which faith is obscured. The clause *whose name is not written*, shows the trial will be so severe, that their election is set over against it as a security (comp. Matt. 24:24.) A smaller group remain with the Lamb; most worship the adversary. The *book of life* belongs to the Lamb (3:5, 21:27.) The ground of our salvation is not our good deeds, but the atonement by his blood; so that Christ is *the Lamb that was slain* (comp. 12:11, 5:9.) Whatever *name is not written* by *him* in the book of life shall never be there. All salvation, including the OLD TESTAMENT saints, depends on the sacrifice of Christ, and those written there have power to overcome Satan and the beast. Salvation is by blood and death, through blood and death is victory (Rom. 8:17, 36, and Rev. 2:10, 12:11.) The *from the foundation of the world*, is not referring to the slaying of the Lamb but the writing of the name in the book, as is clear from 17:8. Here election precedes existence, before the foundation of the world (Matt. 24:24.)

---

4. Heathenism, in Marxism and Darwinism, expressions of Gog and Magog, or the beast from the earth, in its philosophical abstractions, all have elements of the beast, such as a denial of the spiritual, in its earthly nature, and materialistic focus, see p. 142-3—*Editor*.

THE SECOND ENEMY: THE BEAST FROM THE SEA

The divine counsel is immoveable. It is impossible to deceive the elect to their ruin. Parallel is 11:1–despite the world, the temple and its worshippers are preserved. The members of the church are those, who through Christ's blood, by faith, have come to be among the elect. They may be outwardly overcome and even killed by the beast, but they can never apostatize.

FAITH AND PATIENCE FOR THE DIVINE RECOMPENSE

> 9. If any one has an ear, let him hear. 10. He that leads into captivity, shall go into captivity; he that kills with the sword, must be killed with the sword. Here is the patience and the faith of the saints.

According to ver. 9 there is a double point. What is to be *heard* follows in ver. 10. The *he that has an ear, etc.* respects the promises for the churches, which need to be understood spiritually (2:7.) The consolatory truth is a hard one as the natural heart always cleaves to the *visible*. The *if any one has* calls aloud to all, to escape from this natural condition into the Spirit, to enjoy divine consolation, as shows in what follows. Many who have had an ear, lose it when the temptation rises to its highest pitch (Luke 24:25.) The consolation for the ear to hear, is to strengthen desponding hearts to look the beast in the face, till help should arrive. The Lord cannot leave believers so long without consolation and encouragement till the description of the first beast's ferocities could be placed beside those of the second.

10 St John was *a captive* himself in Patmos, it means prisoner of war, Antipas and others were killed by the sword. In ver. 7 persecution appears as *a war.* The deportations first happened under Domitian. In ver. 10 the persecutors of the church experience the vengeance of God, suffering the same evils they had inflicted on the saints (Deut. 32:43 and Ps. 94:12-13.) It is not just *God's* avenging sword, *he who sheds man's blood,* **by man** *shall his blood be shed* (Matt. 26:52.) This is clear from 12:16, 17:16, 18:6. This is not just a *command*, but a prophecy, fulfilled in Domitian, Valerian, and Julian, and in persecuting Rome and the other persecuting monarchies that have trod and still tread in her footsteps. God's procedure is also the rule by which the magistrate works as the servant of God for the punishment of evil doers. Those who deny the magistrate the right of capital punishment have no living sense of the punitive righteousness of God.

Whatever individual or church possesses *patience and the faith*, if they but shine in them, the wicked soon come to an end, and the righteous flourish like the palm-tree. *Patience* prevents men becoming faint and languid in the face of tribulation and persecution (14:12, 1:9, Matt. 13:10.) The sort of patience is *faith*, which keeps its eye on God's lowering sword of vengeance. In what follows John presents this retribution, clothes it with flesh and blood, to help to successfully maintain the conflict with what outwardly appears of an adverse nature.

REVELATION 13:11-18

The third enemy: the beast from the earth —earthly-physical-demoniacal wisdom

SUMMARY

The second *beast* is earthly and demoniacal wisdom. The *lamb's horns* indicate the secret manner it would affect men's minds–like Christ, yet its *speech*, like *a dragon*, betrays its ungodly nature in hatred to Christ and his church. It would be the chief support, herald and advocate for the first beast–its false prophet, inducing earth's inhabitants to worship it. The first beast is worshipped and often mentioned alone, but the second never without the first. Wherever the ungodly state flourishes, the ungodly wisdom is in attendance to strengthen its hands and deck out its pretensions (Ex. 7:11, 2 Tim. 3:8, Dan. 1:20, 2:2,7, Isa. 47.) Pharaoh had his wise men against the Lord and his people. The king of Babylon also has wise men as props of the state, and guardians against misfortune. The influence of this enemy came against the kingdom of God when the first beast came anew after the healing of the deadly wound. If the first beast revives again in Gog and Magog, so will the second revive also.

EARTHLY AND DEMONIACAL WISDOM

> 13:11. And I saw another beast arise out of the earth, and he had two horns like a lamb's horns, and spake like a dragon. 12. And he makes all the power of the first beast before him; and makes, that the earth and those who dwell on it should worship the first beast, whose deadly wound was healed.

The second *beast* came to the help of the first *when* it undertook the war against Christ—hence it is *anti-Christian heathen wisdom*. In Domitian's time the claims made against Christ by the empire were supported by such false, worldly wisdom. The beast is false, ungodly teaching because it is called the *false* prophet (16:13, 19:20, 20:10.)

Daniel describes these world powers opposed to God as *beasts*. It is a humbling name for those who by aerial speculations aspire to stand above common humanity. Human wisdom is *sensual* (Jude 19-the gnostics,) of the soul, the soul being common to man and beast, having merely animal life with no spirit, corresponding to *brute beasts* in Jude 10. Man's wisdom is confined to the soul, and opposed to the region of God's Spirit (Jas. 3:15, 1 Cor. 2:12-14.)

Its origin, *out of the earth* corresponds to its being a beast. In Dan. 7:17 four beasts arising from the sea are four kings who should arise out of the *earth*, in contrast the God of heaven establishes a kingdom in 2:44. The *who is above* stands opposed to *those from beneath*, as is *being born from above* and *born of the spirit* is in opposition to a purely earthly origin (John 8:23, John 3:3,8.)

The want of Spirit, the purely animal, brute nature, characterizes the wisdom not from above, but out of the earth. In things of the Spirit, earth has no productions of its own—heaven or hell, God or the devil are always in the background. Devils proceed out of the mouth of the false prophet (16:13.) The beast ascends out of the medium of the earth from out of hell, full of the Satanic spirit from the abyss. Of the wisdom of the world (Jas. 3:15,) the *earthly* and *devilish* correspond to the *rising out of the earth* here, while the *sensual* applies to the designation of false prophet by the name of *beast*.

It is not like *the* lamb, but *a* lamb. The Lamb has seven horns, indicating greater *power* over the beast's two. In both the horns are imperceptible—the world's wisdom, like Christ's is not palpable. In both the lamb horns do *not* denote meekness. No speech of the dragon is recorded, but its nature is hatred toward Christ and his church, in panting after bloody persecutions. Its watchword is *Ecrasez l' Infame.*[5]

12 The wisdom of the world is the main support of this *power*. Brute force is always impotent. That only which has an ally in public sentiment can have a lasting existence. To secure that the false wisdom puts forth its energies. Intellectual weapons unite with external violence to attack Christianity. He acts as his servant in his interest. To stand *before* anyone simply means to serve him without the collateral idea of good will in the service.

The second *makes* resumes the former *makes* in its making or *exercising* the power of the first beast, bringing the inhabitants to worship the first beast.

The *earth* is named beside and before its inhabitants in a contrast with heaven and its inhabitants. The *inhabitants* of the earth are the earthly minded portion of its inhabitants.

Because the *wound was healed*, the second beast appeals to the first beast's renewed life, with its success in persecutions and the helpless condition of the church, as grounds to worship the first beast. The Roman state was honoured in the idol gods set up when Christianity appeared, yet faith in these gods had already been much shaken. The *healing* was not perfect. The old naive confidence had gone, faith in the avenging and protecting gods no longer dwelt in the heart. Polytheism had become a mythology without doctrine, a lifeless form. Open contempt of the Roman ceremonies and resistance to its laws could not remain unpunished, even though no act was connected with it of a moral nature.

AN IMAGE OF THE BEAST

> 13. And he does great wonders, so that he even makes fire come down from heaven before men. 14. And deceives them that dwell on the earth, because of the signs which are given him to do before the beast, saying to those who dwell upon the earth, that they should make an image of the beast which had the wound of the sword, and became alive. 15. And it was given to him to give spirit to the image of the beast, that the image of the beast should even speak; and that he should make, that whosoever would not worship the image of the beast, should be killed.

---

5. A quote of Voltaire, the 18th century French philosopher, who in a pioneering malice toward Christianity and the royal powers, would sign his letters *Ecrasez l' Infame—Let us crush the infamous thing*, the *infamous thing* being a derisive epithet for Christianity–*Editor.*

CHAPTER 13:11-18 THE REVELATION

<blockquote>13. And he does great wonders, so that he even makes fire come down from heaven before men.</blockquote>

The second beast uses *wonders* to establish the power of the first. The FUNDAMENTAL PASSAGE is Matt. 24:24, where seduction is also through the working of great wonders. Not only false Christs are meant but those who in opposition to Christ lay claim to what belongs only to him. In 2 Thess. 2:9 it is said the adversary's first great manifestation was raising up heathen Rome against Christ, and that his coming is after the working of Satan's lying wonders. These wonders are not false wonders, but Scripture lets the wonders by which the world suffers itself to be deceived be what they give themselves out for, yet laughs in their face. It was this way with the wise men of Egypt, and it is prescribed in Deut. 13:1-3. Soothsaying and witchcraft are rejected, not because of their nothingness, but because they are an abomination (Deut. 18:9.) Unlike true wonders they have a mere natural character mixed with common fraud. As the signs of the Egyptian wise men were occasioned by Moses, so the signs of the false prophets, by Christ. The *fire* is what John and James wished to bring down on those who would refuse Christ.

<blockquote>14. And deceives them that dwell on the earth, because of the signs which are given him to do before the beast, saying to those who dwell upon the earth, that they should make an image of the beast which had the wound of the sword, and became alive. 15. And it was given to him to give spirit to the image of the beast, that the image of the beast should even speak; and that he should make, that whosoever would not worship the image of the beast, should be killed.</blockquote>

14 The little flock have against them a whole deceived world, the huge mass of worldly minded persons on the earth, emphasized by the frequent mention of the *earth's inhabitants*. The repetitions here in regard to the second beast, are more than the first, as all the power of the first beast is exercised through the second, and the heathenish and demoniacal intelligence is a still more frightful enemy than the coercive power of heathendom. Scripture sees the reality of tribulation head on, because it has the strongest consolations, but the world deceives itself regarding the danger, as it sees no alternative but despair.

15 Not images, but an *image* here, yet in the sense a *multitude* of images is meant. The king of Babylon is alluded to, where disobedience to the command to worship his god and image that he had made was punished as high treason. The setting up of the likeness of the emperor rendered the beast and its living representative, the emperor, as omnipresent, placing heathen despotism at the centre of the world. Thus Christians had to choose either martyrdom or apostasy. *And that he should make*, not: *and made*, so that the image is the subject, but, and that *it* made, so the beast, the false prophet is the subject. The *being killed* and *the not buying or selling* can have him alone for its author. Here is the commentary on the words *he spake like a dragon* in verse 11. Dan. 3:6 also—those who did not worship the image were thrown into the fire.

THE NUMBER OF THE BEAST

<blockquote>16. And he makes all, the small and the great, and the rich and the poor, and the free and the bond, that a mark should be given them on their right hand or on their forehead. 17. That no one should be able to buy or sell, but he that has the mark, the name of the beast, or the number of his name. 18. Here is wisdom. Let him that has understanding consider the number of the beast; for it is a man's number, and his number is six hundred and sixty-six.</blockquote>

The *named* are seven—the *all* at the beginning, then the three pairs, a similar seven divided similarly is in 6:15. From the small a rise is made to the great (11:18, 19:18, 20:12.) The mark means *confession*, which drives at public notoriety by some visible mark, like as the revolutionary anti-christian spirit is known by wearing dark red cocades (14:9, 16:2, 19:20, 20:4.) The *hand* show that in all his actions he is to show himself a servant of the beast. The *forehead* is the most open part of the body for display, the mark there is to confess oneself a servant of the beast to the world (7:3, 9:4, 14:1, 17:5, 22:4, Deut. 6:6-8, 11:18, Ex. 13:9, 16.) Allusion is made to Deut. 6:8 where the phylacteries show one should think of God, his commandments and benefits, and be ready to acknowledge him.

17 The aim and result of the mark is that no one is able to *buy or sell* without it, excluding one from society and the means of existence. It consists either of the *name of the beast, or of the number of his name.* The number is equally significant with the name, so by it the nature of the beast is exhibited. In 15:2 are those who obtain the victory over the beast, the image, and the number of his name—the name itself is not specified. It is not a child's play with letters, but a problem which belongs to a more profound spiritual discernment.

18 *Wisdom* which comes from above has an ethical foundation and character, is a prerogative of God and of Christ, is possessed by those who are given the spirit of wisdom and revelation, plus a deeper insight into divine things, and the capacity of apprehending the right in knowledge and duty (Jas. 3:15, 17, 7:12, 5:12, Eph. 1:17, Jas. 1:5, Acts 6:3, Col. 1:9, Wisdom 7:25-26.) *Understanding* is the seat of wisdom, being the mental power to which it belongs (Luke 24:45.) He alone has understanding who has wisdom, whose understanding Jesus has opened by his Spirit. In Dan. 12:10 wickedness and understanding stand opposed to each other.

We are called to *count* the number, but a counting in the sphere of wisdom and spiritual discernment, not in the ordinary sense. The *first* beast is meant. The *number* is the signature of his name and must be in reference to a name. The name is unknown to us without the number. The number has significance even apart from the name. It must stand in an independent relation to the nature of the beast. That alone can be the right explanation of the number which first supplies a name and secondly indicates a direct relation between the number and the nature of the beast. It forms a contrast to a mystical or mysterious number. It is not the number of the name *of a man* because the beast is not a man, not an individual. The FUNDAMENTAL and PARALLEL PASSAGES oppose it.

To discover the name of the beast which furnishes the number 666, we cannot wander after our own imaginations, as John lives entirely in holy Scripture. In the whole of the OLD TESTAMENT there is but one instance in which the number 666 occurs in connection with a name. It is said in Ezra 2:13, *the sons of Adonikam, 666.* The name *Adonikam* must therefore be the name of the beast. It means, fittingly, *the Lord arises,* and agrees with the watchword of the worshippers of the beast, *Who is like the beast? and who is able to make war with him?* It combines all that is described to characterize the beast. It is a name of blasphemy, it corresponds to the mouth speaking great things, and the demand to worship the beast, it points to the saints being carried away into captivity, and killed with the sword. It also agrees with St. Paul, 2 Thess. 2:4 regarding the man of sin. The name, *the Lord arises,* was originally consecrated to the true God and derived from the songs of the church that celebrate him as the Almighty Being, who arises to avenge his enemies. This name the beast appropriates to himself, as his adherents had, in verse 4, claimed for him the name *Michael.*

That a direct relation exists between the number and the nature of the

CHAPTER 13:11-18   THE REVELATION

18. Here is wisdom. Let him that has understanding consider the number of the beast; for it is a man's number, and his number is six hundred and sixty-six.

beast, is seen in that by design the number of the 144,000 appears in the next verse regarding the church. The 666 is the blown up six, swelled and increased to the uttermost, yet still no more than six. It is a subordinate number, as five is half of the perfect number of ten, the six is the half of the twelve, the preliminary step to the seven, therefore in a subordinate relation to the two numbers formed by the combining the three and the four, which are generally consecrated to the church. By the six being carried through units, tens and hundreds, the number marks the soaring pretensions and might of the beast. To the 666 corresponds the *three and a half*, which is the signature of the apparent victory of the world over the church, on account of its relation to the number seven. Irenæus supposes a connection to the image of sixty cubits high and six cubits broad, which Nebuchadnezzar had set up, thereby disclosing a shadowy representation of the nature of the ungodly power of the world, so colossal yet indissolubly bound to the fatal six, the broken twelve and the incomplete seven.

$$\chi\xi\sigma$$

Perhaps there is also an import in the mode of writing the number. It is expressed by the three letters χξσ, kappa, zeta, sigma. The first and last of these three letters are the common abbreviation of the name of Christ. The zeta, ξ, standing in the middle, is like the serpent, under the name of which Satan appears in 12:9, and 20:2. Throughout the whole, therefore, the Antichrist, that is raised up by Satan, is placed before our eyes.

THE BEAST CANNOT BE THE PAPACY

If the beast were the papacy, it must also be the papal persecution of Christianity described in ch. 12, but the description of the persecution by the dragon follows *immediately* after how the power of Satan was broken by the atonement of Christ. If it is a papal persecution, Satan has restrained his rage for a thousand years, and the heathen persecution which John suffered, and which raged for centuries is of no consequence.

The relation of this group to the two groups of the seven seals and the seven trumpets opposes this view. They hold the same theme in common–the oppression of the church, and judgment on the persecutors. The former two are general and introductory, while this later group is detailed. The prophets also use a general announcement preceding the particulars, as in Nahum 1:3-6 and Isaiah 13, where the Lord's purpose to judge the world power precedes the description of the overthrow. If in the last the Papal persecution were meant, then the two early groups must also be the same, but 9:20 describes the sins as having a distinctively *heathen* character. The Apocalypse was written to comfort believers at a time of bloody persecution, not merely for the present but for the church of all ages, however, the subject was the persecuting power during the time then present, and such other future powers as had the same root as that. All the details cannot be said to respect a hostile power of which no suspicion had begun to be entertained. Isaiah predicts for his own time, a deliverance from Assyria, and also from a still future Chaldæan power, even then shooting up, in the same line as the present one. In the time of John, Domitian was persecuting the church, one cannot apply this to the Papacy, as John had throughout in view his companions in tribulation. Prophecy, though not bound to the present, has an actual starting point in the present, must always connect itself with present necessities, questions and complaints, and never can swim loosely in the air. To defend this explanation would be a sheer anachronism.

The dragon is purely worldly, godless, God-opposing, as is his instrument the beast in Dan. 7 and here, *without* the intermixture of spiritual or ecclesiastical properties, or any noble better elements. The Papacy does not fit. The beast here is a composite creature formed out of the different beasts in Daniel. It must comprise the particular phases of the ungodly power of the world which in Daniel was under successive beasts. If the Papacy is introduced this reference to the particular phases of the ungodly power is lost in confusion. On the seventh head there are ten horns, which point back to Daniel, where in 7:24, the ten horns are ten worldly kingdoms, into which the fourth world monarchy falls on its dissolution. If the Papacy is meant this connection is destroyed.

The *adversary*, in 2 Thess. 2, relates to the beast here. He is not a disguised, but an avowed opponent. He does not come in the name of God or of Christ but he exalts himself above all that is called God, intolerant of any god, without hypocrisy or pharisaical appearance. *He sits in the temple of God,* which is the church, not in a pseudo-ecclesiastical sense—it simply means he presses in upon the church from without, seeking the homage of her members, constraining them to worship the emperor and to curse Christ. The first great fulfilment of verse eight, was the overthrow of heathen Rome. The last great phase of the adversary is in Rev 20:7-9, and it is now making way for itself.[6] The name of *the beast* denotes the low, earthly mind opposed to all that is God or godly—regular godlessness, but the zeal for God of Gregory VII or Innocent III lies out of the sphere of the beastly.

If the ten horns are kingdoms yielding homage to the Papacy their being placed on the seventh head makes no sense, as 17:9 shows it is the Roman heathen power. The diadems the beast wears show it is not a spiritual or an ecclesiastical but a purely worldly civil power. The beast bears names of blasphemy–a manifest opposition to God and Christ. The Papacy, however, has always represented itself but as a servant and living organ of God and Christ. The beast is an instrument of the dragon, but the Papacy was never regarded as a purely satanic institution. The name of the false prophet it is said refers to false teachers who have the mask of ecclesiastical authority. But false prophets can be those who speak in the name of other gods, as the prophets of Baal and Aschera. They are not solely limited to wolves in sheep's clothing, but much rather to those who in avowed opposition to Christ laid claim to what belongs only to him. In 17:4-6 zeal is ascribed to the woman for the diffusion of false doctrine, but it is not zeal that is meant here, but thirst for conquest.

Luther says in a letter to two Anabaptist pastors in 1528,

But we acknowledge, that under the papacy there is much Christian good, nay all Christian good, and also that it has come from thence to us; namely, we confess, that in the papacy there is the true Holy Scripture, true baptism, the true sacrament of

---

7. Hengstenberg is most likely referring here to the revolutions in Europe in 1848–*Editor.*

the altar, the true keys for the forgiveness of sins, the true office of preaching, a better catechism than the ten commandments, the articles of the creed, the Pater Noster. I say, that under the Pope, there is true Christianity, nay the real quintessence of Christianity, and many pious and eminent saints.

THE SEVEN HEADS CANNOT BE EMPERORS

Another view is that the beast is both heathen Rome–the seven heads being seven Roman emperors; *and* also the personal Roman antichrist, an eighth head of the beast. Of those seven five at the time of John's vision (17:10) had died; the sixth, Galba, who reigned eight months, was emperor. After the sixth a seventh also comes, who was to reign for a short time. Then it was thought Nero, as the personal Antichrist, should reappear with the kings of the east to destroy Rome. However the beast cannot be the worldly power of Rome. If the beast were the Roman Empire, then *the woman*, who sits upon the beast, must be the *capital city* in contradistinction to the empire, but scripturally world monarchies are represented by their cities—as the Chaldees under Babylon, and in ch. 18 Rome represents the whole empire—with Rome's overthrow so goes the empire. In 19:11-21 entirely different enemies come upon the stage, ten independent kingdoms, opposed by the King of kings. If the *woman* of 17:18 is the Roman kingdom, as the representation of that kingdom, the beast which carries her can only denote the worldly power *generally*, which was then wielded by Rome. If the beast were the Roman worldly power, as contradistinguished from the city denoted by the woman, the woman should have appeared in ch. 13, but there the beast appears *without* the woman.

The beast here with its multiple heads (17:3, 13:1-2) is a composite of the beasts in Daniel 7, the plurality of beasts expressed there is expressed in the multiple *heads* here, the horns of the heads being also derived from Daniel. A copy of this *whole power* of the world cannot be represented here in only *one* of its phases. This contradicts the relation of the Apocalypse with Daniel, which John resumes and supplements, and confuses the symbolism which depends on their uniformity. In 13:2 the one beast is formed of the same parts which in Daniel were distributed among the four beasts. The beast here denotes the world power generally–while the particular phases are found in the heads and horns. When the Roman empire or Nero is understood by the beast, the parallelism among the three enemies of God's kingdom is destroyed. Through the whole of history the two others, the dragon and the serpent, have been represented in their enmity towards God's kingdom. The beast cannot be separated from the dragon, and with its seven heads and horns is given up to the dragon. The second beast has also had his instruments in all ages, from the magicians of Egypt downwards. The ten kings give up their power and authority to the beast in 17:13, but they hate and lay desolate the woman, Rome, in verse 16. Whenever we understand by the beast the power of this world generally, and by the woman that for the present was carried by the beast as Rome *and* the empire, all becomes plain.

The Apocalypse announces the overthrow of the Roman dominion, at a time when there was no indication of it, and unlike in the past where one vast monarchy always supplanted another, it showed that after Rome the ungodly power of the world would present a divided appearance in the ten kings, who, while opposing God's kingdom, will execute upon Rome the recompense of God. The ten horns belong to the beast, but not to Rome, for they destroy her; they are not subordinate vassals, but kings of the earth with their armies (19:18-19,) against whom the Lord himself takes the field, overthrows them and completes the destruction of the heathen ungodly power generally, while the church enters on the enjoyment of a millennium of secure and undisturbed possession of the kingdom.

Satan has seven heads and ten horns as reflecting his visible representative on earth, he is the moving principle of the conquering power of this world in its assaults on the kingdom of God throughout history, he draws the third part of the stars and casts them on the ground (12:4,) overthrowing and subjecting rulers. The dragon gives up his power, throne and great authority to the beast. Now the seven Roman emperors *are too tiny* to reflect such an image. The first four lacked the element of hatred toward the kingdom of God, *Nero was the first to rage against this sect,* says Tertullian. The beast has on his head names of blasphemy, and is full of such names (13:1, 17:3,) names insulting to the true God and Christ. It is a smaller crime to assume titles of false and imaginary deities. In 13:6 the blaspheming of God goes with blasphemy and hostility to his church, and direct blasphemy is spoken of in 16:9,11, 21. The Assyrian king blasphemed (Isa. 36:13-20, 37:10-13) when he exalted himself above God (Isa. 10:9-10,) as did Pharaoh in Ex. 5:2, and Belshazzar drank wine out of the temple vessels in mockery of the God of Israel. In such a one as *Augustus* we find nothing of this sort.

In 17:9, *the seven mountains are seven kings.* Mountains denote not particular kings but kingdoms. The kings are not individuals but *ideal* persons, personifications of kingdoms, *the king of Babylon* or *Rome* etc. The seven hills of Rome symbolize the seven formed worldly power, of which Rome was then the possessor. Seven heads of the beast as the seven hills is incongruous. Immediately before it says *here is the understanding that has wisdom*, the meaning is mysterious to those who have a natural understanding. The *seven heads are seven emperors* view requires no understanding that has wisdom.

The ten horns which denote kings (17:12,) that is ten kingdoms, do not exist along with the heads, but they sit upon the seventh head. The head shows how it agreed with the other heads, but the horns shows that it is a *divided* power. The horns are where horns are to be, and in 12:3 Satan has on his head seven diadems, which is equally understood of the horns, and the horns stand connected with *one* of the heads. As the beast rose out of the sea, the horns first were visible and before the heads, which only appeared afterwards, yet later in 17:3 the heads are mentioned before the horns. There the beast is not seen arising, as he had done in 13:1. The horns are to be viewed as connected with the seventh head, because what in 17:10 is declared of the seventh head or kingdom, stands related to what is said in verse 12 of the ten horns, as the general outline to the filling up. The seventh king denoted by the seventh head had not yet come, and when he had it would be for a *short time.* The same is said of the ten horns, they are ten kings *who had not yet received the kingdom, but they receive power as kings* (to be and act quite independently) *one hour with the beast.* With the fall of the seventh head is coupled that of the beast (ver. 11,) as it is, in like manner, according to ver. 17 and 19:20, with the fall of the ten horns or kings. According to Daniel 7, there were to arise out of the fourth monarchy, the Roman empire, ten kings, represented by ten horns; that is ten kingdoms, symbolized by the ten toes of the image in Nebuchadnezzar's vision (ch. 2): the fourth kingdom was first to be parted into two great kingdoms, the feet; then into smaller ones, the toes. These, and also the horns, must denote kingdoms, because the whole image has to do, not with individuals, but only with kingdoms. In Daniel, however, the ten horns exist, not along with the four beasts, but *upon the head* of the fourth and *last* beast. So here also must they belong to the seventh and *last* head. But if the ten horns or kingdoms belong to the seventh head, then the heads cannot denote royal personages, but only monarchies.

If the first seven Roman emperors are the seven heads, then the overthrow of the Roman state was in the immediate future. But in the time of composition no grounds existed for such an expectation; *Vitellius* ascends the throne, yet the Apocalypse rises to high honour in the church. The naming of *kings* in 17:10 does not mean the discourse is exclusively of the Roman Caesars; no old, valid authority exists for numbering the Roman Caesars from Augustus, on which the hypothesis in question rests; for only thus does Nero become the fifth. In the *XII Caesars of Suetonius*, we find Julius Caesar, from whom the name passed over to the others. In *Dio Cassias,* Augustus is regularly called the *second* Caesar. Josephus reckons from Julius Caesar. The expression, *five are fallen*, in 17:10, does not suit the five emperors, who besides died a natural death. It indicates not individuals, but kingdoms and empires, for whose overthrow the term *falling* is the standing expression in Scripture (18:2, 14:8, 16:19, Isa. 21:9; Jer. 51:8; Amos 5:2.) Falling is used for those who perish in war, not violently in some other way. By Isaiah and Jeremiah the falling is used expressly of Babylon, which in our view is among the five. To the five here is added elsewhere in Revelation a sixth, still in existence, the Babylon of the prophet's time, Rome.

THE BEAST OF CH. 17:8, 11 CANNOT BE NERO

17:8. The beast that thou sawest was, and is not; and shall ascend out of the bottomless pit, and go into perdition: and they that dwell on the earth shall wonder, whose names were not written in the book of life from the foundation of the world, when they behold the beast that was, and is not, and yet is.

11. And the beast that was, and is not, even he is the eighth, and is of the seven, and goeth into perdition.

The view that the beast is Nero goes thus: in ver. 1-7, the beast is the Roman power, and in ver. 8 the beast is *Nero*, the Roman emperor, who, driven from the throne, who was to return as the enemy of Rome; who, therefore, cannot be a concentration of the power of Rome. In ver. 9-10, the beast is *the image of the Roman power*, but in ver. 11 the beast again becomes *Nero*. Further, Nero must appear in ver. 9-10, as also in 13:3, as *one* of the seven heads of the beast; but immediately afterwards in ver. 11 as *the beast itself.* Verse 11, it is thought, must especially point to Nero, who had appeared as one of the seven, was again to appear as the eighth, who, according to the popular opinion at Rome, was to re-appear after his supposed death. But, a quite simple explanation entirely sets aside the reference to Nero. Of the seven, there was one thing prominent in the preceding verses: the *fall*, or *destruction*. Hence, in the clauses, *and he is an eighth*, and *he is of the seven*, is supplied, *in the destruction;* confirmed by the close, *and he goes into perdition*. Meaning that with the overcoming of the seventh phase of the ungodly power of the world, that power generally goes down—comp. 19:20, where subsequent to the fall of Rome, comes the victory of Christ over the ten kings, the beast with the false prophet is destroyed, and so the ungodly power of the world comes to an end. At the close of the thousand years of quiet and secure repose enjoyed by the church (to maintain it to be still future, is one of the sad consequences of conceiving the beast to mean the papacy), there is to arise a new and powerful display of hostility on the part of the world. But the Seer has not comprehended this under the symbol of *the beast*. It is alleged, that Nero must also be meant in 17:11, as also in ver. 8, and 13:3, where *the head of the beast* was wounded to death. This passage, however, cannot refer to Nero. If a beast's head is slain, the beast itself is also slain. But by the death of Nero the beast, the Roman kingdom, was not at all affected. That the wounding to death in the head reached to the whole beast, is clear from 13:3-4, after the healing of the head, the whole earth wondered after the beast and his power.

The whole of the three passages are to be explained by 12:9, which teaches that through the bloody atonement of Christ, Satan is robbed of his power, and by John 16:33, *Be of good cheer, I have overcome the world*. The power of this world, as opposed to the kingdom of God and wielded by satanic influence, *was;* it showed itself active and powerful during the two thousand years before Christ. It is *not:* it was wounded to death through Christ, and had as yet given only a few indications of life. But the prophet perceived, the *I was dead and behold I am alive again*, should also be verified in the case of the antichristian state, in an inferior manner, but not *for ever and ever*. On this riddle the prophet *wondered* (17:6-7)—that the worldly power should be *allowed* to rage so fiercely against the saints. The world itself also, who responded to the word, *I have overcome the world*, looked with wonder (ver. 8,) while it beheld the apparent opposite of this in the revived power of the beast. The antidote to the wondering, presented in ver. 7, by the angel to the prophet, is to look to the approaching overthrow of the persecutors; the ultimate fulfilment of the word, *I have overcome the world*. There is nothing, then, requiring the supposed reference to Nero.

The beast cannot be an *individual*. The four beasts in Daniel are not individuals, but powers. In Eze. 29:3, the great dragon is the *ideal* person of the Egyptian king, the personified kingdom. *The boar out of the forest* in Ps. 80:13, is the king of Assyria. The four beasts in ch. 4 are the Cherubim, not angels but *ideal* creatures, symbols of the earthly creation. The second beast, the false prophet, is an *ideal* person coming in a *multitude* of individuals to an actual existence. But the beast *and* the false prophet are together thrown into the lake of fire. One cannot be an individual, and the other an ideal person! If we compare 17:6, and ver. 8 the re-existence of the beast coincides with the drunkenness of the woman with the blood of saints and the martyrs of Jesus, but only if we understand by the beast the ungodly power of the world.

Here it is an actual death that is spoken of, for the beast returns from the abyss (ver. 8, comp. 11:7;) *it is not* (ver. 11.) The expression, *as it had been killed to death*, refers not to the apparentness of the death, but to the traces of the absolutely mortal wound, after it had returned to life again. This is manifest from the obvious parallelism of the lamb and the beast in 5:6, *I saw a lamb as it had been slain.* The lamb was actually killed. The popular report, however, did not suppose the return of Nero from the dead, but questioned the fact of his death, which very few had witnessed. Nero put an end to himself; but the head of the beast, according to 13:3, was slain to death from a foreign hand.

Finally, this exposition rests on the supposition, that the Apocalypse contains the doctrine of the antichrist being an *individual*. St John, in his epistles, makes no mention of such an one. He expressly states, in 2:18, that the Antichrist is an *ideal* person, to be realized in a *multitude* of individuals; comp. ver. 22, 4:3; 2 John 7. Nor is any mention made of a personal antichrist in the discourses of our Lord regarding his second coming, to which John alludes in his epistles, as they also contain the general plan that is merely enlarged upon in the Apocalypse. They speak only of false prophets and of false Christs, who should arise and draw away many into error (comp. with 2 John 7, Matt. 24:11,24.) In 2 Thess. 2, we shall there also not find the antichrist as an individual, unless we leave out of view the use made in Scripture of the ideal person—which is, indeed, very apt to be done in the present day, when there is so little intimate acquaintance with the OLD TESTAMENT. Most commonly the question is incorrectly put. Some say he is expressly called *the man of sin, the adversary*, and a manner of acting such as is proper only to a person. But the question is not, whether person or not person; but whether *a real* or *an ideal person*, such as we constantly meet with in the Psalms, of *the wicked, the enemy, the adversary*; where also a vicious realism has greatly damaged the work of exposition. But that the subject here is an ideal person is clear, if only no decisive proofs of the contrary can be adduced, from the PARALLEL PASSAGES alone of the NEW TESTAMENT, which have already in part been referred to. In Acts 20:29-30; 2 Peter 2:1; 3:3, Jude 18, where the hostile forces and seducers of the last time are spoken of, it is always of *several*, not of a single individual, that mention is made. So also with Paul himself, besides the passages in his speech and writings referred to, in 2 Tim. 3:13; 1 Tim. 4:1. If everywhere else we find, first, a real plurality in the enemies of Christ, and secondly, this plurality exhibited under the form of an *ideal* person, so that we regard the antichrist not as an individual; but an ideal person consisting of scattered individuals. The mystery of iniquity *cannot* denote a real person. For *mystery* can be used only of *a thing*; and only of such also could it be said, *it already works*. Nor could it properly be said of a person, but only of a tendency or system, that it is *stayed* (letted.) Finally, it is an ideal person also *who withholds* in ver. 7, and before in ver. 6—the personification of the noble powers that then watched and prayed for the church; or the ideal person of the good shepherd, in respect more immediately to the Thessalonians represented by the apostle himself in his writing to them. Of him, and such as him, we must primarily think in this connection (comp. ver. 15; Acts 20:28; 2 Tim. 4:2; 1 Tim. 4:6; 1 Pet. 5:1; Heb. 13:17.)

REVELATION 14

Believers assailed by these enemies consoled by grace, judgments pending on these enemies

CHAPTER SUMMARY

Prophecy everywhere notices distresses, dangers, temptations, in order to fortify the heart against them, *that we through patience and comfort of the Scriptures may have hope* (Rom. 15:4.) The character of this chapter is to administer an *anticipatory* comfort against the great tribulations to come from Satan, the beast from the sea, and the beast from the earth in ch. 12–13.

The preceding description of the beast awakens the question: *Who, then, can be saved?* Faced with such trials the *lead us not into temptation* is weakly prayed. To help believers utter it with vigour was the first object which John, or rather the Holy Spirit, as Paraclete, had to accomplish. And this is done by transporting us out of the tribulations of time with its conflicts and trials, and placing us on the heavenly Zion, with the saints around their Saviour, the warfare finished, steadfast and unmoved in their confession, rejoicing in victory, pure and holy, in spite of all the temptations the earth had presented to them.

The consolation also carries an exhortation to fidelity. Seeing the 144,000 gathered there around the Lamb, with his name and that of the Father on their foreheads–we would strive unto blood to be of their number, and courageously resist everything that might blot out the names from our forehead. The two last verses have a distinctive admonitory import.

This section, while closely related to 7:9-17, is essentially different. There the heavenly glory consoles those who suffer with the world under the mighty hand of God, visiting the world on account of sin; here is a guarantee that fidelity to the Lord can triumphantly overcome all the assaults it endures from the world. The two sections portray two different assaults upon believers. This section only indirectly represents the future glory of believers, or their recompense, or the preservation of the true church upon earth. When the heavenly band appears before the throne in the glory of their steadfast profession, it is on the ground of that steadfastness during the tribulations of time.

THOSE WHO HAVE CARRIED THEIR CONFESSION WITH THEM

14:1. And I saw, and behold the Lamb stood upon the mount Zion, and with an hundred forty and four thousand, who had his name and the name of his Father written on their foreheads. 2. And I heard a voice from heaven, as a voice of many waters, and as a voice of great thunder; and the voice which I heard was as of harp-singers playing upon their harps. 3. And they sing a new song before the throne, and before the four beasts and the elders; and no one could learn the song, except the hundred forty and four thousand who have been redeemed from the earth. 4. These are they who have not been defiled with women, for they are virgins; these are they who follow the Lamb, whithersoever he goes; these have been redeemed from among men, first fruits to God and to the Lamb. 5. And in their mouth is found no lie, for they are without blame.[7]

1. And I saw, and behold the Lamb stood upon the mount Zion, and with an hundred forty and four thousand, who had his name and the name of his Father written on their foreheads.

The words, *and I saw and behold*, indicate the unexpected view of the tender lamb still strengthening his elect in unshakeable fidelity against the savage beast and a subservient world. This power is rooted in the *blood* of the Lamb, who appears here as having been slain (7:14, 12:11, 5:9, 13:8.)

The heavenly *Zion* is here the local position of the heavenly temple, which stands related to the tabernacle, *the tent of meeting*, as substance to shadow; where God and angels meet with men, and the righteous are eternally blessed. John employs Jewish things merely as the symbol of Christian, the earthly mount Zion had become a common profane place. Jerusalem, in the Apocalypse, is never the earthly city. As the voice *from heaven* in ver. 2 is the voice of the one hundred and forty four thousand, so the *mount Zion*, where the Lamb stands with them, is the *heavenly* one. The throne of God is on the *heavenly* mount Zion. The *hundred forty and four thousand* are identical with those in 7:4; as the number of all the true members of the church. There they are in their earthly preservation; here a *triumphant* church, the same *multitude* that *no one could number*, in their heavenly bliss and glory (Heb. 12:22, Rev. 13:6, 7:9-17, 15:2-5.)

If bearing the mark of the beast shows the world one to be a servant of the beast (13:16-17;) here having the *names of Christ and of his Father* on one's forehead, indicates a steadfast confession to the end. This counters anxious doubts regarding maintaining it, in face of the power exercised by the beast over men's minds. He whom they had faithfully confessed on earth, now confesses himself to them. No one shall attain to this blessedness by his own power (19:8.)

2. And I heard a voice from heaven, as a voice of many waters, and as a voice of great thunder; and the voice which I heard was as of harp-singers playing upon their harps.

2 The *harps* belong to the church. The multitude of believers is distinguished from *the elders* attending the throne. The voice of those *redeemed from the earth*, who have reached their destination, sounds from heaven.

In 19:6 the voice of the elect is compared with *the voice of many waters* and *the voice of thunder* from the vast assemblage of persons speaking, singing, playing. In the OLD TESTAMENT it is the voice of the Lord, and the wings of the Cherubim, representatives of what is living on the earth (Eze. 1:24,) also compared to thunder and the noise of a host. The voices' loud praise and thanksgiving, with the *harps* is a call to remain steadfast in temptations.

3. And they sing a new song before the throne, and before the four beasts and the elders; and no one could learn the song, except the hundred forty and four thousand who have been redeemed from the earth.

3 The *new song* is understood from what precedes–that the glorious name is still upon their foreheads, and they stand with the Lamb on Mount Zion, despite the despair in trouble upon earth. The *four beasts*, as representing the bloom of all earth's living creatures, out of whom the redeemed have come, celebrate their triumph. The *elders* always appear where a session is held in matters relating to the church. The *learning* is from Deut. 31:19, 22 where Moses taught the song to Israel. The *no one can learn* the song corresponds to *the new name, which no one knows*, in 2:17. (1 Cor. 2:9.) The *from the earth* is explained by the *out of every tribe and tongue and people and nation* in ch. 5, and here in ver. 4 by the *from among men*.

8. The words, *before the throne of God*, which Luther retained, have probably been introduced into the text by combining together Jude ver. 24 and ver. 3 here.

4 Faith in Jesus always has the keeping of the commandments of Jesus. In the creation, much that is disagreeable and impure exists that reflects the image of sin, that did not originally belong to it, which make us sensible of sin itself. Under the Mosaic law are the several classes of the legally impure: 1. *Impurity arising from death.* Death is the wages of sin; the corporeally dead are those dead in trespasses and sins (Rom. 6:23, Eph. 2:1, Col. 2:13.) 2. *The impurity of the leprosy.* As the head of all diseases in the law it is the symbol of sin. 3. *The impurity of corporeal issues* – like gonorrhea, bloody issues, etc. (Eze. 36:17; Isa. 64:6; Lam. 1:17.) 4. *The impurity of beasts.* Every human evil has its image in the animal creation, and when beholding that, man should look upon himself (Prov. 11:22, Matt. 7:6, 2 Pet. 2:22.)

4. These are they who have not been defiled with women, for they are virgins; these are they who follow the Lamb, whithersoever he goes; these have been redeemed from among men, first fruits to God and to the Lamb.

Now to the third class of legal impurities belongs also *sexual intercourse*, see Lev. 15:18, Ex. 19:15, 1 Sam. 21:4, 2 Sam. 11:4. This legal impurity appears here, from the ancient symbolism, as a figurative description of sinful defilement. The relation of man to woman symbolizes man's relation to sin. Sin is sometimes represented by the woman (comp. Gen. 4:7 with Gen. 3:16,) one must in respect to sin be the man, and it the woman. In Zech. 5:7-8 the woman is *wickedness*. The *wife of the angel* (2:20) is part of the governing body led by false teaching. Gen. 4:7 indicates man should rule over sin, as the man over the woman. By means of the primeval history this figurative representation was quite natural; comp. 1 Tim. 2:14, 1 Pet. 3:7. Our passage agrees with 2 Cor. 7:1. The *hundred and forty and four thousand* are those, who have responded to this exhortation. In 2 Cor. 11:2 the *virgin* state is represented as freedom from sin. If this is not figuratively interpreted, then sexual intercourse and married life is here condemned (1 Tim. 4:3, 1 Cor. 7, Heb. 13:4.) All are such as have not defiled themselves with women, the whole Christian church consists only of virgins. The rejection of marriage is against holy Scripture and the example of the apostles.

Christ often spake of his *followers*, and usually in respect to the connected sufferings, see Luke 9:57-62, Matt. 10:38, Mark 8:34. One must in duty renounce everything to follow him in truth. The Lamb shall feed and lead to living fountains of waters. Here is the consecration, the holiness, by means of which the *first-fruits* were separated from the whole mass of the increase. Num. 18:12 refers only to a part of the first fruits, taken from an entire mass, where one was to take the best. The first-fruits of a tree are not the best, nor the first sheaf. The holy, as contrasted with the common, the rest of mankind, is the point of comparison between the first-fruits and Christians– so Christians are here described as spiritual first-fruits. Parallel in meaning is Titus 2:14, and Jas. 1:18, those begotten in the kingdom of God are standing at the head of humanity. *First-fruits* are parallel to *perfect and entire* (Jas. 1:4, Lev. 19:23-24, Lev. 23:10.) The *one hundred and forty and four thousand* represent the whole church; so that no followers of these first-fruits can be contemplated.

5 Freedom from *lying* is a mark of the elect in the OLD TESTAMENT, see Zeph. 3:13. A liar (1 John 2:4) is one who does not confess Christ, nor exhibit his faith in his works. The crowning point of lying (1 John 2:22) is to deny Christ, with which idolatry and the deification of men, a work of lies (Rom. 1:25,) goes hand in hand, withholding divine honour from him to whom alone it is due, and ascribing it to one to whom it does not belong. What is here ascribed to the honour of Christians, they owe, according to 1 John 2:27, to the anointing, to the Holy Spirit; it is a privilege of the Chris-

5. And in their mouth is found no lie, for they are without blame.

5. And in their mouth is found no lie, for they are without blame.

tian, of the anointed, as generally not to sin (1 John 3:9,) so in particular not to lie. Man's natural inclination to lying has a powerful coadjutor in Satan, the father of lies (John 8:44.) Allusion is made to 1 Pet. 2:22, particularly in the *was found*, which does not occur in the ORIGINAL PASSAGE, Isa. 53:9. The other expression also, *for they are without blame*, has its exemplar in Christ in 1 Pet. 1:19.

In verses 1-5, believers are invigorated by seeing the noble company of those who have carried their confession with them, pure and undefiled, no longer exposed to any trial and temptation. Here the sting is taken out of the temptations by pointing to the judgment which threatens the world that plies the temptations, which in particular will bring to desolation the seemingly omnipotent Babylon by pointing to the frightful temporal, but more especially the eternal punishments, which await the worshippers of the beast. These truths are announced by a threefold angelic message, ver. 6-11. In ver. 12, the admonition is raised from it to continue steadfast in the faith; and ver. 13 sets over against the doleful fate of the worshippers of the beast, the glorious destiny of those who have maintained to the end their fidelity to the Lamb.

A THREEFOLD ANGELIC MESSAGE OF JUDGMENT ON BABYLON

> 6. And I saw another angel fly in the midst of heaven, who had an everlasting gospel, to proclaim a joyful message to those who sit on the earth, and over every nation, and tribe, and tongue, and people.

Another, denotes not a diversity of *person*, but *mission*; as the name of *angel* refers to their mission, not their nature. The *flying in heaven* suits only a real angel. The idea is the nearness of the judgment on the persecutors. This idea assumes flesh and blood, as it were, in the angel here, that the conflict against visible evils might be vigorous and effective.

The subject of this *gospel* we learn from ver. 7; not *the*, but *a* gospel, *a joyful message* of approaching judgments. A king approaching with an army is a terror to his enemies, but a joy for his subjects, who through the judgment are delivered, their life's cause shines clearly. The confident expectation of this judgment shields against doubts and anxieties. For the world it can be *joyful tidings*, for time is still given it to repent. The epithet *everlasting* is applied to the gospel, men's words decay, God's word, his threatenings and promises, are as he is, eternal and unchangeable. When they appear to be impotent, they pass into glorious and terrible fulfilment. Its auditory is *those who sit upon the earth*. The angel's evangelical proclamation over *every nation, etc.* forms the counterpoise to the power of the beast over *every tribe, and people, and tongue, and nation* in 13:7. Here the judgment *generally* is announced, upon all the beast's forms of manifestation, from those that existed in the prophet's time, till the resuscitation of the beast in Gog and Magog.

THE FIRST MESSAGE–ALL FORMS OF THE BEAST

> 7. And said with a loud voice, Fear God and give glory to him, for the hour of his judgment is come; and worship him, who made the heaven, and the earth, and

the sea, and the fountains of waters.

The words, *Fear God, and give glory to him,* contrasts with the fear of the beast and his idols. The *give glory to him* is from Ps. 96:7, in a call, as here, to the tribes of the *heathen* world. The reason follows, ver. 13, *for the time of his judgment is come,* when all must be restored that they have taken away.

The *is come* is in an anticipation, as the call to repent implies the judgment had not quite entered, although it was as good as present. The *judgment* here is the collected force of all the judicial actions, by which till the end of time God is to break the ungodly world. It begins with Babylon, or heathen Rome in ch. 13; the beast is substantially to revive again in Gog and Magog.

Ver. 8 shows it is not the *last* judgment alone. The call to *worship him, who made heaven,* shows the judgment is to fall on the heathen idolaters. Through the work of creation He *who made* is distinguished from false gods, as (Jer. 10:11, ver. 2-7) fear should be cherished, not toward idols, *the gods who have not made the heaven and the earth,* but toward God the Maker. Along with the positive call here to the world-deifying heathenism, which is now again springing into new life, there goes also the negative: *Repent of the works of your hands, that ye may* **not** *worship the gods of gold and silver, and stone,* etc. (9:20,) and above all, not *men,* of whom all other idols are but the reflection and transparent veil. These words do not agree with those who understand by the beast the Papacy, which has always held the first article of the Apostles' Creed– God is *the maker of heaven and earth.*

The description of the objects of God's creative energy completes itself in the number four, as the signature of the world, as also in Acts 14:15.

The mention of *the fountains of water* appears strange at first sight.[8] In 8:10, *springs* of water denote the wells of *salvation,* and also occur figuratively in 16:4. Also under *the sea* we are to couple with what is literally indicated by that name, the sea of the nations–comp. 8:8-9.

We have here a fearful threatening. He who made the heaven, can, and also will extinguish its lights for those who are faithless and unthankful, 8:12; he, who made the earth, can and must and will also by fire and hail desolate and consume it, 8:7; he who made the sea, will change it into blood, 8:8,9; he who made the fountains of water, will turn them into wormwood, 8:10-11, comp. 16:1-9. The Creator of heaven and of earth is the great and terrible God, who can arm every thing against his despisers, and also must do it; as it is contrary to his nature to give his glory to another, and to be satisfied with anything that men are pleased to present to him (see p. 64, 67.)

THE SECOND MESSAGE–THE BEAST IN JOHN'S DAY

8. And there followed another angel, a second, who said, She is fallen, she is fallen, Babylon the great, which made all nations drink of the wine of the wrath of her fornication.

In the preceding verse the judgment *generally* was announced, upon all the beast's manifestations, from that in the prophet's time, till its resuscitation in Gog and Magog; here, on the other hand, is the judgment on that phase of

---

8. Comp. Gen. 7:11, *the same day were all the fountains of the great deep broken up*; the beginning of the great flood, the end of that world; here, the beginning of the end of our world–*Editor.*

CHAPTER 14   THE REVELATION

<small>8. And there followed another angel, a second, who said, She is fallen, she is fallen, Babylon the great, which made all nations drink of the wine of the wrath of her fornication.</small>

the power of the beast, by which the members of the church were *then* harassed and tempted to apostasy. If we were to understand here by Babylon the ungodly power of the world *in general,* the messages of the two angels would not be properly distinct from each other. But as Babylon here is brought into view only as an individual phase of the anti-christian power, what is said more immediately of it, undoubtedly holds good in substance of the other phases that are to follow.

The *second* indicates, as does also the *following* (not *coming*), that the angels, although different, were connected, and that their messages bore respect to each other. *With a loud voice,* it is said in regard to the first and third angel, but not in regard to the second. The announcement here relates to the preceding one as the particular to the general, so the *loud voice* here was unnecessary. In the message of the third angel, when a rise is made from the particular back to the general, it appears again.

Babylon is *heathen* Rome, not *Christian* Rome, for God avenges on Babylon his apostles and prophets (18:20.) It slew Peter and Paul, and sent John into banishment. See 1 Pet. 5:13. The heathen worldly power is the object of the judgment announced by the first angel. But the message of the second angel stands related to that of the first, as the particular to the general. Then, Babylon is only a particular aspect, under which the beast manifests itself, here the beast cannot possibly be the Papacy.

In the OLD TESTAMENT, the worldly powers of the present and the future are not rarely described under the names of those of the past. In 10:11, Zechariah speaks of their future oppressors under the name of Assyria and Egypt. This transference of names carries with it a strong emphasis. It makes the whole of God's earlier procedure start to life again. The word of God, which has once already passed into fulfilment, cannot now be treated as a vain imagination. *Babylon* was first applied in the figurative sense to heathen Rome in 1 Pet. 5:13. The *co-elect* is the associated church settled there, according to 1:2, 2:9; 2 John 13. The epistle was written when Rome had just begun to be a Babylon, in a correspondence to 1 Pet. 5:8, (comp. Jer. 51:37-38.) As the *Nicolaitans* in John point to the second epistle of Peter (2 Pet. 2:15,) so does *Babylon* to the first; in the Apocalypse are other references to the same epistle. For Christians Rome first became Babylon, when it entered on the persecution of the true people of God. In the OLD TESTAMENT, whatever great monarchies might do to worldly kingdoms, it was only when the same came against the Lord's people, that it became an occasion of divine judgment; see, for example, Hab. 2. Here Babylon is called merely *the great;* the *city* is wanting in the best manuscripts. This comes from Dan. 4:30, where Nebuchadnezzar speaks of *Babylon the great.* Allusion is made to Isa. 21:9, *Fallen, fallen is Babylon.* Comp. Jer. 50:2, 51:8. What is predicted here, is represented in 18:2-3 as fulfilled, as also in 16:19.

The *wine of the wrath* is the wine, which consists of wrath. The making the nations drunk with wine is a common image in the OLD TESTAMENT. In Hab. 2:15-16, speaking of the king of Babylon, the sense of ver. 15 is: *Woe to him, who in his wrath makes his neighbour powerless, in order to take advantage of his humiliation.* The wrath is the wine—comp. Jer. 25:15. This figure is likewise applied to Babylon in Jer. 51:7, *The golden cup of Babylon is in the hand of the Lord* (to be now presented to herself, according to Jer. 25:26, hitherto she had presented it to others,) *that makes all the world drunk; the nations have drank of her wine; therefore have the nations become mad.* In Nah. 3:11 it is said of Nineveh, *Thou also shalt be drunken, be hid*– the drunkenness denotes the impotence, the total degradation, the utter vanishing; also Obadiah 16. The point of comparison is always the powerlessness, the helplessness, misery, degradation, shamefulness of the condition. It is more particularly described as that of *her fornication,* by which is denoted the selfishness, that under the veil of love disguises itself, to seek the gratification of its own lust. In Isa. 23:15 Tyrus is named a whore on account of its commercial alliances, and its commercial gain the hire of a whore. It is the making one's self agreeable, *feigning love for the sake of gain.* In Nah. 3:4, the term *fornication* denotes the diplomatic arts of the Assyrian power, by which she insinuated herself upon the nations, in order to ensnare and destroy them under the semblance of love. Among conquering nations there always goes along with their rough power a hypocritical love and friendship, by which they endeavour to wheedle the nations and make them subservient to their purposes. What is described as fornication in Nah. 3:4, is in ver. 1 described as *deceit,* as in Isaiah, selfishness concealing itself behind the appearance of love. The gain sought for there is gain of *merchandise,* here of *countries.* In the same way we are to explain here, *her fornication.* It is added to give additional strength and elevation to the meaning. Without it we might have thought merely of rude force. It showed itself also in the treatment of Christians. In the history of her persecutions we are not so much shocked at their ferocity as at the cunning, by which under the semblance of love it sought to seduce Christians into apostasy.

The subject is *the wine of the wrath,* or *the wrath-wine of her fornication.* Seduction to idolatry, as some have it, cannot proceed from the principle of wrath. That the *fornication* here can only be feigned love for the sake of self-interest, is clear from the reference of 18:3 to Isa. 23, where since *the kings of the earth have committed fornication with her,* is coupled with, *and the merchants of the earth are waxed rich through the abundance of her delicacies,* it cannot be a connection of idolatry with fornication. Finally, in 19:2 it is said, *He has judged the great whore, who corrupted the earth through her fornication.* From the words that follow, *And has avenged on her the blood of his servants,* and from 11:18, it cannot be *spiritual* corruption that is meant here, but only *material,* and such judgment as carries along with it complete destruction.

THE THIRD MESSAGE–THE PAINS OF HELL

> 9. And another, a third angel followed them, and said with a loud voice, If any man worship the beast, and his image, and receive a mark in his forehead or in his hand; 10. The same shall drink of the wine of the wrath of God, which is mixed unmixed in the cup of his wrath; and shall be tormented with fire and brimstone before the holy angels and before the Lamb. 11. And the smoke of their torment ascends up for ever and ever; and they have no rest day and night, who worship the beast and his image, and if any one receives the mark of his name.

The two first messages are preliminary stages to the third, as this last connects itself with ch. 13. Here the aim of all three messages comes clearly out–to strengthen against the temptation which the seeming omnipotence of the beast should present to the followers of the Lamb, and arm them against his seductive arts by the call: *worship not the beast, for the hour of judgment has come, Babylon is fallen, etc.* Fear can only be driven out by a stronger fear.

10. The same shall drink of the wine of the wrath of God, which is mixed unmixed in the cup of his wrath; and shall be tormented with fire and brimstone before the holy angels and before the Lamb.

10 The *drinking of wine* often refers to impending judgment—see FUNDAMENTAL PASSAGE—Ps. 60:3; on which rests Ps. 75:8—regarding the overthrow of the proud enemies of the church; and also Isa. 51:17, 22; and Jer. 49:12, 25:15, where the cup is the misery the king of Babylon was to bring on them. This shows that the wine is mixed in the cup of the wrath of God. It is a mixture with ingredients, which increase its intoxication. The mixed is unmixed with no alleviating mixture. It was a Greek custom to drink wine mixed with water, a weak drink (Isa. 1:22.) Corresponding to this is the element of grace, of compassion.

The threatening ascends to its acme, the punishment of hell. Judgments on the wicked appear in the OLD TESTAMENT under the image of *fire and brimstone* (Gen. 19:24; Luke 17:29, Ps. 11:6; Isa. 34:9-10. FUNDAMENTAL PASSAGES—Matt. 5:22, 13:42, 18:8, Luke 16:24, and, in particular, Luke 12:4-5.) Also the FUNDAMENTAL PASSAGES in the Gospels agree. Both have the practical aim of driving out the fear of man by means of the fear of God. It also is the righteous recompense for the *unrighteous* brimstone-fire of their passion, their wrath, their hatred; comp. 9:17-18. The torment of the fire and brimstone seizes them *before the holy angels and before the Lamb*. That they are the executors of the judgment is clear from 2 Thess. 1:6-9. The angels are designated as *holy*. In 2 Thess. 1:7-10, *the angels of his power* is a corresponding expression. *Holy*—glorious (comp. 4:8,) is an epithet to the angels, in contrast to the impotent creatures on earth, who can give no resistance to the strokes of these servants of the divine vengeance. Christ appears here under the name of *the Lamb*, for the same reason he did in 6:16.

11. And the smoke of their torment ascends up for ever and ever; and they have no rest day and night, who worship the beast and his image, and if any one receives the mark of his name.

11 The words, *the smoke of their torment etc*, and 19:3 refer to Sodom in Gen. 19:28. In that great monument of the righteous judgment of God, there was given a matter-of-fact prophecy of the one before us. Hell would be a fable, if it had not such earthly types. Sodom and Gomorrah gives assurance of an earthly judgment. From what they have no rest, enjoy no relief, is to being tormented with fire and brimstone. The meaning is, *and they have there no rest*. Chapter 20:10 shows the hell-torments, as the contrast to the heavenly rest of the saints here in ver. 13. The threatening is a frightful one, but it is assured in the word of the Lord, Matt. 25:41.

NEGATIVE AND POSITIVE REASONS FOR PATIENCE

12. Here is the patience of the saints, those that keep the commandments of God and the faith of Jesus. 13. And I heard a voice from heaven saying, Write: Blessed are the dead, who die in the Lord, from henceforth. Yea, saith the Spirit, that they may rest from their labours, for their works follow with them.

The verse contemplates the point of view from which the preceding description is to be considered, the end it is intended to serve, which was to strengthen believers in patience, in the willing endurance of all that they had to suffer for Christ, while steadfastly adhering to their confession. If the hour of judgment is approaching, and Babylon is destined to destruction, and torments awaiting the worshippers of the beast, then the *patience of the saints* is in its proper place. Bengel: *It is patience, when one adapts himself to all that he has to suffer, and will comply with nothing that is forbidden.*

That under *the commandments of God*, faith in or toward Jesus holds the foremost place, in which the fulfilling of all the rest has its root, 1 John 3:23.

13 In the preceding verse we have the negative reason assigned for patience, here is given the positive reason, the eternal *blessedness* of the faithful. The *voice from heaven* speaks of those who die *in the Lord*– perhaps one of the just made perfect testifying, or one of the elders (7:13-14.)

The command to *write* is repeated twelve times in the Revelation, to indicate the things it refers to are important. He writes, not of their escape from distress, but of the *blessedness* of the felicity of heaven; in what follows they are blessed from their *resting from their labours*. It is said: *the dead*, to determine the sphere of blessedness. The faithful are never described in Scripture as dead, the dead are the unbelieving as opposed to the believing (Matt. 8:22, Rom. 8:10, comp. 3:1.)

The *Lord* is the Lord Jesus; see 1 Thess. 4:16; 1 Cor. 15:18, where the discourse is of the dead and such as sleep in Jesus. The being *in the Lord*, is explained by John 15:4. Those that *die in the Lord* are not the martyrs alone; but the blessedness of dying in the Lord is celebrated, to inspire faithfulness even unto death; the blessedness belongs to the 144,000, the whole Christian host, in contrast with the worshippers of the beast, who have no rest day and night. The *from henceforth* means *even now;* not merely in the new Jerusalem one day to be set up on the earth, but from the very moment of their departure to heaven. The penitent thief prayed that the Lord would remember him in his kingdom of glory on the earth. But the Lord grants him paradise that very day. In calling Jesus *Lord*, he was one who died in the Lord. For it is to die in the Lord, when one in the immediate prospect of death confesses to him with full confidence as the Lord. This word, *from henceforth*, is an antidote against those who dream of a sleep of the soul. The soul's life in Christ can suffer no interruption (John 5:24); if there is, eternal life itself is indirectly denied. The *from henceforth* is a strong shield which may keep the Christian from falling away under all temptations. If in this now he must die for the faith, he attains from henceforth to a life, in comparison of which the life he surrenders may be regarded as a death.

Yea, saith the Spirit; the Spirit catches up the words that were uttered by the voice from heaven. The *Spirit* is the Spirit by which John was inspired. Hence, we are to supply from the preceding, *blessed are the dead who die in the Lord;* and the following words, *that they may rest from their labours,* where the blessedness is denoted (comp. 2:2, John 4:38, 1 Thess. 1:3, 3:5; 1 Cor. 3:8, 15:58.) The *labours* are those in the service of the Lord; in particular those undergone in the conflict with the beast, as the *following works* are the product of the labours. It is not said *their works follow after,* but, *they follow with them.*

THE HARVEST

14. And I saw, and behold a white cloud, and upon the cloud sat one, who was like a Son of man; he had a golden crown upon his head, and in his hand a sharp sickle. 15. And another angel went out of the temple, and cried with a loud voice to him that sat on the cloud, Send thy sickle and reap, for the hour for reaping is come; for the harvest of the earth has become dry. 16. And he, who sat upon the cloud, thrust in his sickle on the earth, and the earth was reaped.

In ver. 6-13, the temptation, which the beast carried along with it, has had its sting taken out by the reference to the judgment, which threatens the world that plies the temptation. Here, the judgment, as already entered, presents itself to John under a double image–that of *the harvest*, ver. 14-16, and that of *the vintage* and *the wine-press*, ver. 17-20. What in history is realized in a whole *series* of judicial acts, which at last run out into the final judgment, is here, comprehensively, brought together in one great harvest, one great vintage and pressing of the grapes. Here, as also in the FUNDAMENTAL PASSAGE, Joel 3:13, we cannot refer to a single phase of the judgment. It leaves nothing over for a future judgment; the range of the judgment is an unlimited one; its sphere is the whole earth; and its severity also is such as to admit of no further increase. The practical aim is, to give courage before the world, to *consider its end*, Ps. 73:17. Whoever, looking beyond its seeming almightiness, will fix his eye on the *white cloud*, and the *Son of man* on it with his *sharp sickle* can afford to laugh at the threatenings of the world; he knows, that it will soon itself suffer something far worse than it can inflict on him; and that he should be party to its punishment, if he were to follow its guidance. The Spirit would strengthen us like Stephen beholding the glory of God, when he speaks through John as here. Any one, that will take these to himself, will find himself cured of that natural cowardice, which still clings to all, even the most courageous, and shall be enabled to ride upon the high places of the earth.

14. And I saw, and behold a white cloud, and upon the cloud sat one, who was like a Son of man; he had a golden crown upon his head, and in his hand a sharp sickle.

14 The *cloud* brings a *judgment* in view (comp. *on the clouds* at 1:7.) The cloud is *white* because of the glory of him who comes in judgment. The *with power and great glory* in Luke 21:27, and Matt. 24:30 corresponds to this cloud. On the words, *and on the cloud sat one, who was like a Son of man*, comp. 1:13. Here, as there, allusion is made more immediately to Matt. 24:30. But the proper FUNDAMENTAL PASSAGE is Dan. 7:13.

The *crown* is everywhere in the Revelation the sign of royal dignity, of dominion. Christ bears it as *the King of kings and the Lord of lords*, to whom, consequently, all judgment is committed.

The *sickle*, the instrument of reaping the harvest, Christ bears as *the Lord of the harvest* (Matt. 9:38, comp. Mark 4:38.) The harvest denotes the spiritual harvest, the gathering of souls into the kingdom of Christ (Matt. 9:38; John 4:35.) Then, it signifies *the end of the world*, when the righteous and the wicked shall be gathered to their own dwelling (Matt. 13:30, 39; Mark 4:29.) Finally, it denotes *the harvest of wrath*, when the sin and wickedness of men has become ripe for visitation and just punishment. The proper FUNDAMENTAL PASSAGE is Joel 3:12-13, where, in the description given of the judgment on the heathen, all judgments on the enemies of the church are combined into one grand image. The ripeness, the fullness of the vats denotes the fulness of the guilt. The whole address in ver. 13 is directed to the mighty ones, the angels, with the angel of the Lord at their head. In like manner, Isa. 27:11, and Jer. 51:33 denotes the harvest of punishment. The special allusion to Joel is clear from this, that here, precisely as there, the harvest and the vintage are immediately connected with each other. Joel 3:13 forms the foundation of this whole section; consequently the application of the image there furnishes the key for the one made here. In ver. 15 there is a literal allusion to Isa. 27:11. The *sharpness* of the sickle shows, that we have to do with a judgment. Where Christ appears on a *cloud* the work at hand is always a judgment. The name

BELIEVERS ASSAILED BY THESE ENEMIES

of *the Son of man* is chiefly used when Christ appears for judgment–comp. John 5:27, and Rev. 1:13. The *golden crown* (angels do not bear crowns) and the sharp sickle are the symbol of his judicial power toward the enemies of his church.

15-16 Christ also appears as an angel in 7:2, 10:1, 18:1, 20:1. That Christ can receive a command from or through an angel is shown in that the activity of the Son always takes its impulse from that of the Father, see John 5:30, 5:19, 27. In the *angel* who here brings to Christ the commission of the Father, his dependence on the Father, to whom he is united in nature, and whose will is not alien to him, has assumed flesh and blood.

The heavenly *temple* is the symbol of the church; and the seat of God, in so far as the church is concerned. The command to reap goes forth from the temple, the misdeeds to be punished are such as had been committed against the church. The reason for the call is *the hour is come* and *the harvest of the earth is dry* (2:4, 7:30, 8:20, 16:21, 25, 32, 17:1.) The measure of iniquity has become full (Gen. 15:16; Matt. 23:32, Matt. 24:28.) Here we see the comprehensive character of this judgment. The harvest of Babylon is only a part and beginning of this harvest. The last great harvest day is described in 20:9. In 14:7, *the hour of his judgment is come*, as *at hand*, but here it is *already* entered.

15. And another angel went out of the temple, and cried with a loud voice to him that sat on the cloud, Send thy sickle and reap, for the hour for reaping is come; for the harvest of the earth has become dry. 16. And he, who sat upon the cloud, thrust in his sickle on the earth, and the earth was reaped.

THE VINTAGE AND THE WINEPRESS

> 17. And another angel went out of the temple in heaven, who had also a sharp sickle. 18. And another angel went forth from the altar, who has power over fire, and cried with a loud cry to him who had the sharp sickle, and said, Send thy sharp sickle, and cut the clusters of the vine of the earth, for its clusters have become ripe. 19. And the angel struck with his sickle at the earth, and cut the vine of the earth, and threw (the cut-off clusters) into the great wine-press of the wrath of God. 20. And the winepress was trodden without the city, and blood came out of the wine-press, even unto the bridles of the horses, a tract of a thousand six hundred stadia broad.

The harvest and *the vintage*, along with *the treading of the grapes*, are too connected to admit of more than one harvester. In ver. 15 the angel is described as *another*, here also it is *another*, but the same *another*. The name *angel* here respects the *mission* not the person. In verse 14 the Son of man on the cloud had a sickle, here the angel has a *sickle*, therefore the angel here also is Christ. It is too great a work for an ordinary angel. The one who treads the winepress, according to Isa. 63, can be no other than Christ, as the connection with 19:15 affirms. That the angel proceeds *out of the temple*, shows that Christ appears for the good of his persecuted church, with the sickle. The sickle is regarded here as used both in the harvest *and* the vintage.

18 The *altar* is the altar of burnt-offering. That the *angel* goes forth from it may be explained by Amos 9:1, also Eze. 9:2, where, at the Lord's command, who comes to deliver his people, appear the ministers of his righteousness stepping into the temple beside the brazen altar. Hence, with Amos, this altar is the place of transgression. There lie the un-atoned iniquities of both houses of Israel, instead of a treasury of love and faith embodied there in sacrifice. In that place of transgression the Lord appears for the purpose of glorifying himself in the destruction of those who would not glorify him in their lives. In explanation we refer to 6:9-10, where the angel comes forth

18. And another angel went forth from the altar, who has power over fire, and cried with a loud cry to him who had the sharp sickle, and said, Send thy sharp sickle, and cut the clusters of the vine of the earth, for its clusters have become ripe.

from the altar to avenge the blood of the saints which had been shed upon the altar. He comes *out of* the altar and not *from* it, as if ascending from its base, because in ch. 6 the souls of the martyred saints lay there. Ch. 16:7 also, where the altar speaks, favours this as the place where was shed the blood of saints and prophets. In ch. 9:13 the punishment of the world is sought from the golden altar, as the place of the prayers of God's people.

The angel *has power over fire*. Fire being the symbol of divine wrath and judgment (comp. on 4:5, 8:5.) In ver. 19 the wrath of God corresponds to this fire, this is founded in the reference to the fire of the altar. The fire of God's wrath consumes those accused before God by the fire of the sacrifice of his saints; comp. 8:5, where, in like manner, the wrath-fire is used in reference to the fire of the altar, but the fire there is the fire of prayer, here the fire of sacrifice. In the full sense God alone has power over fire (comp. 16:8,) the angel's power is that of a subaltern.

19. And the angel struck with his sickle at the earth, and cut the vine of the earth, and threw (the cut-off clusters) into the great wine-press of the wrath of God. 20. And the winepress was trodden without the city, and blood came out of the wine-press, even unto the bridles of the horses, a tract of a thousand six hundred stadia broad.

19-20 What the *winepress* is for common *clusters*, that is the wrath of God for these. The *city* can only be *the holy city* (11:2,) Jerusalem, which in the Revelation always designates the church. That *the wine-press was trodden out of the city*, indicates the members of the church are not under the judgment, which is executed on the world as opposed to the church. PARALLEL is 7:1-8, where believers are preserved amid the judgments on the world. The despised and hated *city* is now the only place of security and deliverance; but its gates are shut against its despisers and enemies. What is said of the triumphant church in 21:27, 22:15, holds true also of the church militant. Comp. Isa. 66:24. In 20:9 the *city* is besieged by those who are here thrown into the wine-press. *Blood* comes forth from the *wine-press*. Wine is called in the OLD TESTAMENT *the blood of grapes*, not for its red colour, but because it is prepared from the juice and strength of grapes. But these grapes yield real blood (Gen. 49:11, Deut. 32:14, comp. Isa. 63:3-6.) So deep is the sea of blood which comes from the destruction of all the wicked, it *reaches* even to the bridles of the horses. The warlike forces, the horses, may be those of the heavenly hosts (comp. 19:14-15,) accompanying the treader of the wine-press in his vengeance. We are here to take for our starting-post the holy city, before whose gates the sea of blood—a sea, not a river (as also in Eze. 32:6, Isa. 34:3)—begins, and completes a circle of *1600 stadia*. The number denotes a judgment *encircling* the whole earth. Four, the signature of the earth, is first multiplied by itself, and then again by 100 (comp. on 4:6, 7:1, 9:14, 13:7, 14:6.) Quite similar is the formation of the 144,000; the fundamental number is twelve, first multiplied by itself, and then by 1000. Similar also is the formation of the number 666.

That this must mean the length of Palestine proceeds on the false supposition that it is a *stream* of blood, instead of a *sea* of blood. Besides, this is not the length of Palestine; so that we are thrown on mere conjecture, to which no licence is given in the Apocalypse. Throughout the Apocalypse no signification is attached to Palestine.

GROUP 5

THE SEVEN VIALS

The seven plagues that accompany the beast, the ungodly power of the world, through the course of centuries

REVELATION 15–16

REVELATION 15–16

The seven plagues that accompany the beast, the ungodly power of the world, through the course of centuries

GROUP SUMMARY

The *fourth* group delineates the conflict waged by the three enemies of the kingdom of God against it; the *sixth*, how they are one after another vanquished. The *fifth* forms a sort of *prelude* to the latter. The kingdom of God has no absolute *past;* all the old deeds of God become new again in it, whenever the circumstances recur, which called them forth. Thus, here, the Egyptian plagues revive again, by which in ancient times the beast, whose fury had now begun to exhibit itself in the days of John, was visited in its *first* form of manifestation, and was at last crushed.

The Seer beholds seven angels, who have the last seven plagues, 15:1. In the presence of these angels and their work, the just made perfect sing, with anticipative confidence, the praise of God, ver. 2-4. Then the seven angels proceed forth from the temple of God, and seven vials are given to them filled with the wrath of God, ver. 5-8. How the seven vials, one after another, are poured out, and what effects proceed from them, is represented in ch. 16, at the close of which we find the power of the world shattered.

SEVEN ANGELS WITH THE SEVEN PLAGUES

> 15:1. And I saw another sign in heaven, great and wonderful; seven angels, that had the last seven plagues; for with them is finished the wrath of God.

Here it is a *great and wonderful sign* on account of the height of the matter denoted by it. A new scene begins. As *seven angels* are mentioned indefinitely, we cannot consider them as identical or different with the angels of the seven trumpets. John sees merely the seven angels, and only afterwards the temple and their proceeding out of it. This does not imply they had been shut up in it. The instruments of the plagues that the angels have are the seven vials, given to them at ver. 7. The verse serves as a superscription. John may have already seen the seven angels, ver. 2-4 implies it was intelligible to him, if he had not previously seen them. The song of praise, sung by those who stood on the *sea of glass*, refers to what they were to do, and forms a commentary on the appearance of the angels. Chapter 8:2 is analogous, where he sees the angels with the seven trumpets, then in 8:3-5 follows a sort of prelude, the vision of the angel with frankincense, then follows the work of the seven ministers of divine vengeance.

The prophet sees *the angels who have the seven last plagues*. They are so called *because by them is the wrath of God finished*. This is proof for the division of the

CHAPTER 15   THE REVELATION

1. And I saw another sign in heaven, great and wonderful; seven angels, that had the last seven plagues; for with them is finished the wrath of God.

Revelation into groups. After these seven plagues no others can come because *the wrath is finished* (comp. Isa. 9:20; Dan. 11:36; Lam. 4:11.) The subject of discourse is of the *last plagues* generally, of the finishing of the wrath of God. The song on the sea of glass implies that the end is *absolutely* reached. And if the chapters that follow (17—20) delineate judgments of God, the only explanation is that a *co-ordinate* series is introduced, that at ch. 17 we have a new beginning. By these seven plagues the worldly power is completely annihilated. But other aspects of this great drama should necessarily disclose what we expect after the vision of the three enemies in 12—14. These plagues are all inflicted on the *first* beast and *his worshippers;* of the fate of the *second* beast, and Satan, we learn nothing here. Even in regard to the first beast, we do not receive a complete answer to the questions arising from ch. 12—14. The beast is here always represented as a whole, and as the object of the judicial severity of God. But in 13:1 mention is made of the heads and horns of the beast of which some disclosure is to be given. We expect to find, not merely the judgments on the beast, the ungodly power of the world in general, but the judgments also on its *individual phases*. Now, all this we do find in 17—20, to which the present group stands in the relation of *a prelude*.

The *last* judgments of God are represented also by the two groups of the seven seals and the seven trumpets. They each bring things to a termination, exhibiting the ungodly world prostrate on the ground. The difference between the present group and these earlier ones is merely, that the former take for granted what is described in 12—14; that here the judgments alight on the ungodly power of the world, while there the object of the judicial severity of God is more *generally* delineated. There *ungodliness*, here the *ungodly power of the world*. It accords with this, that the seven plagues are here brought in. This has respect to the plagues of Egypt (comp. Ex. 9:14,) the object of which was not the ungodly world in general, but specially the ungodly world-power. The plagues and the beast go together. Because the name of *plagues* was formerly appropriated to denote the judgments of God on the first phase of that power, so here also the judgments that were impending over it are called by the name of *plagues*. The expression, *is finished*, is used in anticipation; it shall be finished, when all the seven shall have taken effect.

THE JUST PRAISE GOD WITH ANTICIPATIVE CONFIDENCE

> 2. And I saw as a sea of glass mingled with fire, and them that had gotten the victory of the beast and of his image, and of the number of his name, that they stood on the sea of glass and had the harps of God. 3. And they sing the song of Moses, the servant of God, and the song of the Lamb, and say, Great and wonderful are thy works, Lord God Almighty; just and true are thy ways, thou king of the heathen. 4. Who would not fear thee, Lord, and glorify thy name? For thou alone art godly. For, all nations shall come and worship before thee; for thy judgments are become manifest.

The *sea* denotes the great flood of the wonderful works of God, of his righteous and holy ways, of his judicial acts manifested among men. The *glass* denotes their blamelessness and purity; and the sea being *mingled with fire*, indicates the vision is chiefly about God's wrath, his punitive righteousness. Both symbol and song anticipate what the seven angels accomplish with the seven plagues. That those, who stand on the sea of glass, have to do with the impending work of the seven angels, that the sea is a symbolical embodiment of their work, and that their song celebrates it, is evident from the narrative beginning with the angels, and again returning to them after the interlude of ver. 5, but also from the correspondence between the words in ver. 3, *great and wonderful are thy works*, and those in ver. 1, *a sign great and wonderful.*

The *stood on a sea of glass*, alludes to Ex. 15:1, where Moses beside the Red Sea, with the children of Israel, sings a song to the Lord—comp. *they sing the song of Moses and the Lamb*, in ver. 3. The Red Sea, in which the Egyptians drowned, hence an image of the righteous judgments of God, was a type of this sea of glass. The subjects are the *conquering*, not those who *have* conquered, to John the victory was still in process of *being*. Comp. *these are they who come out of the great tribulation*, in 7:14. The words are literally: the conquering *out of* the beast. Hence before the victory they were in the power of the beast, as 11: 7, *and it* (the beast) *shall overcome them and kill them.*

Harps of God, consecrated to his praise, occur only here. The parallelism of the section 7:9, 14:1-5, places the scene in heaven. The just made perfect, who after overcoming by blood and death, celebrate the earthly triumph of the cause, which they had served on earth, and the judgments of God, by which he brings to destruction its enemy, the beast.

3 From ver. 2, *standing on the sea,* the *harps*, indicating its lyrical character and laudatory matter, we understand by *the song of Moses* the song of Ex. 15, not the prophetical song in Deut. 32. This is clear also from the mission of the angels, celebrated by this song, whose work was to renew the plagues of Egypt, with the overthrow of Pharaoh being celebrated in that song of Moses; which was also the song *of the Lamb*–the song not belonging to the Lamb as its author, but giving glory to him as the Saviour of his suffering people. It is for the Lamb's sake, that the seven angels are sent by God to destroy the world, and relieve his saints. Hence the song of Moses is the song which celebrates the salvation obtained for the church through his instrumentality–compare Ex. 14:31, where Moses is called the *servant of God.* In Ex. 15 Moses is not expressly called the author of the song. By the analogy of Ex. 15:1, and by Rev. 14:1, where the Lamb stands at the head of his people on Mount Zion, it appears the Lamb sings this song with his people. The addition alone *of the Lamb* forbids us to expect a literal agreement with the song of Moses. A new salvation, a new song. Isaiah too, who, in ch. 12, applies the song of Moses to the Messiah's salvation, has merely verbal allusions, the allusion here supplied by the express reference to the song of Moses, that is wanting in the prophet. But it is common to this song of the Lamb and the song of Moses, that in both alike the power of the heathen world is the object of the judicial energy of God. Habakkuk 3 also is such another variation of the song of Moses. It begins with the prayer, that God would revive his work in the midst of the years; then praises God for fulfilling it, since he had made the old new again, which there, as well as here, is *anticipated by faith.*

On the words, *Great and wonderful are thy works, Lord God Almighty*, comp. Ps. 92:5-6. They are the works and purposes of God for the deliverance of his people, in the destruction of their enemies. See also Ps. 66:3, where they are his judgments on the proud heathen world. *Great* and *wonderful* because he has given the feeble victory over the apparently omnipotent. The *Lord God, Almighty* implies the divine nature is the source of the actions; comp. on 1:8.

CHAPTER 15 — THE REVELATION

3. And they sing the song of Moses, the servant of God, and the song of the Lamb, and say, Great and wonderful are thy works, Lord God Almighty; just and true are thy ways, thou king of the heathen.

On the words, *just and true are thy ways,* comp. Ps. 145:17. The justice or righteousness is manifested in his giving his church salvation, to his enemies destruction. The truthfulness of God's ways refers to his faithfulness in keeping promise, and also his omnipotence. The *justice and truthfulness* of the ways of God are perceived in his making himself known as *the king of the heathen.* The heathen are the power which opposes the glorification of his righteousness and truth. When this power is laid prostrate, at the end of the seven plagues, then the complaining against the justice and truthfulness of his ways will be stopped. In confirming this reading, the designation of God rests on Jer. 10:7, with which the first words of the following verse begins. The whole subject of that chapter of Jeremiah, which is, that not idols, but God, must be feared, is by such a reference quickened into new life in the soul.

In seasons of tribulation the church often doubts the greatness of God's works, the justice and truth of his ways; to *doubt* whether he really were the *king of the heathen.* Now this doubt is dispelled by deeds; the clouds, which veiled the glory of God from her eyes, are made entirely to vanish.

4. Who would not fear thee, Lord, and glorify thy name? For thou alone art godly. For, all nations shall come and worship before thee; for thy judgments are become manifest.

The *fear* comprehends reverence. That God is everywhere to be feared, and his name to be glorified, has its foundation in the truth, that he alone is holy.

The word *godly,* when used of men, denotes a tender and solemn regard toward God and the relations appointed by him; when used of God (in the NEW TESTAMENT, only here and 16:5), it denotes regard to his own character and the government of the world as grounded therein. In 16:5 it is used on his regard for *justice,* which he maintains through his judgments. It differs essentially from *holy.* For this denotes the absoluteness that is in God, and comprehends not merely sinlessness, but also omnipotence. *Uprightness,* when used of God, much more nearly corresponds to what is meant by *godly.* But God is called godly, not only in contrast to men, but also to the heathen gods, which violently broke through the limits of the moral order of the world. Indeed, according to the FUNDAMENTAL PASSAGE, Ps. 86:8-9, the contrast with heathen gods is taken into account, which is opposed to the proper idea of the divine and so must necessarily be abolished.

That God alone is godly is affirmed in that *all heathen shall come and worship before him;* and this because his righteous deeds, 19:8, or his *judgments, have become manifest.* Their coming is of itself also a proof that God is godly, for it could take place through God making known his righteous character. In Ps. 86:8-10 the maintaining of the glory of God is made primarily to appear from the coming of the heathen—comp. Zeph. 2:11; Zech. 14:9, 16. But they come because God's greatness manifests itself in glorious deeds, corresponding to the word, *for thy judgments are become manifest.* In consequence of the righteous procedure of God all heathen *are* already come. The *all heathen* receives its limitation from what follows, 16:19, 21, according to which the heathen to the very last harden themselves against the judgments of God that fall upon them, and repent not to give him glory. The heathen referred to, therefore, are only those who among all sorts of people fear God and do righteousness (Acts 10:35.)

THE SEVEN PLAGUES ACCOMPANYING THE BEAST
THE ANGELS PROCEED WITH VIALS FILLED WITH WRATH

5. And after that I saw, and the temple of the tent of the testimony was opened in heaven. 6. And the seven angels went out of the temple, who had the seven plagues, clothed in pure white linen, and girt about their breast with golden girdles. 7. And one of the four beasts gave to the seven angels seven golden vials full of the wrath of God, who lives for ever and ever. 8. And the temple was full of the smoke of the glory of God and of his power; and no one could go into the temple, till the seven plagues of the seven angels were finished.

The *after that I saw*, indicates that here the main scene begins, *that* before being an introduction, a *prelude*. Such a portal for this group draws a broader line between it and the preceding vision, rendering it independent.

What is signified by the opening of the *temple*, and the procession of the angels out of it, may be understood from *the tent of the testimony*. It is not the *temple* of the testimony, because the OLD TESTAMENT mentions the *tent* of the testimony; it is rather the temple in its property as the tent of testimony. The tabernacle was called the *tent of the testimony*, because it contained the ark with the testimony–the law of God which testifies against sin. Here the import is in the punishment of those who have transgressed the testimony; comp. on 11:19. The commandments of God are not a dead letter, but a living force, which falls on the despisers of it, and crushes them to the dust. When the temple of the tabernacle is opened in heaven it is dreadful for the world, but joyful, though mingled with trembling, for the church.

6 The angels have the seven plagues even before the seven vials are given to them. This is clear from the words, *who had the seven plagues*, but also from their going forth out of the tent of testimony. This implies that they had already been entrusted with the work of vengeance. In the *clothing* of the angels their mission is represented. The clothing cannot, as in Christ (in 1:13,) or Michael (Dan. 10:5,) refer to the person, but only to the business.

The *linen* clothing is mentioned on account of its shining whiteness. In 19:8, the righteous deeds of the saints are denoted by pure and bright clothing. So also here, the righteous deeds of the angels and indirectly of God— comp. ver. 4. To the *pure* corresponds in ver. 3 the *just and true are thy ways*; to the *white*, glittering, the *great and wonderful are thy works*; comp. the difference between washing and making white at 7:14. The sea of the divine judgments and deeds of righteousness is compared in 4:6 to glass and to crystal: *as a sea of glass, like to crystal*. To the glass, denoting blamelessness, corresponds here the *pure*; to the crystal, denoting terribleness, awfulness, glory, the *white*. The pure and white also holds in respect to the *gold*. It is employed here on account of its glittering purity, as in 1:13, comp. 21:18, 21. In Job 37:22 the bright pure splendour of the sun is called figuratively *gold* (NRSV *golden splendour*,) and to it is compared God's frightful majesty.

7 That the vials are presented to the angels by one of the four beasts, is explained by 16:1, *Pour out the seven vials of the wrath of God on **the earth***. The cherubim act here as the representatives of the living creatures of the earth, comp. on 4:6, on which the judgments of God are to alight, as in 6:1, 6.

The symbol of the *vials* rests on the passages of the OLD TESTAMENT, which speak of the *pouring out* of the wrath of God; comp. the *pour out* in 16:1. The pouring out has respect to the *copiousness* of the display of God's wrath. The

CHAPTER 15   THE REVELATION

<small>7. And one of the four beasts gave to the seven angels seven golden vials full of the wrath of God, who lives for ever and ever.</small>

vials serve as vessels, from which it may be copiously poured out. The two FUNDAMENTAL PASSAGES, in which the pouring out of the wrath of God occurs in reference to the heathen, are Zeph. 3:8, and Ps. 79:6, (comp. the passage, which depends on this in Jer. 10:25.) By the connection there, the heathen and the kingdoms are particularly those hostile toward Israel, consequently the same as those, which are here threatened by the vials. The expression *pour out* points back to Ps. 79:3, *have shed their blood round about Jerusalem.*

The vials being of *gold* indicates that the wrath is not opposed to righteousness, but rather forms the energetic exercise of it. The purity and the splendour are here also, as in ver. 6, the properties of gold.

The two FUNDAMENTAL PASSAGES lead us to regard the contents of the vials as of a fiery nature, and in the Revelation also fire is the common symbol of wrath. That God *lives for ever* (comp. on the expression: *who lives for ever and ever,* at 1:18, 4:9-10, 10:6,) was given even in Deut. 32:40 as a pledge that he would completely avenge his own and his people's enemies. In Heb. 10:31 it is represented as a fearful thing to fall into the hands of the living God. With God's eternity his omnipotence is inseparably bound up. To the wrath of the Eternal here corresponds the wrath of the Almighty in 19:15.

<small>8. And the temple was full of the smoke of the glory of God and of his power; and no one could go into the temple, till the seven plagues of the seven angels were finished.</small>

8 *Smoke* in the Revelation is always the product of fire, 8:4, 9:2, 14:11, 18:18, comp. Ps. 148:8; and so also here, as *fire* was all but expressly named in ver. 7. When the golden vials are full of the wrath of God, this is visible by the symbol of fire. In the Revelation it is constantly a sign of God's wrath. The smoke proceeding from the fire of God's wrath, is said to be the smoke *of* (literally, *out of) the glory of God, and of his power.* The temple was *full* of the smoke of God. In Hab. 2:14, the glory of the Lord is an angry one, manifesting itself in judgments. So also in the FUNDAMENTAL PASSAGE, Num. 14:21; and here in ver. 10, and in 16:19, where this wrathful glory appears before the community. It is confirmed by Isa. 6:4, *and the house was full of smoke,* where Isaiah cries out before an angry God, *Woe is me, for I am undone.* The message he receives is one of wrath. Of the same description, too, is the smoke in Ex. 19:18. The whole manifestation there also was an angry one—comp. Heb. 12:18. It called aloud to Israel, that his God was a consuming fire, that no one could escape who might venture to set at nought his commandments. Smoke is never a symbol *of God's presence rich in grace,* or *a covering of the divine majesty.*

The *second part* rests on Ex. 40:34-35. Comp. also 1 Kings 8:10-11. The cloud there corresponds to the smoke here, and produced the same effect; although we must still carefully distinguish between them. That the cloud bears also a threatening character in the pillar of cloud and fire, is plain from the correspondence between the fire by night and the cloud by day (Num. 9:15-16.) Out of the cloud destruction came forth on the Egyptians (Ex. 14:24.) In the pillar of cloud the Lord came down to execute judgment on Miriam and Aaron (Num. 12:5.) But there, as well as here, the threatening carries a promise. If Israel is truly Israel, it affects only the enemies, and is to him a pledge of salvation. The God of energetic zeal for righteousness is his God. So here; that the temple is full of smoke, and no one is able to go into it, this is a sign that the Lord in love to his own was going to destroy their enemies. Besides, we see quite plainly in Isa. 6 the reason why none could enter in. If God manifests himself in the whole glory of his nature, in the whole energy of his punitive righteousness, the creature must feel itself penetrated by a deep feeling of its nothingness—not merely the *sinful* creature, as there in the case of Isaiah, but also the *finite*, according to Job 4:18, 15:15. Comp. on the words in 1:17, *and I fell down at his feet as dead.*

THE COMMAND TO POUR OUT THE SEVEN VIALS

> 16:1. And I heard a great voice out of the temple, which said to the seven angels, go away and pour out the seven vials of the wrath of God upon the earth.

The *loud voice* out of the temple can only, according to 15:8, be the voice of God, in whom the judgment to be executed for the welfare of the church begins. In Eze. 9:1 a similar call proceeds from God, *with a loud voice,* to the ministers of divine judgment; comp. there ver. 8, 7:8. The same voice which here delivers the commission to pour out the vials, says, after they have been poured out, in ver. 17, *It is done.* The voice is clearly God as it proceeds *out of the temple from the throne.* Here the same definiteness in the description was not necessary, as the verse relates to 15:8. To the earth belongs also the sea, in the sense in which it occurs at ver. 3.

THE FIRST VIAL: JUDGMENTS ON THE EARTHLY MINDED

> 2. And the first went away and poured out his vial on the earth. And there came an evil and grievous sore on the men, who have the mark of the beast, and worship his image.

In ch. 8 the word *angel* is repeated (8:7.) Here the style is briefer: *the first, the second,* etc, and *the seventh poured out his vial.* The vials make short work.

In ver. 1 the *earth* is used locally, but here, as the sea is distinguished from the earth, as are the rivers, there must be *an earth upon the earth* marked specially for the first vial. It indicates the *earthly minded,* the men who alienate themselves from heaven. In 13:12 *the earth and those who dwell on it* means not those who locally and corporeally abide on earth (the pilgrims on it dwell in heaven, 13:6,) but *the earthly minded* upon earth. This *earth* is formed by *the men who have the mark of the beast,* who have themselves become beast-like. In 13:11 the designation there of a beast corresponds to the *out of the earth.*

The *evil and grievous sore* refers to the sixth Egyptian plague, the boil *that cannot be healed* (Ex. 9:8-12, Deut. 28:27, 35.) It is mentioned among loathsome diseases, difficult to cure, but not fatal. It was in the knees and legs, and affected men and cattle. Those affected by it could not *stand* before Moses. It is an image of a *distressed condition,* as in ver. 11, sores are again mentioned with *pains,* as a consequence of the *darkness* over the kingdom of the beast.

The introductory groups have to do in general with the judgments of God on *the wickedness* of the world, while here the representation advances to the judgments on the *ungodly power* of the world, first in the general, then in ch. 17, in regard to its particular phases.

THE SECOND VIAL: THE SCOURGE OF DESTROYING WAR

> 3. And the second poured out his vial in the sea, and it became blood as of one dead, and every living soul died, that is in the sea.

The *sea* is the sea *of the peoples, the restless wicked world* (comp. on 13:1,) not a *literal* sea, which is no sphere for God's punitive and avenging agency. Compare on 8:8-9. That the *sea* is the subject in the expression, *and it was*, is plain from the words in the passage referred to, *and the third part of the sea became blood*. Here, as in 8:8-9, there is a reference to the first Egyptian plague; Ex. 7:20. It possessed a symbolical character; indicating the blood of the Egyptians should be shed, if they did not repent. If the blood has the appearance *as of* that of the dead, we are not to think of the blood-*colour* of the water, as in point of fact it *is* the blood of the dead, not the fact itself, but its symbol. Here it is the blood shed in war, as is evident from the symbol of the sea, out of which the beast arose. In 20:13 the dead that are in the sea, are those who perished violently in political conflicts. The scourge of destroying war is placed before our eyes by a double image—the *changing of the sea into blood*, and the *dying of the living creatures in the sea*. In the Egyptian plague the changing of the sea into blood caused the dying of the fish. So this may be referred to those who perish in battle, while the dying of all the living creatures in the sea are the greater number of those who die in consequence of the war, by distress, hunger, sorrow, and disconsolateness.

THE THIRD VIAL: PROSPERITY TURNED TO BLOODSHED

> 4. And the third poured out his vial on the rivers, and on the fountains of waters, and they became blood.

The water of *the rivers* is an image of prosperity, and good fortune; the *fountains of waters* indicate the source of a prosperous condition. The same symbol is in 8:10-11, where at the third trumpet a star falls on the rivers and fountains of water. There *the third part of the waters became wormwood*, here: *they became blood*. The correspondence between the second and third vial and the second and third trumpet is intentional, showing the internal connection between the two groups, yet the correspondence is only in part. That the rivers and fountains, named in Ex. 7:19, become blood, shows, that in the place of a prosperous and flourishing state there has come the shedding of blood. Similar is Ps. 42:3, *My tears have been my meat day and night*, instead of eating I weep; Ps. 80:5, *Thou feedest them with bread of tears*, instead of bread with tears; Ps. 88:18, *My acquaintances, the place of darkness*, the dark region of the dead has come into the place of all my acquaintances.

In the first Egyptian plague there was a twofold symbolical element. It first points to the shedding of guilty blood as a punishment for the shedding of innocent blood–the death of the firstborn, the drowning in the Red Sea, touching the *life* of the Egyptians. The second element is contained in Ex. 7:21, *And the river stank, and the Egyptians could not drink of the water of the river*–a prophecy of all that should damage the *prosperity* of Egypt, of which the water of the Nile was an emblem, since upon it the Egyptians wholly depended. Both the elements are found in Ps. 78:44, *he turned their streams into blood, and their waters they drank not.* How the threatening contained in the second symbolical element was fulfilled, is shown in ver. 45-48, and that of the first, ver. 49-51.

THE ANGEL OF THE WATERS: THE SUSTENANCE OF LIFE JUSTLY DENIED

> 5. And I heard the angel of the waters say, Thou art righteous, who is and who was, the godly, because thou hast judged thus. 6. For blood of saints and prophets have they shed, and blood hast thou given them to drink; they are worthy! 7. And I heard the altar say, Yea, Lord God Almighty, true and righteous are thy judgments.

The *epiphonem* in these three verses is attached primarily to the *third* vial; but the second is closely connected, and the first a prelude to the last two. The seals are divided by *four* and *three*. This *epiphonem* serves to separate the *three* vials from the *four*. So the three first vials are united by their brevity–one verse. The four last begin with the sun, and conclude with the air, while the three first keep *below*—to the earth, the sea, the rivers and the fountains. The ninth verse, *and they blasphemed the name of God* cannot be a boundary line as it occurs again at the fifth, ver. 11, and at the seventh, ver. 21, but rather connects the four last plagues together, and divides them off from the three first.

The *angel of the waters* here represents the whole host of angels, serving God, and *so far* is a purely ideal form, which only belongs to the vision, as the *speaking altar* in ver. 7, and in reality becomes manifest in a multitude of individuals. The *angel of the waters* has a delicate bond to the one in John 5:4.

In the address to God: *who is and who was, the godly,*[9] those attributes of God are particularly specified, which were manifested by his judgments, and from which these judgments flowed. *Here* we have still not reached the last end; four vials are yet to follow. But still, *who comes,* would not be properly suitable here, as it had been laid aside at 11:17. Here respect is not had, as in 1:4, 8, 4:8, to what the Lord is going to do in the future; but what he *has* done. Here the old God proved by deed, that he still lived. The *godly* is applied to God, in his regard for the moral order of the world, which admits of nothing alien, opposed to or rising above him, but only what conforms to his own nature, comp. on 15:4.

6 The judicial rule, according to which God appears as righteous in the judgments, which he here threatens, was laid down in Gen. 9:6, *Whoso sheddeth man's blood, by man shall his blood be shed,* where in connection with ver. 5 it is declared, not what *should* be done by man, but what God would accomplish by means of his righteous judgments; comp. on 13:10. Since the rule holds with God, blood for blood, so should it also hold with those in judicial authority, comp. Ex. 21:23.

Upon the distinction between *saints* and *prophets,* corresponding to that of righteous persons and prophets in Matt. 10:41, comp. at 11:18. Among the prophets the first place is held by the apostles, whose blood was shed upon the altar—Peter and Paul; comp. on 1:1; and also in Matt 10:41 the term *prophets* comprehend the apostles, comp. ver. 40. That Rome takes the lead in the guilt and the punishment, appears from 18:24.

---

9. Luther's text improperly prefixes, *Lord,* and instead of *the godly,* has *and holy,* or *godly.*

CHAPTER 16   THE REVELATION

<small>6. For blood of saints and prophets have they shed, and blood hast thou given them to drink; they are worthy!</small>

In the declaration, *blood hast thou given them to drink*, we must supply, *instead of the water, which they formerly enjoyed;* as the angel speaks of water. The drinking of *blood*, is brought into notice here, not as a *crime* (as it is in 17:6,) but as a *punishment*; as it is also in the FUNDAMENTAL PASSAGE, Isa. 49:26. In place of the pleasant drink of water they are made to take the horrid draught of their own blood; their prosperous condition disappears, and in its stead a bitter but righteous doom impels them to rage against one another.

<small>7. And I heard the altar say, Yea, Lord God Almighty, true and righteous are thy judgments.</small>

7 In 6:9-10 the souls of those who were slain for the word of God are lying under the altar of the heavenly sanctuary, having been offered on the altar.[10] From there they cry, *Lord, holy and true, how long dost thou not judge and avenge our blood on those who dwell on the earth.* In 14:18, the angel comes out of the altar, in vengeance for the blood shed on the altar. *Here* the altar *itself* rejoices in anticipation of the revenge. The altar itself might as well be said to speak here, as *the blood* in Gen. 4:10.

The *yea* expresses agreement with the preceding speech of the angel of the waters, in order that the two voices of *the angel of the waters* and of *the altar* may not fall out with each other; comp. 14:13. Without omnipotence (comp. 4:8, 15:3, 19:6) the judgments of the *Lord God Almighty* would not be true and righteous. The *truth* here also refers not merely to fidelity in regard to the promise (comp. on 6:10, 15:3); it stands opposed to all mere show and superficiality, that attaches itself to human judgments.

THE FOURTH VIAL: THE SUFFERINGS OF THIS LIFE

> 8. And the fourth poured out his vial on the sun, and it was given to him to scorch men with fire. 9. And the men were scorched with great heat, and blasphemed the name of God, who has power over these plagues, and repented not to give him glory.

The *sun* is here, not as light-giving (8:12 is not to be compared,) but in respect to his *scorching* power; so that 7:16 is parallel, *the sun shall not light upon them, nor any heat,* and the FUNDAMENTAL PASSAGE of Isa. 49:10. As in 8:12, the splendour of the sun represents a happy condition, its darkening, distress, so here the sun is the image of the sufferings of this life.

It is not of the natural *scorching* of the sun's rays here, as the whole preceding portion, the earth, the sea, the water, is in a *figurative* sense—but also from the addition, *with fire*. Fire is the divine wrath and judgment (14:18.) When we consider the sun figuratively, the fire poured out of the vial (comp. 15:7) is homogeneous to the fire of the sun.

That we must not render, *it was given to it*, the sun, but *it was given to him*, the angel, is clear from 7:2 (comp. also 4:8.) But it was given him *so, through* the sun, inflamed to an unusual heat by the vial. The *heat*, figurative of sufferings and assaults, is found also in Jer. 17:8; 1 Pet. 4:12.

In regard to the fate of the members of the church in this vial, the solution is given in ch. 7. The preservation of the children of Israel during the plagues which fell on the Egyptians, among whom they dwelt, and with whose fate their own seemed inseparably bound up, has the import of a matter-of-fact prophecy for all times. Here the word holds that is written in Jer. 17:7-8.

<small>10. Instead of: *and I heard the altar say*, Luther has, following an ill-supported reading—*and I heard another angel out of the altar say.*</small>

THE SEVEN PLAGUES ACCOMPANYING THE BEAST

9 Because the men had blasphemed, *the men were scorched with great heat.* The *blaspheming* is connected with all four plagues, except the sixth—as the catastrophe was *nearly* prepared, so the occasion for blaspheming was not fully given. The *being* of the Great God; it presses itself upon them with power, as a frightful load. But because they deny the sin, they rage against him as a tyrant; and blaspheme him, because they cannot murder him. *The heart of Pharaoh was hardened* is the refrain in the Egyptian plagues. This shows there is no inherently beneficial power in suffering, no other aim for divine, or human punishments, than that of retributive righteousness. The heathen ascribed their misfortunes to the neglected worship of their gods. But this was a self delusion, they were exasperated because the hand of the Christian God lay heavy upon them.

In regard to the blasphemers, ch. 15:4 shows the suffering does not prove to *all* a curse, many find it a blessing, and, like the penitent thief, are filled with contrition, when they receive what their deeds have deserved. But with them we shall find something existed before which is quickened to life. What was dead and corrupt remains under pains and sufferings as it was, or, if any change takes place, it is for the worse.

They blaspheme *the name of God* (comp. on 13:6,) not the Deity, but the God who has shown his deeds, the God of Jesus Christ, the God of the church, which inflames the worshippers of the beast to more wrath, that she constantly confesses this same God to be the author of the calamities under which they groan. That they blaspheme the name of God *because* he has the power over these plagues is shown by ver. 11, because of *their pains and their sores;* and ver. 21, *men blasphemed the Lord* because *of the plague of hail.*

On the words, *and they repented not,* comp. 9:20. The repentance is placed in this, that men give glory to God, if they recognize that the suffering is a deserved punishment of sin, and, therefore, it serves to glorify God, who is sanctified by the judgment. Where man is unyielded, proud and defiant, there God also does not yield, and in such a conflict man must be consumed. For a moment Pharaoh gave God glory, in Ex. 9:27, when he said to Moses and Aaron, *The Lord is righteous, and I and my people are wicked.* But it did not last long. *When Pharaoh saw that the thunder and the rain ceased, he sinned yet more, and hardened his heart, he and his servants.*

THE FIFTH VIAL: SMITING THE RULERS

> 10. And the fifth poured out his vial on the throne of the beast, and his kingdom was darkened. And they bit their tongues for pain. 11. And they blasphemed the God of heaven because of their pains, and because of their sores, and repented not of their deeds.

The former plagues fall upon the circumference of the kingdom of the beast, but this strikes its centre and the circumference at the same time. The preceding plagues affect the *throne,* as they distress the *subjects;* this descends from the throne to the subjects. When God seeks to destroy a people, it is most effectual by smiting the rulers.

The throne of the beast is situated at different places in different times; the beast has seven heads (comp. on 13:1, Isa. 47:1, Ps. 94:20.) Among the Chaldees it was at Babylon. At the time of the Seer it was at Rome. At the end of

10. And the fifth poured out his vial on the throne of the beast, and his kingdom was darkened. And they bit their tongues for pain.

time, after the thousand years, it will be in some sort of way under Gog and Magog. But wherever it may stand, it will be struck by the fifth vial. For, like all the others, this has a comprehensive character; it accompanies the ungodly power of the world through the whole of its history. That the throne of the beast is not the *capital city*, but the governing power, appears from 13:2, and also from 2:13. Comp. Jer. 13:13, *the kings that sit upon David's throne.* Rome was not the throne of the beast at the Seer's time, but the throne stood there, and the Roman emperor occupied it.

In consequence of the pouring out of the vial on the throne of the beast, *his kingdom is darkened* in an abiding, not a transient, darkness. Here the *kingdom* stands here in the sense of the governing power (John 18:36; and 1:6,9, 17:12,18.) On the *darkening* comp. Ps. 105:28 where it is said of Egypt, *He sent darkness, and darkened*, it is figuratively the doom of displeasure and calamity from the first to the last plague. There is only an allusion to the last plague but one in Egypt. The darkness which covered the Egyptians is the image of the divine wrath. Comp. Wisdom 17:21, *Over them was spread a heavy night, an image of that darkness which should come upon them.*

The subject in, *they bit*, are the possessors of the throne, and those with them. One bites his tongue to deaden the *passive* pain by means of an *active* one. In ver. 11, *because of their pains*, etc., *because of their darkness*, that is, their pains and their sores.

11. And they blasphemed the God of heaven because of their pains, and because of their sores, and repented not of their deeds.

11 They blaspheme the God of heaven, who brings upon them this suffering, even though they cannot come at him (comp. Ps. 2:4.) There is a verbal reference to 11:13, where it is said of the members of the church, *and they gave glory to the God of heaven.*

THE SIXTH VIAL: GOD ARMS HIS ENEMIES

12. And the sixth poured out his vial on the great river Euphrates, and its water was dried up, that the way might be prepared of the kings from the rising of the sun.

From the rising of the sun, east beyond the Euphrates, conquering hordes came from the earliest times upon lower Asia, especially Canaan—comp. on 9:14. *Euphrates* is here mentioned under the sixth vial, as there under the sixth trumpet. From there, in vision, come the hosts of the enemies of the church, here represented under *Jerusalem* (comp. on 14:20,) to be understood *typically*, comp. 9:14, in that the object of the assault is only *typical* Jerusalem, and from ver. 14, where, in the room of the kings from the rising of the sun, come the kings of *the whole earth*, putting the *actual* in immediate juxtaposition with the *typical* description.

The typical preparations of a *way* through water (the Red Sea and the Jordan) were for God's people, so also through the Euphrates itself in Isa. 11:15-16, and the leading through the sea and the Nile in Zech. 10:11. The preparation of the way serves the same design here, though the Lord *appears* here to do for the enemies of his people what elsewhere he did only for his people, as the drying up of the Euphrates is a result of *the pouring out of a vial.* All the vials were poured out in behalf of the church, for the destruction of her enemies, and to prepare for her final victory, as is shown in ver. 16, where we see that the way through the Euphrates is opened to the kings, *only that they may get to the place of their overthrow.* Verses 13-15 take into account the hellish-human machinery, the subordinate importance of which is manifest from the single fact, that it is hemmed in on both sides by the divine agency.

The *Euphrates* is mentioned here merely in respect to the hindrance it presented to the march of the ungodly power of the world into the holy land, against the holy city, against the church. This hindrance—to the terror of all persons of little faith, to the triumph of the world and the strengthening yet more of its enmity to God and Christ—is removed by God himself; what would arrest it is by him taken out of the way—as when, for example, in the time of the Seer, Peter and Paul, the pillars of the church, were beheaded, John himself banished to Patmos, and the church, thereby left exposed to the seductions of heathenism. But when faith is well nigh disposed on account of such things to give way, and the world is preparing to deal out the last blow against the church, then comes the place of Armageddon.

Precisely as God here *dries up* the Euphrates for the enemies of his church, did God, according to Isa. 43:17, lead Pharaoh's host to pursue after Israel. Scripture shows that *every step which the ungodly world takes for the destruction of the church, stands under the divine direction*—not merely the divine permission; God does not simply overthrow the enemies of his church, but also arms them, and that the success of their plans belongs not less to him than their discomfiture; *so that we have everywhere to do only with God.* Here, too, it is not prophesied what was to be done once, but what was to be continually repeated anew, so long as the conflict of the beast with the church should last, which substantially revives again in Gog and Magog. We have also in this vial, as in all the rest, a collective representation before us of that which in history realizes itself by degrees, and in a succession of acts and scenes. He who has properly received into his heart the contents of this book, can look on with painful delight while he sees one bulwark of the church after another laid prostrate, so that it might seem to be going into remedyless destruction.

HOW THE ENEMIES WERE SUMMONED

> 13. And I saw out of the mouth of the dragon, and out of the mouth of the beast, and out of the mouth of the false prophet, three unclean spirits as frogs. 14. (For these are spirits of demons, which do wonders) which go forth over the kings of the whole earth, to gather them together to the war of that great day of God the Almighty.

The words, *for these are, etc.*, can only be regarded as a simple parenthesis. The expression, *which go forth*, must be immediately joined to, the *frogs*. For the statement, *I saw out of the mouth*, requires the supplement of, *to go forth*, εκπορευεσψαι; which is done by the expression: *which go forth.*

While verses 13 and 14 delineate the activity of the enemies of God in the matter, in a regression they go back to *the first beginnings.* In ver. 12, the kings with their people have come on their way against the holy city, as far as the Euphrates. *Here* it is reported how they are summoned to the expedition. They are the kings of the *whole* earth; as 20:8, where Satan is represented as deceiving the nations in the *four* quarters of the earth.

The *dragon*, or Satan as the prince of this world, the *beast*, and the *false prophet*, known earlier as the *second beast from the earth*, have all been repre-

13. And I saw out of the mouth of the dragon, and out of the mouth of the beast, and out of the mouth of the false prophet, three unclean spirits as frogs.

sented in ch. 12 and 13 as the enemies of Christ and his church. The undertaking to which they stir up can therefore only be directed against Christ and his church. All three struggle for their existence.

Out of their mouth proceed *three unclean spirits*. Out of the *mouth*, not because the *speech*, but because the *breath* belongs to this—comp. Isa. 11:4. The proper dispenser of this impure, seductive spirit is the dragon. It goes out to the kings of the earth, not merely through its organs, the beast and the false prophet, but also *directly;* Satan is not *confined* to them. Therefore there are *three* spirits.

14. (For these are spirits of demons, which do wonders) which go forth over the kings of the whole earth, to gather them together to the war of that great day of God the Almighty.

14. The dependence of the spirits of the beast, the false prophet, and the dragon, is clear from ver. 14, where these spirits are *spirits of demons*, under Satan as their head. In 20:7 the whole work of seduction is ascribed to Satan, where he goes forth, to deceive the nations–the unclean spirits do not proceed from the whole three as on one footing of independence. Real influences proceed from Satan as well as from Christ. Men are placed mid-way between the *good* spirit, that is of Christ, and the *bad* one, that proceeds from Satan, see on 12:7, 13:11.

In 9:2, the *smoke* denotes the hellish spirit, which comes up to the earth. According to Zech. 13:2 the *false* prophets as well as the *true*, the worshippers of idols as well as those of God, stand under the dominion of a power lying beyond them, to which they have surrendered themselves by a free act of their own will.

In 1 Kings 22, the spirit of prophecy, personified yet appearing in a corporeal form, offers to deceive Ahab by putting false prophecies into the mouth of the prophets. This shows that the *false* prophets as well as the *true* stand under the influence of a power, that exists out of their own nature. By the parable of the tares among the wheat (Matt. 13:38-39,) Satan is in possession of the minds of his followers in like manner as Christ of his.

Christ stands opposed to the dragon (comp. 12:10;) Christian rulers form the contrast to the beast; and the contrast to the false prophet is found in Christian instruction and the office of witnessing, comp. 11:3.

The *frogs* respect the plagues of Egypt where uncleanness, and loathsomeness is noticed; belonging to the unclean animals, as symbols of sin. The parenthetical *for there are (exist) spirits of demons, which do signs*, makes preparation for ver. 15, and is like a call, *Watch and pray*, to stir us up to watchful zeal, we contend not with flesh and blood, but evil spirits (Eph. 6:12.) Left to ourselves we are undone, we need to seek in the *height* help against the *depth*.

All manifestations of God's judgment on the wicked, are concentrated here into one image–*the day of God*. In ch. 19 it is not the *entire* conflict of that great day, which is there described, but only a *single scene* of it. Another important scene, the overthrow of Rome, *precedes* it, and it is likewise to be *followed* by an important scene, the catastrophe of Gog and Magog.

KEPT FROM THE PUNISHMENT OF NAKEDNESS

15. Behold I come as a thief. Blessed is he who watches and keeps his garments, that he may not walk naked, and they may not see his shame.

THE SEVEN PLAGUES ACCOMPANYING THE BEAST

Here Christ is the speaker, see 3:3 and the Gospels. The words are immediately connected with ver. 14, the *great day of God the Almighty*, it is the day of Christ, the Father has committed all judgment to the Son. One outwardly belonging to the church, yet internally united to the world, shall also be condemned with the world. Believers, too, are in the world, and the world has a troublesome ally in their hearts. When the world fights against the Lord and his anointed, it will be difficult for them to watch, and keep their garments. Nothing can here preserve them but an eye fixed to the coming of the Lord. The great day of the Lord is the collective result of all his judgments on the ungodly world. Historically it manifests itself in an entire series of calamities. At each of them, and also those which are now before our eyes, the word, *Behold I come quickly, etc.*, a sort of miniature representation of the seven epistles, acquires new meaning; the letters, which in ordinary times are *dark*, then become transparent.

Clothing is a symbol of the *state and condition;* sinners bear filthy clothing, the justified pure, the righteous have white. The address is to Christians, so that the garments denote the *Christian state.*

The blessedness consists in keeping our garments beforehand (comp. on 1:1, 7,) and not being destitute of a Christian state before all the world, in its disgrace and humiliation. The *nakedness* is not the guilt, but the *punishment*; through the judgment the already existing nakedness, becomes a matter of public shame. The seeing of the shame appears often in the OLD TESTAMENT as a threatening and punishment, as in Isa. 3:17, 47:3, Hos. 2:10, Nah. 3:5.

GOD IS SANCTIFIED IN GOG

16. And he gathered them together into the place, which is called in the Hebrew Armageddon.

The subject is *God the Almighty*. At the close of ver. 14, every thing was connected with the Almighty: *of that great day of God the Almighty,* who was also the subject in ver. 15. Christ there announced his coming, here he comes in *his* name. We understand God as the subject also by the FUNDAMENTAL PASSAGE, Joel 3:2, *And I gather all peoples and bring them into the valley of Jehoshaphat,* Joel calls it *the valley of the judgment of God,* here it is *Armageddon,* comp. Ezek. 38:3-4, 39:1-6, where also the Lord leads the enemies of his church into his land, in order to judge them there; 38:16, *I bring him up on my land, that the heathen may know me, when I am sanctified in thee, Gog.*

Armageddon means *the mountain of Megiddo.* In the valley of Megiddo, Pharaoh, the type of the ungodly power of the world, had once killed the pious Josiah, who in Zech. 12:10-11, appears as a type of Christ, ver. 11: *At that time there shall be a great lamentation in Jerusalem* (over Jesus, who, like Josiah, was slain by the hand of the heathen, on account of the sins of his people,) *like the lamentation of Hadadrimmon in **the valley of Megiddo***. God gathers the heathen together, yet from their own design, as with ver. 12, where they *desired* to pass the Euphrates, and by means of the vial the Euphrates was dried up for them. What they once accomplished there against Josiah, they would now again accomplish against Jesus; he, the risen one, must there receive from them the stroke of death, and his church must go down with him to the grave, as formerly the theocracy was borne to the grave with Josiah. But the ancient

CHAPTER 16   THE REVELATION

<small>16. And he gathered them together into the place, which is called in the Hebrew Armageddon.</small> heathenish wicked deed shall not be *renewed* in Armageddon, but be *avenged* (comp. 1 Kings 21:19, 23; 2 Kings 9:33,) because it is God, who gathers them together into this place, to which they themselves also hasten; and in ver. 14 the great day of God the Almighty breaks in at Armageddon.

There is a *human design* that lies in the background, for which the place carried an inviting aspect, as it had been the theatre of an earlier overthrow of the church and of its former head, who by name and position typified the present head. Mention is made of *the valley of Megiddo* only in the passages which refer to the death of Josiah. Nothing properly corresponds to the valley, but the mountain. The death of Josiah, in Zech. 12:10-11, is cited by John in his Gospel, 19:37, and alluded to in this book, 1: 7. The reference to *the victory of Pharaoh* suits the Egyptian character of the whole group.

Its being said, *which is called in the Hebrew*, shows, that not simply a proper name is brought forward, but that the word has an element in it which must be explained out of the Hebrew. That no Greek explanation is appended, shows, in connection with the fact of Megiddo presenting no obvious derivation, that this Hebrew element can only stand in the syllable, Ar (the Hebr. הר), which required no explanation.

The sixth vial of necessity breaks off here to what immediately prepares for the final catastrophe of the seventh. With the actual irruption of the great day of God the Almighty, with the overthrow of the kings of the earth, which suddenly takes place, all—the drying up of the Euphrates, and also the fatal day of Armageddon, which announced the overthrow of Christ—all is *out*, nothing more remains as an object for the avenging severity of God. As regards the substance, it is reported in the seventh vial on this overthrow. Still, the *clothing* there is of a different description.

The seven vials form of themselves a separate whole, and there can be no continuation of what is broken off here, as in the one who sits on the white horse. Besides the battle in 19:11 is only a partial, particular phase of the conflict described here, in which all the conflicts of the worldly power against Christ and his church are comprised into one whole.

THE SEVENTH VIAL: THE END OF THE UNGODLY WORLD POWER

<small>17. And the seventh poured out his vial upon the air; and there went out a loud voice out of the temple from the throne, which said: It is done. 18. And there were lightnings and voices and thunders, and there was a great earthquake, such as has not been since men were upon the earth, such an earthquake so great. 19. And out of the great city there were made three parts, and the cities of the heathen fell.
And Babylon the great was remembered before God, to give to her the cup of the wine of the wrath of his anger. 20. And all islands fled away, and no mountains were found. 21. And a great hail as an hundredweight fell from heaven on the men; and the men blasphemed God upon the plague of hail, for its plague is very great.</small>

In ver. 1 merely, *a loud voice out of the temple*, where from what goes before shows the voice to be God's. Here this is rendered still more evident by the *from the throne*. In ver. 1 the commission was to pour out the seven vials of God's wrath on the earth. Now it is fulfilled; for the inevitable result could be anticipated (comp. on 11:17.) The word, *it is done*, at the same time carries along with it the end of the ungodly world and its power, for, according to 15:1 the wrath of God is filled up with these seven plagues. Ezekiel 9:11 is similar. We must not explain, *It has been*. For, then we should want a definite subject. The vials are not limited to Rome, as in what follows, Babylon the great appears only as a particular point, which was struck by the judicial severity of God under this seal.

18 We may compare 11:19, also ver. 21. The seventh vial agrees exactly in its main features with the seventh trumpet. Here again we have arrived precisely at the same point at which we found ourselves there, clearly the whole book cannot be a continuous representation. At the same time, however, there is a difference between the vials and the trumpets. The particular in the vials comes more distinctly out on the ground of the general. Peculiar here are the contents of ver. 19-20, the reference to the *God-opposing powers of the world*, while the trumpets, like the seals, have to do simply with *godless men*.

That the *lightnings* should go first is clear from what was remarked at 11:19.[11] By the *earthquake* is denoted the shaking of the ungodly powers of the world. On the expression: *such as has not been*, comp. Ex. 9:18, and Dan. 12:1, on which also Matt. 24:21 rests. The expression in this last passage, *since the beginning of the world*, serves to explain that in Daniel, *since there was a nation*.

19 The division of the verses is here unhappy. Ver. 19 should properly have ended with *fell*. Then each verse would have begun with the *particular*, whose fall was of especial importance in respect of the present of the Seer, and from that would have risen to the *general*.

Babylon the great corresponds to the great city, and the *islands* and *mountains* correspond to the cities of the heathen. *Three parts*, after the number of the powers that bore rule in it—the dragon, the beast, and the false prophet; to each a part. That with the threefold division we are to suppose a complete prostration concurring, is plain from the cause that produces it, the earthquake; and also from the parallel *falling* which is spoken of the great city itself, in 14:8, 18:2. *Two cities* have in the Revelation the name of *great*—Jerusalem in 11:8, and Babylon, that is Rome in all the other passages, and very commonly, 14:8, 17:18, 18:10, 16, 18-19, 21.

The designation of *the great city* is used neither of Jerusalem nor of Babylon without something in the context to indicate with certainty what precisely is meant. Hence the following expression, *and Babylon the great*, must be a resumption, as otherwise the common epithet of *the great* would be attended only with perplexity. The pain of uncertain conjecture in the Revelation belongs only to those who voluntarily surrender themselves to it. In the Apocalypse Jerusalem always denotes the church. But this can never become wholly degenerate and fall away; and as little can it be the subject of consuming judgments—comp. 11:13. The heathen are to be regarded, according to 11:18, as full of wrath, raging against the church of Christ. For this they here receive their reward. From the connection with the great city, *the cities of the heathen* are here to be conceived as possessors of the power of the heathen world. In the designation of Babylon as *the great* there is a reference to her guilt, since she had only become great through her disregard of what is just and right. Babylon denotes *heathen* Rome as proved at 14:8. *Babylon was remembered*, alludes to Ps. 9:12. On the words, *to give her the cup*, etc., see on 14:10.

---

11. Luther follows the reading: *voices and thunders and lightnings*, which has arisen from an unseasonable comparison of 8:5.

In the expression, *of the wrath of his anger*, also in 19:15, the anger is the genus, and the wrath, the species—the intense feeling that appears in the energy and rigour of the mode of action. This is a necessary accompaniment of *fulness of love*.

20. And all islands fled away, and no mountains were found.

20 The *islands*, like the *mountains*, denote *kingdoms*; comp. on 6:14. As kingdoms by *islands* respect is had to their separate existence, while as *mountains*, they exercise dominion over others. The addition *of the heathen* in ver. 19 is to be understood also here. Along with the islands and the mountains the sea also has vanished. The *last* event, which is comprised in the comprehensive representation, is the destruction of Gog and Magog in 20:7-10.

21. And a great hail as an hundredweight fell from heaven on the men; and the men blasphemed God upon the plague of hail, for its plague is very great.

21 On the *hail* comp. on ch. 11:19. Instead of: *as an hundredweight*, properly, as large as a *talent*. The talent weighed between fifty and sixty pounds.

They still *blaspheme*, therefore, dying. For this hail leaves no one in *life* who is struck by it of the enemies still left by the other plagues. The deadly character of the hail is clear in that no mention is made, as in the PARALLEL PASSAGES, of their repenting of their works along with their blaspheming. They no longer have *time* to repent. But even when dying they can still blaspheme.

Under the seventh trumpet *the time for the dead to be judged* had also come; comp. 11:18. But this is not said in respect to the seventh vial, however nearly it otherwise touches on the seventh trumpet. For the seven vials or plagues, after the example of those of Egypt, do not alight on individuals as such, but on the powers of the world; they all, therefore, belong to the earth (comp. 16:1.) Hence, in *this* group the wicked feeling that prompted the still unpunished blasphemy cannot be met. We are thus pointed forwards to the *following* group, at the close of which, in 20:12, the dead who have not died in the Lord shall be *judged according to their works*.

GROUP 6

THE DESTRUCTION OF THE THREE ENEMIES OF GOD'S KINGDOM

REVELATION 17:1–20:15

REVELATION 17:1–20:15

The destruction of the three enemies of God's Kingdom

INTRODUCTION

As the fourth group (chapters 12—14) represents the conflict of the three enemies against the Lamb and those who follow him with preliminary indications of their overthrow, so this sixth group (17:1—20:15,) to which the fifth formed a sort of prelude, represents *the judgment on the three enemies*. In doing this, it does not stand merely at what is altogether general, but goes as far into detail as it could properly do without transgressing the limits which separate prophecy from history. *In many respects we have here the most important part of the book before us.* The striking clearness and accuracy with which we have here unfolded to us the most important evolutions in the history of the church, during the times which we can now look back upon, strengthens our faith in looking forward with confidence to the one event announced here, which still belongs to the *future*, ch. 20:10.

Whoever has attained to a right apprehension of the meaning of this group will find it a tabernacle into which he can retreat in tempestuous times. It is capable of affording an inexpressible rest and confidence to the soul.

The arrangement is as follows. In representing the conflict waged by the three enemies against Christ and his church, a descent is made from Satan down to the two beasts; but here, inversely in representing Christ's victory, a rise takes place from the two beasts to Satan. In the first beast, again, it rises from the destruction of the two last heads, which, in St John's time, were still present and future, the two last phases of the ungodly power of the world, in its heathen state, to the destruction of the beast itself.

In the time of the Seer, the beast oppressed the church through the *sixth head*, the Roman monarchy; and through the possessor of this monarchy, the great whore, the Babylon of that time—Rome. The judgment of the great whore, the destruction of Rome as the heathen mistress of the world, is unfolded in ch. 17. And now the ungodly power of the world must be directed by God through its *seventh* and *last* phase, which, as had already been imaged in ch. 13, by the ten horns on the seventh head, was to possess, not a *united*, but a *divided* character, consisting of ten kings or kingdoms. These, as in ver. 14, by way of anticipation, were to war with the Lamb, and the Lamb was to overcome them. The overthrow of heathen Rome, which is announced in ch. 17, is vividly portrayed in ch. 18. The prophecy makes no advance here. The aim is to imprint deeply what had already been represented in ch. 17. In 19:1-4, the whole of this first part, so important and consolatory for those who were sighing under the persecutions of Rome, and struggling with her seductions, concluded, by the *te deum laudamus* of the just made perfect, celebrating God's righteous judgment upon Rome.

This *first* song of praise of the heavenly church, which magnifies the grace of God contemplated as already past, is immediately followed up in ch. 19:5-10 by a *second*, which *in anticipation* gives thanks for what was still to be done, even to the setting up of the kingdom of Almighty God, and the celebration of the marriage feast of the Lamb; so that it forms the introduction to all that follows. The following portion represents how these anticipations are gradually realized. By means of the two songs of praise the whole of the group is divided into two great halves—the first containing the victory over the enemy, that at the time of the Seer pressed so hard upon the church; the second, the victory over all the other enemies.

First, in 19:11-21, in further enlargement of what was indicated in ch. 17, we have *the victory of Christ over the ten kings,* the instruments of his judgment on Rome. Along with these, as the last phase of the *heathen worldly power,* the ten horns on the seventh head of the beast out of the sea, the beast himself also, the heathen state, goes down, and his tool likewise, the beast out of the earth, the false prophet, the God-opposing wisdom of the world.

Of the three enemies of the kingdom of God in ch. 13, two now lie prostrate on the ground. Ch. 20:1-6 represents how the third, Satan, is rendered for a time harmless. He is shut up for a thousand years in hell, and allows to the church, during that thousand years, a secure and unimperilled existence.

At the end of the thousand years opportunity is given to Satan anew for seduction; the earth again rises up against heaven; the church on all sides is heavily oppressed; but fire comes down from heaven and consumes her oppressors *(he who reads, let him understand.)* Satan is for ever disarmed of his power, and the final judgment overtakes all, who during the course of time have acted in a hostile manner toward the Lord and his church, 20:7-15.

Now, since all the enemies of the kingdom of God have been brought to desolation, the opening song of praise has found its realization, the Almighty God has taken to himself the kingdom, the joyful time of the marriage of the Lamb has come, and the only thing that remains as an object for the seventh and last group is, the solemnization of this marriage.

REVELATION 17

Announcing the overthrow of Rome, the sixth head

CHAPTER SUMMARY

Chapter 17 divides itself into *three parts*, marked by the angel commencing his discourse with the word, *he spake, etc.* three times.

In the first part the judgment of the great whore, that sits upon the beast with the seven heads and ten horns, is shown. The two others give the signification of the symbol. The first treats, in preparation for the second, after the introduction in ver. 7, of the beast in ver. 8, of his seven heads in ver. 9-11, of the horns in ver. 12-14. The second treats of the whore and the judgment that is held upon her, ver. 15-18.

THE JUDGMENT OF THE GREAT WHORE

17:1. And there came one of the seven angels who have the seven vials, and spake with me and said, Come, I will show thee the judgment of the great whore that sits upon the many waters. 2. With whom the kings of the earth have committed fornication, and they that dwell on the earth have been made drunk with the wine of her fornication. 3. And he brought me into a wilderness in the Spirit. And I saw a woman sitting on a scarlet coloured beast, that was full of names of blasphemy, and had seven heads and ten horns. 4. And the woman was clothed with purple, and scarlet colour, and gilded with gold and precious stones and pearls, and had a golden cup in her hand, full of abominations, and of the filthinesses of her fornication. 5. And on her forehead a name written: mystery, Babylon the great, the mother of harlots, and of the abominations of the earth. 6. And I saw the woman drunk with the blood of saints, and with the blood of the witnesses of Jesus. And I wondered very much when I saw her. 7. And the angel spake to me, wherefore dost thou wonder? I will tell thee the mystery of the woman and of the beast, that bears her, which has the seven heads and the ten horns.

One of the angels having the seven vials, points to a close connection between this sixth vision and the fifth. The judgment of the great whore, which forms the theme here, was comprehended in the seven vials. In the last plague, which annihilated the ungodly power of the world, *Babylon the great* is named as a chief object of the judgment of God (16:19,) hence, what is said here of that can only be a *more extended representation of a particular point;* and to indicate this one of those angels appears as the leader. It is the same angel that shows John, in 21:9, the bride, the Lamb's wife. This is because he here shows the judgment of the great whore in reference to the parallelism between the two women—one of whom is brought down, the other raised up. The second passage, 21:9, literally agrees with verse 1.

The angels *still have* the seven vials, and the vials are still also full, so the judgment was still future. The *come,* is like the *come* to Lazarus in John 11:43,

CHAPTER 17   THE REVELATION

1. And there came one of the seven angels who have the seven vials, and spake with me and said, Come, I will show thee the judgment of the great whore that sits upon the many waters.
2. With whom the kings of the earth have committed fornication, and they that dwell on the earth have been made drunk with the wine of her fornication.

before her is seen the destruction of her enemies, and her own resurrection to new life. The angel would *show* John the *judgment* of the whore. What John says of the beast, of his heads and horns, serves as a foundation for what he has to say of the *woman*; which serves as a preparation for the judgment. The Seer sees immediately in ver. 3 the woman in the wilderness, and obtains the explanation in ver. 16, that thereby her *desolation* is denoted.

2 Babylon, or Rome, is called *the great whore* on account of her selfishness which conceals itself behind the appearance of love, on account of the diplomatical and deceitful arts, by which she extends her dominion. This is clear from 14:8, where she *has made all the heathen drink of the wrath of the wine of her fornication. Fornication* here does not refer to apostasy from God. Babylon still appears standing, and in 16:19 is called *the great*—an internal connection subsists between the greatness of the whore and the greatness of Babylon; as in 14:8, the greatness of Babylon is brought into remembrance with her fornication. If the fornication denotes *cunning policy*, then the *being great* in that implies being great in general: the great whore is at the same time the great mistress of the world. So it turns here, not upon a moral property alone, but also upon the great *power* which must be brought to an end by the judgment.

Her *judgment* here implies that her doing, her *guilt* had already been treated at length already–in 14:8 in a passing way, and in 13:3-8, where are described the severe persecutions which the Roman power, the sixth head of the beast, inflicts on the church. The great whore is only so far different from the sixth head, as this head denotes the Roman power, while the whore is *the great city* in which that power concentrates itself–Rome.

3. And he brought me into a wilderness in the Spirit. And I saw a woman sitting on a scarlet coloured beast, that was full of names of blasphemy, and had seven heads and ten horns.

3 The *wilderness* is an image of the state into which the woman was to be brought, where her judgment is fulfilled. In Jer. 51, the threatening is that ancient Babylon should be turned into a wilderness; and in Isa. 21:1, Babylon, on account of the approaching desolation, is called the *desert of the sea*. What is said here of Babylon, respects every worldly power that treads in her footsteps. The church is continually called anew to stand unmoved amid the proud triumphs of that power, and allow herself to be carried by the Spirit into the wilderness, to see there *the ruin* hidden behind the greatness.

The beast is here indicated in a cursory manner, and in terms that interconnect with ch. 13; so that we are to borrow what is needed. Here the Seer has not to do with the *beast*, but with the *woman, who sits upon the beast*, especially the judgment to be passed upon her. If the beast and the woman are the same—Rome and its empire, how then can the woman sit upon the beast? If the beast is the ungodly power of the world in general, then Rome, the possessor of that at the time of the prophet, should naturally appear sitting on the beast.

The scarlet coloured beast corresponds to the *red* dragon in 12:3. The moral quality of the beast is found in its *godlessness* (13:1,) and its blasphemy, and here its *scarlet colour*–the colour of blood. In ver. 6 the woman is drunk with the blood of saints and witnesses. See Isa. 1:18. With the godlessness, hatred toward true piety goes hand in hand. The *scarlet coloured* denotes a *quality*, a blood-thirsty disposition, but not a *property* like royal pomp and glory.

4. And the woman was clothed with purple, and scarlet colour,

4 The *apparel* and the adorning of the woman is significant of *the rich and proud pomp of a sovereign*. In regard to the *golden cup*, comp. at 14:8, Jer. 51:7, *the golden cup of Babylon is in the hand of the Lord*. The cup can only be filled with what makes those to whom it is given *helpless*, in an *overpowering*, a

THE ANNOUNCING OF THE OVERTHROW OF THE SIXTH HEAD, ROME

reducing to a state of *impotence*. Hence it is not the abominations of idolatry, but only of *political enormities*. The *abominations* and *filthinesses*–the wine of the cup, are then *the shameful transactions of that love feigning policy by which Rome reduced the nations to a state of impotence*. The *golden* points to the glory of the person who has the cup, and who presents it to the nations, that they may drink of it.

5 The *name*, which she has *written* on her *forehead*, is not a title which she takes to herself, but the expression of her nature. The name consists of a whole sentence, and ver. 6 also belongs to it. A *mystery* is a matter lying absolutely beyond the common, natural understanding. The mystery of Babylon consists in that its greatness still continued after the appearance of Christ, and in its oppressing his confessors. The secret is *told*, ver. 7, through announcing that this greatness is not an *abiding* one; but destined to destruction. To the secret corresponds the *great wondering* of the seer in ver. 6. An end comes at the same time to the mystery and the wondering. In Ps. 73 the victory and the unveiling of the mystery comes there, by the Psalmist recovering from his error, and going into the sanctuary to see the secrets, closed to natural understanding (ver. 16-17.) The solution of the mystery there, too, is found by *marking their end*. It is merely an enigma and certainly no mystery to suppose that by Babylon is meant Rome, especially after 1 Peter 5:13. Babylon as *the great*, or *the mother of harlots*, as much as *the great whore* in ver. 1, practises through the widest bounds, a policy the most cunning and destructive to the nations. All, who practise the same within narrower bounds, are, as it were, her daughters. The *abominations* here also can only be *political* enormities, including what she did against the church, for the root of her conduct in that respect was not false religious zeal, but *despotism*, as is further brought out in ver. 6.

6 The *witnesses of Jesus* are not those who testify of Jesus, but those who belong to him, as *the testimony of Jesus* is the testimony which belongs to him. By means of a rise here, the saints–the witnesses, that quality of the slain appears which makes the mystery more penetrable, still heightens the guilt of Rome. They had been killed in their very service on *account* of their confession. Not those, who generally delivered a good confession, but such as filled the *office* of witnessing by profession. As here the saints and the witnesses of Jesus are connected, in 18:20 the *prophets* and the saints; in 19:10, to have the *testimony of Jesus*, is explained by *having the spirit of prophecy;* that also in 11:3, the two witnesses are *prophesying*, not representing Christians generally, but the *teaching office*. In 11:18, Christians are divided into *two classes*, prophets and saints, the great and the small. The *first* place among the witnesses, according to 18:20, is held by the *apostles*.

The *wondering* of John corresponds to Babylon being designated as a *mystery* in ver. 5, as from ver. 7, *wherefore wonderest thou? I will show thee the mystery*. The mystery of the woman must be the object of wonder, in that it abides in its greatness, notwithstanding its fearful guilt. In a contrast is the wonder of the Seer, and those whose names are not written in the book of life in ver. 8. If he wondered at the power of the beast, still unimpaired after Christ, then his wondering infers he did not know what to make of the woman. In 13:3 the object there of the astonished wondering is the heathen, and specially the Roman power appearing still unbroken after Christ had come. The angels with the seven vials were *a sign great and wonderful*, and correspond

and gilded with gold and precious stones and pearls, and had a golden cup in her hand, full of abominations, and of the filthinesses of her fornication.

5. *And on her forehead a name written: mystery, Babylon the great, the mother of harlots, and of the abominations of the earth.*

6. *And I saw the woman drunk with the blood of saints, and with the blood of the witnesses of Jesus. And I wondered very much when I saw her.*

with the wondering of John upon the woman. The judgment on the beast, the whore, is, as it were, the counter-wonder to the beast, the whore herself.

<small>7. And the angel spake to me, wherefore dost thou wonder? I will tell thee the mystery of the woman and of the beast, that bears her, which has the seven heads and the ten horns.</small>

7 The *wherefore didst thou wonder?* here corresponds to Matt. 14:31, *O thou of little faith, wherefore didst thou doubt?* Human nature is always riveted to the visible. John *wondered* because the overthrow of the gigantic mischief had not yet been accomplished, its power still existed in undiminished force. The *wherefore* shows, that the wondering is a groundless, foolish one. That wondering of Jesus at unbelief in Mark 6:6 corresponds to the wondering here.

The mystery of the whore is *that she is made desolate;* the mystery of the beast, *that it goes into perdition.* The mystery of the beast is merely indicated here to connect it with the whore. The chief object here is the judgment on the whore, which is immediately and wholly disposed of; the beast is mentioned only in the *second* place, a general sketch merely is given in ver. 10-11, to be completed later in 19:20. The subject of *the beast* is handled in ver. 8, of his *seven heads* in ver. 9-11, his *ten horns* in ver. 12-14, of *the whore* in ver. 15-18, which all show what is said of the beast serves as foundational to that said of *the woman.* That the chief subject is discussed in ver. 15-18, is expressly indicated by the new beginning, *and he spake to me.*

THE BEAST

> 8. The beast which thou sawest, was and is not, and shall ascend out of the abyss, and go into perdition; and they that dwell upon the earth shall wonder, whose names are not written in the book of life from the foundation of the world, when they see the beast that it was, and is not, and again shall be present.

The beast *was,* it held its being upon earth, so long as the dominion of Satan as the prince of this world was unbroken. By what his *not being* was accomplished, appears from 13:3, *and I saw one of his heads as killed to death.* As the *deadly* wound there, so here the corresponding *not being* must have its ground in the atonement of Christ. Further, if it is Christ who puts an end to the beast's coming again out of the abyss and his resumed existence on the earth (comp. ver. 14, 19:11, especially ver. 20,) in him also must its *not being* have its cause. The *not being* is continuing during the coming again and renewed being, because ver. 11, the whole duration of the beast is denoted by the two stages of *having been* and of *not being.*

On the *abyss,* that is, hell, see on 9:1. Chapter 11:7 mentions the beast's ascending from hell. See on the *ascending* at 13:1. That the *it shall (is going to) ascend,* and the corresponding, *it shall again be,* had a foundation in the present, and that an *increase* belongs to the future, is clear in that the Apocalypse was composed at a time of organized bloody persecution against the Christians. *Perdition* is the perdition of hell. The beast goes to *its own place;* what comes out of hell, goes to hell. In John 17:12, Judas is called the son of perdition, corresponding to the *child of hell* in Matt. 23:15, and also 2 Thess. 2:3, comp. 1:9. In 19:20, *they were both cast alive into the lake of fire, etc.* On the words, *and they shall wonder . . . from the foundation of the world,* comp. 13:8. Election is brought in to meet the great temptation. As the second *was and is not* corresponds to the first, so the *and shall again be present,* corresponds to *shall ascend out of the abyss.* It is not said, *shall be,* but, *shall be present.* The wound was an absolutely mortal one, as will be shown by the end. It comes

THE ANNOUNCING OF THE OVERTHROW OF THE SIXTH HEAD, ROME

again out of the abyss, from which it derives, as it were, its last power, but only as a kind of spectre. The emphasis rests on the expression, *again shall be present*, when they see, that the beast, which was and is not, again shall be there.[12]

THE SEVEN HEADS OF THE BEAST

> 9. Here belongs the understanding, that has wisdom. The seven heads are seven mountains, on which the woman sits, and are seven kings. 10. Five are fallen, one is, the other is still not come, and when he comes, he must abide a short time. 11. And the beast, which was and is not, he is an eighth, and is of the seven, and goes into perdition.

The *here belongs* is properly *here is*, meaning that wisdom here has its right place, intimating a problem is presented here, which requires profound spiritual insight, as in 13:18. The *mountains* are to be understood spiritually, as 13:3 says that one of the heads was killed to death, which does not suit a mountain, as say the seven hills of Rome. In ver. 3 the woman *sitting on a scarlet-coloured beast* corresponds to the sitting on the mountains here. If by the first Rome is the holder of the world's power, then the sitting upon the mountains will also have the same meaning. Symbolically *mountains* signify *kingdoms*. This is plain from the explanation *seven kings*, or *kingdoms*. The seven phases of the ungodly power of the world were definitely marked at 13:1. The seven hills of Rome could only be a symbol of the seven-formed worldly power. That the *kings* here are not individuals, but ideal persons, personified *kingdoms*, is clear from the expression: *mountains*, denoting not single rulers, but kingdoms. In ver. 12 also, kings stand for kingdoms. That the heads of the beast here are called *kings* is against the opinion that the beast is the papacy.

10 Of the seven kings mentioned *five* belong to the period already past; and of the two others one was then present on the stage of history, and the other had still not entered on it. The *falling* denotes the overthrow of the kingdoms; comp. 18:2, 14:8. The five kings, or worldly kingdoms, that had already fallen at the time of the Seer, are the kings of Egypt, Assyria, Babylon, Persia and Greece.

The *one that is*, accordingly, must be the sixth great monarchy, the Roman, for this existed at the time of John. The being, *one is*, denotes here the contrast to the being fallen, the being *as king*. Otherwise, a contradiction would be presented to ver. 8, 11, where the *not being* of the beast is affirmed. With the beast the power also of this sixth head is broken, the head which received the deadly wound. The beast is no longer what it was, but it has still not gone into destruction. The one king does not stand as the five preceding kings stood before their fall; he is, as he even now can be, in the *non esse* of the beast. The Lord said, *I have overcome the world*. In that lies the foundation of the difference between the one and the five. When *the other* is *come*, then *the sixth falls*, that is now the king of Rome. As the *seventh* shall abide but a *short time*, then

---

12. The reading καιπερ εστιν, *although it still is*, is to be rejected. It gives, properly, no right sense. By it the wondering must turn upon the *not being*; for the being would only be incidentally noticed; *although it is*, cannot signify as much as, *and still is*. But 13:4 is against it, as there only a wondering of astonishment can be meant, such gaping admiration as a lost world feels toward the beast. So also here, ver. 6, by which the wondering can only refer to the *power* of the beast. And, lastly, the correspondence between the *again shall be present*, and *shall ascend*, is decisive against this reading, which is at any rate badly supported, and on external grounds also is deserving of rejection.

CHAPTER 17   THE REVELATION

<small>10. Five are fallen, one is, the other is still not come, and when he comes, he must abide a short time.</small>

with the one then being it was likely to continue still a long time, to exercise the church in patience.

The kings are *ideal* persons, as the seventh king in ver. 12 is a compound of ten kings. *He has not yet come,* because his time has not yet arrived (John 7:8; comp. ver. 6, 8:20.) When it is said that he shall remain only *a short time,* the subject is the duration of the seventh power as a God-opposing one. To the declaration here, *he must abide a short time,* corresponds in ver. 12 the statement, *as kings they receive power one hour with the beast.* The end to this abiding is represented in 19:11.

<small>11. And the beast, which was and is not, he is an eighth, and is of the seven, and goes into perdition.</small>

11 The words, *which was and is not* form the basis of that which was to be declared of the destiny of the beast. If it has received its death-blow from the atonement of Christ, if its existence from that time is only an apparent one—if, with all its swaggering, it is but a bloodless spectre—its end can only be palpable *destruction.* The destruction of the beast, with all that belongs to it, is the theme of the whole group. It was only destruction that was spoken of in what immediately precedes: five have already fallen; the one that is, must fall; the seventh, that had not yet come, is to continue but a short time. So that at the words, *is an eighth,* there is implied, *in destruction.* If there stood merely, *he is of the seven,* we would suppose he personally belonged to the seven (Acts 21:8;) as it is decidedly against the manner of the Revelation of John to put forth enigmas for the solution of which it does not itself provide the means, and to leave space to uncertain conjecture. But as the words *is an eighth* precede, the relation to the seventh is withdrawn from the *personal* sphere, and by the connection limited to the *issue,* in what precedes all has respect to the destruction of the parties in question, as with the appended statement confirms, *and goes into perdition,* and like the seven, or with the seven, the beast goes also into perdition. With the seventh phase of the ungodly power of the world, itself also ceases, the heathen state generally comes to an end. We have a commentary on what is meant here in 19:11-21. There the conflict of the seventh head or king against the kingdom of God is delineated. In this conflict, according to ver. 20-21 the beast also is comprehended, and is cast into the lake of fire (corresponding to the *perdition*), whereas before, the beast *survived* its particular heads, and soon appeared again on the stage of conflict with a new head.

From the interpretation now given every thing in this verse refers to the destruction of the beast. The current exposition is quite different. It finds the announcement here, that after the seven heads of the beast the *personal antichrist* shall appear. But if the beast were a proper independent power, *along with* and *after* the seven heads, then what was to be said on it would not belong here which deals merely with the seven heads. It must still be made the subject of discourse elsewhere in its proper place. If ver. 9-11 treat of the heads of the beast, this verse cannot contain anything new; it can only bring clearly and distinctly out, what had already been indirectly contained in the preceding part. If the heads of the beast are only seven then it is self-evident that with the seventh head the beast itself goes to destruction, for without a head the beast can have no existence. Then, those who understand *antichrist* here by the beast either feign an eighth head, without any textual foundation for it, and against the limitation of the heads to the number seven, or remark the beast consists of eight *pieces*–the seven heads are for themselves, and the eighth piece is the whole body and therefore the beast itself (11:7) with his feet, mouth, etc. But the beast needs its head, with its mouth with which it blasphemes, its teeth as that with which it tears. As formerly the heads were not without the body, so now the body cannot be without the head, in a diminution of its frightfulness. But the NEW TESTAMENT elsewhere knows nothing of a *personal* antichrist—see p. 152.

Finally, the words, *and goes into perdition* resume with intentional literality the *and go into perdition* in ver. 8. Now, if the beast there is the whole of the worldly power as opposed to God, it cannot denote antichrist here as an individual. The identity with ver. 8 is clear from the *was and is not,* which itself also does not suit a personal antichrist, for such had not been before.

THE TEN HORNS OF THE BEAST

> 12. And the ten horns, which thou sawest, are ten kings, which have not as yet received kingdoms; but they shall receive power as kings one hour with the beast.
> 13. These have one mind and give their power and their authority to the beast.
> 14. These shall war with the Lamb, and the Lamb shall overcome them—for he is a Lord of lords, and a King of kings—and with him the called, and chosen and believing.

The angel turns now from the heads to the *horns*. The beast, according to ver. 7, has *ten horns*. All beasts have them on the *head*. But if they could exist only on one of the heads, it must be the *seventh,* for this was spoken of in the preceding context in ver. 10-11. We see this also by comparing the *which have not as yet received a kingdom,* with those in ver. 10, *the other is not yet come;* and comparing the *one hour* here, with *he must abide a short time* there. The seventh phase of the ungodly power of the world, denoted by the ten horns on the seventh head, is to be a divided one, in contradistinction to all the earlier ones, especially to the sixth, the Roman—as a proof, that the Revelation is really what its name imports, and did not owe its origin to a conjecture formed after the analogies of the past.

The horns are *kings*. We are not to think of *individual kings* but *powers.* For the horn is the symbol of power, victorious strength. In Daniel 7 the ten horns are the ten kingdoms, into which the fourth great monarchy, the Roman, was to fall. In Dan. 8:8 and Zech. 1:18-21 powers, or monarchies, are denoted by horns. If kings are kingdoms in ver. 9, they must also be so here. The number ten is a round one, showing it was not exactly and definitely ten, but around that number. The heads denote *world-monarchies,* of which there was always but one at a time on the theatre of history. But the horns denote a *constellation* of powers, existing *independently* beside each other. Their boundaries are of a somewhat fluctuating nature.[13]

The word *kingdom* is used here in an *active* sense, of the government, the kingly rule and authority. We are not to explain *a* kingdom, but rather: *which had not yet received kingdom or dominion.* The matter concerns not *a* kingdom, but worldly dominion. It concerns not the existence of nations with their respective governments, but *that they were no longer to come forth as the reigning*

---

13. Berengaudus (9th century) designates the kingdoms by which the Roman Empire was destroyed as the Vandals in Africa, the Goths in Spain, the Lombards in Italy, the Burgundians in Gaul, the Franks in Germany, the Huns in Pannonia, the Alans, and the Suevi. He also included the Persians and Saracens. Bossuet has some excellent remarks in regard to the number ten: *There appeared much about the same time Vandals, Huns, Franks, Burgundians, Suevi, Alani, Heruli, to whom succeeded Lombards, Germans, Saxons; more than all these the Goths, who were the real destroyer of the empire.*

power on the theatre of the world's history. Not existence, but reigning power is what first belongs to the future. The expression, *one hour,* is explained by the ολιγον, a little, short time, in ver. 10. History delivers for the *one hour,* a remarkable confirmation. The first appearance of the *German* tribes on the stage of public history almost entirely coincides with the commencement of their conversion to Christianity. But the short continuance is here affirmed of their power *with the beast.* Since after the overthrow of these kings through Christ (comp. ver. 14 and 19:11,) no new human monarchy is mentioned, since also this overthrow is to be accomplished only by Christ, and his church, therefore, that on the power, which the ten kings receive with the beast, another will follow, which they shall receive from Christ.

As kings, that reign not merely over their own subjects, but over the world. For the context treats of the dominion of the world; it is with the different phases of this, that the prophecy is occupied. The word, *with the beast,* is involved in the nature of the subject, and would have to be supplied, if it were not expressed. The character of their dominion, as opposed to God and Christ, is implied above in the circumstance, that they are *horns on the head of the beast.* The *admission* of the kings is inseparably connected with the *abolition* of Rome. But the beast is not affected by this change. As Rome at an earlier period received power with the beast, so now the kings receive the same. It is a change in the phases of the worldly power, while this itself continues for the time unchanged. Those, who understand by the beast heathen Rome, and those likewise who understand by it the papacy, are involved in no small perplexity by the expression here *with the beast,* and also by ver. 13. They suppose, that the ten kings shall hold only at *first* with the beast and that they shall afterwards rise up against her. But it is against this view, that in ver. 12-14, the matter of the horns is so far cut off, that in ver. 15-18, where the whore is the subject of discourse, nothing absolutely new can be introduced in regard to the horns, nothing can be brought in, which has not a point of contact with something in the portion preceding ver. 15. But such would be the case if the beast were heathen Rome, or the papacy. Then, here it would be friendship, there, quite suddenly and immediately, enmity. Not to mention that according to ver. 16, not merely the horns, but also the beast itself, shall hate and persecute the whore, Rome.

13 The expression, *with the beast,* is enlarged upon and explained. *One mind,* in reference to what is here under consideration, and which is expressly brought out in the second part of the verse (comp. ver. 17.) For otherwise the being of one mind is against the nature of evil. Sin is as certainly the mother of division, as selfishness is inherent in its very nature. If the beast is the God-opposing power of the world, impelled by a thirst of conquest, and a desire of dominion, then in the circumstance of their *giving their power and authority with one mind to the beast,* the foundation is laid of their unanimity in seeking to destroy Rome. The new possessors of the worldly power could only stand in an attitude of hostility toward its former possessors. But another consequence also springs from it, and one unfolded in what immediately follows—their war against the Lamb.

14 Our eye rests with deep emotion upon this passage; for it presents an insight into the destiny of our own race, which at the time lay profound-

ly concealed.[14] The verse has altogether a provisional character. The proper theme here is only the *judgment of the whore*, and nothing of a particular and definite nature can be introduced respecting the ten kings, excepting what they have to do concerning this judgment. Here we have an indication of the *farther* doings and fate of the ten kings. The instruments of the divine *wrath* are destined to become vessels of divine *grace*. The filling up of the outline here is given in 19:11-21, where the war of the ten kings against Christ, and his victory over them, is particularly described.

[14. These shall war with the Lamb, and the Lamb shall overcome them—for he is a Lord of lords, and a King of kings—and with him the called, and chosen and believing.]

The *war* of the ten kings *against Christ* manifests itself in their assaults on his church (comp. Acts 9:4-5.) Christ is the proper object of the conflict, and proper author of the victory. Believers are represented as sharers in the *victory*, and are also sharers in the *conflict*. Among the first witnesses for the war of the ten kings against Christ are the numerous martyrs who fell among the Goths in the persecution of Athanarich.[15] They were followed by a train of others, among whom appears Boniface.

The Lamb shall overcome them; Berangarius remarks at the beginning of the ninth century, *We know that these tribes have, with few exceptions, received the yoke of Christ.* Even in the fifth century, Orosius says, that in the East and the West the churches of Christ were filled with Huns, Suevi, Vandals, Burgundians, and an incredible number of believers from among other barbarous nations. Kortüm, in his history of the middle ages, surveys the progress of Christ's victory,

After the German-Arian confession had lost all its public importance, by the subjection of the Eastern Goths and Vandals, and the desertion of the Western Goths, Burgundians, and Longobards, the orthodox church attained to a purer form among the Irish, Scots, and Anglo-Saxons, than elsewhere, by the proscription among them of intolerance, the limitation of outward pomp in Divine worship, and the striving towards a cultivated and moral condition, not through fire and sword, but through doctrine and instruction. Persons reared under such principles, possessing a fearless spirit and a quick intelligence, and distinguished by a blameless walk, seldom failed to accomplish the end of their laborious and disinterested missions among rude but vigorous barbarians. This course was followed in the seventh century among the Germans of the high-country, by the Scotch Columba and Gallus, out of whose hermitage arose the monastery that became so active in the interest of Christianity and civilization, among the Bavarians by Emmeran, among the East Franks and Thuringians by Kilian, among the Frisians by Willibrod, among the Hessians by the Anglo-Saxon Winfred (Boniface), who was the centre of the new ecclesiastical direction of the eighth century, for the whole of north Ger-

---

14. Hengstenberg wrote for a German audience, yet the English are descended from the Angles and Jutes, and other continentals also find their roots among these tribes, from which Christianity has truly found a prominence for a thousand years. Initially it was the English St. Winfred or Boniface who brought the gospel to the Germans–*Editor.*

15. August, The City of God, Book 18, ch. 52, *The king of the Goths, in Gothia itself, persecuted the Christians with wonderful cruelty, when there were none but Catholics there, of whom very many were crowned with martyrdom, as we have heard from certain brethren who had been there at that time as boys, and unhesitatingly called to mind that they had seen these things?* Quadi, Marcomanni, and others, passed the Danube in the 4th century, spread desolation with fire and sword, broke down churches, scattered about the bones of the saints, etc. Of the irruption of Radogast, with his 200,000 men into Italy, the devastation was frightful; villages, towns, churches, lay in ashes; no sanctuary, no monument of art, could escape the fury of these equally warlike and zealous worshippers of Odin.

many. In East France the archbishopric of Mentz (748), whose diocese ... gave strength and order to the straggling efforts of the missionaries that chiefly came from the Anglo-Saxons, became nurseries of milder manners, and of advancing commerce and knowledge, but, at the same time, props of the state of things that were meanwhile gradually forming by the encroachments of the bishopric of Rome.

<small>14. These shall war with the Lamb, and the Lamb shall overcome them—for he is a Lord of lords, and a King of kings—and with him the called, and chosen and believing.</small>

The words, *King of kings and Lord of lords*, point to the foundation of Christ's victory. The Lamb conquers because he is *the Lord of lords;* believers conquer because they are with the Lamb. Allusion is made here, as in 19:6 to 1 Tim. 6:14-15. John ascribes to Christ, which is there declared of the Father. The allusion to that passage goes with what immediately follows in the passage. John ascribes to Christ nothing more than what he assumes to himself in Matt. 28:18. The addition, *and with the called and chosen and believing* (properly, *and who are with him, called, etc.,*) is of great importance. Rome, too, fought with Christ, and was conquered by him; not there, however, are the *chosen* the instruments, but the ten kings are so, who execute his work without knowing and wishing it. The *called, etc.*, being mentioned as the instruments of Christ's victory, shows the victory here can be no bloody and destroying one, but that it was to be won by properly Christian arms, as in Eph. 6:10. The true members of Christ are described by these three marks, the first and last palpable, the second hidden, and manifesting itself in the first and third, so that where these are it cannot fail. The expressions are rather Paul's than John's. But Paul had rendered them familiar to those for whom John wrote, so that they are a sort of proper names.

THE WHORE FOUNDED ON THE BEAST

<small>15. And he says to me, The waters which thou sawest, where the whore sits, are peoples, and multitudes, and nations, and tongues. 16. And the ten horns, which thou sawest, and the beast, these shall hate the whore, and shall make her desolate and naked, and shall eat her flesh, and shall burn her with fire. 17. For God has given it to their hearts, to do his mind and to do one mind, and to give their kingdom to the beast, till the words of God shall be fulfilled. 18. And the woman, that thou sawest, is the great city, which has kingdom over the kings of the earth.</small>

What was just said of the beast, the heads, and horns, merely served as a foundation for what was to be said here of the woman, Rome. In ver. 1 the *peoples* are brought into view in respect to the advantage they afforded to the mistress of the world, imaged by *the waters*, indicative of the advantage of an extensive worldly dominion. The contrast is formed by the dry and naked *wilderness*, and by what is said in ver. 16, that they shall make her desolate, eat her flesh, and burn her with fire. The prophet first sees the *woman*, according to ver. 3, in the wilderness. There too, he must have seen the waters upon which she still sits—present tense. They served as a symbol of her *vanished* glory, as the sitting of the woman on the beast in ver. 3 also denotes an already vanished condition. This makes the wilderness appear all the more dismal. She simply sits upon the beast upon or by the waters. The enumeration of the *peoples, etc.*, is *four*, the signature of the *earth*. In the PARALLEL PASSAGES quoted at 13:7, in place of the *multitudes* or masses, which occur only here, we have *tribes*, once *kings*; comp. at 5:9. Here, where only an advantage is taken into account connected with dominion, the reference to the masses of the governed is the more suitable.

16 The angel says to John, in ver. 1, *Come, I will show thee the judgment of the great whore.* This showing takes place even in ver. 3. The angel conducts John in spirit into the wilderness, and lets him there see the woman. Here the meaning of what is shown to John and seen by him, is disclosed. Here, what was now seen as present belonged to the future. The ten horns are known to us already from the preceding verses as the new holders of the worldly power. Here the judgment of the woman is expressly declared, what in the preceding portion had been already indicated, that the horns shall put an end to the woman. The ten horns sit upon the seventh head. It is thereby intimated, that the new holders of the ungodly power of the world, with all their independence and self-sufficiency, are still bound to each other by a certain *unity*. We must, therefore, only think of nations of the Germanic race, and such as were immediately conjoined with them.

On the expression, *and the beast,* comp. ver. 12 *with the beast*—all the undertakings of the ten kings are placed under the auspices of the beast. The ουτοι, *these,* is employed with as much emphasis as the *he* in ver. 11. It is designed to direct attention to those who were destined by God to avenge the poor cause of Christ upon the persecutor Rome.

The *whore* here represents not the city Rome as *opposed* to the kingdom, but the city as the mistress and centre of the kingdom, so that every assault, which is directed against the land, is also directed against it; every injury which affects the kingdom, also affects it. They shall make her bare or *naked*, while before she had been arrayed in purple and scarlet, and bespangled with gold and gems and pearls, sitting upon her throne. The *flesh* is in the plural: *her much flesh*. By the flesh is denoted the material power and the kingdom. The powerful and rich evil-doer appears even in the OLD TESTAMENT as thick and fat—comp. for example Ps. 73:4, 7. The *being made desolate or waste* not unfrequently occurs also of persons, since these are represented under the image of a city prostrated by enemies, or of a devastated country. So in Judges 5:27; Ps. 17:9; Sir. 16:4. Accordingly we should refer also the words: *and shall burn her with fire*, not primarily to the city, but to the woman, of whom it is also spoken in 18:8. The fire is here, according to 8:7, not so properly material fire, as the fire of war.[16]

17 They *appear* to accomplish their own mind. The reference to this mind or purpose of their own, on the part of the kings and the beast, and the respect to the second *mind*, has effected, that here the subject of discourse is God's mind instead of his *purpose*. The beast is too far distant to be the subject of discourse in the preceding verses, while the destruction of the woman is expressly described as the determinate purpose of God. Comp. the words in ver. 1, *I will show thee the judgment of the great whore,* and in ver. 12, they *receive power as kings.* That they *do one mind,* stands in the closest connection with this, that they do the mind of God. *They give their kingdom to the beast*

---

16. Jerome, who lived at the time of the fulfilment says, in his ep. 123 ad Ageruchiam: *A few of us have hitherto survived them, but this is due not to anything we have done ourselves but to the mercy of the Lord. Savage tribes in countless numbers have overrun all parts of Gaul. The whole country between the Alps and the Pyrenees, between the Rhine and the Ocean, has been laid waste by hordes of Quadi, Vandals, Sarmatians, Alans, Gipedes, Herules, Saxons, Burgundians, Allemanni and—alas! For the commonweal!—even Pannonians.*

17. For God has given it to their hearts, to do his mind and to do one mind, and to give their kingdom to the beast, till the words of God shall be fulfilled.

for the destruction of Rome, and also to make war upon the church. This proceeds from their own unconverted state, by which God turns them so, that they should come forth on the theatre of the world's history. The sins, which they there committed, in the horrors they inflicted on Rome and the war they waged against the church, belonged to themselves. But the impulse awakened in their minds by God served, not only to execute his judgment on Babylon, but also to bring about their own conversion, and along with it the fulfilment of the word of God. We are not to substitute the mere *permission* of God in the place of putting it into their heart. It is a humiliation of God to ascribe to him only the part of an idle *looker-on* in the most important events of the world's history. What *words of God* is meant, is rendered more specific, partly from the PARALLEL PASSAGE in 10:7, *the mystery of God should be finished, as he hath declared to his servants the prophets,* and partly from ver. 16 and ver. 14. By these we are taught to limit the expression to the *promises of victory given to the church.* These pass into fulfilment, first when Rome is overthrown by the ten kings, and then when they themselves are overcome by the Lamb, and are received into the bosom of the Christian church.

18. And the woman, that thou sawest, is the great city, which has kingdom over the kings of the earth.

18 In regard to *the great city,* see on 16:19. It is the city, which had dominion in the time of the Seer, that is spoken of. It never once means: which *then* has. In the presence of the great city, which then had dominion over the kings of the earth, John must necessarily have expressed himself otherwise, if he had not meant *that* city, which all his first readers would naturally think of, but another one. Besides, if the kings are worldly kings, then the kingdom, which the woman has, will be a worldly kingdom. Papal Rome, too, has never had for the papacy the same importance, which heathen Rome had for the Roman empire. The pope has never been, like the emperor, only the representative of Rome, so that the dominion might be attributed, not to him, but to Rome, as is done here.

REVELATION 18

The overthrow of Rome, the sixth head

CHAPTER STRUCTURE

The destruction of the Babylon of the time then present was announced in ch. 17. But the bare announcement was not enough respecting an event so difficult for John's contemporaries to believe. The reality that oppressed them needed to be met with an ideal reality in a provisional draught on history. When God's people were captive under threatening oppression the old prophets portrayed the destruction of Babylon in great detail and length (Jer. 50-51,) or delineated the restoration of the temple that had been destroyed (Eze. 40–48) for it to serve as an interim temple, in order to meet their despair. In the same manner ch. 18 served for those under the oppression of Rome.

The chapter falls into three chief divisions. First, the appearance of the angel with great power, who comes down from heaven, and announces the fall of Babylon as accomplished, ver. 1-3. Then, the announcement of the voice from heaven, ver. 4-20. Finally, the appearance of the angel, who throws a great stone into the sea, and then explains the meaning of this symbolical transaction, ver. 21-24. The first and the third parts may be regarded as an introduction and conclusion. The voice from heaven forms the main burden of the prophecy. This voice first addresses the people of Christ, that may be in Babylon, ver. 4-5, and then the instruments of God's judgment upon her, ver. 6-8. It next describes in ver. 9-10, the mourning of the kings; in ver. 11-16, the mourning of the merchants of the earth; in ver. 17-19, the mourning of the mariners on the sea over the downfall of Babylon; and at the close, in ver. 20, calls upon the heaven with its inhabitants, the members of the church, to rejoice over her. So that the conclusion returns to the beginning; for the whole had begun with an address to the members of the church.

ANGEL ANNOUNCES THE FALL OF BABYLON

> 18:1. And after these things I saw another angel come down from heaven, who had great power, and the earth was enlightened with his glory. 2. And he cried in strength and said, She is fallen, she is fallen, Babylon the great, and has become an habitation of demons, and a hold of all unclean spirits, and a hold of all unclean and hateful birds. 3. For all heathen have drunk of the wine of the wrath of her fornication, and the kings of the earth have committed fornication with her, and the merchants of the earth have been made rich by the power of her luxury.

First in ver. 1-3, Christ the conqueror of Babylon proclaims her downfall. That the other angel is no other than Christ is clear from 10:1. The angel proclaims the victory as already accomplished over Babylon. The *great power and glory* shows the announcer of the victory over Rome was also the author of it. Its downfall is carried up to God in 17:17 and 19:1, and as God does

CHAPTER 18 THE REVELATION

everything for Christ, so he does it through Christ, the ten kings war against Christ, he must show himself to be the King of kings and the Lord of lords in its destruction.

The *earth being enlightened by Christ's glory* corresponds with 10:1, *his countenance was like the sun.* Glory is a prerogative of the Father and his Son (John 1:14, 2:11,12:41; Rev. 1:16, 21:23, comp. also Hab. 3:3, and the earth is full of his praise, Ps. 50:1-2, 94:1-2.) He can then be no other than the Lord of the earth. The FUNDAMENTAL PASSAGE, is Eze. 43:2, *the earth was enlightened by his glory.*

2. And he cried in strength and said, She is fallen, she is fallen, Babylon the great, and has become an habitation of demons, and a hold of all unclean spirits, and a hold of all unclean and hateful birds.

2 Christ here proclaims his victory over Rome, which was still future, yet it served to comfort believers. Matt. 28:18 tells of the great power of Christ. What is declared there of the voice of Jehovah in Ps. 29:4, *The voice of the Lord is in strength*, is here transferred to the voice of Christ, exactly as in ver. 1 that is affirmed of Christ, which in Eze. 43:2 is spoken of Jehovah. The power in the calling afforded a pledge in the doing for those oppressed by the power of Rome.

In regard to the words, *Fallen, fallen etc.* comp. 14:8, 16:19.[17] In regard to the *demons* see at 9:20, 16:14. In Isa. 13:21 it is said of ancient Babylon being fallen, *And bucks dance there*, in connection with owls and ostriches; and Isa. 34:14, *And one buck calls to another, there also reposes the night-spectre and finds rest to itself.* In Egypt the heathen gods were called *bucks* and then *evil spirits* (comp. Lev. 17:7; 2 Chron. 11:15.) The LXX in Isa. 13:21 has, *and demons shall dance there;* and in Baruch 4:35 it is said, *and has been inhabited by demons for a very long time.* In Lev. 16, Satan is *Azazel*, the *separated*, and the he-goat is sent to him in his abode in the wilderness. In Matt. 12:43, the waste and dry places are the seat of evil spirits. In Luke 8:27 the man who had demons, *abode not in the house, but was in the tombs.* In 16:13-14 unclean spirits are mentioned before demons, and are placed among unclean birds, their dwelling, that is haunts of desolation, is where such birds must resort (comp. Ps. 102:6, Isa. 13:21-22, 34:14, Jer. 50:39, Zeph. 2:14.) The *habitation* is a freer place, while the *hold* is a place of custody (2:10, 20:7,) mentioned in connection with the unclean spirits. It is the law of their nature that banished them there, as a ruined existence is at home among the ruins.

3. For all heathen have drunk of the wine of the wrath of her fornication, and the kings of the earth have committed fornication with her, and the merchants of the earth have been made rich by the power of her luxury.

3 One reason for the downfall of Rome was her oppression of the nations. In 14:8, 17:2 it is her fornication, and so on to ver. 23, the power of her *luxury*, is brought into notice, as the means of extortion for her oppression. On the *wine of the wrath of her fornication,* the love-feigning policy whereby Rome destroyed nations, see at 14:8. On the *committing of fornication with Babylon by the kings,* which is considered as pressed on them, see 17:2.

ANNOUNCEMENT OF VOICE FROM HEAVEN TO GOD'S PEOPLE IN BABYLON

4. And I heard another voice from heaven, which said, Go out of her, my people, that ye be not partakers of her sins, and receive not of her plagues. 5. For her sins

---

17. The preterite in 14:8, 16:19 is a prophetic one; it denotes a fact which even as a part of the vision was still future. But here it is used of a fact which, viewed in respect to the vision, had now entered, comp. 17:3. For the vision the victory was in the preceding chapter a completed fact; the judgment of the great whore was already put in force; the woman was already placed in the wilderness; only the exposition there makes use of the futures. Seeing this and the continuous use of the preterites in the discourse of the angel, it is clear that proclamation is here made of what has already been done.

reach to heaven, and God remembers her iniquities.

We have now in ver. 4-20 the *voice from heaven*. It is not another *angel*, but another *voice*, which must be the voice of *Christ*. In verses 1-3 the storm has discharged itself, the angel had come down from heaven, but here the voice is heard from heaven, as the storm hangs lowering.

The call to the people of God rests upon Jer. 51:6,45, on which also Zech. 2:7 rests, and points to Gen. 19:15,17. Here the second clause, *that ye be not partakers etc.*, explains the first, *Go out of her. Sins* here are punishments of sins. As in the FUNDAMENTAL PASSAGES, the call is not literally to leave Rome, as here it is representative of the Roman Empire. It serves to show that Babylon's destruction is great and certain, to remove the fear of Babylon. The Lord will certainly preserve his people in the midst of judgments, as in 7:1-8, or in the case of Lot, Gen. 19.

5 It marks the highest degree of sin, when it is *reaching to heaven*, pressing before God's throne, and calling down his vengeance (comp. 2 Chron. 28:9, Ezra 9:6, Gen. 4:10, 18:21, 19:13, Jon. 1:2.) The fundamental passage is Jer. 51:9, *for her judgment reaches unto heaven, and extends even to the clouds.* The reaching up of judgment presupposes the reaching up of sins, as in Ps. 36:5 (comp. 57:10,) where in contrast the goodness and faithfulness of God reaches to the clouds and heaven. Here God remembers her iniquities as literally her sins have reached up and adhered to heaven. The sins are great.

THE INSTRUMENTS OF GOD'S JUDGMENT UPON BABYLON

> 6. Render to her as she also has rendered, and double double according to her works in the cup, which she has mixed, mix to her double. 7. How much she hath made herself glorious, and has been luxurious, so much torment and sorrow give her. For she says in her heart, I sit as queen, and am no widow, and I shall not see mourning. 8. Therefore shall her plagues come in one day, death, and mourning, and hunger, and with fire shall she be burned; for strong is God the Lord, who judges her.

The voice from heaven, which in ver. 4-5 has addressed the people of God, turns now to the instruments of vengeance, which we learn from 17:16, to be the ten kings. The FUNDAMENTAL PASSAGE here is Jer. 50:29. She has *rendered* to harmless innocent behaviour, with cunning, bloodshed and servitude. By *the double* in the OLD TESTAMENT is denoted *abundance*. The recompense corresponds to the measure of guilt (comp. Ex. 21:24, Matt. 7:2.) It is doubled to her because her works were an aggravated wickedness. In Jer. 50:21, ancient Babylon is called *the land of double revolt* (Merathaim,) Kushan has the surname of Rishathaim, *the double wickedness* (comp. Matt. 23:15.) The FUNDAMENTAL PASSAGE is Jer. 16:18 (comp. 17:18.) On the *mixing* see 14:10, and the image of *the cup* see 14:8, 18:3.

7 At the words, *how much, etc.*, we are to supply, *at the expense of others*. The words, *for she says, etc.* contain the reason for the heavy sentence against Babylon which was pronounced in the preceding verse. The reason is, the presumptuous security in which she trod beneath her feet all divine and human rights. The FUNDAMENTAL PASSAGE is Isa. 47:8, *who says in her heart, I am, and none else beside me; I shall not sit as a widow, neither shall I know the loss of chil-*

dren. The *widowhood* is the state of desertion, helplessness and humiliation; she is a *personae miserabiles.* Comp. Lam. 1:19-20, Bar. 4:12.

<small>8. Therefore shall her plagues come in one day, death, and mourning, and hunger, and with fire shall she be burned; for strong is God the Lord, who judges her.</small>

8 The four *plagues* are mentioned with respect to her glory upon the earth, being one from every corner of the earth. *Death*—which carries off a great part of her people (not pestilence, but the hand of enemies), *mourning,* and *hunger* with the survivors. On the *burning* see 17:16. *God the Lord* confronts the imagined goddess of the earth. Rome means strong, but *strong* is God the Lord the author of the judgment.

THE MOURNING OF THE KINGS

<small>9. And the kings of the earth, who have committed fornication, and have lived luxuriously with her, shall weep and lament over her, when they see the smoke of her burning. 10. And they shall stand afar off, for the fear of her torment, and shall say, Woe, woe, the great city, Babylon the strong city. For in one hour is thy judgment come.</small>

In ver. 11 *the kings of the earth* have placed by their side *the merchants of the earth,* as opposed to those who traffic on the seas; and the common contrast to both is formed at the close in ver. 20 by the heaven and its inhabitants. Earth and sea lament, heaven rejoices. The kings of the earth, as opposed to the heavenly inhabitants are earthly minded. Their lament is not of love, but the grief that arises from self interest. Their mistress with all the advantages they derived from her, has fallen.

With all the three, kings, merchants, mariners, *they stood afar off;* and the lamentation begins with *Woe, woe, the great city;* and concludes with, *because in one hour.* The FUNDAMENTAL PASSAGES are Eze. 26:16-17, and Eze. 27:35. Tyre and now Rome was the centre of the world's commerce, the fulfilment of the prophecy on Tyre is a pledge of the certainty of that pending Rome.

Here is as Abraham, who in Gen. 19:28, saw from afar the smoke of Sodom and Gomorrha. In Jer. 50:1 the land of the Chaldeans is mentioned along with Babylon–the city is referred to as representative of the kingdom. So here Babylon comprehends in itself the whole kingdom–comp. 17:18, so the *burning* cannot be literal, but an emblem of its whole destruction.

10 *They stand afar off,* as it is impossible to render help, as the Almighty himself contends with Rome, its punishment makes them shudder. They are afraid to partake of her sins and receive her plagues. The double *woe* corresponds to the double double in verse 6.

THE MOURNING OF
THE MERCHANTS OF THE EARTH

<small>11. And the merchants of the earth weep and mourn over her, because no one any more buys their cargo. 12. The cargo of gold and silver and precious stones and pearls; and of linen-stuff, and purple and silk and scarlet; and all thyine wood, and every kind of vessel of most precious wood, and of brass, and of iron, and of marble. 13. And cinnamon (and amomum) and perfumes and ointment and frankincense, and wine and oil, and fine flour and wheat, and cattle and sheep; and of horses and of chariots and of bodies; and souls of men. 14. And the harvest of the desire of thy soul is departed from thee; and all that was full</small>

and glorious, has perished from thee, and thou shalt no longer find such things. 15. The merchants of such wares, who have been enriched by her, shall stand afar off for fear of her torment, weeping and mourning. 16. (And) saying, Woe, woe, the great city, that was clothed with fine linen and purple and scarlet, and gilt with gold and precious stones and pearls; for in one hour is so great wealth laid desolate.

12 The FUNDAMENTAL PASSAGES for this and the following verses are Isa. 23 and especially Eze. 27, against Tyre. As preparation is made for ver. 9-10, by ver. 3, *And the kings of the earth have committed fornication with her*, so also for verse 11 by *and the merchants of the earth have become rich by the power of her luxury*. The features here do not suit Papal Rome, as if she stored spiritual wares, as here she does not sell the wares; which serve rather for her use and consumption. The *cargo* is that of ships freighted for merchants. The wares, as follows, are divided into seven classes.

12 First come *hard* materials for show and ornament; then the *soft* (comp. 17:4)—both placed at the head because Babylon was not, like Tyre, a common commercial city, but merely as the mistress of the world drew the merchandise of the world. The hard materials are *four*, the signature of the earth, and so are the soft; purple and scarlet, the clothes of the dominant people. Then we have material for expensive furniture, and furniture made from it, then four kinds of articles or vessels. *Thyine wood* was a fine scented ever green tree for costly furniture. It is connected together with ivory.

13 We have here first articles of perfumery. Whether *amomum (odours)*, stood originally in the text or not, is doubtful. If not, then we have four aromatic substances. After this three pairs of articles of food, then articles of conveyance. Chariots here is the latin word *rheda*. Bodies are united with *horses and chariots* as capable for *bearing* men as sedan bearers, and separated from the *souls of men*. Tyre trafficked in men's souls (Eze. 27:13.)

14-16 After the wares, which were brought from without, mention is made of domestic goods; then all this enumeration is collected into *all that was fat and glorious*. The mourning of the merchants is interrupted, to be resumed here, it is given to show that *all* the glory of Rome had departed. The *harvest* denotes the fruits which ripen in harvest, in the OLD TESTAMENT the contrast is made between desolations and the joy of the vine dresser and reaper, comp. Isa. 16:9-10 and Jer. 48:32-33. The *full* or *fat* is used of the produce of the land (Isa. 30:23) as enumerated in the immediately preceding, the rest is comprised in the term *glorious*, aside from a part of verses 12-13. What the worldly have enjoyed is taken away in death, *departed* and *perished*, and they are left without a drop of water. Ver. 15 would possess the character of a needless repetition, if ver. 14, as several have supposed, stood in the wrong place. The expression, *such wares*, refers more immediately to the *full and glorious* in ver. 14.

THE MOURNING OF THE MARINERS ON THE SEA

17. And every shipmaster, and all who sail for one place, and sailors, and whosoever work the sea, stood afar off. 18. And cried, when they saw the smoke of her burning, and said, Who is like the great city! 19. And they threw dust upon their heads, and cried, weeping and mourning, and said, Woe, woe, the great city, by which all were made rich, who have ships in the sea, from her costliness; for in

one hour she is laid desolate.

17. And every shipmaster, and all who sail for one place, and sailors, and whosoever work the sea, stood afar off.

The classes named are four. *Those who sail for one place* are such as pursue a determinate course. The words, *whosoever work the sea* comprehend all that are here under consideration. The figure *work the sea*, has its analogies in Isa. 23:3, where the many waters appear as the harvest field which bears for Tyre the corn of Egypt, and in Eze. 27:33.

18-19. 18. And cried, when they saw the smoke of her burning, and said, Who is like the great city! 19. And they threw dust upon their heads, and cried, weeping and mourning, and said, Woe, woe, the great city, by which all were made rich, who have ships in the sea, from her costliness; for in one hour she is laid desolate.

The FUNDAMENTAL PASSAGE for the lamentation of the mariners is Eze. 27:32, *Who is like Tyre, like the destroyed in the midst of the sea*, the reference is simply to the earlier glory. *Who, it is asked, is like her in this?* Comp. Isa. 47:8, where Babylon says, *I am and none besides*. In Ezek. 27:30, it is said of the mariners, *And they cry aloud over thee, they lament bitterly, and throw dust upon their heads, and wallow in ashes*. This is symbolic of a humbled condition (comp. Ps. 102:9.) On the *by which were made rich* see Eze. 27:33. The *costliness* is her pomp and glory, her luxurious mode of life.

THE CALL TO REJOICE OVER BABYLON

20. Rejoice over her, Heaven, and ye saints, and ye apostles, and ye prophets, for God has judged your judgment on her.

This verse forms the close of what is said by the voice from heaven, all that proceeded from ver. 4. John merely sees and hears; and does not speak. The *joy* forms the contrast to the mourning of the earthly-minded over the downfall of Rome. *Heaven* is the dwelling-place of the militant and triumphant church (12:12, 13:6.) The *saints* are the genus, the *apostles* and *prophets* the most eminent species (comp. on 11:18.) Here the prophetical dignity is shown to be highest in the apostles. Apostles and prophets are personally identical, prophecy also culminates in the apostleship. The apostles can only mean the twelve (comp. 21:14.) *Your* judgment; comp. 17:1, 20:4, your condemnation or doom, which here corresponds to 6:10, *judge our blood*, which he had shed. Ch. 13:10 is parallel, the doom of Rome was spoken of in 13:7, where he makes war with the saints, and kills them. The saints respond with *joy* to this call in 19:1-4. Here is an allusion to Jer. 51:48, *and heaven and earth rejoice over Babylon*.

AN ANGEL THROWS A GREAT STONE INTO THE SEA

21. And a strong angel lifted up a stone as a great mill-stone, and threw it into the sea, and said, Thus with violence shall Babylon the great city be thrown, and be no more found.

In Jer. 51:63-64 Jeremiah gives to Seraiah, who was going to Babylon, the commission to read his prophecy there, after which he was to bind a stone to it and throw it into the Euphrates, and say *thus shall Babylon sink, and shall not rise*. Allusion is made to Matt 18:6 and Mark 9:42, *but who shall offend these little ones, etc*. This quote points back to the Jeremiah passage, which also refers to Ex. 15:4-5, comp. Neh. 9:11. In this last FUNDAMENTAL PASSAGE it says *he threw them into the sea, they sank down in the floods as a stone*. In the place of the sea Jeremiah substitutes the Euphrates. In the declaration of

Christ, the sea returns again, and the sea is here also. The strength of the angel has its basis in the greatness of the stone and its heavy force where it settles on the bottom, no more to be found, the *no more* occurs six times in succession in emphasis. The great city has completely and without a trace perished.

THE SPEECH OF THE STRONG ANGEL CONTINUED

> 22. And the voices of the harp-singers, and musicians, and pipers, and trumpeters, shall no more be heard in thee; and no craftsman of any craft shall any more be found in thee; and the sound of a mill-stone shall no more be heard in thee. 23. And the light of a candle shall no more shine in thee; and the voice of the bridegroom and of the bride shall no more be heard in thee. 24. And in her was found the blood of prophets and saints, and of all those who had been slain on the earth.

In ver. 22-24 the speech of the strong angel continues, to explain his symbolical action. The FUNDAMENTAL PASSAGE here is Jer. 25:10, *And I destroy from them the voice of mirth and the voice of gladness, the voice of the bridegroom and the voice of the bride, the sound of the mill-stones and the light of the candle;* comp. 7:34; Isa. 24:8; Ezek. 26:13. The vanishing of all *joy* forms here the beginning and the end, the joy of marriage as the highest (Jer. 33:11,) and in the middle all commerce and life, which now ends. The individuals representing joy form two pairs first, the *harp-singers* (14:2) and the *musicians*, vocal and instrumental music; and again, of the latter, two related kinds are specified. On the first words comp. Isa. 23:8, where it is said of Tyre, *whose merchants princes, whose traffickers the honourable of the earth.* The *merchants* are not the master merchants in Rome but the commercial people who deal with her (see verses 3 and 15.) The second *for* gives the ground for the first. That the merchandise with Rome produces so rich gain is because she has drawn all nations into her net, so all the world's treasures flow into her lap. Verse 3 and 14:8 mentions only one crime of Babylon.

24 The first cause of judgment is the selfish ambition which planted herself in the centre of the world, out of which proceeds her guilt spoken of in our verse, the second also in verse 24 proceeds. She persecutes the church because this will not yield to her pretensions.

Sorcery is the means by which injury is done secretly to a neighbour, Babylon drew the nations into her grasp with bewitching guile (as in Gal. 3:1) to destroy them. Here agrees the fornication, deceitful and cunning policy (14:8, 18:3.) Other sorcerous arts were used–comp. 13:14. They have been deceived for her deification, and to submit to her dominion.

We are to compare Jer. 51:35, especially verse 49, *As Babylon shall fall slain, ye slain of Israel, also Babylon fall slain, ye slain of the whole earth.* The prophets and saints are to be ranged under the slain of Israel, beside the slain of the whole earth. In John's time Rome was the great destroyer of men, in her ambitious striving to oppress all nations. The *blood* is *in her* because it has been shed by her.

REVELATION 19:1-4

Praise song at the fall of Rome

VERSE STRUCTURE

In response to the call of the voice from heaven in 18:20, the church of *the just made perfect* here celebrates God's judgment on Rome. First, the multitude of believers come forth praising and giving thanks in ver. 1-3. Then, in ver. 4, its heads and representatives, the four and twenty elders. These are joined by the four beasts, as representatives of all creatures on earth, that had fallen under the dominion of the oppressor of the world. With this full-toned conclusion, the subject of Rome's overthrow is brought to a close.

MULTITUDE OF BELIEVERS PRAISE AND THANK GOD

> 19:1. After these things I heard as a voice of a great multitude in heaven, who said, Hallelujah! The salvation, and the glory, and the power is our God's. 2. For true and righteous are his judgments, for he has judged the great whore, that corrupted the earth with her fornication, and avenged the blood of his servants out of her hand. 3. And they spake a second time, Hallelujah, and her smoke goes up for ever.

The saints were called to rejoice, in 18:20, that God had avenged them on Babylon; here they express joyful praise for this grace. To the church of the just made perfect belongs *the great voice in heaven* in 12:10, and 11:15, and here in verse 6. More on the great multitude is understood from 7:9.

The *as a voice* shows that here this is only a likeness, having a visionary quality, still to sound in future in reality when the great whore was judged.

Hallelujah is here only in the NEW TESTAMENT; fifteen of the Psalms either begin or end with Hallelujah. Here allusion is made to Ps. 104:35 where the sinners are consumed from the earth and the wicked shall be no more, the sinners being the heathen host opposed to the Lord. The church, on earth, under suffering from the world, stirs up faith and confidence with their Hallelujah, while the church above cries triumphant over the world power.

The Lord is the only possessor of salvation. There is an allusion here to Ps. 3:8, as at 7:10, *Salvation is the Lord's*. The whole doxology rests upon the doxology of the Lord's Prayer in Matt. 6:13, *Thine is the kingdom etc.* There redemption out of evil is grounded in the glory and power of God, here the power and glory are deduced from the redemption out of evil. Instead of the kingdom, which still had not fully come into being, there stands anticipatively *salvation*, the allusion to *the kingdom* follows in verse 6, as also in verse 3 there is the *forever,* and the *Amen* in verse 4. There is another allusion to the *Paternoster* in 12:10, where its realization is anticipated by faith. Here it is entered into reality in part in the kingdom, its full realization, the dominion, still awaits. In 11:15 is still another allusion, the *it has become* there rests upon the *it is* of the Lord's Prayer. There are many allusions to Matthew's gospel in the Apocalypse–1:7, 2:7, 3:3, 5, 6:12, 11:11-13, 14:11, 18:21.

2 That God's judgments are true and righteous, his glory and his power is again established through the judgment on Rome. His truth and righteousness lays the basis for his being the sole possessor of salvation.

The great whore's *fornication* is her cunning policy by which she sought to bring the world and Christians to destruction (comp. 14:8, 17:1-2.) The *that corrupted the earth* is seen in 11:18, *and to corrupt* (destroy) *those that corrupted* (destroyed) *the earth.* The FUNDAMENTAL PASSAGE is Jer. 51:25, where it is said to ancient Babylon, *Behold I am against thee, thou corrupting mountain, saith the Lord, who dost corrupt the whole earth*—the mountain, a symbol of the mighty kingdom. From this, which itself refers to Gen. 6:11-13, we are not to think of *moral* corruption.

The clause, *he has avenged the blood of his servants out of her hand*, shows the offence, complained of in 6:10, is now set aside. It resembles 2 Kings 9:7 where the *out of the hand* allusion is made through it to Deut. 32:43, *He avenges the blood of his servants.* To avenge *out of the hand*, is also in 15:2, *to conquer out of the beast.* When the blood remained unavenged, she had it, in her hand. By means of the revenge it is withdrawn from her.

3 That is repeated, which was designed to be made emphatic and strong; comp. Ps. 62:11, and Job 33:14. *Her smoke goes up forever* is similar to Ex. 15:21 where the women's chorus repeat what Moses had said, *horse and rider are thrown into the sea*, bringing a seal of completion to the fact.

Edom is the type of the ungodly heathen world, and in Isa. 34:9-10, her smoke shall go up forever. Ch. 18:9, 18 is to be compared here, but not the torments of hell of 14:11.

BEASTS AND ELDERS JOIN IN PRAISE AT CLOSE OF ROME'S OVERTHROW

4. And the four and twenty elders and the four beasts fell down, and worshipped God that sat upon the throne, and said, Amen, Hallelujah.

The *four and twenty elders* represent the multitude of believers, as the point of view is the revenge on the blood of God's servants. The four beasts represent the living creation upon earth in thanks for the redemption of the earth as it was corrupted by the great whore's fornication. The earth is quiet as in Isa. 14:7. We see the beast's *Amen* in 5:14, the angels' in 7:12.

The *Amen, Hallelujah* is from Ps. 106:48 and concludes the prophet's announcement of the fate of heathen Rome. By Babylon, the heathen Rome is denoted. Iraenius expected the partition of the Empire by the ten kings. Tertullian saw that John meant Babylon as Rome, as great as Babylon, and a persecutor of the saints. Lactantius says, alluding to the Apocalypse, that in referring to another name Rome's downfall was meant. Jerome also considered it so. Orosius (*B.VII.c.2*) represents the Roman state as the antitype and continuation of the Babylonian. An objection would be why would God punish Christian Rome for heathen Rome's sins? When John wrote, heathenism reigned uncontrolled, and continued to be deep rooted when the prophecy went into fulfilment. Constantine transferred the seat of empire to Byzan-

CHAPTER 19:1-4   THE REVELATION

4. And the four and twenty elders and the four beasts fell down, and worshipped God that sat upon the throne, and said, Amen, Hallelujah.

tium, in despair of extirpating heathenism properly from Rome. Jerome saw Rome as the capital of all superstition. Even in the fifth century it was still its centre. The state could not be regenerated, the renewing power of Christianity could take effect only on individuals, in 18:4 the *people* of Christ in Rome are addressed, the state was not to be a truly Christian one. If it had, it would not have been overthrown. As the great whore in her imperial power and majesty she was destroyed, yet the city itself continued to stand, unlike ancient Babylon.

Materials of another kind were to be sought for the formation of a Christian state, and these were found in the people of the ten kings of the Apocalypse, the German tribes. What was historically realized in the course of centuries is in this prophecy compressed into one scene.

REVELATION 19:5-10

Anticipatory victory celebration over the other enemies

VERSE STRUCTURE

In these verses we have the porch to the building of 19:11—20:1-15. A voice from the throne, the voice of the Lord of the church, calls upon the whole people of God to praise him, ver. 5. The church responds to this call; by faith anticipating what is to come, she rejoices in that the kingdom of God has entered, the marriage of the Lamb has come, the bride appears in suitable apparel, ver. 6-8. The angel next to John affirms the truth of the facts, which form the theme of the heavenly song of praise, ver. 9. John is gladdened, testifies his regard to him, who had communicated it on behalf of himself and the church, and the angel returns his acknowledgment, ver. 10. This is not a continuation of the preceding song of praise raised over the destruction of Babylon, which was seen in vision as already accomplished. There is a difference in the contents, and the preceding scene was brought to a close. But we find in other parts of the Apocalypse songs of praise, which anticipate what is to come, comp. 15:2-4, 11:15-18.

VOICE FROM THRONE CALLS ALL BELIEVERS TO PRAISE HIM

19:5. And a voice went out of the throne and said, Praise our God, all his servants, and ye that fear him, small and great.

According to 16:17, the *voice from the throne* belongs to him, who sits upon the throne, so it is not the Father, as the call is to praise our God, so it must be from Christ, who sits in the throne with his Father (7:17, 3:21, 22:1, 3.) The Lamb calls on those with him to give thanks in 15:3-4. It cannot be from the cherubim as they are not upon the throne. As *proceeding* from the throne it shows its equality to God in power and glory. The godhead of Christ assures us of the security of a coming salvation. The *small and great* are mentioned in 11:18.

CHURCH RESPONDS, REJOICES IN THE MARRIAGE

6. And I heard as a voice of a great multitude, and as a voice of many waters, and as a voice of loud thunder, saying, Hallelujah! For the Lord our God, the Almighty has taken the kingdom. 7. Let us be glad and rejoice and give him the glory; for the marriage of the Lamb is come, and his wife has made herself ready. 8. And it was given to her to be arrayed in a clothing of fine linen, shining, pure.

**6. And I heard as a voice of a great multitude, and as a voice of many waters, and as a voice of loud thunder, saying, Hallelujah! For the Lord our God, the Almighty has taken the kingdom.
7. Let us be glad and rejoice and give him the glory; for the marriage of the Lamb is come, and his wife has made herself ready.**

For the linen are the righteousnesses of the saints.

Here is the accomplishment of what was called for in ver. 5. On the *voice of many waters, etc.* see at 14:2. The *to reign* means to take the government (11:17,) and this is consummated by ch. 20. The subject of praise is, first, the Lord has taken the kingdom and overthrown his enemies, and second, in verse 7-8, the marriage is come, the glorification of the church comes. In 12:10 the kingdom of God has come, after the atonement; 11:17 is directly parallel. There we have the general plan announced, here the filling up. The *let us rejoice and be glad*, seems to allude to Matt. 5:12 (comp. 1 Pet. 4:13.)

7 Giving honour and *glory* is ascribing it to God as existing (comp. on 4:9, 11:13, 16:9.) To give glory is to give *the* glory, that glory which God has manifested.

This group reaches no farther than to the immediate approach of the wedding. We distinguish between the arrival and the celebration, as the wife has made herself ready, so the wedding has not begun, it only comes when the wedding day dawns. As in John 3:29, we have a reference to the Song of Solomon (comp. 3:20.) The *marriage* here is not the marriage feast, where individual believers are spoken of, but here is the marriage itself, the *Lamb's wife* being the entire church.

There is implied here the quiet concealed glory which Christ has with his church from the first foundation through the age (Matt. 28:20.) It is a time of absence for the bridegroom (Matt. 9:15,) the ten virgins expect his return, in Eph. 5:25-27 the church is adorned for a *future* marriage. The name of *the Lamb* indicates that his relation to his church is founded on the bloody atonement, from which the state of glory has its root. We are here beyond the last victory over Gog and Magog, the marriage is already at the door. The betrothed was sometimes called the *wife* of the bridegroom (comp. Deut. 22:23; Gen. 29:21; Matt. 1:20; ch. 21:9.) The *making ready* is the great object of the church, prepared with oil in the lamp—the Holy Spirit, that is in having the name of a Christian, an *anointed* one. Special allusion is made to Matt. 25:10.

8. And it was given to her to be arrayed in a clothing of fine linen, shining, pure. For the linen are the righteousnesses of the saints.

8 The white clothing is not the glory as received in reward, as that is future. The *pure* is added to the *shining* as the washing is distinct from the making white in 7:14. The shining white *linen* points to the excellencies of the saints (see 3:18, comp. 7:14,) which proceeds as a gift from Christ (Eph. 5:25-27,) as the spiritual preparation of the wedding garment in Matt 22:12.

The *shining* denotes the glory of the holy life of the righteous; the pure, their freedom from sin. The *linen clothing* signifies the righteousnesses of the saints. The rule of justice is the law of Moses (Matt. 5:17,) the clothing the symbol of men's state, by *righteousnesses*, is the whole moral condition, of which actions are the outward expression. Allusion is made to 18:12, 16, comp. 17:4, where the clothing of the great whore is described.

ANGEL AFFIRMS THE TRUTH OF THE PRAISE

9. And he says to me, Write, Blessed are they that are called to the marriage feast of the Lamb. And he says to me, These words are true, (they are the words) of God.

That the speaker is an angel, appears from ver. 10. It can only be the angel mentioned in 17:1, as no other angel has spoken to John; and the same shows him the bride (21:9.) These are *blessed,* but those who are not, by implication stand under a woe (comp. Luke 14:24 with verse 14, Matt 25:12.) The individual members of the church are here the invited guests. The *blessed are they* corresponds to 14:13, *the dead who die in the Lord.* The *these words* or *sayings* refer to verses 5-8, that is the great and consolatory truths of the coming of the Lord's kingdom, the marriage of the Lamb, the suitable preparation of the bride, and her appearance in the linen attire of righteousness, as given to John in divine revelation by the angel. When Christ seems to have cast off the church, the whole authority of God is needed to fill it with joy about the future wedding, and when sin darkens, God's promise of being made ready assures.

JOHN GLADDENED BY THE MESSAGE, ANGEL ACKNOWLEDGES

10. And I fell before him at his feet to worship him. And he says to me: See thou, do it not! I am thy fellow-servant and of thy brethren, who have the testimony of Jesus. Worship God. For the testimony of Jesus is the Spirit of prophecy.

The angel was to John the mediator, respecting the marriage of the Lamb, and in his humility he forgets the crucial importance of his role as a prophet and apostle. They in honour prefer one another, as between Jesus and the Baptist (Matt. 3:14,) Jesus is baptized by John, or Cornelius falls before Peter (Acts 10:25-26,) and Peter raises him up, *I also am a man.* The *worship* here is anticipative, while in 22:8-9 is contemplated as finished. There is a distinction between civil and religious worship, that due to God, paid directly or to those who bear his image, his representatives, the possessors of his gifts and offices, and the proskinesis, which is yielded without and in opposition to God. God is honoured in those who bear his image, fulfil his offices, in father and mother, the men of grey hairs (Lev. 19:32,) in princes (Ex. 22:28,) in judges (Deut. 1:17, Ex. 21:6, 22:7-8) and heavenly messengers. The honour ascribed to John, is because he had *the Spirit of prophecy, and the testimony of Jesus,* that being the testimony which Jesus delivers. Every Christian has this testimony, it is in the fullest sense in the prophets and apostles. In 22:8, John falls to worship the angel, who says he is of the prophets. John here is regarded not as a Christian here, but as prophet and apostle, his brethren are prophets (22:6,) God's servants. The angel rejects the worship in order to place the apostolical and prophetical ministry equal with angels. The *worship God* has nothing in common with the Lord's *Thou shalt worship the lord thy God, and him only shalt thou serve.* Here it is only God's grace and office that are worshipped in the angel, there it is an opposing rival power with God. The dissuasion is based in the consideration that the worship trenches on God's honour, not on God's glory. The testimony of Jesus is all one with the spirit of prophecy. The testimony *concerning* Christ is at the same time the testimony *of* Christ, and *prophecy* has its source in the *Spirit* of prophecy—these correspond to each other. Christ testifies in the prophets through his Spirit (1 Pet. 1:11.)

REVELATION 19:11-21

The victory of Christ over the ten kings, seventh head of the beast with ten horns, instruments of judgment against Rome

CHAPTER SUMMARY

Christ, appearing at the head of his heavenly hosts in the full glory of his nature, is first described at length. Ver. 11-16 shows what Christ's opponents had to expect. The angel in the sun calls the birds to a feast on the corpses in ver. 17-18. The description of the battle is so brief, compared to that of Christ for its length; implying there can be no sustained conflict against him, who slays with the breath of his mouth. According to ver. 19 the beast and the kings of the earth are assembled together with their hosts to fight against Christ. But in ver. 20-21, the beast and the false prophet are cast into the lake of fire, and a great slaughter takes place on the *human* enemies of Christ.

The kings of the earth are described as the opponents of Christ in ver. 19. By ver. 15, they are to be regarded as *heathenish;* as they are subordinate to the beast, the ungodly power of the world in its *heathen* state.

This group, which represents the victory of Christ over the three enemies, first deals with the victory over the beast. This beast has *seven heads,* seven phases of the worldly heathen power. Of these seven five had already fallen before the time of John (17:10): the Egyptian, Assyrian, Chaldean, Medo-Persian and Grecian. The fall of the *sixth* head, the Roman, has been shown in the preceding portion; it had to give way to the present, which according to 17:12, is introduced through the *seventh* head with ten horns, the ten kings, the seventh phase of the worldly power in its heathen state, which unlike the earlier ones is to have a *united* character, but a *divided* sovereignty. These ten kings are the only powers with the beast, which still remain on the field, understood as the *kings of the earth*. Their war with Christ and their overthrow has been described in 17:14, and with it the beast goes into perdition (comp. ver. 20.) The ungodly power of the world exists only in its particular phases.

The destroyers of the Roman empire were the Germanic tribes. The battle of Christ here cannot be the quiet effective power of the word alluded to in 17:14, but a second power which accompanies the word. It holds with nations as with individuals, that they who are chastised exercise repentance; the way in to the kingdom is through tribulation; that the wine-press alone brings out the wine; that the seed takes root in fields opened up by God's plough of judgment. All here bears the impress of anger, blood and death; yet behind the clouds of wrath is the sun of divine grace. The eyes of Christ are as a flame of fire; the sword, which goes out of his mouth; his iron rod, his garments stained with blood, the wine-press of his wrath, which he treads—all plainly show Christ's mission here is more immediately of wrath and judgment.

John has given us a key. Christ's description here, in 19:11, presents an intentional verbal reference to 6:2, *and behold a white horse,* which indicates the battle of Christ here bears the same character as there, where Christ's weapons are hunger, pestilence, and especially bloody discord. The history of the times, when the northern tribes roved about, shows this vision passed into reality. The oppression of the Huns was the occasion of the western Goths being converted to Christianity. For the Germanic tribes, Attila was *the scourge of God.* 162,000 died at the battle of Chalons. The eastern Goths suffered in Italy from the Franks. Among the Picentians, 50,000 men were starved with hunger; even killed one another to obtain food. Leuthar, who invaded Italy in the mid sixth century died of pestilence with most of his men in the Venetian territory; many went mad and gnawed their own flesh. So it was that many battles and distresses occurred in those times which served to break the hardness of the German nations and soften their spirit.

WHAT THOSE WHOM HE WENT FORTH TO BATTLE HAD TO EXPECT

> 19:11. And I saw heaven opened, and behold a white horse; and he that sat upon him was called Faithful and True, and in righteousness he doth judge and make war. 12. His eyes were as a flame of fire, and on his head were many crowns; and he had a name written, that no man knew, but he himself. 13. And he was clothed with a vesture dipped in blood: and his name is called The Word of God. 14. And the armies which were in heaven followed him upon white horses, clothed in fine linen, white and clean. 15. And out of his mouth goeth a sharp sword, that with it he should smite the nations: and he shall rule them with a rod of iron: and he treadeth the winepress of the fierceness and wrath of Almighty God. 16. And he hath on his vesture and on his thigh a name written, King of kings, and Lord of lords.

Heaven is opened, so Christ may descend to earth with his hosts, contrast 4:1. He who sits on the *white horse* is Christ, as 6:2 shows. This contrasts with the ass of Matt. 21:1-11, the first coming in meekness, but when despised he appears in terror to the ungodly.

The names of Christ are four. 1. He is called *faithful and true;* 2. he *has a name written, which he alone knows;* 3. his name is called, *the Word of God;* and 4. *he has a name written, King of kings, and Lord of lords.*

The designation *the true* bespeaks almightiness and essential Godhead (comp. at 3:7, 6:10, 15:3, 16:7.) Also with the name *Faithful,* faithfulness or credibility presupposes omnipotence. All men lie (Ps. 116:11, Ps. 62:9, 108:12,) the Lord alone is faithful and worthy of confidence.

Parallel to *and in righteousness* is Ps. 45:4, where the divine hero rides to the protection and deliverance of the meek, the righteous. Christ's warring proceeds not from irritated passion, but righteousness.

12 The *eyes as a flame of fire,* flashing indignation, denote the energetic character of Christ's punitive righteousness.

The diadems (crowns) correspond to the crown, in 6:2 and 14:14, their *manifoldness* to the name *King of kings, and Lord of lords* in verse 16; and also respects the ten horns of the beast in 13:1, who have ten diadems for ten kings. Christ has many diadems, having conquered all the earlier phases of heathen power from Pharaoh on. The names of blasphemy by which an independent

12. His eyes were as a flame of fire, and on his head were many crowns; and he had a name written, that no man knew, but he himself.

dominion is usurped over the earth, which are written upon the heads of the beast, and now the seventh head also, are blanched before the name of Christ. John sees the name but cannot read nor express it (Matt. 11:27,) it is known only to Christ. In Judges 13 Manoah asks after the name of the angel, the answer, ver. 18: *Why do you ask after my name, and it is wonderful?* indicates not a particular name, but a fathomless depth, transcending human comprehension. The church embraces a great part of Christ's riches, but not all, we wonder and adore before the mystery. The high priest bore the name of the Lord on his forehead, so the name is likely to have been on the *head*.

13. And he was clothed with a vesture dipped in blood: and his name is called The Word of God.

13 The *garment dipt in blood* points to Isaiah. 63:1-3, comp. here 14:20. The *blood*, is that of the enemies of God's people. A transition from Christ to his *army*, both on *white horses*, is made through the clothing. Heb. 4:12 supplies a bridge between the clothing and the name (comp. 1:16,) in which they both convey a destroying character, Christ as the mighty warrior. Genesis 1 and Ps. 33:6 shows what the word of God accomplishes, the creation, or the ten kings, cannot oppose him. The name *Jesus* shows his grace, but the older name *the Word of God* his majesty. The external word reveals what one is in his mind. This name appears in John's gospel and his epistle also.

14. And the armies which were in heaven followed him upon white horses, clothed in fine linen, white and clean.

14 Compare here *the called, the chosen and the believing* in 17:14; although the church exists in heaven, and the armies in heaven denote the believers, here Christ comes in a judicial capacity, this train of Christ is rather the angels (Matt. 16:27, 25:31, 26:53, Luke 9:26, Mark 8:38, 2 Thess. 1:7, Luke 2:13.) Here it is the crushing power with which Christ, as governor of the world, with his angels, beats all resistance of his adversaries, through the means represented in ch. 6; there it is the peaceful mission of the church which scatters the seed of the word in the fields that have been ploughed by the judgments of God. The glittering *white* of the angels' pure white linen symbolizes their work, white the glory, the purity, his righteousness, as Christ displayed in 1:15.

15. And out of his mouth goeth a sharp sword, that with it he should smite the nations: and he shall rule them with a rod of iron: and he treadeth the winepress of the fierceness and wrath of Almighty God. **16.** And he hath on his vesture and on his thigh a name written, King of kings, and Lord of lords.

15-16 *And out of his mouth goeth a sharp sword, that with it he should smite the heathen.* The tending of the heathen with the staff of iron and the treading of the winepress belong to the future in verse 20, and serve to explain the *sharp sword.* This sword is the all powerful agency of Christ in judging and destroying (comp. 1:16, 2:12, John 18:5 with Acts 9:4-5.) The iron staff dashes the heathen in pieces (Ps. 2,) and has already occurred in 2:27, 12:5. The *wine press* is that of God's wrath (comp. on 14:19,) Christ the one who puts it into motion, presses the wine out. The wine is the blood of his enemies, in 14:19, the symbol of the winepress expresses the energy of the wrath, and here the fierceness explains and conveys it. The sword commonly is found upon the garment on the thigh, as a symbol of a ruler's personality and position, and along with this, glory and majesty (Ps. 45:3-4.) The sword is always as the man who carries it. In 17:14 Christ is denominated a *King of kings, and a Lord of lords* with respect to the ten kings (1 Tim. 6:15.)

THE BIRDS FEAST ON THE CORPSES

17. And I saw an angel standing in the sun; and he cried with a loud voice, saying to all the fowls that fly in the midst of heaven, Come and gather yourselves together unto the supper of the great God; 18. That ye may eat the flesh of kings, and the flesh of captains, and the flesh of mighty men, and the flesh of horses, and of them

that sit on them, and the flesh of all men, both free and bond, both small and great.

Here we have *an angel standing in the sun.* The birds are invited to the feast before the slaughter, because the outcome is inevitable. The FUNDAMENTAL PASSAGE is Eze. 39:17-20, the prophecy against Gog is applied to the ten kings. The *sun* is the natural image of the glory of God and Christ (comp. on 1:16, 10:1, 12:1) and so fit for an *angel* to announce the victory of God.

The *great supper of God* contrasts to the marriage supper of the Lamb in verse 9. The *flesh of kings* here is similar to 6:15, 13:16. Here we have four parties, the last again composed of four, corresponding to the four of the second and third division.

THE BEAST AND THE KINGS ASSEMBLE TO FIGHT AGAINST CHRIST

19. And I saw the beast, and the kings of the earth, and their armies, gathered together to make war against him that sat on the horse, and against his army.

The kings stand under the direction of the beast—comp. on 17:13, bound together only by their earthly temperament; and hence mention is made of *armies.* On the other hand, Christ has with him only one *army.*

BEAST, FALSE PROPHET THROWN INTO FIRE, SLAUGHTER ON ENEMIES

20. And the beast was taken, and with him the false prophet that wrought miracles before him, with which he deceived them that had received the mark of the beast, and them that worshipped his image. These both were cast alive into a lake of fire burning with brimstone. 21. And the remnant were slain with the sword of him that sat upon the horse, which sword proceeded out of his mouth: and all the fowls were filled with their flesh.

The beast was seized, which had tried to seize Christ in his members (John 7:30, 32, 44, 10:39.) The beast and false prophet are not human individuals, but purely ideal forms; they were alive without corporeal death. A human person cannot proceed *alive* into hell. Distinction must be made between form and reality, as in 20:14, death and hell are cast into the lake of fire, they are purely ideal forms, as *fire and brimstone* point to the overthrow of Sodom and Gomorrha, alluding to the Dead Sea as the earthly image of hell.

21 The rest, as those in verse 18, were slain by Christ's sword (comp. 2 Thess. 2:8,) and sent to hell in the final judgment (comp. 20:12-15) if they have not in the intermediate state been saved (1 Pet 3:20.)[18]

---

18. The Rev. Patrick Fairbairn, translator of the original commentary, expressly declared his objection to this comment.

REVELATION 20:1-6

Satan harmless as church reigns a thousand years

CHAPTER SUMMARY

Of the three enemies of God's kingdom, Satan alone now remains. The ground, however, has been taken from under him by the overthrow of the beast and the false prophet. He is bound for a thousand years by the power of Christ, so that he can no farther deceive the nations, ver. 1–3. Thus, therefore, the church of Christ celebrates on earth a glorious triumph; and even the faithful witnesses and confessors, who do not live to see the beginning of the thousand years, so that they cannot reign with Christ upon the earth, do not altogether vanish during the thousand years; they exist in heavenly bliss, and reign in heaven with Christ over the earth, ver. 4-6. With such prospects for the church of Christ in earth and heaven, who would then be afraid any more of the great dragon and his associates? They can neither arrest the victorious career of Christ on earth, nor intercept the enjoyment of the heavenly bliss.

SATAN BOUND A THOUSAND YEARS FROM DECEIVING THE NATIONS

20:1. And I saw an angel come down from heaven, who had the key of the abyss, and a great chain on his hand. 2. And he seized the dragon, the old serpent, who is the devil and Satan, and bound him a thousand years. 3. And cast him into the abyss, and shut and sealed over him, that he might no more deceive the heathen till that the thousand years were completed; afterwards he must be loosed for a short time.

What happens here with Satan relates to the ten kings and the beast; and follows necessarily from it. The dominion of the God-opposing principle was broken in the ten kings, partly through severe judgments of God (19:11-21,) partly through the peaceful mission of the church (17:14.) They are no longer in enmity against God and Christ and the church; so the beast is not on the stage, whose last *instruments* they were. From the whole doctrine of Scripture touching the relation of Satan to human affairs, it was thus only that Satan could find room for his seductive agency, and in the same way it must again be taken from him after it was given. The existence of the beast and its heads forms the basis of Satan's dominion over the earth (comp. 12:3, 13:2.) The sphere of Satan upon earth extends precisely as far as the sphere of the inclination to meet him on it. Believers pray, *Lead us not into temptation, but deliver us from the evil* (the evil enemy;) and this prayer has the testimony and promise that God does not lead his people into temptation, but rather delivers them from the tempter. He allows them to be exposed to no more

SATAN HARMLESS AS CHURCH REIGNS A THOUSAND YEARS

than human temptations. Satan is only the prince *of the world*. Such alone are deceived by him, as will suffer themselves to be deceived by it. For these it is a deserved punishment, if they are given up to Satan, and they are gradually led farther than they were disposed to go. *Every one*, says St. James, *is tempted, when he is led away and enticed by his own evil lust* (1:14.) Also *Resist the devil, and he will flee from you* (4:7.) If the earth were to watch and pray for a thousand years, Satan should have nothing on it. What is said here of the operations of Christ, repeats itself in the case of every individual, who stands in faith, watches and prays. If we separate what Christ here does against Satan, from the preparation and basis laid for it in what precedes, the question then arises, why should Christ not have bound Satan earlier? and also, why should he not have thrown him at once into the lake of fire, but allowed him to get free again after a thousand years?

1-2 The *angel* here is Christ, who in 1:18 has the keys of hell and death, here the *key of the abyss*, and has come down from heaven to lay hold of *Satan* and throw him there. It is the work of Christ to bind Satan (Matt. 12:29.) The *abyss* is hell, from where Satan makes excursions upon the earth, as mentioned in Luke 8:31, where the spirits were in expectation of their fate, not yet upon them, but now so. The *great chain on his hand* makes many coils upon Satan, signifying the impress of God's will.

Christ's underlying victory against Satan described in 12:9 under four names there, the four, the number of the world indicating Satan as prince of this world, are repeated again here. The *dragon* is first in order, but at the end of the thousand years it is not the dragon but Satan and the devil that is loosed, because in his property as the dragon, and the beast, he has been cast into the lake of fire. A new phase of enmity in an essentially different character is with us at the end of the thousand years.

The *thousand years* being mentioned six times, shows a real importance is attached to the number itself. Although it has a floating character as far as determining its exact parameters, a commencement date most suited is the year 800 when the Pope placed the crown on the head of Charlemagne inaugurating the western Christian empire.[19]

3 It is *sealed* securely over Satan, as the prison house is a subterranean one. In Matt. 27:66 the grave of Jesus was sealed, and to ensure his unchanging purpose Darius the King sealed the lions' den with his signet ring–Dan. 6:17 (compare the *chain on his hand* in verse 1.) As if it is *Today to me, tomorrow to thee!* for Satan in his work against Christ and his people.

He may no longer deceive–not the deceiving of individuals, but the nations in their unchristianized state, the destruction of the Christian state that had been settled among them. It is not the seducing to sin generally, but to open unbelief, heathenism and opposition to Christ and his church, as it had been in the time of the beast under Rome and the ten kings.

Satan is first mentioned here as the *dragon*, coming into view as the animating principle of the ungodly power of the world. The two last names, *the devil and Satan*, indicate his hostility toward the church.

As was spoken of Elijah in Matt. 17:12, *He has come already, but they did not know him*, holds here, as the church has held dominion for a thousand

---

19. Perhaps an end may be seen when Napoleon, gorged with power, ignored the Pope and crowned himself Emperor on the 8th December 1804; or, after the defeat by Napoleon at Austerlitz, on the 6th August 1806, the Emperor Francis II dissolved the Holy Roman Empire–*Editor.*

years. Death still reigns in the millennium, with the fundamental relations introduced by sin, which is connected with the working of Satan. The war of the dragon against the seed of the woman ceases, she is not shut up in the wilderness, the field of the world is open to her, her man-son rules the nations, which are no more deceived by Satan, but subject to Christ and free from persecutions.

The heathenish state of mind forms the condition to Satan's work of *deceiving*. This condition was for a time destroyed by Christ's victory over the ten kings. The deceiving can only return by a return first to heathenism, then Satan makes himself known as the organising principle of the opposition to the kingdom of God.

AN INTERLUDE: FAITHFUL WITNESSES REIGN IN HEAVEN WITH CHRIST

> 4. And I saw thrones, and they sat upon them, and judgment was given to them; and the souls of those who had been beheaded for the testimony of Jesus, and for the word of God, and who had not worshipped the beast, nor his image, and had not received his mark on their forehead and on their hand. And they lived and reigned with Christ the thousand years. 5. The rest of the dead, however, did not again live till the thousand years were finished. This is the first resurrection. 6. Blessed and holy is he that hath part in the first resurrection: on such the second death hath no power, but they shall be priests of God and of Christ, and shall reign with him a thousand years.

Verses 4-6 contain an interlude, as verse 7 clearly joins to verse 3:

3. And cast him into the bottomless pit, and shut him up, and set a seal upon him, that he should deceive the nations no more, till the thousand years should be fulfilled: and after that he must be loosed a little season.

7. And when the thousand years are expired, Satan shall be loosed out of his prison.

What is given to the saints points to the blessed time, the approaching period of ascendancy for the church, in much the same way the martyrs were given when they passed out of this life in an earlier period, in 6:11. John shows that the earlier departed saints are solemnly inaugurated into the heavenly inheritance during the millennial kingdom.

Ch. 4:4 and Matt. 19:28 casts light on who it is that sits upon the thrones– the four and twenty patriarchs and apostles, in which tribes the apostle recognizes the whole Christian church. In Dan. 7:9-10 around the throne the books are opened, the judgment is composed under the representatives of the covenant people, who receive full judicial power, in judgment on the church, and the sentence is this: that the faithful witnesses must *live and reign with Christ*. The *souls* are the murdered souls, not souls in the intermediate state, but in the moment of death, showing that their living again is consequent to the divine sentence and their claim to the divine recompense. It is properly the *killed with the hatchet*, in respect to the Roman executions. So we are to think primarily of the martyrs under the persecution of Rome, who had remained stedfast with Christ, and not worshipped the beast.

Jesus is the personal word of God, so *the testimony of Jesus* is also the word of God. John saw how they *lived* and came to not merely bare life, but the blessed resurrection life, as promised as the crown in 2:10 (19:19) and the white garment of 6:11. Christ *reigns* in the *thousand years* from the beginning to the end, because his enemies who contended for the dominion, the beast, the false prophet, the dragon, have now become his footstool. His members take part in this dominion. The godless, the rest of the dead however take no part in this, but are in hades and torment. The judgment of verses 12-13 is only on the ungodly, and they must pass into the final torment at the end.

5 The *first resurrection* is the first stage of blessedness immediate on departing this life (14:13, John 14:2-3, 13:36, 17:24,) the second when they enter the New Jerusalem–comp. 6:11 (19:9 expanded in 21:22–comp. 3:12, Matt. 19:28, John 5:25, 28-29, 6:39-40.) John denotes the two stages by the same name, distinguished by the first and the second, so one must of necessity be wanting in literality, as two resurrections are inconceivable. To understand this as a literal resurrection has no other support in scripture, which knows only a general resurrection. It only suits the heavenly state of blessedness. The design is to draw a parallel between the two stages. With resurrection there is also the life, the chief point is not the local rising out of the grave, but the transition to a new and glorious state. It is taken in general here so the two degrees of bliss are denoted by the same word. Resuscitation, revivification are described as a resurrection in Heb. 11:35, with Elijah, and is in the purely spiritual territory in Eph. 2:6, Col. 3:1.

6 The *holy* here denotes, not the moral quality, but the glorious state of the children of God even in this life, yet more distinctly unfolded in the future world. Parallel to *over such the second death has no power* is John 11:26, *He that believes upon me shall never die.* The sufferings of now are nothing in light of the good of the first resurrection.

We now have the thousand years reign behind us. We stand at the loosing of Satan out of his prison and his excursion to deceive the heathen in the four quarters of the earth to gather them together to battle (20:7-9.)

The conviction during the Middle Ages was that the thousand years dated from Christ's birth, and so there was great expectancy for Christ's return. The current exposition of chiliasm, that the millennium is still future, was taught by the Lutheran Bengel (1687-1752,) and adopted by the Pietists. The sects have always had a great predilection for chiliasm, but the church has been disinclined to adopt it. In the nature of the sects there lies a practical denial of the confession, *I believe in one holy catholic church.* They confine to within the circle of their party what is good and Christian, and are unable to see the divine in strange garb, which it often assumes, and so they transfer the thousand years to the future, to a state imagined more satisfactory to what has been in the past. Chiliasm rests on things incompatible–corporeally risen saints are on the earth, the resurrection is separate to the earth's regeneration, the risen glorified church is attacked by mortal men at the end, the final apostasy presupposes the trend of sin through the period. Chiliasm is the natural consequence of believing the beast is the papacy, for the millennium only begins with the destruction of the beast (19:20;) as the papacy is still with us, then the millennium must be future. This false view of the beast has ensured chiliasm has obtained an almost universal diffusion through the church. If the earth is to get more corrupt and wicked it is a great consolation that the thousand years are now behind us, and the final conquest is in the immediate offing.

REVELATION IS NOT A PROGRESSIVE WHOLE

It is a fundamental error of exposition to regard the Revelation as a progressive whole, proceeding in regular order from beginning to end. It is rather to be viewed as composed of a number of independent groups, each complete in itself, each bringing out particular points, thus supplementing one another. The last end for instance is referenced at points throughout the book–6:12-17, 8:1, 11:15 and 14:14-16.

Now, the independent groups are altogether seven as follows:
1. The seven epistles to the churches.
2. The seven seals.
3. The seven trumpets, ch. 8:2–11:19.
4. The three enemies of the kingdom of God–Satan, the beast, and the false prophet, and their war upon it, ch. 12–14.
5. The seven vials, ch. 15–16.
6. The judgment on the three enemies, beginning with the beast and the false prophet, and rising from them to Satan, ch. 17–20.
7. The New Jerusalem.

To ascertain the time the thousand years belongs we go to a new beginning at ch. 17, where it follows immediately on the destruction of the beast and the false prophet. By these we understand the ungodly heathen power and wisdom, and therefore the millennium cannot be future, as the heathen power has ceased to exist in the lands of the Roman world.

This sixth group has a chronological development from beginning to end. The sixfold repetition of the number shows it is to be taken in good earnest, as the ten always bears in scripture the character of a round number, as also is the thousand as a multiplicand of ten, and never a symbolical one.

The last phase of the heathenish power concerned the ten kings or peoples who overthrew the Roman Empire. We understand these as the Germanic peoples, whose conversion is represented in ch. 19 under the image of their conquest by Christ in a great battle, so the commencement of the millennium must be coincident with the conversion of the Germanic tribes. The thousand years then coincides with the German ascendancy, in which the European tribes have raised and carried forward the new European Christian life in a vigorous and beautiful manner. Since the time of the French revolution, there has been a great falling away, and it has been plain that Satan has been completely loosed from his prison and gone forth to gather the heathen to battle. The point now remains that the falling of fire from heaven is imminent (see ver. 9.)

OBJECTIONS TO THE VIEW

In objection to this view it is alleged that 20:1-3 cannot have been fulfilled in the past, as the deceiving of the heathen has carried through the past, so it must end in the future. But here is not Satan's deceiving in the general, but deceiving with a view of stirring the heathen to an open attack on the kingdom of Christ, for the purpose of destroying it, to threaten its destruction. That the agency of Satan and sin should have altogether ceased during the thousand years is belied by this more narrowly bounded definition of the deceiving. With all its corruptions, severe conflicts and losses for individuals, it was on the whole the period of Christ's undisputed sway. That a great change has begun at the end of it is clear from the histories. During the thousand years there have been no conflicts which resemble those that precede and come after it. As for Islam, it had left the original ground of Christianity untouched.

To regard the papacy after an unhistorical mode of viewing it, as on a level with ancient and modern heathenism, has led to the abandoning of the historical ground in determining the position of the thousand years. Besides, the papal dominion comprehends only part of the thousand years, which period also embraces the whole springtime of the evangelical churches. The reformation had presupposed the existence of glorious powers of life, though in a slumbering state at times. Now we no longer stand within the thousand years, we have about us the Gog and Magog of unbelief.[20]

Another objection is from verses 4-6 where the righteous are resurrected at the beginning of the thousand years and continue on earth through it. As it has not happened before, men perceive it as still future. But this leads to a perfectly monstrous combination of things incapable of union, the church partly mortal, partly glorified and risen on the unrenewed earth, entangled in conflict, the glorified saints estranged from their rest.

This section before us is entirely similar in structure. It leads us from the earth, and the triumph granted there to the cause and the servants of Christ, to heaven, to see the glory of those who departed before the thousand years. Their resurrection is ascribed to these, in a figurative sense, of a transition into a new and glorious existence. The Apocalypse points to the blessedness the redeemed enjoy even before the general resurrection. The passages, 1 Cor. 15:22-23; Luke 14:14; 1Thess. 4:16, do not say the righteous shall be raised at the last day before the wicked. The resurrection only comes at Christ's coming, and is not connected with the thousand years, but rather with the time of the New Jerusalem. The change on the living is coupled by Paul with the resurrection of saints that are asleep, which can only take place with the general regeneration, with the new heavens and the new earth. Finally Luke 18:8 testifies that in the last times apostasy shall be widespread, not a church of risen saints. What is said of the thousand years is brief, and John hastens on to the section of the glory of the New Jerusalem, so it is manifest that in the thousand years we are to seek no heaven upon the earth.

---

20. The passing of time since the first publication of this book in 1852 serves only to affirm these assertions—*Editor.*

REVELATION 20:7-10

The final destruction of Satan

This passage shows, as indicated in verse 3, that at the end of the thousand years there should be a great change in the relation of Satan to the earth. After the thousand years he is loosed from the abyss, deceives Gog and Magog, that is the heathen over the whole earth, to come and fight against Christ and his church, and initially he succeeds and lays siege to the camp of the saints and the beloved city. But fire from heaven consumes them, and Satan, the last of the three enemies of Christ and his church, is thrown into the lake of fire.

The reason of his being loosed is connected with his being bound. The earth watched and prayed for a thousand years. If the earth should cease to do so, it must necessarily fall into temptation. Where God is no longer present, Satan is sure to come among the children of disobedience and the backsliders, as in Matt. 12:43-45, Eph. 2:2. Shameless profligacy and covert unbelief would give rise to carnal security and profane mockery in a germinating heathenism.

TWO RELATED PROPHECIES
DANIEL'S LITTLE HORN, GOG AND MAGOG

This passage has in common Daniel's prophecy regarding the little horn uprooting the three great horns (Dan. 7:8,) with its hatred against God and his church, the changing of times and laws, in order to abolish all holy and profane, divine and human institutions and laws, its success in overcoming three kingdoms, getting the church into its power, and the end of the world with its overthrow. The other passage is the prophecy of Ezekiel against Gog, the king of Magog, the chief prince of Meshech and Tubal, in ch. 38-39.

Daniel's prophecy regards a future fact in world history, while Ezekiel's Gog and Magog has an ideal composite character, representing all the enemies of God. Ezekiel had prophesied Israel's return from exile and oppression, and countered the doubt regarding a permanent recovery. It has no literal historical fulfilment, in that unrelated peoples from diverse regions are called to the expedition; and a king is formed of Gog, out of the land Magog, which alone is mentioned in Genesis 10:2, where the enemies of God's kingdom are spoken of in general terms. John also viewed it this way. In 19:17-18 the victory over the ten kings is one fulfilment of it. He changes a king, Gog, into a people, Gog, together with Magog, removing the national and the local limitation which Ezekiel attaches to it, considering Gog and Magog as the heathen in all the earth.

SATAN LOOSED TO DECEIVE OVER ALL THE EARTH

20:7. And when the thousand years are finished, Satan shall be loosed out of his prison. 8. And he will go forth to deceive the heathen in the four corners of the earth, Gog and Magog, to gather them together to the war, the number of whom is as the sand of the sea. 9. And they went up on the breadth of the earth, and encompassed the camp of the saints and the beloved city. And fire came down out of heaven from God, and consumed them. 10. And the devil that deceived them was cast into the lake of fire and brimstone, where the beast and the false prophet are, and shall be tormented day and night for ever and ever.

Here the future is announced beforehand, carrying us to the farther side of the *thousand years.*

The Lord releases *Satan* with the key of the abyss, without whose will Satan cannot move a step, as Job shows (1:8-12,) and without whose permission they could not even enter into swine (Matt. 8:31.) In punishment of ingratitude and apostasy, he sends to those who have lost their love for the truth, through Satan, strong delusions, that they should believe lies (2 Thess. 2:11, comp. Rom. 1:25.) The evil enemy is called *Satan,* and in verse 10, the *devil.* The *dragon* is no longer on the stage, but the heathen state corresponds, and culminates in the heathen kings. So far however matters are not to come again. The Christian state may be perforated by the evil and in part destroyed where the mass yields to the seductions of Satan, but he cannot pluck the Christian state up by the root, and establish himself again as the dragon, as he had before. He no longer has that name, so the anti-Christian world receives the name of Gog and Magog. Even in Ezekiel, Magog bears the character, not of a regularly constituted state, but of a horde of plunderers. Gog appears as the head of Magog, is viewed as a distinct people, acting in concert with Magog. The prison is the abyss, the loosing of Satan in comparison to the thousand years is only to be for a short time. (See p. 133, regarding the *little horn* of Daniel 7.)

8 Satan accomplishes his work through the unclean spirit (16:13.) The *corners* represent the whole people from the beginning to the end, whatever is bounded by them (Isa. 11:12, Eze. 7:2, Job 37:3.) In the FUNDAMENTAL PROPHECY of Ezekiel, *Gog and Magog* form the epexegesis to the nations in the four corners of the earth, Gog is the centre (38:5-6.) But here the ground of Gen. 10:2 is abandoned, Gog and Magog are all the heathen, *as the sand of the sea* in number, as were the Canaanites, the Midianites and the Philistines (Josh 11:4, Judg. 7:12, 1 Sam 13:5.)

9 The *going up* is war talk as to ascend and take a height. Those deceived by Satan are scattered over all the earth, others dwell un-seduced with them, and it is these against whom they now go forth, as if the meek would not inherit the earth. The camp is in the city (Acts 21:34, comp. ver. 37, 22:24, 23:10, 16, 32); the church in Moses time externally presented a military camp, *the camp of the saints* is the essential warlike condition of the church (Eph. 6:10, 1 John 2:14, 5:4.)

The *beloved city* is Jerusalem, in the Apocalypse a symbol of the church. This echoes Luke 19:43, the same state of things a punishment, for if the church had done her duty Satan would not have deceived her; but with all its failings it is still the beloved city, as in ancient Jerusalem it is a house of prayer, to which God hears and brings *fire down from heaven* (comp. 8:3-5, in an allusion to Gen 19:24, Eze. 38:22, 39:6,) unexpected, quick, frightful and overwhelming.

10 In 12:9 Satan is cast down from heaven to the earth, in 20:3, into the abyss, hell; here, at last into the lake of fire and brimstone, the deeper hell (comp. at 19:20.)

REVELATION 20:11-15

The final judgment on the servants of Satan and the beast, the removal of the present constitution of the world

The three enemies of God's kingdom have disappeared. There must now still follow the final and ultimate decision respecting the fate of those, who submitted to their influence in ver. 12-15; and all, too, of the irrational creation, which had been pressed by them into the service of sin in ver. 11, must be put out of the way. This being done, all is then prepared for the new earth, on which righteousness dwells, for the new Jerusalem coming down out of heaven from God; and, therefore, for the beginning of the seventh and last vision.

> 20:11. And I saw a white great throne, and him who sat thereon, before whose presence the earth and the heaven fled away, and no place was found for them. 12. And I saw the dead, the small and the great, stand before the throne, and books were opened, and another book was opened, which is (the book) of life. And the dead were judged according to that which was written in the books, according to their works. 13. And the sea gave the dead, that were therein, and death and hell gave the dead, that were therein; and they were judged every one according to their works. 14. And death and hell were cast into the lake of fire. This is the second death, the lake of fire. 15. And whosoever was not found written in the book of life, was cast into the lake of fire.

The *white throne* corresponds to the white *cloud* in 14:14. The *white*, as also the crystal clear jasper (4:3) symbolizes the glory of the judge. A *great* throne, in contrast to the thrones in ver. 4, on account of the glory and greatness of God. He *who sits*, only one is sitting, God the Almighty Creator in the undivided unity of his being, here without respect to the diversity of persons in the Godhead. The *no place* indicates a complete removal, a vanishing away, as at 12:8, 16:20. A real *flight*, as at Ps. 114:3-4 and finally at 21:1, so that the new creation take their place. The old order ceases (Matt. 24:35, 19:28, and 2 Pet. 3:7, 10-12,) the judgment of the ungodly is connected with the destruction of *the heavens* and *the earth* (1 John 2:17, John 6:39, 12:48,) which has become altered by the fall, changed into a dwelling for human and satanic wickedness (Gen. 3:17-19, 5:29,) the heavens often red and troubled, clothed in darkness, made of iron, earth as brass, land unyielding, labour lost, angels leaving their first estate in high heaven (Matt. 16:3, Isa. 50:3, Lev. 26:19-20, comp. Deut. 11:17, 28:23, Jude 6, 2 Pet. 2:4.)

12 Here it is not all the dead, but the ungodly *dead*, raised before the throne, who even while in the body were still dead (Matt. 8:22.) Those that had slept in Jesus before the thousand years then lived and reigned with Christ. Those who died in the Lord in the thousand years and in conflict with Gog and Magog are not included here. To avoid confusion a distinction needs to be observed between substance and dramatic form when comparing this with

the sheep and the goats of Matt. 25:31-32. Here also the scene of judgment merely forms a part of the representation. The apostle regards the *dead* as *judged* already in John 5:24, 8:51 and 1 John 3:14, in 11:18 the *dead* are the lost dead. As for *the small and great* compare 11:18, 13:16. All the fear they awakened has vanished away!

The words *and the books were opened*, is from Dan. 7:10, where another judgment is spoken of. The books are those of guilt, condemnation and death–of unforgiven sins. The *book of life* is opened to show that they had not been written there, where guilt has been purged away by the blood of the Lamb. Many books to the one shows that but few are saved, or *the book* is simply the names, but *the books*, the long array of evil deeds and works. The judgment is here as in 11:18, and the PARALLEL PASSAGES quoted there from the Gospel of John, which declares believers to be free from the judgment (3:18, 5:24,) a condemnatory one.

This verse does not advance, but supplies and completes. The words, agreeing with the close of verse 12, repeated, show we are at the same point. Verse 6 described the salvation of believers as the first resurrection, so it is not used in regard to the raising of the ungodly. According to the style of Revelation the righteous partake of a double resurrection, but the wicked none at all. As the privilege of believers it is so in the gospel (comp. 6:39-40, 44, 54 and Luke 14:14, 20:35.)

13 The *sea* in the Apocalypse is the sea of the peoples, the wicked restless world. It is not the literal sea that is meant. The *dead*, whom the *sea* conceals, are those who were slain in the spirit of brotherly hatred, Cain against Cain, those who are related to *death and hell*, which phrase shows that the sea is the receptacle of the lost dead.

14-15 *Death* here is an unblessed death, the continuation and punishment of spiritual death, connected with *hell* (1:18, 6:8,) or Hades, the place of torment for the ungodly. *Death* here is the death of final perdition. As long as death reigns over unbelievers, believers must also be subject to death as commonly accepted. The *second death* is for the wicked, the second blessed resurrection for the righteous. The first death is the state of man under the dominion of sin and the wrath of God. Its dominion stretches over two lands, one in time, in this life (Luke 15:32, 1 John 3:14,) the other when separated soul from body into the common receptacle of departed, impure souls.

In regard to *the lake of fire* (19:20, 20:10,) the oven of fire in Matt. 13:42,50 corresponds. Here the final hell is erected, in a parallel to John 15:6, *He that abides not in me, is cast forth as a branch, and is withered; and men gather them, and cast them into the fire, and they are burned.* In ver. 14 the final hell is, as it were, erected, here it receives its wretched inhabitants.

Jesus, help now, for the sake of thy wounds, that I may be found written in the book of life!

GROUP 7

THE NEW JERUSALEM

The description of the new Jerusalem

REVELATION 21:1–22:5

REVELATION 21:1-8

The description of the new Jerusalem

INTRODUCTION

The sixth group, in ch. 17–20 represented the judgment upon the three enemies of God, of the Lamb, and the church. It closes with the completion of their overthrow in the destruction of the chief enemy, Satan; with the last judgment on their servants, and the removal of all that has pressed in upon the creation through sin.

Everything is now prepared for the entrance of the last phase of the kingdom of God, for the foundation of the new earth, on which righteousness dwells, for the erection on it of the kingdom of glory, for the solemnization of the marriage of the Lamb, to the threshold of which we were brought by the song of praise in 19:6-8, that anticipated the contents of 19:11–20:15.

This sacred closing history is the subject of the present group. That the hope may become truly living, the object of it is vividly delineated by John to the church, that she might take up more successfully the conflict with the visible, which is apt to induce despair, as was done in former times by the Holy Spirit, who spake through the prophets of the OLD TESTAMENT, that the minds of believers might have the glory of the future exhibited to their view to free them from care, anxiety and grief. So, for example, Ezekiel in ch. 40–48, and Isaiah in ch. 40. There is an unmistakeable reference to these OLD TESTAMENT representations in the description given here of the new Jerusalem, by which we must seek only for the beginning of their fulfilment in the first appearance of Christ. Christian hope is still always justified in repairing to them for strength and refreshment.

CHAPTER SUMMARY

John sees the new heaven and the new earth, ver. 1; then he sees the new Jerusalem coming down from heaven, ver. 2. Thereupon he hears a double voice, one that of the just made perfect, the citizens of the new Jerusalem, who informed him, and through him the church, what is implied in this, and what blessed hope it presents, ver. 3-4. The other voice, that of him who sits on the throne, first announces that he is going to make all things new, and then, after testimony respecting his supreme majesty and absolute credibility, declares that invincible faithfulness alone can attain to a participation in the benefits of the new world, while the lake of fire is appointed as the doom of apostasy.

That this section has the character of an introduction, and a prelude, is clear from ver. 10, where the prophet still, as in ver. 2, sees Jerusalem coming down from heaven, whereas, if we had a continued representation before us, he would have seen it as already come down. With ver. 9 begins the chief burden of the group, in which that briefly indicated in ver. 2, is more largely unfolded, proceeding from a similar starting point. The introduction first shortly represents the chief matters of the group; then it refers to the practical point of view that these are to be considered, *that we may run with patience the race that is set before us*. If the old Jerusalem, the militant church, is heavily tried and afflicted to invoke despair and renunciation, as was the case at the time when the Revelation was seen, then for our consolation and support, we must keep our eye on the new Jerusalem, and the wells of living water, which are there opened for the thirsty.

JOHN SEES THE NEW HEAVENS AND EARTH

21:1. And I saw a new heaven and a new earth. For, the first heaven and the first earth were passed away, and the sea is no more.

The *new heaven* and the *new earth* is first mentioned by Isaiah in 65:17 —to which 66:22 refers, and of which is said respecting the earth in Isa. 11. In 2 Pet. 3:13 we have reference to these promises. In substance the *regeneration* corresponds, or the *renewing of the world* in Matt. 19:28, which is presupposed in 2 Cor. 5:17. As the corruption began with persons, and then passed over to the other parts of creation, the renewing also must proceed in the same way. In the germ, therefore, there is to be seen the new heaven and the new earth in the first appearance of Christ, and the new powers of life brought into operation in him and conferred on the human race. The commission of his militant church for centuries has been to rear occupants for the new earth, citizens for the new Jerusalem. The announcement of the new heaven and the new earth joins on immediately to 20:11, where the destruction of the present heaven and the present earth was predicted; *for the first heaven and the first earth had passed away*. The desolations which sin has effected on the old earth and heavens vanish, the kernel remains. Nature will not be annihilated, but purified; all corruption abolished; the work of God remains, but set free from its dross. It will be such a change as if a destruction of what previously existed, showing quite plainly how deeply the effects of sin have been imprinted on the heavens and the earth. The *sea* is the sea of the *peoples*, the wicked restless world—comp. at 20:13 where along with the sea, there brotherly hatred, which led men to kill one another also vanishes from the creation. By it sea and death are connected with each other. There is no longer any sea, after those not in the book of life are cast into the lake of fire (20:15.) The sea disappears along with the wicked (Isa. 57:20.) The vanishing of the natural sea is not meant; as according to Gen. 1, it belongs to creation in its original state, here that alone is removed from heaven and earth which was the effect of sin. The sea occupies a prominent place in the praises found in the OLD TESTAMENT respecting *the Creator's* greatness—for example Ps. 104:25-26.

THE DESCRIPTION OF THE NEW JERUSALEM

THE NEW JERUSALEM COMES DOWN FROM HEAVEN

2. And the holy city the new Jerusalem, I saw come down out of heaven, from God prepared as a bride adorned for her husband.

First the new heaven and the new earth is mentioned, then the *new Jerusalem*. The former is the condition of the latter. Hence they are guilty of folly, who expect on the old earth a triumphant *and* glorious church. *The holy city*—so is the church of the future world named here and in 22:19, because she shines forth in her virtues (comp. on 19:8) and the glory lent her by God. The *holy* was applied even to the old Jerusalem—the church in her militant state (comp. 11:2); but it belongs to the new in so surpassing, and transcendent a sense, that it is called simpliciter *the holy city.* In Isa. 52:1 Jerusalem is called *the holy city* in the sense of the august and glorious, and in regard to its glorified state after the appearance of salvation. A *threefold* Jerusalem is peculiar to the NEW TESTAMENT. First, the *heavenly Jerusalem* (Heb. 12:22, comp. 11:10, 16, 13:14,) or the *Jerusalem that is above* (Gal. 4:26,) the heavenly community of the righteous. Then a Jerusalem here below, in the present life, the church in her militant state. Finally, the new Jerusalem on the glorified earth, with the introduction of which the two others vanish, which has in common with the first its heavenly character, and with the second a dwelling on the earth. In the Revelation, the heavenly Zion is mentioned with its 144,000 of perfectly righteous (14:1-5;) the militant church is indirectly denoted as Jerusalem (comp. on 11:2,) the holy city (20:9;) the beloved city; but John has reserved the name *Jerusalem* for the *new* Jerusalem, of which it is used here in ver. 10 and in 3:12. It never once denotes the militant church, much less that lifeless corpse, the literal Jerusalem.[21] That the new Jerusalem, a glorified Jerusalem, forms the contrast to *the beloved city* in 20:9 (which is warred against—the militant church), not to the literal Jerusalem, is evident in that the latter is never mentioned in the Apocalypse, while the militant church is indirectly represented as Jerusalem. The new Jerusalem is mentioned for the consolation of those under the oppressions that befell the militant church, and *not* because of the loss of the literal Jerusalem. Never is the heavenly Jerusalem as such designated by the name of the new Jerusalem. It is the new Jerusalem only in so far as it coming down in place of the old. The new Jerusalem *comes down out of heaven from God.* The city comes actually down to the earth. It comes down out of heaven in a *double* respect. First, in so far as till then the great number of its citizens, the just made perfect, had been preserved in heaven for their future inheritance upon earth, which corresponds to 11:12 (comp. at 20:5.) The descending of the new Jerusalem forms the counterpart to the removal of the ungodly out of the provisional state of misery into the final, the lake of fire, 20:13-15. Then again it does so, in so far as the church of the future has its origin in God, who makes all things new, ver. 5. There is a correspondence with 20:9, *and fire came down from heaven and consumed them.* That coming down out of heaven from God prepares the

---

21. Bengel: *John in his Gospel always writes* ιεροσολυμα, *when referring to the ancient city; in the Apocalypse always* ιερουσαλημ, *of the heavenly city; the latter is the Hebrew term, original and more sacred; the other, at that time common, Grecian, more polished* (comp. 1:19, 2:13, 4:45, 5:1, 2). *Paul makes the same distinction when refuting the Judaizers in Gal. 4:26* (comp. with 1:17, 2:1, Heb. 12:22,) *although elsewhere he speaks promiscuously, and as a mark of respect and favour uses* ιεροσολημ *when writing to the Romans and Corinthians.*

2. And the holy city the new Jerusalem, I saw come down out of heaven, from God prepared as a bride adorned for her husband.

way for this, and is its essential prerequisite. The *preparation* refers partly to the glorious virtues with which she is adorned in whose lustre she shines (comp. on 19:7-8,) partly to the glorious distinctions she has from God, as they are more fully unfolded in ver. 9. The *prepared*, etc. corresponds to the *holy* at the beginning. In Isa. 61:10 the church in the glory of the future state is already compared to the ornamented apparel of a wedding-season. According to 22:5, *And they shall reign for ever,* there can be no doubt that this form of the church is the last. We are led also to infer the same from the glory of the description, which excludes all further advance.[22]

THE VOICE OF THE JUST

3. And I heard a great voice from heaven, which said: Behold the tabernacle of God is with men, and he will dwell with them, and they shall be his people, and God himself shall be with them as their God. 4. And he will wipe away all tears from their eyes, and there shall be no more death, nor sorrow, nor crying, neither shall there be any more pain; for the first things are passed away.

The *voice from heaven* proceeds from amongst the citizens of the new Jerusalem, ver. 2, who are coming down from heaven. Chapter 19:1 shows the great voice as the multitudinous host in heaven. This is confirmed by the analogy of 11:15, 12:10, 14:2, 15:2-4, 19:1, 6.

The *tabernacle* is the centre of the city, not the city itself. Therefore: *behold, here* it is. Instead of the whole the most excellent part is taken into account. God's presence among his people in ancient times manifested in the symbolical form of a tabernacle, in which he dwelt in the midst of his people. What is there used as a *symbol* occurs here as an *image*. Ver. 22 shows it cannot be an external sanctuary. Ver. 11 corresponds as to substance, the new Jerusalem's distinguishing feature is that God is present there in the fulness of his glory. There is nothing absolutely new that is promised here: its foundation is seen in Ex. 29:45, Lev. 26:11-12. And when Ezekiel, in 37:27-28, promises, *And my dwelling shall be over you, and I will be your God, and ye shall be my people; and the heathen shall know that I the Lord sanctify Israel, when my sanctuary in your midst is perpetual,* he certainly did not mean the new Jerusalem merely of the Revelation; a prelude of the fulfilment was in the manifestations of divine grace, at the return from the captivity, and in the appearance of Christ. The *behold the tabernacle of God is with men* in 7:15, is verified for believers in the heavenly glory; according to 12:12, 13:6, believers even now dwell with God in his heavenly tent, though still in the militant church. In the new Jerusalem the presence of God among his people is so glorious, more intimate, gracious and peculiar in manner, that all earlier manifestations are eclipsed. Here is a reference to John 1:14, where it is said of the Word, *he dwelt among us.* This latter is the sure foundation of the former. The sum of God's covenant with his people is: *I will be your God, and ye shall be my people.* In place of: *God himself will be your God,* as we might expect from the books of Moses, it is said: he will be *with* them, or *among* them as their God, an allusion to the name *Immanuel* in Isa. 7:14, comp. Matt. 1:23.

22. Bengel: *It is not the new city of the millennium, but one perfectly new and eternal, as is shown by the series of visions, the magnificence of the description, and the contrast in regard to the second death,* 20:11-12, 21:1, 2, 5, 8, 9; 22:5.

THE DESCRIPTION OF THE NEW JERUSALEM

4 The *he will wipe away all tears from their eyes,* already occurred in 7:17, referring to the heavenly section of the church. Now the flow of her tears is for ever stayed. After the tears *death* is mentioned, which brings bitter weeping. It comes into the world through sin (Gen. 2:17; Rom. 5:12,) it must again cease through the complete victory over sin (1 Cor. 15:54.) As *tears* precede death (in the FUNDAMENTAL PASSAGE Isa. 25:8, the destruction of death precedes, and the ceasing of death follows,) so it is again succeeded by *mourning,* which is also connected with death in 18:8. The *crying* is not that of persons fighting, but of those oppressed, overpowered, despairing, Isa. 65:19. On the expression *no more,* till now it had not wholly ceased.

THE VOICE FROM THE THRONE

> 5. And he that sat upon the throne said, Behold I make all things new. And he says: Write, for these words are certain and true. 6. And he said to me, It is done. I am the Alpha and the Omega, the beginning and the end. I will give to him that is athirst of the fountain of the water of life freely. 7. He that overcomes shall inherit these things; and I will be his God, and he shall be my son. 8. But the fearful and unbelieving, and the abominable, and murderers, and whoremongers, and sorcerers, and idolaters, and all liars, shall have their part in the lake, that burns with fire and brimstone, which is the second death.

H*e that sat upon the throne* is God in the undistinguished unity of his being (comp. on 20:11.) *And he says,* etc., the change of tense—he *says* between the double *said*—and the similarity to 19:9 (in both passages, the command to write, and the assurance of truth) show, that here, as well as there, the *angel* is the speaker. On the call to *write,* which points to the high importance of the word spoken, see at 14:13. The *behold I make all things new,* is difficult for the natural mind to understand, how a change should take place, especially so when the old order of things oppresses on the church in John's day. So, the angel adds the reason, *for these words are certain and true;* the *ground* of confidence being that these are the words of God (comp. 19:9.)

6 After the interruption by the angel the discourse is again resumed of him, who sits on the throne. He said *to me.* What was said by him that sat on the throne in ver. 5, was also spoken for John. The express addition of the *to me* here is explained by the hortatory character of the termination of the discourse in ver. 7-8. In John the church is addressed. In the Revelation, the *it is done* is mentioned twice. First at the completion of the wrath of God in 16:17, and here at the making of all things new. The connection is that nothing more remains to be wished for by believers, the whole work of God is completed. The reality was still future, yet the future is spoken of as immediately present. The new heaven and the new earth are spoken of as already come at ver. 1, and in ver. 2, Jerusalem is seen coming down.

The *Alpha and the Omega* indicate, that in the beginning God made the heaven and the earth, as in 14:7. The *Omega* and the *end* is what is chiefly respected here (comp. at 1:8.) God is the Alpha and the beginning, he is also the Omega and the end. That he really is so, is made manifest by this corresponding renewal of creation.

It is done (it was so), was the word uttered in the beginning after every creative act; and the same, *It is done,* is repeated now at the end, in regard to the work of renewal. God is himself called *the beginning and the end,* because, as

6. And he said to me, It is done. I am the Alpha and the Omega, the beginning and the end. I will give to him that is athirst of the fountain of the water of life freely.

the beginning, so also the end yields him unconditional obedience, his decrees are assuredly carried into effect, on all the seal of his nature is impressed, all bears witness to his glory. In 1 Cor. 15:28, similarly it is said, *God will at last be all in all.* On *I will give to him that is athirst,* etc., see on 7:17, comp. also 22:17. The *thirsting* are those who are in need of salvation; the *water of life* denotes *salvation.* The *freely,* without his own doing and labouring, is from Isa. 55:1, referring to the Messiah's salvation, the final accomplishment of which is brought in here. Jesus himself alludes to this passage in John 7:37, *If any man thirst, let him come to me and drink,* in glorious fulfilment here. All that is here said to ennoble the period, when God makes all things new, is at the same time *an evidence of poverty in respect to the thousand years' reign, which belongs to the old world.* In it still the thirsty did not drink to satisfaction from the fountain of the water of life. Sadness and longing continue even in it to be the inseparable accompaniments of the state of believers.

7. He that overcomes shall inherit these things; and I will be his God, and he shall be my son.

7 The practical aim of this whole group meets us in this verse, which is to strengthen the church groaning under the cross, in view to the coming glory she may stand fast amid temptations.[23] The quintessence is contained in Rom. 8:18. Strong emphasis is to be laid on the *he that overcomes* (comp. at 2:7.) Victory must be wrung from all opponents, who are many. The contrast to the persons overcoming is formed by all who are mentioned in ver. 8. At John's time the chief enemy was fear for the persecuting world, as that there the *fearful* are the first to be named. The FUNDAMENTAL PASSAGE is Matt. 19:29. Every one *that overcomes shall inherit the whole* of the promise.

8. But the fearful and unbelieving, and the abominable, and murderers, and whoremongers, and sorcerers, and idolaters, and all liars, shall have their part in the lake, that burns with fire and brimstone, which is the second death.

8 The FUNDAMENTAL PASSAGE for what follows is 2 Sam. 7:14. The words in ver. 15 serve as an explanation. In place of *Father* there, *God* is put here; comp. 2 Sam. 7:24, 1 Cor. 6:9-10. The characters named form four pairs—the four, the signature of the earth, to which belong these different tendencies of those who live in the world (Col. 2:20.)

The series commences with the *fearful,* the faint-hearted, who shrank from the danger and the cross. We have nothing to be so much afraid of as *fear*—comp. the OLD TESTAMENT warning given respecting it in Deut. 20:1-8. Allusion is made to Matt. 8:26, which also points to Deut. 20; comp. John 14:27, *Why are ye fearful, ye of little faith!* comp. Mark 4:40, *Why are ye so fearful? how is it that ye have not faith?* The word δειλον occurs only in these three passages. There also the *fearful* stands connected with a little faith or none. Fearfulness unites with *unbelief* as its inseparable companion. There is no courage without faith, for the foundation of courage is confidence in God's help, bringing invincible strength. Here the fearful, who allow their courage to sink, and the unbelieving, are declared to be characters that the Lord has no pleasure in. The transition from the first class to the second is not so abrupt, as might at first sight appear. When the light of faith is extinguished, a frightful darkness arises, in which all sins have their being. People, who withdraw from the conflict, are capable of becoming abominable characters, murderers, whoremongers, etc. The *abominable* are those who give themselves to actions of an abominable kind, comp. at 17:4-5, as like *murder. Murderers* stand related to the abominable, much as idolaters do to liars. What is abominable is much more comprehensive in the law (comp. Lev. 18:26-27) to admit that sodomy here is particularly described (as in Lev. 18:22.) Besides, according to

---

23. Luther: *all things.* The *to me,* which Luther adds, ought to be deleted, according to the best authorities.

1 John 3:15, brotherly hatred even is of the same nature with murder, as being this in its germ and root.

Whoremongers and *sorcerers* have this in common, that their attempts on the well-being of a neighbour, unlike those of the murderer, are made covertly. Sorcery appears also in 9:21, as the means of hurting one's neighbour thus, and especially in regard to his life (comp. also 18:23.) *Fornication* is in the law presented under the aspect of injury done to a neighbour, and so also here in 9:21. In the last pair the *idolaters* are the species, *liars* the genus: and generally *all liars*. Idolaters are liars, they change God's truth into a lie, and have given glory and worship to the creature along with the Creator (Rom. 1:25; and on the idea of a lie, see on 14:5.) It is indifferent, whether idolaters worship idols, or mammon and their belly (Eph. 5:5, Col. 3:5, Phil. 3:19.)

REVELATION 21:9-22:5

The lengthened description of the new Jerusalem

THE MAIN THEME

After the introduction we have now the main theme of the group, the lengthened description of the new Jerusalem. After St. John had, in ver. 9-10, been transferred to the immediate neighbourhood of the new Jerusalem, he begins his description, in ver. 11, with the glory of God, which illuminates it. On this follows its greatness and lofty walls, its twelve gates, and the twelve foundations of the gates, in ver. 12-14. In ver. 15-17, he gives us the measurement of the city and of the walls. In ver. 18-21 the grandeur and glory of the city, as appearing in its material, in the walls, in the buildings, in the foundations of the walls, in the gates, and finally in the streets. In ver. 22-27 we see the glory of the city in regard to its inhabitants; first of all, the Lord God Almighty and the Lamb, ver. 22-23; then, coming down to the human inhabitants, the elect portion of the heathen world with its kings, ver. 24-26; finally, in ver. 27, the exclusion of all those, whose presence would darken its bright splendour. In 22:1-5, the Seer unfolds the blessedness of the inhabitants of the new Jerusalem, and the glorious privileges they enjoy—the water of life, and the tree of life, their glorious and never interrupted fellowship with the Lord, their reigning for ever and ever.

JOHN TRANSFERRED TO THE NEW JERUSALEM

> 21:9. And there came one of the seven angels, who have the seven vials full of the seven last plagues, and spake with me and said, Come, I will shew thee the bride, the Lamb's wife. 10. And he brought me in the Spirit to a mountain great and high, and showed me the city, the holy Jerusalem, coming down out of heaven from God.

Why the *showing* should be given to one of the angels, who had the seven vials, may be seen at 17:1. The epithet, *the bride*, determines what follows, *the Lamb's wife;* shows, we are to understand the *betrothed*. That the bride of the Lamb is here spoken of (in allusion to the Song, comp. 3:20,) shows that the glory of the church is here beheld in its *becoming* and *beginning*; and corresponds to John's seeing, in ver. 10, as in ver. 2, the new Jerusalem *coming down*, which is in a manner the bridal procession.

10 In the wilderness, where John had been carried, was the whore; on the *mountain, great and high* to which he is now brought, is *the city* itself, in view of all the nations (ver. 16, Matt. 5:14.) Ezekiel, in 40:2, after the overthrow of the city and temple, was carried to Israel in vision to a very high mountain, *whereon there was like the building of a city toward the south.* In Ezek. 17:22-23 a high lofty mountain is spoken of in respect to the future

glorification of the kingdom of God: *the Zion,* which when viewed spiritually, appeared very high, grows in the future to a measureless elevation (comp. Ps. 48:1-5, Ps. 68:15-16, Eze. 20:40. comp. Isa. 2:2.) The last FUNDAMENTAL PASSAGE is Micah 4:1, where the future surpassing glory of the church is represented under the symbol of Zion's elevation above all mountains.

The *old* Jerusalem is so little thought of in respect to the *new,* that the latter is here simply called *Jerusalem.* Bengel remarks, *The angel would show John the bride; he shows him a city; before he had said, he would shew him the great whore, and showed him the city Babylon.* The *inhabitants* of Babylon and Jerusalem are respectively meant. 19:7-8 shows that by the bride is intended the church's *members.* In the city also the *inhabitants* hold the most important place. But the body, the outward state, in which the soul resides, comes also into consideration, as well as the soul itself.

THE GLORY OF GOD ILLUMINATES THE CITY

11. Which had the glory of God: her light like to the most precious stone, like a crystal-clear jasper stone.

The description of the city begins with the most glorious element belonging to it, the presence of *God.* The name of the city henceforth is: *Jehovah therein*—present in the fulness of his glory, protection and favour; such was the statement with which Ezekiel had concluded his whole delineation of the new temple and the new Jerusalem. What he *ended* with is here made the *beginning.* God is present—this was the fundamental distinction of the OLD TESTAMENT church from the heathen world. The rendering of this presence efficient was the highest privilege of the church of the NEW TESTAMENT during the present life. But in the new Jerusalem the presence of God shall manifest itself in a way hitherto unknown.

Of *the glory of God* and Christ John speaks in the Gospel and the Apocalypse with great frequency (comp. at 18:1.) The glory of the Lord is always only where the Lord himself is; *it is the Lord in his glory.* It is said here, in ver. 22, *the Lord God the Almighty is its temple;* in 22:5, *God the Lord will shine upon them.* These passages stand related to the one before us, as Isa. 60:19, to Isa. 60:1. In John 12:41 it is said, *This spake Isaiah, when he saw his glory.* According to Isaiah 6:1 he had seen *the Lord* sitting upon his throne high and lifted up. God was there present with all his riches, and with all splendour.

Her light is not diverse from the glory of the Lord. It can only be *seen* as light; as in ver. 23, *the glory of the Lord* enlightened *it,* finally from 4:3, the Lord himself, on account of his glory, is compared to the *jasper-stone.* In this light, allusion is not made to the lamps of the temple, but to the great lights of heaven, as is clear in that this word is used of the lights of heaven, and the PARALLEL PASSAGE, ver. 23, comp. to Gen. 1:14. It never properly means *splendour,* as some put; in the Hellenistic and NEW TESTAMENT usage it always bears the sense of *light.*

With St. John the *jasper* is the noblest of precious stones; as is evident from 4:3, and vers. 18 and 19. Perhaps he idealized it, lent it the character of transparency and of bright splendour; and that afterwards the usage changed. Dioscorides and Psellas also speak of a crystal kind of jasper.

THE WALLS, GATES & THE TWELVE FOUNDATIONS

> 12. It had a wall great and high, it had twelve gates, and upon the gates twelve angels, and names written thereupon, which are the twelve tribes of the children of Israel. 13. On the east three gates, on the north three gates, on the south three gates, and on the west three gates. 14. And the walls of the city had twelve foundations, and upon them twelve names of the twelve apostles of the Lamb.

A *wall* is often employed in the OLD TESTAMENT as an image of protection and safety (1 Sam. 25:16, Prov. 18:11; Eze. 22:30; Zech. 2:5, Isa. 26:1.) The *great* and *high* strengthen this; the former referring to the length and thickness. The walls represent *the security of the new Jerusalem against assaults*, with which the old Jerusalem, the militant church, received in the latter days; and also the divine protection securing the church. The old Jerusalem had wanted walls great and high—comp. Eze. 38:11, where Gog and Magog come up against those *who dwell without walls, and have neither bars nor gates*. The dangers against which the walls protect are only *conceivable* and *possible* ones, for the enemies have all been cast for ever into the lake of fire. The walls around the temple of Ezekiel 40:5 had a different purpose, as in 42:20, they needed not be great and high. The *walls great and high* embody the promise given in Isa. 54:14, *Thou shalt be far from oppression, for thou shalt not fear; and from terror, for it shall not come near thee.*

The *gates* serve for an entrance to the citizens into the new Jerusalem (22:14.) The angels *on the gates* are here with reference to the protection of the righteous, as is clear from the parallelism of the angels on the gates with the walls great and high (Ps. 91:11; Matt. 18:10; Luke 16:22; Heb. 1:14.) The gates stand constantly open (ver. 25.) Nothing of a hostile nature might pass into the city. The *angels*, like the walls, are a *symbol* of the divine protection against all enemies: for *real* enemies are no longer to be found in the new Jerusalem.

According to Eze. 48:31-34, the new Jerusalem has twelve gates, according to the *names of the children of Israel*, three on each side. The gates and the tribes correspond with the names of the twelve tribes on the gates. It indicates that the new Jerusalem is a great unity having its root in God, the last form of the holy catholic church, the union of the head with all his true members; and therefore meets the narrow-mindedness which now in the militant church would single out some particular part and set it forth as the true church of Christ. The church in all its parts is denoted by the twelve tribes of the children of Israel, not in a Jewish, but an Israelitish-Christian sense, which points to the continuity of the church, belying the antagonism between Judaism and Christianity. The names of the twelve tribes were engraved on the stones on the priest's ephod; here the names of the apostles are upon the stones or foundations of the city, and the names of the twelve tribes upon the gates, Eze. 48:31. The names of the twelve apostles guard against the misapprehension of the twelve tribes of Israel, for the apostles were Christ's ambassadors to all nations, Matt. 28:19.

13 The *gates* are avenues for the chosen to go into the city; comp. on ver. 12 and ver. 25, constantly open. Their being directed to all the quarters of heaven, points to the ecumenical character of the new Jerusalem. That the east should be first in order (in Eze. 48:31, it is the north) and the west

last, is to be explained by means of a reference to the word of the Lord in Matt. 8:11, *many shall come from the east, and from the west, and shall sit down with Abraham, Isaac and Jacob in the kingdom of heaven.* Also in the word in Isa. 43:5-6, to which the Lord alludes, the east forms the beginning, and the north precedes the south; comp. Luke 13:29.

14 Every twelfth part of the walls between the gates had a foundation-stone stretching along the whole length exposed to view. The *foundations* mark their immoveable stedfastness, according to Heb. 11:10, *he looked for a city, which has foundations.* Upon the foundations stand the *names* of the *twelve apostles*; indicating that the twelve apostles by their immoveable steadfastness hold the foremost place, the main channel for the protecting grace of God. If still in the new Jerusalem they are so, then in every age they are the bulwark, by which all real assaults are driven back. It lets us know, whither we should turn ourselves, if we have not yet come to know it. This passage and Matt. 19:28, where the twelve apostles appear as the heads of the church in *the regeneration*, which is all one with the new Jerusalem, stands against those, who see the apostleship as a perpetual office, who expect the deliverance of the church by her submission to pretended *new* apostles. The Lord knew only of *twelve* apostles. *The twelve apostles for ever,* this is the solution with which we meet them on the basis of these passages. The FUNDAMENTAL PASSAGE here is Eph. 2:20, *built on the foundation of the apostles and prophets, Jesus Christ himself being the chief corner-stone* (which points back to Matt. 16:18;) where the apostles themselves are called the foundation stones of the church, their names here also stand on the foundations only because on them in a quite peculiar manner rests the security and steadfastness of the church. By *the prophets* are meant, not those of the OLD, but those of the NEW TESTAMENT. That they are personally identical with the apostles, is evident from the PARALLEL PASSAGES, Eph. 3:5, 4:11, and from the considerations formerly advanced on 1:1.

That John reckoned Paul among the apostles is clear from the relation in which the Revelation stands to St. Paul—comp. at 1:4-5, 3:14, 17:14. This passage itself rests on a Pauline foundation. The appointment of Matthias was only a provisional one, as is clear from the way it took place, and the external qualifications, which (Acts 1:21-22) were taken into account. It stood in force only till the Lord himself should be pleased, by his own immediate choice, to fill up the vacant ground.

That they are designated apostles, messengers, *of the Lamb*—so Christ is here called on account of the atonement by blood, through which he founded his church (19:7.) In this way the honour, which is bestowed on them, reverts unconditionally to him; precisely as in Matt. 16:18 the word addressed to Peter as the representative of the apostles, *on this rock will I build my church*, was said on the ground of his confession to Christ as the Son of the living God; and as Paul, in Eph. 2:20, still expressly points to Christ as the proper cornerstone. The apostles are deeply penetrated by a consciousness of the dignity of their office–in John ch. 17 they appear as the spiritual foundation of the whole Christian community.

THE MEASUREMENT OF THE CITY AND WALLS

15. And he that spake with me had as a measure a golden reed, that he might

> measure the city, and its gates and its walls. 16. And the city lies foursquare, and its length is as great as its breadth. And he measured the city with the reed, twelve thousand stadia. 17. And he measured its walls an hundred and four and forty cubits, man's measure, which is angel's measure.

<small>15. And he that spake with me had as a measure a golden reed, that he might measure the city, and its gates and its walls.</small>

Allusion is made to the angel with the measuring-rod in his hand in Eze. 40:3. The *reed* is of *gold* on account of the glory of what was to be measured. The *measure* of the gates is not expressly given afterwards. They must be understood to be of the same height with the walls.

16-17 The purpose to measure the city forms the kernel of this verse. Being a complete *square*, the whole circuit was ascertained, whenever one side was measured. But because the height also was of importance, it is added, that the dimensions here were equal to those already given concerning the length and breadth. A square of a similar kind is formed also by the new city of Ezekiel, 48:16, 20. The square was regarded among the ancients as the symbol of *the complete, the perfect*. It has respect also to the ecumenical character of the new Jerusalem, indicating that an equal right to it was presented to all the four quarters of the earth. The *length* of each side was *12,000 stadia*: the twelve, the signature of the church, here multiplied by a thousand, in ver. 17 by itself (see at 7:4.) As the immense extent of the new Jerusalem—300 geographical miles—points to the multitude constituting the triumphant church, rendering *many mansions* absolutely necessary, so does the enormous height point to its glory.

Here, as in the words immediately preceding, it was precisely the height of the city that was spoken of. The expression, *man's measure, which is angel's measure*, may be explained from the remarks at 13:8. Angels, when they measure, do it only for men, man's measure is at the same time angel's measure, and the *hundred and four and forty cubits* are common cubits.

THE GRANDEUR OF THE CITY IN WALLS, BUILDINGS, GATES AND STREETS

> 18. And the building of its wall was jasper, and the city was pure gold like to pure glass. 19. The foundations of the wall of the city are adorned with all precious stones. The first foundation a jasper, the second a sapphire, the third a chalcedony, the fourth an emerald. 20. The fifth a sardonyx, the sixth a sardius, the seventh a chrysolite, the eighth a beryl, the ninth a topaz, the tenth a chrysopras, the eleventh a hyacinth, the twelfth an amethyst. 21. And the twelve gates were twelve pearls, every several gate was of one pearl. And the street of the city was pure gold, like transparent glass.

The subject of ver. 18-21 is the glory and splendour of the new Jerusalem. First here, the *wall* and *city* attract the eye, the city high above the walls; then downwards, the foundations of the walls and gates; lastly, the streets of the city. The FUNDAMENTAL PASSAGE for here is Isa. 54:11-12, where its glory is described, *Behold I lay thy stones with fair colours, and lay thy foundations with sapphires. And I make thy battlements of rubies, and thy gates of precious stones, and all thy borders of select stones.* The *building* here forms the contrast to the *foundation*, in ver. 19, and denotes what is built on it.[24] The building

---

[24] The word ενδομησισ, properly *in-building*, occurs only here. The building on, in respect to its firm and close connection with the foundation, might be called an in-building.

THE LENGTHENED DESCRIPTION OF THE NEW JERUSALEM

consists only of *one* material, the most glorious among stones, the *jasper* (see at ver. 11.) A great variety, however, is found, in respect to the *foundations*. There the jasper takes the first place. This must be regarded as the most glorious imaginable. The *city*, as distinguished from the *wall* here, and the *street* in ver. 21, can only denote its mass of houses. These, however, are not believers themselves, but their places of abode. The *gold* comes here, as in 17:4, in respect to its *splendour*. It denotes the glory, with which the elect shall be crowned by God for their fidelity. The comparison of *gold* and *glass* stands in the purity; the transparency of the glass symbolizes purity. The gold, by the purity, is distinguished from gold which is not pure; the glass, by the purity distinguishes it from other objects, which are not pure. With the gold, not its splendour or transparency, but its absolute purity and homogeneity are the qualities regarded.

19-20 Each precious stone both formed an ornament and constituted the foundation; *the first foundation was a jasper,* etc. That the precious stones here are taken into account merely as *precious* stones, appears from, *with all precious stones,* which distinctly brings out the point in view; the entire contents of ver. 18-21, the subject of which throughout is the glory of the new Jerusalem; the comparison of 17:4, where the gold, the precious stones and the pearls, with which Babylon was adorned, precisely as here the Jerusalem of the future, which is to inherit the glory of the world, serves to indicate its splendour; so also the comparison of Eze. 28:13, where precious stones are employed along with gold to adorn the king of Tyre; finally, the comparison of the passages, presently to be referred to, in the books of Moses. For, that the precious stones in these, on which the names of the tribes of the children of Israel were engraved, were intended merely to symbolize the glory of the people of God; is the most natural meaning attached to precious stones.

The precious stones which form the foundations have respect to the apostles because in ver. 14 the names of the twelve apostles are engraved on the foundations, as the analogy of the precious stones in the books of Moses, on every one of which was engraved the name of one of the tribes of Israel (comp. 1 Kings 10:2, 10-11, Tob. 13:20, Isa. 54:11-12.) They have no particular correspondence to individual apostles; the order of the apostles is not settled, neither the symbolical meaning of the different stones. That the order of the tribes was not determined by the stones on the high priest's breastplate, as the glory denoted by the stones belonged to the individuals as parts of the whole; precisely as the blessings of Jacob and Moses that speaking generally is only individually applied to particular tribes as they belong to the whole. So by the variety in the precious stones is symbolized the richness of the glorious gifts of God, which unfolded themselves in the apostles.

The first stone, the *jasper*, supposes an allusion to Peter, who took the first place among the apostles, in Matt. 10:2 he is expressly marked as the *first*. As the foundations represent the apostles, the precious stones denote the glory they enjoy in the new Jerusalem as in Dan. 12:3. So also is 1 Cor. 15:41. In Isa. 54:11-12 the precious stones are a consolation for the church while the storms of life were over her. But the precious gifts with which the apostles were endowed is a foundation for the glory with which they shall display in the new Jerusalem. But the special FUNDAMENTAL PASSAGE here is Ex. 28:17-20 (comp. the repetition in Ex. 39:10-13,) regarding the breastplate of the high-priest. Similar is the number twelve, and the stones are the same. Though they have all a different position, with one exception, they are the same, as given in the LXX, and Ezekiel. The *chrysopras* alone is new here, which was formerly placed on the vacant part of the anthrax, although anthrax and chrysopras are different. There is a red chrysopras, which approaches in colour to the anthrax. The glory of the people of God, symbolized by the Mosaic precious stones, finds in the precious stones of the Revelation its last and fullest realization, where they symbolize the glory of the apostles. But the distinction is very nearly removed by the circumstance, that the apostles are the heads of the church, and in them this is honoured and glorified. St. John departs from the order of Moses, he sets the jasper in the very first place, which there holds the last. The reason is, that there is no mystery in the arrangement, so we regard it as in Moses as a matter of indifference (see similar indications in 13:18, and here ver. 17.) A *polemical* connection respects the precious stones; in Eze. 28:13, itself alluding to Ex. 28, the proud splendour of the king of Tyre is denoted, which is an irony on the promises to Israel; and a reference also to 17:4, where the woman appears with gold and precious stones and pearls, the same number three that occurs here in ver. 18-21. The world may possibly for a time carry itself proudly, in a transient glory; but the church can look on with a quiet and composed spirit, for she knows that it must soon come to an end.

<small>20. The fifth a sardonyx, the sixth a sardius, the seventh a chrysolite, the eighth a beryl, the ninth a topaz, the tenth a chrysopras, the eleventh a hyacinth, the twelfth an amethyst.</small>

<small>21. And the twelve gates were twelve pearls, every several gate was of one pearl. And the street of the city was pure gold, like transparent glass.</small>

21 The description of the new Jerusalem is not to be taken in a realistic sense. Its glory is only represented under images derived from what is most glorious on the earth as is evident from the expression: each of one *pearl*.

The *street*, in contrast to the *city* in ver. 18, stands here, as in 11:8, 22:2, for the *streets*. The whole of the streets are thrown together into one ideal street. It does not mean the city, only one street, as this is not expressly said. The transparency of *glass* is mentioned as a sign of its purity, and it is the purity of gold, which alone is taken into account (comp. at ver. 18.)

THE GLORY OF THE CITY IN REGARD TO ITS INHABITANTS–FIRST GOD AND THE LAMB

<small>22. And I saw no temple therein. For, the Lord God, the Almighty, is its temple, and the Lamb. 23. And the city needs not the sun and the moon to shine in it, for the glory of God did lighten it, and its light is the Lamb.</small>

The *temple* was the brightest ornament of the typical Jerusalem (comp. Ps. 122:1, Jer. 7:4.) To dwell spiritually there was the greatest boon godly persons could enjoy in life. This view of the temple is founded in God's pledge of gracious fellowship with his people. Whoever sought him under the old covenant, could find him only in the temple, in which God confirmed his word spoken in Ex. 25:8, *they shall make me a sanctuary, and I will dwell in the midst of them*, comp. 29:40, 46, *and I dwell in the midst of the children of Israel*. The name of the temple in its first form, *Ohel Moed, the tent of meeting*, shows it was where God was to meet with his people (comp. Ps. 23:6, Ps. 27:4, Ps. 84:3.) All Messianic hope was a proof of poverty in respect to the temple. The temple pointed forwards to a real union between God and his people, which took place in Christ. If the union of God with his people formed the kernel of the sanctuary, the manifestation of Christ must stand related to it as the body to the shadow. By means of it God truly dwelt among his people. He took from them and among them flesh and blood. To this typical relationship, John alludes in 1:14. In 2:19, also, Christ appears as the anti-type to the temple. A similar indication is found also in Col. 2:9, *In him dwelleth all the fulness of the Godhead bodily,* where Christ is referred to as *the true tabernacle*—comp. besides Col. 1:19. With the personal manifestation of God in Christ, however, we must combine his dwelling among his people by his Holy Spirit, which stands related to the former as a stream to its source (comp. Matt. 28:20, and especially 1 Tim. 3:15; 2 Cor. 6:16.) Because in the militant church the presence of God is still not perfectly realized, from the bodily presence of the Lord having been soon withdrawn from it again (comp. 12:5,) and from the agency of his Spirit being subjected to manifold restraints, it is only the triumphant church that is to be regarded as the full anti-type of the OLD TESTAMENT type. There only the words, *Behold the tabernacle of God is with men,* will find their complete and perfect realization.

We have an OLD TESTAMENT PARALLEL PASSAGE in Jer. 3:16-17. The ark of the covenant was the heart of the temple, the centre of the Old Covenant, yet it is to be forgotten, as belonging to the beggarly elements, to the image and shadow, with an entire annihilation of the earlier form of God's kingdom, like that of the seed-corn, which dies to bring forth fruit, or of the body, which is sown in corruption, that it may be raised up in incorruption.

As the temple was the symbol of the church, it must be in the new Jerusalem; as certainly as the church also is in heaven (comp. 7:15, 11:19, 14:15.) That the temple *once* existed, is a pledge of its everlasting continuance, as no divine institution can be of a merely temporal nature (Matt. 5:17.) That the temple is only in a certain sense wanting in the new Jerusalem, is evident even from the assertion here. For, the temple is not simply denied to it; it is accorded as well as denied. The designation of God: *The Lord God the Almighty,* points to the glory of the compensation. Where he is in the whole glory of his being, with the fullness of his gifts, there the loss of the poor temple with its imperfect manifestation of God's presence is to be considered real gain.

The same glorious properties are ascribed to the Almighty God *and* the Lamb (ver. 23, 22:1, 3, 7:10. Comp. 5:13, 6:16, 7:10.) Through the Lamb the Almighty God has become for the church the reality of the temple. Till John knew the Lamb the temple was to him his one and all. That the Lamb still did not exist, was the cause of the old temple's poverty, of the imperfect manner in which it displayed God's presence. Immanuel! so was it proclaimed at the moment of Christ's appearance in the flesh; it was proclaimed more loudly when he finished the atonement; and so yet again, most gloriously of all, will it be proclaimed in the new Jerusalem.

23 In verse 22 the *glory of God,* streaming forth from the Lamb, eclipsed the earthly temple; here that glory darkens the natural light. The FUNDAMENTAL PASSAGE is Isa. 60:19-20. We may compare besides Isa. 24:23. The *sun and moon* are ashamed there, because they are outshone by the uncreated light. The sun and the moon are both denoted a light, the sun does not correspond to the Lord, nor the moon to the Lamb. In Isaiah 24:23 the Lord forms the contrast to *both* the sun and moon. Here instead of the sun and the moon the glory of the Lord enlightens it, and *the Lamb is its light.* The city has the glory of God only because and insofar as it has the Lamb. That the moon receives her light from the sun, is never accounted of in Scripture, but

very often the smallness of her light is compared with the sun's.

THE HUMAN INHABITANTS-THE ELECT

> 24. And the heathen shall walk through its light, and the kings of the earth bring their glory into it. 25. And its gates shall not be shut by day; for there shall be no night there. 26. And they shall bring the glory and the honour of the nations into it.

The FUNDAMENTAL PASSAGE is Isa. 60:3, *And the heathen walk in thy light* (not: *to thy light*), *and kings in the brightness which goes forth on thee*. And the preceding verse: *The Lord goes forth over thee, and his honour appears upon thee*. The *light* is the glory of the Lord manifesting itself in the church, which is to shine forth in the new Jerusalem in full and cloudless splendour. The light irradiates the way so much for the *heathen*, that *they walk*, as it were, *through* it; or *by* it. The εθνη in the usage of the Revelation are always *heathen* nations, in their natural or christianized state; comp. at 20:3. Here it is *converted* heathen, those in the book of life. When John saw the Apocalypse, they still actually were heathen. They are not without the city; but being *within* the city they shall be illuminated by its light, according to ver. 25, and all of Isa. 40. All are either in the new Jerusalem, or in the lake of fire (ver. 8.)

The *kings of the earth bring their glory* into the new Jerusalem. The *bringing* is symbolical, as it were, coming in procession; as also in 22:14, the entrance of citizens into the gates of the city. The kings had formerly brought their glory into the kingdom of grace (comp. 15:4, 17:14.) The glory can be brought into the new Jerusalem only in so far as it can be glorified; all false glitter and earthly pomp must disappear. But in the kingdom of glory there reigns no *levelling equality*. It would otherwise stand below the kingdom of grace, and be like the land of shadows, *where there is no order,* Job. 10:22. As among the angels there are distinctions of rank and order (comp. at 8:2,) so shall there be among glorified men. If all were ruled according to a bare democratic uniformity, the *teachers* could not have the position that is assigned them in Daniel, nor the apostles the position indicated respecting them in ver. 14, 19. The heathen and kings are brought into view here as an ornament of the new Jerusalem. The kingdom of God should, according to its idea, be universal in its dominion. But this idea was very imperfectly realized during the OLD TESTAMENT; and still also in the militant church much is wanting for its realization; indeed, in St. John's time it had scarcely so much as begun. The worldly power stood then in all its pomp and glory looking with indifference on the kingdom of God, or even manifesting hostility towards it. This contrast between the idea and the reality must, if it were to be regarded as a permanent one, shake faith. St. John meets here the ground of offence thence arising. In the new world the bearers of the worldly power shall either have become impotent, and have been consigned to eternal misery, or they shall have entered with their peoples into the kingdom of God. From this investigation, also, it becomes obvious, why it is that only the heathen with their kings are mentioned among the citizens of the new Jerusalem, and not also the elect portion of the Jews. The latter did not require any special mention.

25-26 The words, *for there shall be no night there*, intimate why the *day* merely is spoken of, as city *gates* are commonly shut at night.

The words, *and they shall bring*, etc. give the reason why the gates stand continually open, that the glory and honour of the heathen may enter into the new Jerusalem, which in St. John's time was so hard a matter for faith. The FUNDAMENTAL PASSAGE is Isa. 60:11, *And thy gates stand open continually, day and night they shall not be shut, to bring to thee the riches of the heathen, and their kings shall be led.* Neither here, nor in the passage before us, is any respect had to *rest* and *security*, as the reason for the gates standing open. Day and night in Isaiah is as much as *continually*. The night, in the sense in which it is here said to have ceased, is there also brought to an end, ver. 20. The difference between the two passages is merely in the letter. Ver. 7 is to be supplied from ver. 20. *There will be no night there*, namely, because the glory of the Lord shall constantly enlighten it—comp. ver. 11, 23, 22:5. Night denotes a state destitute of blessing, when the gracious presence of the Lord is withheld. The militant church is in this respect subjected to a continual alternation. The sad word, *and it was night*, John 13:30, is often quite overlooked. Allusion is made to Isa. 60:20.

THE HUMAN INHABITANTS-
THOSE WHO WOULD DARKEN ITS SPLENDOUR

> 27. And there shall not enter into thee any thing whatever common, and which does abomination and lies; but only those that are written in the Lamb's book of life.

Instead of *anything whatever common*, it is properly, *all general.* By Adam's fall human nature has become wholly corrupt. So that the general has at the same time become the *common*, the *unclean*. Separation is needed, if one would not live with the world, and be judged with the world (2 Cor. 6:17.) The Pharisees derived their name from this separation. What they sought after in the flesh, must be sought after by Christians in the Spirit.

Abomination is similarly mentioned in 21:8, 22:15, comp. also at 17:4-5. In regard to the notion of *lie* as meant by John, see at 14:5, 21:8.

In regard to the *Lamb's book of life*, see at 13:8. It is implied that all who are not written in the Lamb's book of life, have been addicted to the previously mentioned sins; while such as have been atoned for by the blood of the Lamb, and have accordingly been written in his book of life, are free from them.

THE GLORIOUS PRIVILEGES OF THE BLESSED

> 22:1. And he showed me a river of the water of life, shining like crystal; which went from the throne of God and of the Lamb. 2. In the midst of the street of it, and on both sides of the river, the tree of life, which bore twelve fruits, and brought forth its fruit every month; and the leaves of the tree for the healing of the heathen. 3. And there shall be no more curse; and the throne of God and of the Lamb shall be in it, and his servants shall serve him. 4. And they shall see his face, and his name shall be on their foreheads. 5. And there shall be no night there, and they need no lamp, nor the light of the sun; for God the Lord will shine upon them, and they shall reign for ever and ever.

The *water* signifies, according to the author himself, *life*, that is, salvation, blessedness (comp. on the notion of life in John at 7:17.) The great full-

1. And he showed me a river of the water of life, shining like crystal; which went from the throne of God and of the Lamb.

ness of life, which belongs to the glorified church, is represented here in its pouring forth as a *river*, as in Ezekiel 47. The glorious nature of the life is represented by the *shining like crystal*. St. John had the conviction, that man, as he believes in the Son of God, is thereby raised from death to life. Yet John is not so sure and conscious of its power and blessedness as to preclude the need for hope in the Christian. The tone of depression that pervades his Gospel is a proof of the contrary, as also the entire description of the Christian state in the last discourses of Christ: *The world hates you, you shall have tribulation in the world, you need the Comforter to support you under all your distress and sorrow, your eye must be on the eternal blessedness and glory, that your heart may not be appalled* (John 14:2-3, 17:24, comp. 1 John 2:25, 28, 3:2.) St John is no idealistic visionary. There are not two lives, but only one life, which begins the moment we attain to faith in Christ, and continues through all eternity—though this life, during our sojourn in the world, is still interwoven with manifold troubles and interruptions, both of an inward (1 John 1:8) and an outward kind. Only in the future state of being will the germ of life fully develop itself. Life in the present state of being is as plainly recognized in the Revelation as it is in the Gospel. To be living and not dead is the Christian state (Rev. 3:1.) In the Revelation the future phase of the divine life is brought out, the Gospel must represent, what we have already received through Christ, the Revelation what he will yet give to his servants. Add to this, that the Revelation was seen at a time when dark shadows had settled down on the life of Christians.

The type of the *river* here is the river that at first watered paradise. As in Gen. 2:9-10, the river and the tree are connected with each other. In Ps. 36:8, this river is the type of streams of delight, which God's love pours down to refresh his people. *Here* the true anti-type is transferred to eternity. Comp. Joel 3:18, *A fountain goes out of the house of the Lord, and waters the valley,* also Eze. 47, where a stream flows out of the sanctuary, and after vivifying the desert, empties into the Dead Sea; finally, Zech. 14:8. The fountain is the fountain of blessing, of salvation, of life, the waters quickening the desert of man's necessities. Here these promises are finally and gloriously fulfilled. The worst manifestation of death is being morally dead; the worst side of human misery is enmity or indifference toward God. This side of death and misery, which Ezekiel, Joel and Zechariah take into account, still contemplates the salvation of Christ as *one* whole, comprising in it the life—its bestowal celebrated by John in the Gospel—*that* side has here been *already done away*. The river of life is for those, who have died in the Lord, and have washed their robes and made them white in the blood of the Lamb. The river is for quenching the thirst, or satisfying the desire of blessedness, as in 21:6, 22:17.

2. In the midst of the street of it, and on both sides of the river, the tree of life, which bore twelve fruits, and brought forth its fruit every month; and the leaves of the tree for the healing of the heathen.

The river goes *from the throne of God and of the Lamb*, in accordance with the declaration, *All that the Father hath is mine*. Comp. at 7:17, according to which the Lamb is in the midst of the throne. God is thus set forth as in Christ, the dispenser of life or blessing. Christ is called *the Lamb*, because through his labours and blood he has won for us this *crown* of all his gifts.

2 Besides *thirst* the Lord's people are in this life also liable to *hunger* (comp. Matt. 5:6; Rev. 7:16.) Hence life or salvation is here represented as the *fruit of a tree*, as in the preceding verse it had been imaged by water. That the tree should be called the *tree of life*, because the participation of its fruit imparts life, is clear from Gen. 3:22, *And now, lest he should stretch forth his*

248

hand and take also of the tree of life, and eat and live for ever. There can be no doubt that allusion is here made to this paradisiacal tree of life from 2:7, *He that overcometh, to him will I give to eat of the tree of life, that is in the paradise of my God.* It is also referred to in Ezek. 47:7, *When I turned back, behold on the border of the river there was wood very much, on both sides;* and ver. 12. By an unseasonable comparison of Ps. 1:3, Jer. 17:8, several understand by the trees the *righteous*; and that the waters are the outpouring of the Spirit. But this is only a *part*—an important one for Ezekiel—in the *whole* of life or salvation. The tree in Ezekiel is the tree of life. The variety of the trees in Ezekiel and here on both sides of the river seems to contrast with Genesis, where only one tree of life is spoken of. But this latter point admits of some doubt. It is said *the tree of life which is in the midst of the garden;* and at any rate it had conjoined with it as a type *every tree that is pleasant to the sight and good for food,* which the Lord is said, in the immediately preceding context, to have made to spring out of the earth, and which supposedly, in ver. 10, to have grown on the banks of the river. We must still think of these trees as trees of life in the more general sense, the tree of life only as such in the highest degree. In Ezekiel the tree of life stands only on both sides of the river; here it stands also in the middle of the street. But as the tree of life stands connected with the water of life, this cannot mean a second quite separate position. We are rather to suppose the river flows through the street, and that the tree of life stands on both sides of the stream.

The tree *yielding new fruits every month* simply indicates, that in the new Jerusalem the enjoyment of life shall be without interruption, where death is not constantly breaking in violently upon life. We are not to think of *different kinds* of fruits. Luther has put improperly *twelve sorts* for *twelve*. It is not said that *the leaves* of the tree *shall* serve *for the healing of the heathen;* but the power is only attributed to them generally, of producing healing. Healing implies *disease*. But this belongs only to the present life. Into its gates they only enter who have made themselves *ready* (19:7-8, comp. 21:2.) No intermediate state is to be thought of as possible, where all the circumstances are of a fixed character, and no room is left for change. To bring the enjoyment of *the leaves* within this present life is also the more natural, since in 2:7, which points to the future world, it is only the eating of the fruit that is spoken of. The *leaves* are *inferior* to the fruit. The fruit is nobler than the leaves; if, then, the leaves are so sanatory, how efficacious must be the fruit? The powers of life, which descend from the Jerusalem above on this poor earth for the healing of wretched sinners, are a foretaste of the surpassing blessedness, which may be expected in the new Jerusalem by the just made perfect.

3 The first words are taken from Zech. 14:11, *And they dwell in it, and there shall be no more curse in it, and Jerusalem is securely enthroned.* In the new Jerusalem the penal justice of God will no more find an object; his whole procedure toward her will be an uninterrupted manifestation of his love and righteousness. The idea of *cursing* is always that of the forced consecration to God of those who had obstinately refused to consecrate themselves voluntarily to him—of the manifestation of the divine glory in the destruction of those, who during their life-time would not reflect it, and therefore would not realize the general destination of man, the design of all creation. God sanctifies himself *upon* all those, in whom he is not sanctified. The destruction of every thing on earth, which will not serve him, proclaims his praise. God

3. And there shall be no more curse; and the throne of God and of the Lamb shall be in it, and his servants shall serve him.

3. And there shall be no more curse; and the throne of God and of the Lamb shall be in it, and his servants shall serve him.

constantly declares anew to his militant church what he said of old in Joshua 7:12. Times of revival are followed by times of decay; in which the true city becomes an harlot, and iniquity is ascendant; and then, God proves himself to be the jealous God, who visits the iniquities of the fathers on the children.

The clause, *and the throne of God and of the Lamb shall be in it,* is very closely connected with that, which declares, *there shall be no more curse.* Because there is no more curse, that is, no more an object of cursing, the gracious presence of God and of Christ shall no longer withdraw, as with the Jews, as the curse began to alight on them, *Behold your house is left unto you desolate; ye shall not henceforth see me, till ye shall say, Blessed is he that cometh in the name of the Lord* (Matt. 23:38-39;) and so does he virtually speak from time to time to his church. The more the time happens to be one of cursing, this verse is consolatory for the true members of the church. It is said, *His servants shall serve him,* not, *their servants shall serve them;* according to the word, *I and my Father are one.* Up to this the Seer wrote what he had seen; here writing in such a manner could no longer suffice, and the description must take the form of prophecy.

4. And they shall see his face, and his name shall be on their foreheads.

4 To see God's *face* means to enjoy God's favour. In 14:1, the chosen bear *the name of God on their foreheads* as a mark of their proved *fidelity.* But here it is written on their foreheads as a *reward*—a pledge of their right to participate in all the benefits of the kingdom of glory.

5. And there shall be no night there, and they need no lamp, nor the light of the sun; for God the Lord will shine upon them, and they shall reign for ever and ever.

5 In 21:25 the *night* denoted the absence of blessing, when the gracious presence of the Lord is withdrawn, because of iniquity. Here once again this thought returns at the close, to console those who find themselves enveloped in night. By the *day* is denoted the time of grace and salvation, by the night the time of perdition, entering when grace is withdrawn. See John 9:4, *the night cometh when no man can work.* In John 11:9-10 Jesus sees no danger in going where the Jews had lately sought to stone him, it was still *day,* and no danger was to be feared, this arises only when the *night* comes, in which the light of the world appears not. Luke 22:35-36 is to be compared, as the Lord there points out the difference between the time when God imparts his grace and when he withdraws it. In John 13:30, it is said, *But it was night when he went out.* The natural night to John was a symbol of the spiritual night, when the light of grace does not shine, and the power of darkness begins (Luke 22:53;) when the hour has arrived for a desperate attack on the kingdom of God. The *and there shall be no night there* presupposes that the alternation of night and day in the spiritual life of the church shall have finally ceased in the new Jerusalem. So long as this still continues, the church must be exercised by the cross, as must also individual believers. We must let the night fall upon us, though the longing of our heart must be toward the time, when it shall be perpetual day. We could not, besides, properly enjoy the day as yet, because we are constantly apprehensive of the night coming, which often breaks so suddenly in upon us.

In regard to the *reigning* of believers, see on 1:6, 5:10, 20:6. *Here,* when the meek shall possess the earth, the kingdom of the elect shall reach its highest elevation. If till then it has reigned, with its divine head, in the midst of its enemies, thenceforth its enemies shall be for ever completely subdued, and there shall be nothing more to withstand the full establishment of its dominion. In Ps. 49:14, it is said of the wicked, *As sheep they are laid in hell, death feeds on them, and the righteous reign over them in the morning.* There the wicked, notwithstanding their *destruction*, are the object of that ruling, which is to be exercised by the righteous. So also here.

Bengel says, *Thus far of the holy city Jerusalem! Would that we may enter therein! Would that we even were therein! Now it is in our power to attain to a happy portion, if we will but turn our back on a lost world, and renounce the service of the prince of the world. There is need for a good, instant resolution to act, under the impulse of grace. But whoever has set his face steadfastly to go toward this Jerusalem, shall abide in it, and shall never err from the way of life.*

CONCLUSION

Come Lord Jesus!

REVELATION
22:6-21

REVELATION 22:6-21

CONCLUSION
Come Lord Jesus!

The conclusion of the book, in correspondence with its introduction, expressly points to its high *importance*, and at the same time applies its consolatory and refreshing fundamental truth of the coming of the Lord once more to the hearts of all saints.

THE ASSEVERATION OF TRUTH AND CERTAINTY

22:6. And he said to me: These words are certain and true. And the Lord the God of the Spirits of the prophets has sent his angel to shew to his servants what must shortly come to pass. 7. And behold, I come quickly. Blessed is he, who keeps the words of the prophecy of this book.

The asseveration of *truth* and *certainty* was made, like Daniel (8:26,) in 19:9, in respect to the great consolatory truths of the coming of the kingdom, of the marriage feast, and the preparation of the bride; and in 21:5, in respect to the *behold I make all things new*. Here it stands at the close of the whole book. The words, *and the Lord the God of the Spirits of the prophets*, assign the reason of the confidence. What John has to communicate to the church belongs not to *him*; but it ascends through the medium of the angel to the Most High God. In 19:9, *These words are true, of God,* the expression, *of God,* corresponds.

There is a reference to the beginning of the introduction in 1:1. This intentional connection intimates that the conclusion of the book begins here. As the introduction showed the high importance of the book, the conclusion also begins with the same topic. If there by the *servants* of God the *prophets* are to be understood, so also here. The *his servants* are represented by *John*. As God has all human spirits in his hand, so has he in particular the Spirits of each particular prophet (comp. 1 Cor. 14:32;) so that what they experience proceeds from him; and this God has communicated to his servant John through his angel the future, which is unfolded in this book. The *Spirit of the prophets* is the Spirit of prophecy, which rests on them (comp. 19:10.) It is *one* Spirit that moves in all the prophets (1 Pet. 1:10-11, 2 Pet. 1:21.) But individual prophets have each their own Spirit, differing according to that measure of the Spirit's grace, which is severally given to them.

The expression, *shortly*, is here; *what must come to pass*. This *shortly*, which is again resumed in ver. 7, contains a *second* reason for the high importance of the book. Threatenings and promises, soon to be fulfilled, demand of all wakeful attention, so as not to be *too late*. The expression, *what must shortly come to pass*, which was already explained at 1:1, shows, that this verse does not even *primarily* refer to what immediately precedes, to what lies beyond the thousand years' reign; but that it applies to the whole of the book. It also

> 7. And behold, I come quickly. Blessed is he, who keeps the words of the prophecy of this book.

coincides with the *introduction* of the book, which then emphatically stamps this as the *conclusion* of it.

7 Ver. 3 of the introduction corresponds. There the person who reads is pronounced blessed, *for the time is near. Here* the order is reversed: *I come quickly, therefore, etc.* The *behold I come quickly,* is spoken from the person of Christ (comp. ver. 20.) The person sent only speaks from the person of the sender, as in Gen. 19:21-22. The *angel,* as he is, and because he is the angel of God, so also the angel of Christ (comp. ver 16.) There was no reason given for bounding off the sphere of God in respect to that of Christ. In the FUNDAMENTAL PASSAGE also of Malachi the Lord comes in the covenant-angel.

The threefold, *behold I come quickly,* here and in ver. 12, 20 (comp. 3:11, 2:5, 16,) refers to Mal. 3:1, *The Lord whom ye seek, will suddenly come to his temple, and the covenant-angel, whom ye desire, behold he comes, saith the Lord of Hosts.* In no other passage of the OLD TESTAMENT is the idea of *coming* so prominently brought out; first, he will come suddenly; and then again at the end, with solemn emphasis, *behold he comes.* It contains all the three words of the clause before us: the *behold,* the *coming,* and the *quickly* (suddenly.) He, who now seems to be absent, will soon appear in the person of his heavenly messenger. This announcement received its final fulfilment in the appearance of Christ, in whom the angel of the Lord, the Logos, became flesh. We are not to seek this final fulfilment, either in the state of humiliation, or in the state of exaltation alone, but in both as an inseparable whole. The appearance of Christ in humiliation contained in the germ every thing as to blessing and cursing which in his state of exaltation he has either already brought, or will yet bring into accomplishment. The thought in Malachi is that the Logos is always, from Malachi's time onwards to the end of the world, irrepressibly carrying forward a plan, in which, as circumstances perpetually require his interposition, so he is ever ready to interfere either for salvation or for judgment. John also points to the same prophecy in 1:9, 15, 27 of his Gospel, speaking of Christ manifest in the flesh, and in 21:22, the expression, *I come,* refers to Malachi, precisely as here, of the *future* coming of the Lord.

The *behold I come quickly,* denotes the gladsome character of Christ's appearing in regard to the fulfilment of all the promises and threatenings of this entire book. Bengel: *This word I come admonishes us of the whole subject-matter of the book, and so everything in us should be raised and elevated, that the whole Apocalyptic heaven may, in a manner, turn round, before our eyes.*

In 1:3 the *words of the prophecy* alone are mentioned. But here there is added: *of this book.* This addition shows, that the completion of the book kept pace with the receiving of the Revelation. The book, also repeatedly mentioned in the following verses, must already be completed as to its main part.[25]

TREMBLING BEFORE THE WORD OF GOD

> 8. And I John am he, who heard and saw these things. And when I heard and saw, I fell down to worship at the feet of the angel, who showed me these things. 9. And he said to me, See thou do it not; I am thy fellow-servant, and of thy brethren the prophets, and of those who keep the words of this book. Worship God.

---

25. Also in Deuteronomy, where its speedy conclusion comes in view, Moses speaks of it as a *book*; first Deut. 17:18-19, then 28:58, 29:20-21, 27.

These two verses also have respect to the high importance of the book, and press it on the readers to take up the right position in regard to it. A trustworthy man, a tried organ of divine communications, *John*, whom Jesus loved, expressly assures us, that he has not spoken of his own, but only what he *has heard and received.* And this same John, carried away by the lofty theme of the Revelation, throws himself down before the angel, who had conveyed to him such a wonderful message. In regard to the expression: *I John*, see at 1:1, 4, 9. John had placed his name in the title of his book, in the superscription to the seven churches, and at the beginning of his narrative. Now at the close he names himself still again. As people set their names to important original documents, to prevent all error and uncertainty respecting them, so John does the same here. He does so in his Gospel also, 21:24, where often he mentions his name (13:23, 19:26, 21:20,) *covertly*, allowing the *I* to fall back; while here, according to the custom of the prophets (see on 1:1,) he comes boldly forward, with his *I John.*

Common to the Revelation and the Gospel, with the emphatic assurance of the truth and trustworthiness of the matters reported (comp. ver. 6 here, and the PARALLEL PASSAGES, with John 19:35, 21:14,) there should be a special reference to the *seeing* and *hearing* (1:14, 19:35, 1 John 1:1-2, 4:14.) We must here lay the emphasis on the name *John*, and on the *heard* and *saw.*

In 19:10 the offered *worship* had respect to the joyful message concerning the universal dominion of God, which was certainly at hand, the marriage of the Lamb, and the preparation of the bride: here, on the other hand, it is done in respect to the whole subject-matter of the book. The only other difference is, that here, in addition to the prophets, those also are mentioned who *keep the words of this book,* who stand in a blessed society and brotherhood. The angels are servants of God, in respect to their office, and so also are the *prophets.* Those, therefore, who *keep the words of this book,* are the servants of God in his vineyard. The *keeping* manifests itself in those, to whom it belongs, by their not appearing faint and lifeless in the testimony of Jesus (comp. at 14:12;) to have the testimony of Jesus as a calling in the church (comp. at 6:9, 12:17.) *Or*, we are to regard those, who keep the words of this book, as annexed to the prophets, so that the angel is only in so far their *fellow-servant*, as they are comprehended *under* the *prophets* as their heads.

THREATENINGS AND PROMISES NEAR TO FULFILMENT

10. And he says to me: Seal not the words of the prophecy of this book, for the time is near. 11. He that is unjust, let him be unjust still; and he that is filthy, let him be filthy still; and he that is righteous, let him do righteousness still; and he that is holy, let him be holy still. 12. Behold I come quickly, and my reward is with me, to give to every one as his work shall be. 13. I am the Alpha and the Omega, the first and the last, the beginning and the ending. 14. Blessed are they that do his commandments, that their power may be to the tree of life, and to enter by the gates into the city. 15. Without are dogs, and sorcerers, and whoremongers, and murderers, and idolaters, and all who love and do a lie. 16. I Jesus have sent my angel to testify these things to you upon the churches. I am the root and the race of David, the bright morning-star. 17. And the Spirit and the bride say, Come! And he that hears, let him say, Come! And he that is athirst let him come; he that wills, let him take the water of life freely. 18. I testify to every one, who hears the words of the prophecy of this book. If any one adds thereto, God will add to him the plagues which are written in this book. 19. And if any one

take away from the words of the book of this prophecy, God will take away his part from the tree of life, and from the holy city, which are written in this book. 20. He who testifies these things says: Yea, I come quickly. Amen, come Lord Jesus. 21. The grace of the Lord Jesus Christ be with all saints.

<small>10. And he says to me: Seal not the words of the prophecy of this book, for the time is near.</small>

The book is of great importance. For its threatenings and promises are drawing near to their fulfilment. He who does not consider it, shall certainly lose salvation, and be unexpectedly overtaken by the threatened plagues. The words, *And he says to me,* shows that the discourse of the angel here takes a new beginning. *Seal not.* Daniel was told his prophecy was to be a shut and sealed book; until the church of the future should make a right use of it (comp. at 10:4.) It is otherwise with our prophecy. Its contents are more accessible; and concerned the circumstances of the time, and were immediately beginning fulfilment.

That *the time is near,* not merely in respect to the first readers and hearers of the Revelation, but for all time. Much of what is announced in the Revelation is of a kind which has its fulfilment continually repeated anew, and reaches through all history. So, especially, the vision of the seven seals, and the vision of the seven trumpets. But in particular the word, *the time is near,* holds in respect to the times, in which the special catastrophes announced in the Revelation are ready to break forth. It holds quite peculiarly in respect to our own times, in which the last and the greatest special pre-intimations are proceeding with giant strides toward their accomplishment.

<small>11. He that is unjust, let him be unjust still; and he that is filthy, let him be filthy still; and he that is righteous, let him do righteousness still; and he that is holy, let him be holy still.</small>

11 Verse 11 stands in the middle, between the declaration that the time is near, and the announcement, *Behold I come quickly;* and its meaning is to be determined by its position. That the wicked should continue to be wicked, and the righteous to be righteous, is alike agreeable to the will of God. If the second is no mere permission, but a manifestation of will on the part of God, so must it be also in respect to the first. If they will have it so, let it be so; if it is right in their view, so is it also in God's. He will take care that they do not escape from him. If they will not sanctify him, he will sanctify himself upon them; and that not merely in the future world, but also soon in this. There is a similar announcement in Eze. 2:7. The righteous stand opposed to those that do injustice, and the holy to the filthy. The nature of sanctification consists in the separation, whereby one keeps one's self undefiled from the world. To do righteousness for exercising it, is an expression peculiar to St. John (comp. 1 John 2:29, 3:7, John 3:21, where he speaks of *doing* the truth.) The FUNDAMENTAL PASSAGE is Gen. 18:19, where doing righteousness appears as the mark of a true descendant of Abraham, and a condition necessary for obtaining the divine blessing (comp. Isa. 56:1, 58:2, Ps. 106:3.)

<small>12. Behold I come quickly, and my reward is with me, to give to every one as his work shall be.</small>

12 Luther has: and behold. On the word, *I come quickly,* comp. ver. 7. The *My reward is with me,* is taken from Isa. 40:10, 62:11, where Jehovah is the speaker. So we can apply from 2 John 8, the admonition, See that we lose not what we have wrought, but that we receive a full reward. The *reward* comprehends here the recompense of the wicked. On the words, *to give to every one, etc.,* comp. Rom. 2:6, who shall give to every one according to his works, enlarged upon in what follows. Here the work simply is mentioned; Bengel remarks: The whole doing of a good or bad man is a single work and business, Matt. 16:27. Ver. 12 lays the foundation for the two declarations in ver. 13 and 14. As the beginning belongs to God in Christ, so also does the

CONCLUSION—THE NEW JERUSALEM

end; blessed then are they who do his commandments, ver. 14, but woe to sinners, ver. 15.

13 The *Omega* and the *ending* are here to be accented (comp. at 21:6, 1:8.) We must take heed we stand well with him, to whom the end belongs. It is a piece of folly to attach one's self to those, who expatiate only for a time in the *middle*. The speaker here, as in 1:8, is *simply God in the undistinguished unity of his being, or God in Christ*. That Christ is also *the Alpha, the beginning, the first*, and consequently *the Omega, the end, the last*, is evident alone from the fact, that he is *the Word of God* (comp. on 19:13,) *the beginning of the creation of God* (3:14.) But the angel cannot, without specific intimation, be regarded as speaking now from the Father, and again from the Son; and where he does not speak in his own person, or the speaker is not more definitely described, as at ver. 16, there it can only be God in Christ.

13. I am the Alpha and the Omega, the first and the last, the beginning and the ending.

14 The meaning is, *blessed **therefore** are they;* for the benediction rests on the circumstance, that God in Christ is *the Alpha and the Omega*. Were it otherwise, they would be the most miserable of men (1 Cor. 15:19.)

To *keep* or *do God's commandments*, his will, his law, is a mode of speech frequent with St. John (12:17, 14:12, John 7:19, 4:34, 6:38, 7:17, 9:31.) Among these commands faith in Jesus, is the foremost. A similar benediction pronounced on *doing* is found in John 13:17. The *his* shows that the angel is speaking here in his own person. In the words, *that their power may be*, etc, the manner in which the blessedness is to be realized is more accurately determined (comp. on 14:13.)

No other entrance can be found into the new Jerusalem, but through the *gates*. The glory of the gates here referred to, described in 21:21, here again comes especially into view. Allusion is, perhaps, made to Ps. 122:1-2.

14. Blessed are they that do his commandments, that their power may be to the tree of life, and to enter by the gates into the city.

15 In 21:8, those whose part is to be in the lake that burns with fire and brimstone, form four pairs—the four being the signature of the earth—the *fearful and unbelieving*, the *abominable and murderers, whoremongers and sorcerers, idolaters and all liars*. In 21:27 those excluded from the kingdom of God are *three. Here* the excluded are *seven*, and the seven is divided by the four and the three; as similarly in Isa. 1:4 there are to be found seven designations of sinful and corrupt ways, divided into four and three.

The *dog* is in Scripture the symbol of the disgustingly impure, the shameless, those who are altogether deserving of contempt, as in the Mosaic law, in Deut. 23:18 it designates *base and disgusting filthiness*; a genus for the species of abominations in ver. 17. The chief quality here is the impurity; comp. Prov. 26:11, *as a dog that returns to his vomit*, 2 Pet. 2:22; Matt. 7:6. The dog-like spirit (comp. Phil. 3:2) manifests itself in wrath and biting (comp. Ps. 22:16; Matt. 7:6.) This is indicated by the juxtaposition of *sorcerers* with dogs, who are persons who seek to hurt their neighbour secretly. Several understand by dogs *the effeminate, and abusers of themselves with mankind*, of 1 Cor. 6:9, but this is not specifically described. *Whoremongers* are here associated with *murderers* as adulterers are in the law of Moses. In 21:8 *whoremongery* is considered under the aspect of an injury done to a neighbour. *Idolaters* here also are the *kind*, liars the *species*—comp. at 22:8. The *doing* a lie stands opposed to *doing the truth* in John 3:21.

15. Without are dogs, and sorcerers, and whoremongers, and murderers, and idolaters, and all who love and do a lie.

16 The subject-matter of the book ascends through the medium of the angel to *Jesus*. Whoever apprehends his glory (*I am the root, etc.*) cannot doubt the truth of its contents; but firmly expect the fulfilment of its promises. The

16. I Jesus have sent my angel to testify these things to you upon the churches.

16. I Jesus have sent my angel to testify these things to you upon the churches. I am the root and the race of David, the bright morning-star.

these things refer to the whole contents of the book. *To you,* my servants, who are represented by John, the prophets (comp. on 22:6,9, 1:1.) *To testify,* not that he, but that *I* may testify, comp. 1:2. *Upon* the churches (the επι as in 10:11; John 12:16,) the churches being regarded as the *object* of the testimony. The whole book is occupied with the future affairs of the church, that is the Christian churches generally, not merely the seven of Asia; for to these only the seven epistles specially belonged. Even in these epistles the promises do not respect alone the seven churches, but the churches generally. The book closes in ver. 21 with, *The grace of the Lord Jesus Christ be with* **all saints**.

The *root* of David, as in 5:5, is the product of the root, the sprout from the root, that in which the family of David, that had sunk into the lowest depression, again bloomed forth. Because Jesus is the root, he is also *the race of David*. In him alone is the race preserved from vanishing. The race of David is more than his offspring; it indicates that the race of David should, save for Christ, have ceased to exist. The race of David is here brought into view in respect to the unconquerable strength and everlasting dominion promised it by God (comp. Luke 1:32-33.) What he testifies, in whom the glorious race of David culminates, will assuredly go into fulfilment. Jesus is called the *bright morning-star* in allusion to Isa. 14:12, on account of his glorious dominion; comp. on 2:28. The practical result of the verse is this: *You must, therefore, firmly believe what in this book is said of my coming, of the water of life, etc. For, the saying, whatever he has promised, he holds sacred, stands good with respect to me; I shall not feed my people with empty hopes.*

17. And the Spirit and the bride say, Come! And he that hears, let him say, Come! And he that is athirst let him come; he that wills, let him take the water of life freely.

17 What the book contains of the coming of the Lord, etc. is certain, ver. 16. And, therefore, *the Spirit* responds here to the word of Christ: *Come!* then comes the call of the Spirit to every one, who hears the *come,* to accord with it, then invites the *thirsty* to enjoy the promised salvation.

The *Spirit* is not the Spirit that dwells in all believers (Rom. 8:26,) but the Spirit of *prophecy* (19:10,) the Spirit of the prophets (22:6,) in which John was on the Lord's day (1:10, 4:2,) which also speaks through John in 14:13, and which utters the promises in the seven epistles. The *bride, i.e.* the church (comp. 19:7, 21:2, 9) stands related here to the church, as elsewhere the saints to the prophets, comp. at 18:20. *The saints are the genus, the apostles and prophets, who are personally identical, are the most distinguished species of these,* 11:18, 16:6, 17:6, 18:24. There is no change of person here as to the *Come* uttered by the Spirit, and the *Come* uttered by the bride, but the Spirit himself, and John his organ, proclaims the *Come* as the bride's representative. This *Come* uttered by the organ of the church in her name is a *fact*—she *speaks*—and on it follows the call to all the members of the church, to accord with this *Come.* He that hears—not generally the words of the prophecy of this book, by comparing ver. 18 and 1:3, but the *Come* of the Spirit and the bride.

On the words, *And he that is athirst let him come,* comp. John 8:37, and the remarks made at 21:6. If the contents of this book really belong to the true and faithful witness, the thirsty need but to come; such simply as have the *will,* may receive the water of life. For now all is ready.

18-19 The natural man must not find much that he would find, and, again, find much that he would not. Hence comes the disposition to make additions and omissions. Such adders and omitters are here meant, as those who said, *Where is the promise of his coming?* (2 Pet. 3:4;) or, *Let him make speed and hasten his work, that we may see it* (Isa. 5:19;) or those

CONCLUSION—THE NEW JERUSALEM

who maintained, that it was unprofitable to remain faithful unto death (2:10,) or that people should freely eat of things sacrificed to idols, and commit fornication. That such additions and omissions are here referred to, as belong to the proper kernel of the book, such as would substitute for the narrow way presented in it a broad one, or would in some respect extinguish the light of hope, that shines in it for Christians, as Hymaeneus and Philetus, who said the resurrection was past already (2 Tim. 2:17;) is clear from the spirit of this book. It is also confirmed by the PARALLEL PASSAGES of the OLD TESTAMENT. It is said in Deut. 4:2, *Ye shall not add unto the word which I command you, neither shall ye diminish ought from it, that ye may keep the commandments of the Lord your God, which I command you;* and an example is given in ver. 16-19, where they are warned against a seduction to the worship of images and the host of heaven. Deut. 12:32, *Whatsoever thing I command you, observe to do it; thou shalt not add thereto nor diminish from it,* stands connected with a warning against total apostasy, against participation in the Canaanite idolatry, and mixing it up with the service of Jehovah. In Prov. 30:5-6, *Every word of God is purified, he is a shield to those who trust in him.* (But) *add not thou to his words, lest he reprove thee, and thou be found a liar,* such additions to the promises of God (for these are more especially referred to) are meant, as when, after the manner of Satan in Matt. 4:6, the protection, which God has promised to his people, so long as they walk in his way, is applied to those, who would strike out a way of their own—additions, therefore, which are based on a moral perversion. That there were persons in the Christian church disposed to make additions and omissions of the kind referred to, is clear from the seven epistles. Balaam and Jezebel had then revived again. Heathenism is smuggled into the church with great zeal (see at 2:6.) In times of persecution and oppression, such as that in which the Apocalypse was written, there is a peculiar temptation to such additions and omissions. Whoever surrendered himself unconditionally to the truths set forth in this book, put himself in direct opposition to heathenism, and drew upon himself its persecuting violence. And any one that lacked the spirit of martyrdom, must add or take away. There was therefore sufficient reason for such an earnest threatening as is here uttered. The dominion of the world carries along with it a powerful incentive to the adding and taking away. One plies every effort to take off the edge from the word of God, and to strike a shameful agreement with the world. Proofs enough of this are not wanting unfortunately even in the province of a theology of faith. When these words are correctly understood, none can take offence at them but those who regard the title, *Revelation of Jesus Christ,* as a mere assumption. The idea contained in them is simply this: As men deal with the word of God, so does God deal with them, and justly so, 3:10. Quite similar is Gal. 1:8-9, which passage may serve as a commentary. It is not accidental, that the warning occurs toward the close of the first, and toward the close of the last book of the canon, whose author clearly perceived that it was given him to shut up the canon; as little as it is accidental that paradise meets us at the beginning of Scripture, and at the end the new Jerusalem. The warning uttered in the first and the last book substantially applies to all, that lies between the two.

In the word, *God will add,* the divine recompense is brought clearly to view by the similarity of the expression: *He that adds, shall have plagues added to him, he that takes away, from him shall blessings be taken away.* The two go

---

18. I testify to every one, who hears the words of the prophecy of this book. If any one adds thereto, God will add to him the plagues which are written in this book. 19. And if any one take away from the words of the book of this prophecy, God will take away his part from the tree of life, and from the holy city, which are written in this book.

18. ... God will add to him the plagues which are written in this book. 19. And if any one take away from the words of the book of this prophecy, God will take away his part from the tree of life, and from the holy city, which are written in this book.	inseparably together—on the one side the experience of the plagues and the loss of salvation, and on the other, deliverance from the plagues and the inheritance of salvation. The *plagues, which are written in this book*, are such as were to befall the ungodly world. By his profane rashness in adding, the offspring of his carnal state of mind, he shows that he has belonged to the world, and not to the church; and hence must be at last condemned with the world, and not preserved with the church. By the word *part* the destiny and inheritance are denoted (comp. John 13:8.) This was hitherto *beside* the tree of life, and *in* the holy city. But now it shall be taken away from both, and he receives instead his part in the lake of fire, which burns with fire and brimstone (21:8.)

The *tree of life* and the *holy city* are mentioned also at ver. 14, and in these two stands the sum of the blessedness written at the beginning and at the close of the book, 2:7, 3:12, 21:2, 22:2. The words, *who are written in this book*, refer to the tree of life and the holy city, as also the plagues standing over against them are described as being written in this book.

20-21 In ver. 20 we have the parting words of Jesus and John. In ver. 21 the latter dismisses his hearers. *He who testifies these things* is Christ (comp. at 1:2, 5.) The *Amen, come Lord Jesus*, is spoken by the Spirit through Jesus, or by John in the Spirit. The *I come quickly*, is the sum of the prophetic announcements of the book. That the church with full confidence may say the *Amen, come Lord Jesus*, is the great practical design of this book.

20. He who testifies these things says: Yea, I come quickly. Amen, come Lord Jesus.
21. The grace of the Lord Jesus Christ be with all saints.

THE END

INDEX A

List of passages specially noticed or illustrated in the preceding work

GENESIS
2:9-10, 3:22, 4:7, 6:11-13, 9:6, 19:28, 49:9,

EXODUS
3:13-16, 7:20, 9:8, 11, ch. 15, 19:6, 24:10, 28:10, 40:34-35,

LEVITICUS
26:11-12

NUMBERS
14:21

DEUTERONOMY
6:6-8, 23:18

JOSHUA
Ch. 6

1 KINGS
19:11

2 KINGS
9:7, 9:22

EZRA
2:13

PSALMS
2:9, 36:8, 45:1, 45:3-4, 46:3-4, 48:3-4, 49:14, 69:28, 86:8-9, 89:28, 99:1, 104:35, 107:33-34,

PROVERBS
30:5-6

ECCLESIASTES
5:6

SONG OF SOLOMON
4;7, 4:17, 5:1-2, 8:6

ISAIAH
6:4, 11:1, 11:12, 14:27, 22:22, 23:3, 24:3, 34:4-5, 42:4, 42:19, 44:6, 44:26, 48:13, 49:2, 49:20, 51:16, 54:11-12, 57:3, 60:4, 60:11, 60:19-20, 61:6

JEREMIAH
3:16-17, 16:18, 17:18, 49:36, 50:1, 51:13, 51:25, 51:63-64

EZEKIEL
1:1, 1:4, 1:7, 1:22, 3:3, 8:2, 9:4, 10:2, 12:23, 25, 14:21, 17:22-23, 26:15-16, 28:13, 32:34, 34:42, 37:27-28, 40:2, 47:7,9,12, 48:1-7, 23-29

DANIEL
3:1, 7:2, 7:9-10, 7:13, 7:45, 7:20, 10:6-7

HOSEA
2:6, 12:8

JOEL
3:12-13, 3:18

AMOS
9:1

MICAH
4:1

NAHUM
2:9

HABBAKUK
2:14, 2:15-16, 2:20

ZEPHANIAH
2:11

HAGGAI
1:13, 2:6

ZECHARIAH
1:7-17, 1:9, 2:13, 4:1, 4:6-7, 4:10, 6:1, 12:10, 14:8, 14:11

MALACHI
3:1, 4:2, 4:5-6

MATTHEW
2:1-12, 6:13, 8:26, 18:6, 24:6, 24:6-8, 24:42-43, 26:64, 27:66

MARK
4:40, 14:51-52

LUKE
10:18, 11:21-22, 18:7-8, 23:43

JOHN
5:4, 9:4, 11:9-10, 13:30, 13:48-49, 14:21, 23, 16:12, 16:14-15, 19:34

ACTS
10:10-17

ROMANS
11:26

1 CORINTHIANS
14:6, 15:22-23

2 CORINTHIANS
12:1

GALATIANS
1:12

EPHESIANS
3:3, 3:5-6

COLOSSIANS
1:15-18, 1:24

1 THESSALONIANS
4:16

2 THESSALONIANS
2:4

1 TIMOTHY
2:14

HEBREWS
4:12

JAMES
3:15

1 PETER
5:13

JUDE
Ver. 9

INDEX B

Principal words and topics in the preceding work

A

Abyss, a designation of hell, 102
Adonikam, the mystical name of the beast out of the sea, 145
Angel, why applied as an epithet to Christ, 130-131
Angel, sometimes applied to Christ, 21, 42, 82, 108-110, 112-113, 128, 130, 162, 163, 201, 216, 219, 253
Angels, of different ranks, 21, 104, 105, 162-3, 226, 246
Angels of churches, the presiding and ruling power in these, 44, 47, equivalent to king, 73
Antichrist, an ideal person, 152
Apocalypse, when written, 3-10
Apocalypse written during a time of general persecution, 4-5
Apocalypse written when executions and banishments were suffered, 5, 7
Apocalypse written in the time of Domitian, and shortly before his death, 3-10, 117, 141, 142, 146
Apocalypse, the immediate future deferred in it, 21
Apostles, also prophets, 241, 257
Apostles, the number twelve bears respect to twelve tribes, 116, 240, 243
Apostles, only twelve, 241
Armageddon, its meaning, 181
Asia, seven churches of, 4, 11, 29-30, 34, 39, 46-58

B

Babylon, means heathen, 53, 89, 137, 157, 158 Rome in the Revelation, 135, 157, 158.
Babylon, first applied to Rome in the New Testament by Peter, 158
Babylon, why called the great whore, 187
Balaam, teachers of his doctrine same as Nicolaitans, 4
Balances, symbol of scarcity, 77
Beast, its symbolical import, 136
Beast from the sea, its heads, 134-138
Beast, its horns, 1, 13, 129, 134, 136, 137,
Beast, its deadly wound, 142, 192, 193
Beast, its name and number, 145, 147
Beast from the earth, 142-144, 153
Beast, what it symbolizes, 134, 137, 142
Beast, why represented with two lamb's horns, 143
Beast not the Papacy, 146-147
Beasts, the four around the throne symbolical representations of creation, 63-66
Beginning of creation, in what sense spoken of Christ, 33
Black, symbolical of mourning, 77
Blasphemy, names of what, 137
Blessedness, a double stage of in the Apocalypse, 221
Blood, drinking of as a punishment, 176
Book with seven seals, 68-75
Book, why none but Christ could open it, 69

C

Chalkolibanos, its meaning, 41, 45
Cherubim, how far they could join in the song of the redeemed, 71
Cherubim not angels, 63, 151
Church, her unbroken continuity in all times, 83, 240
Crystal, a symbol of terrible majesty, 63
Corners of the earth, what meant by, 64, 225
Cold and hot, what they denote when used spiritually, 57
Crown, a symbol of royal dignity, not of victory, 49, 76, 104, 162
Cup of wine of fornication, 158-159, 190-191, 202

D

Dan, why omitted in the enumeration of the tribes of Israel, 83
Darkness, a symbol of displeasure, calamity, 178
David, key of, symbolizes the power over God's kingdom, 55
Day of God, its comprehensive import, 180
Death and the dead sometimes used only in a bad sense, 227
Demons, mean only evil spirits, 107
Diadems, why many on Christ's head, 215
Dogs, symbols of impurity and malice, 256
Dragon, a symbol of the worldly power, 129
Double punishment, what, 226-227
Drunk, what meant in prophecy by making so, 158

E

Eagle, a symbol of the Lord, 132
Earthquakes and storms, symbols of God's destroying power, 118
Eating a book denotes the full appropriation of its contents, 108, 109-111
Eating things sacrificed to idols, why forbidden, 50, 52
Egypt regarded as a source of religious corruption, 113
Egypt, plagues of, the prototype of God's judgments under the trumpets, 113
Elders, the twenty four, representatives of the Old and New Testament church, 62
Emperor's image an instrument of persecution, 144
Equality of condition not to exist in the heavenly world, 246
Euphrates regarded as the region that sent forth God's instruments of vengeance against his church, 105, 178
Euphrates, what meant by the drying up of, 178
Eye-salve, a symbol of the grace of the Holy Spirit, 58

F

Faithfulness, as a divine quality of Christ, 215
Falling from heaven, what it denotes, 100, 102,

Fire, the symbol of divine wrath, 41
First and last, what meant by it as applied to Christ, 36, 48, 146
First-fruits, the symbolical meaning of, 153
Fornication, what meant by, when used of kingdoms, 159, 190
Frankincense, symbol of prayer, 71-72
Frogs, symbol of impurity, 180

G
Garments emblematic of the state, 181
Garments, white, indicative of heavenly glory, 54, 62
General designations sometimes mixed up with particular ones, 78-79, 90, 94, 96, 127, 129, 134, 146, 158, 168, 183, 187, 192, 212
Gentile and Jewish Christians regarded as entirely on a footing, 83, 85, 114
Germanic tribes, their troubles and disasters before conversion to Christianity, 199, 214-215
Glass, a symbol of purity, 243
Glorifying God in suffering, what, 169, 177
God directs, not merely permits what is done by the enemies, 179
Godly, its meaning when applied to God himself, 170
Gnostics, their affection into seeing into depths, 51-52
Gnostics, their licentious doctrine and practices, 47, 50
Grass, emblem of the common people, 99, 103

H
Hades always means the place of torment, 227
Hair very long a sign of barbarism, 104
Hallelujah, 208
Harvest, its symbolical meaning, 162
Heathenism, conflict with it, the prominent thing in the Apoc., 1
Heretics of an ethnicising, not of a Jewish stamp, referred to in the seven epistles, 47
Holiness, expresses God's peerless exaltation, 65
Horns, symbols of victorious power, 136

J
Jasper, an emblem of divine glory, 226
Jerome's view of Babylon, 209
Jerusalem, influence of its fall on Christianity, 9, 117
Jerusalem, a threefold mentioned, 233
Jerusalem, literal, never referred to in Apoc., 114, 116-117, 164, 183
In Apoc. Jerusalem always designates the church, 183
Jerusalem, the new, what meant thereby, 233
Jezebel, a symbolical, not historical name in Apoc., 51
Images of heathenism, their connection with the gods they represented, 144
Incense, a symbol of prayer, 71-72
John, the apostle, the John of the Apoc., 3-5
Islands denote kingdoms, 79

L
Lamps, symbolical meaning of, 40
Last end throughout book, 222
Legal impurity from death, leprosy, bodily issues, 155, from beasts, 155

Life, full import of it in Apoc. and other writings of John, 161, 221, 247-248
Life, why likened to a river, 247
Lightnings and thunders denote warnings of judgment, 62
Linen white, symbolical of righteousness, 171, 212
Literal interpretation of temple, Jerusalem and Jews erroneous, 114
Locusts represent a hostile invasion, 102
Lord's day, first of the week, 38
Loud voice, indicative of power in action, 69, 82
Luther's remarks on the Papacy, 147
Lying, its wide import in John's writings, 155-156

M
Manna, what a type of, 50
Manna, why called hidden, 50
Marriage, not condemned or discountenanced in Scripture, 155
Marriage, church's with Christ, 212
Matthias, his relation to the twelve apostles, 241
Megiddo, victory at, by Pharaoh over Josiah, 181
Michael, import of the name, 21, 41, 42, 109, 130-131, 139, 145
Moon, image of created, inferior glory, 245
Morning star, an image of dominion, 53
Mosaic law; its external arrangements for bringing sin to remembrance, 155
Mountains, symbolical of kingdoms, 183-184
Mystery, its meaning, 191

N
Name of God, what meant by, 139
Name of God, what to blaspheme, 139
Nero, not the beast of the Apocalypse, 8, 148, 150-152
Nicolaitans, same as Balaamites, 4
Night, what an emblem of, 247, 250

O
Orosius, his view of Babylon as Heathen Rome, 209

P
Pale horse, significant of wan death, 77
Palms, emblems of joy at feast of tabernacle, 85
Panther, of what symbolical, 137
Paul, reckoned one of the twelve, 241
Pillar in God's temple, and pillar-like, an emblem of stability, 56
Polycarp, probably at Smyrna when the Apocalypse was written, 49
Polytheism, its slight hold on men's minds in the age of the apostles, 143
Prophecy, how imparted, and to whom, 19

R
Rainbow, a symbol of grace after wrath, 109
Rationalistic view of the temple, and Jerusalem, in the Revelation, 114
Revelation, what it means, 19
Root of David, its import as applied to Christ, 70

S

Saints, a name not for distinguished, but merely true Christians, 120
Sardius, an emblem of penal justice, 62
Satan, his power not independent, 136
Satan, the extent of his influence, 180
Satan, how restrained so as never again to become the dragon, 225
Satan represented as offensive till Christ's death, afterwards defensive, 131
Satan, his being thrown out of heaven indicative of the weakening of his power, 131
Sea, a symbol of the restless nations, 82, 109, 126, 132, 135, 136, 149, 157, 227, 232
Sea of glass, a symbol of God's wonderful works, 62, 168-169, 171
Seals on a book, symbolical of secrecy, 69
Sealing a vision denotes the concealment of its contents, 69
Sealing the forehead denotes confirming, 154, 250
Seven spirits, indicative of God's operations externally, 31, 32
Shaking of heaven and earth, 78, 81, 183
Showing, its meaning, and what it refers to, 21
Smoke, its symbolical import, 172
Sorrows in the church the forerunners of great deliverances, 29, 86
Sodom, the image of a church deeply corrupt in morals, 113
Speculative errors not always the most dangerous, 54
Stars, symbols of rulers, 79
Suffering sometimes merely penal, not sanctifying, 177
Sun, an image of divine glory, 82, 128
Sword of Christ, its symbolical import, 41-42, 50, 214, 216

T

Tabernacles, feast of, its symbolical import, 88
Temple, a symbol of the true church, 56, 111, 115, 116, 125, 139, 163, 244-245
Temple, measuring of, indicates the preservation of the church, 111
Trees represent kings and nobles, 99
Ten horns or kingdoms, 195, 196
True, a divine predicate, 55
Trumpets, why used in God's service, and referred to in Apocalypse, 95-96
Truth, as affirmed of Christ, 209, 215

V

Vengeance, why sought for by the martyrs and executed by God, 8
Virgins, what meant by such in Apocalypse, 155

W

Weeping in John, a sign of weakness of faith, 69
White, an emblem of splendour, 41
White stone, of what emblematical, 50
Winds, symbols of God's judgments, 79
Wine of wrath, what, 158
Wine mixed and unmixed, 160
Wisdom of the world, its relation to the world's power, 142-143
Wisdom, its wonders, 144
Witnesses, two ideal persons, 112, 191
Witnessing regarded as prophesying, 191
Woman, a symbol of the true church of all ages, 83, 128

APPENDIX
THE 70 WEEKS OF DANIEL
—condensed and adapted from Hengstenberg's Christology.

Daniel wrote this prophecy, Dan. 9:24-27, when the seventy years of Babylonian captivity were about to end. His tender love to his people is shown in the phrase *and over thy people, and over thy holy city*. God knows Daniel's love toward his city, and God's covenant people. It is Daniel's city and people, much as it is the Lord's city and people.

> Seventy weeks are cut off over thy people, and over thy holy city

Seventy is the number of jubilee, a time of liberty. In the ancient Israelite society, at the end of a seventy year period all debts were to be remitted, and all slaves emancipated. These 70 weeks are *cut off* over this people and their city. The seventy year period is here marked out like a tailor would cut out the material for a piece of clothing; it is a complete period, *cut off* from subsequent duration. The phrase *seventy weeks* means not a literal seventy weeks, but given the nature of the case, 70 weeks of *years*, in other words a period of 490 years. It is a complete period without any dismemberment, that is *cut off* in whole material for the fulfilment of what follows.

> to shut up transgression and to seal sin and to cover transgression and to bring everlasting righteousness and to seal up vision and prophecy and to anoint a holy of holies.

A series of particular things are fulfilled in this time of 490 years, such things being, to shut up transgression, to seal sin, to bring everlasting righteousness, to seal up vision and prophecy, and to anoint a holy of holies. Here is not to do with judgment, only a divine blessing and prosperity is intended. Transgression and sin is shut up and sealed by forgiveness, existing sin is removed out of sight. Here is a time when God will not regard men as sinners, but as righteous. From its eternal origin and duration it will be an everlasting state, an everlasting righteousness. All the vision and prophecies regarding the sealing of sin are also sealed up in their fulfilment. In the epistles the salvation of believers is described in terms of *sealing* (2 Cor. 1:22, Eph. 1:13, Eph. 4:30.) As the disciples declared, *We have found him of whom Moses did write.* With the anointing of a holy of holies we have the antithesis to the desolation of the sanctuary. The omitted article, *a holy of holies*, designates the object in its widest universality. The anointing took place at the baptism of Christ, Matt. 3:16. The word *anointing* is not here a literal but a figurative term for the gifts of the Holy Spirit. The *holy of holies* is the new temple, the church of the new covenant. When Christ rose from the dead, he led captivity captive, and gave gifts unto men, see Eph. 4:8, the offices of ministry.

> And thou shalt know and understand from the going forth of the word to restore and to build Jerusalem until an Anointed One, a Prince, are seven weeks and threescore and two weeks, street is restored and built and firmly is it determined, and in a time of distress.

The *going forth of the word* is the publication of the decree, the divine decree from God. This decree embarks at the same time as the deed happens. It is the decree to restore and build Jerusalem. The word *restore* means to cause to return, to bring back. It is a complete restoration of the temple and city, which had been destroyed by the Babylonians. The going forth of the word is *until an Anointed One, a Prince*. This anointed one is an exalted king, Christ. The kings of Israel were anointed as theocratic rulers, as in 1 Sam. 10:1. That this Prince is Christ is clear from Acts 3:15, 5:31. It is *until* an Anointed One, a Prince, with a period determined of seven weeks and threescore and two weeks. The end of this period is at the time the anointing takes place at Jesus's baptism, where he appears as the Messiah, in Matt. 3:13-17.

We have a twofold determination of time. After seven weeks we have the completed restoration of the city, and after a further threescore and two weeks the appearance of the Anointed One. The *street* is restored and built. *Street* here is a singular object in its widest extent. The *firmly determined* prophecy is a consolation for pious Israelites, that the death of the Anointed One is a causal connection with the desolation of the temple. As for this being *a time of distress* we have the testimony of Nehemiah in 9:36-37.

> And after the sixty two weeks will an anointed One be cut off and [there] is not to Him.

The remaining week, or seven years, follows the anointing of the Holy One. The dominion of the Anointed One over his people was destroyed when by their crime he was violently put to death. He was *cut off,* as Isaiah in 53:8 had prophesied. The mark of the Messiah was to be a Prince over Israel. The *and* [there] *is not to him,* means he is no longer ruling over Israel as he has been killed by his own people. Here we have the negative consequence of the cutting off of the messiah, that is, the cessation of his dominion over his people. The positive consequence of the desolation of the city and temple is connected. The shepherd's staff is broken, as in Zech. 11:9-12.

> and people of a Prince who comes, will lay waste the city and the sanctuary and it will end in the flood and until the end is war, a decree of ruins.

The *prince who comes* is another prince, the Roman, Titus, who laid waste the city and sanctuary, the *flood* here is a designation of a warlike expedition. A *decree of ruins* designates the utter destruction of a city.

> And one week will confirm the covenant with many,

Here a *week* is a space of time, in which it is said to do what really is done within it. The end of the week has no bearing on the matter, it is merely a space of time within which something is accomplished. The covenant shows demonstrations of mercy, and the *many* of which it is concerned with are the objects of the former promises. The prince has no connection with this week.

> and the half of the week will abolish sacrifice and meat offering,

The death of the messiah, does away with the Levitical service, which *sacrifice and meat offering* represents, it is done away with and the old covenant is abolished. Three years were to pass from the anointing at Christ's baptism until his violent death. The temple then was to be superceded by the perfect offering of Christ, Matt. 23:38 declares.

> and over the summit of abominations comes the destroyer, and that, till what is completed and cut off shall drop down over the desolated [one].

The wing is figuratively the summit of the temple, desecrated by abomination. The seizure of the highest part presupposes the possession of the rest. The old temple is now an abomination caused by the profanation by the covenant people. The phrase, *comes the destroyer,* conveys the fixed determination to inflict suffering. The Jews, not the heathen, are the proper authors of the desecration of the temple, as in Dan. 11:31, Luke 21:21.

Here we have the only tenable view of this prophecy, the original fall of the temple in 70AD.

See Hengstenberg's Christology for the full essay with analysis of the timing and dates. The futurist interpreters use this prophecy to supplement their understanding of the Revelation. I include this appendix to show readers that this prophecy is to be understood differently to futurist claims, that it cannot suffer intrusions of millennia—Editor.

www.ingramcontent.com/pod-product-compliance
Lightning Source LLC
Chambersburg PA
CBHW031411290426
44110CB00011B/335